An Introduction to Autodesk Inventor 2013 and AutoCAD 2013

Randy H. Shih
Oregon Institute of Technology

ISBN: 978-1-58503-728-5

Schroff Development Corporation
P.O. Box 1334
Mission KS 66222
(913) 262-2664
www.SDCpublications.com

Publisher: Stephen Schroff

Trademarks

The following are registered trademarks of Autodesk, Inc.: Autodesk Inventor, 3D Studio, ADI, Advanced Modeling Extension, AME, AutoCAD, AutoCAD Mechanical Desktop, AutoCAD Development System, AutoCAD LT, Autodesk, Autodesk Animator, AutoLISP, AutoShade, AutoVision, and Heidi.
The following are trademarks of Autodesk, Inc.: ACAD, Autodesk Device Interface, AutoCAD DesignCenter, AutoTrack, Heads-up Design, ObjectARX and Visual LISP.
Microsoft, Windows are either registered trademarks or trademarks of Microsoft Corporation.
All other trademarks are trademarks of their respective holders.

Copyright 2012 by Randy Shih.

All rights reserved. No part of this book may be reproduced, stored in a retrieval system, or transcribed in any form or by any means -electronic, mechanical, photocopying, recording, or otherwise - without the prior written permission of Schroff Development Corporation.

IT IS A VIOLATION OF UNITED STATES COPYRIGHT LAWS TO MAKE COPIES IN ANY FORM OR MEDIA OF THE CONTENTS OF THIS BOOK FOR EITHER COMMERCIAL OR EDUCATIONAL PURPOSES WITHOUT EXPRESS WRITTEN PERMISSION.

Shih, Randy H.
    An Introduction to Autodesk Inventor 2013 and AutoCAD 2013/
Randy H. Shih

ISBN 978-1-58503-728-5

The author and publisher of this book have used their best efforts in preparing this book. These efforts include the development, research and testing of the material presented. The author and publisher shall not be liable in any event for incidental or consequential damages with, or arising out of, the furnishing, performance, or use of the material.

Printed and bound in the United States of America.

Table of Contents

Autodesk Inventor 2013

Chapter 1
Getting Started

Introduction	1-2
Development of Computer Geometric Modeling	1-2
Feature-Based Parametric Modeling	1-6
Getting Started with Autodesk Inventor	1-7
The Screen Layout and Getting Started Toolbar	1-8
The New File Dialog Box and Units Setup	1-9
Autodesk Inventor Screen Layout	1-10
Application Menu	1-11
Quick Access Toolbar	1-11
Ribbon Tabs	1-11
Online Help Panel	1-11
2D Sketch Toolbar	1-12
Graphics Window	1-12
Message and Status Bar	1-12
Mouse Buttons	1-13
[Esc] - Canceling Commands	1-13
Autodesk Inventor Help System	1-14
Data Management using Inventor Project files	1-15
Setup of a New Inventor Project	1-16
The Content of an Inventor Project File	1-19
Leaving Autodesk Inventor	1-19

Chapter 2
Parametric Modeling Fundamentals

Introduction	2-2
The Adjuster Design	2-3
Starting Autodesk Inventor	2-3
The default Autodesk Inventor Screen Layout	2-5
Sketch plane – It is an XY Monitor, but an XYZ World	2-6
Create Rough Sketches	2-8
Step 1: Create a Rough Sketch	2-9
Graphics Cursors	2-9
Geometric Constraint Symbols	2-10
Step 2: Apply/Modify Constraints and Dimensions	2-11
Dynamic Viewing Functions – *Zoom* and *Pan*	2-14
Modifying the Dimensions of the Sketch	2-14
Step 3: Completing the Base Solid Feature	2-15
Isometric View	2-16

Dynamic Rotation of the 3-D block - 3D Orbit	2-17
Dynamic Viewing - Quick Keys	2-19
Viewing Tools – Standard Toolbar	2-20
Display Modes	2-24
Orthographic vs. Perspective	2-24
Disable the Heads-Up Display Option	2-25
Step 4-1: Adding an Extruded Feature	2-26
Step 4-2: Adding a Cut Feature	2-31
Save the Model	2-34
Questions	2-36
Exercises	2-37

Chapter 3
Constructive Solid Geometry Concepts

Introduction	3-2
Binary Tree	3-3
The Locator Design	3-4
Modeling Strategy - CSG Binary Tree	3-5
Starting Autodesk Inventor	3-6
Base Feature	3-7
GRID intervals Setup	3-8
Model Dimensions Format	3-11
Modifying the Dimensions of the Sketch	3-11
Repositioning Dimensions	3-12
Using the Measure Tools	3-13
Completing the Base Solid Feature	3-16
Create the Next Solid Feature	3-17
Create a CUT Feature	3-21
Create a PLACED FEATURE	3-24
Create a Rectangular Cut Feature	3-26
Save the Model	3-28
Questions	3-29
Exercises	3-30

Chapter 4
Model History Tree

Introduction	4-2
The *Saddle Bracket* Design	4-3
Starting Autodesk Inventor	4-3
Modeling Strategy	4-4
The *Autodesk Inventor Browser*	4-5
Create the Base Feature	4-5
Adding the Second Solid Feature	4-8
Create a 2D Sketch	4-9
Renaming the Part Features	4-11

Adjusting the Width of the Base Feature	4-12
Adding a Placed Feature	4-13
Create a Rectangular Cut Feature	4-15
History-Based Part Modifications	4-16
A Design Change	4-17
Assigning and Calculating the Associated Physical Properties	4-20
Questions	4-22
Exercises	4-23

Chapter 5
Parametric Constraints Fundamentals

CONSTRAINTS and RELATIONS	5-2
Create a Simple Triangular Plate Design	5-2
Fully Constrained Geometry	5-3
Starting Autodesk Inventor	5-3
Displaying Existing Constraints	5-4
Applying Geometric/Dimensional Constraints	5-6
Over-Constraining and Driven Dimensions	5-10
Deleting Existing Constraints	5-11
Using the Auto Dimension Command	5-12
Constraint and Sketch Settings	5-16
Parametric Relations	5-17
Dimensional Values and Dimensional Variables	5-19
Parametric Equations	5-20
Viewing the Established Parameters and Relations	5-22
Saving the Model File	5-23
Using the Measure Tools	5-24
Questions	5-28
Exercises	5-29

Chapter 6
Geometric Construction Tools

Introduction	6-2
The Gasket Design	6-2
Modeling Strategy	6-3
Starting Autodesk Inventor	6-4
Create a 2D Sketch	6-5
Edit the Sketch by Dragging the Sketched Entities	6-7
Add Additional Constraints	6-9
Use the *Trim* and *Extend* Commands	6-10
The *Auto Dimension* Command	6-12
Create Fillets and Completing the Sketch	6-14
Fully Constrained Geometry	6-15
Profile Sketch	6-17
Redefine the Sketch and the Profile	6-18

Create an OFFSET Cut Feature	6-22
Questions	6-25
Exercises	6-26

Chapter 7
Parent/Child Relationships and the BORN Technique

Introduction	7-2
The BORN Technique	7-2
The U-Bracket Design	7-3
Starting Autodesk Inventor	7-4
Sketch Plane Settings	7-4
Apply the BORN Technique	7-5
Create the 2-D Sketch of the Base Feature	7-7
Create the First Extrude Feature	7-11
The Implied Parent/Child Relationships	7-12
Create the Second Solid Feature	7-12
Create the First Cut Feature	7-16
Create the Second Cut Feature	7-17
Examine the Parent/Child Relationships	7-19
Modify a Parent Dimension	7-20
A Design Change	7-21
Feature Suppression	7-22
A Different Approach to the CENTER_DRILL Feature	7-23
Suppress the Rect_Cut Feature	7-25
Create a Circular Cut Feature	7-26
A Flexible Design Approach	7-28
View and Edit Material Properties	7-29
Questions	7-31
Exercises	7-32

Chapter 8
Part Drawings and Associative Functionality

Drawings from Parts and Associative Functionality	8-2
Starting Autodesk Inventor	8-3
Drawing Mode - 2D Paper Space	8-3
Drawing Sheet Format	8-5
Using the Pre-Defined Drawing Sheet Formats	8-7
Delete, Activate, and Edit Drawing Sheets	8-9
Add a Base View	8-10
Create Projected Views	8-11
Adjust the View Scale	8-12
Repositioning Views	8-13
Display Feature Dimensions	8-14
Repositioning and Hiding Feature Dimensions	8-16
Add Additional Dimensions – Reference Dimensions	8-18

Add Center Marks and Center Lines	8-19
Complete the Drawing Sheet	8-22
Associative Functionality – Modifying Feature Dimensions	8-23
3D Annotations in Isometric Views	8-26
Questions	8-34
Exercises	8-35

Chapter 9
Symmetrical Features in Designs

Introduction	9-2
A Revolved Design: PULLEY	9-2
Modeling Strategy - A Revolved Design	9-3
Starting Autodesk Inventor	9-4
Setup the Display of the Sketch Plane	9-4
Create the 2-D Sketch for the Revolved Feature	9-5
Create the Revolved Feature	9-9
Mirroring Features	9-10
Create a Pattern Leader Using Construction Geometry	9-12
Circular Pattern	9-17
Examine the Design Parameters	9-19
Drawing Mode – Defining New Border and Title Block	9-19
Create a Drawing Template	9-22
Create the necessary Views	9-23
Retrieve Dimensions – Features Option	9-26
Associative Functionality – A Design Change	9-28
Add Center Lines to the Pattern Feature	9-30
Complete the Drawing	9-31
Questions	9-34
Exercises	9-35

Chapter 10
Assembly Modeling - Putting It All Together

Introduction	10-2
Assembly Modeling Methodology	10-3
The Shaft Support Assembly	10-4
Additional *Parts*	10-4
(1) Collar	10-4
(2) Bearing	10-5
(3) Base-Plate	10-5
(4) Cap-Screw	10-6
Starting Autodesk Inventor	10-7
Placing the First Component	10-8
Placing the Second Component	10-9
Degrees of Freedom and Constraints	10-10
Assembly Constraints	10-11

Apply the First Assembly Constraint	10-13
Apply a Second Mate Assembly Constraint	10-15
Constrained Move	10-16
Apply a Flush Constraint	10-17
Placing the Third Component	10-19
Applying an Insert Constraint	10-19
Assemble the Cap-Screws	10-21
Exploded View of the Assembly	10-22
Editing the Components	10-24
Adaptive Design Approach	10-25
Delete and Re-apply Assembly Constraints	10-29
Setup a Drawing of the Assembly Model	10-31
Create a Parts List	10-33
Edit the Parts List	10-34
Changing the Material Type	10-36
Complete the Assembly Drawing	10-38
Bill of Materials	10-39
(a) BOM from Parts List	10-39
(b) BOM from Assembly Model	10-40
Questions	10-41
Exercises	10-42

Chapter 11
Introduction to Stress Analysis

Introduction	11-2
Problem Statement	11-4
Preliminary Analysis	11-4
• Maximum Displacement	11-5
Finite Element Analysis Procedure	11-6
Create the *Autodesk Inventor* Part	11-7
Create the 2D Sketch for the Plate	11-8
Assigning the Material Properties	11-10
Switch to the *Stress Analysis* Module	11-11
Create an FEA Simulation	11-12
Apply Constraints and Loads	11-14
Create a Mesh and Run the Solver	11-16
Refinement of the FEA Mesh – Global Element Size	11-18
Refinement of the FEA Mesh – Local Element Size	11-20
Comparison of Results	11-23
Create an HTML Report	11-24
Geometric Considerations of Finite Elements	11-25
Conclusion	11-26
Summary of Modeling Considerations	11-26
Questions	11-27
Exercises	11-28

AutoCAD 2013

Chapter 12
Getting Started

Introduction	12-2
Development of Computer Aided Design	12-2
Why use AutoCAD® 2013	12-5
Getting Started with AutoCAD® 2013	12-7
AutoCAD® 2013 Screen Layout	12-8
Application Menu	12-9
Workspace Switching	12-9
Quick Access Toolbar	12-9
AutoCAD Menu Bar	12-9
Graphics Window	12-10
Graphics Cursor or Crosshairs	12-10
Command Prompt Area	12-10
Cursor Coordinates	12-10
Status Toolbar	12-10
Ribbon Tabs and Panels	12-10
Draw and Modify Toolbar Panel	12-11
Layers Control Toolbar Panel	12-11
Annotation Toolbar Panel	12-11
Layout/Model Toolbar	12-11
Viewing Toolbar	12-11
Mouse Buttons	12-12
[Esc] - Canceling Commands	12-12
On-Line Help	12-13
Leaving AutoCAD® 2013	12-14
Creating a CAD File Folder	12-15

Chapter 13
AutoCAD Fundamentals

Introduction	13-2
Starting Up AutoCAD® 2013	13-2
Drawing Units Display Setup	13-4
Drawing Area Setup	13-5
Using the *InfoCenter* to Get More Information	13-6
Drawing Lines with the *LINE* Command	13-7
Visual Reference	13-9
GRID ON	13-10
SNAP Mode ON	13-11
Using the *ERASER*	13-12
Repeat the Last Command	13-13

The CAD Database and the User Coordinate System	13-14
Changing to the 2D UCS Icon Display	13-15
Cartesian and Polar Coordinate Systems	13-16
Absolute and Relative Coordinates	13-16
Defining Positions	13-17
The *Guide Plate*	13-18
Creating *Circles*	13-22
Save the CAD File	13-24
Close the Current Drawing	13-25
The *Spacer* Design	13-26
Start a New Drawing	13-26
Drawing Units Setup	13-27
Drawing Area Setup	13-28
Using the Line Command	13-30
Using the *ERASE* Command	13-32
Using the Arc Command	13-32
Using the Circle Command	13-34
Saving the CAD Design	13-35
Exit AutoCAD	13-35
Review Questions	13-36
Exercises	13-37

Chapter 14
Basic Object Construction Tools

Introduction	14-2
Starting Up AutoCAD® 2013	14-2
Dynamic Input	14-3
The RockerArm Design	14-6
Activate the Startup Option	14-7
Drawing Units Display Setup	14-8
GRID and *SNAP* Intervals Setup	14-9
Drawing Area Setup	14-10
Referencing the World Coordinate System	14-11
Creating *Circles*	14-12
Object Snap Toolbar	14-13
Using the *LINE* command	14-14
Creating a *TTR Circles*	14-16
Using the *TRIM* Command	14-18
Using the *Polygon* Command	14-20
Creating a Concentric *Circle*	14-22
Using the QuickCal Calculator to Measure Distance and Angle	14-23
Saving the CAD file	14-27
Exit AutoCAD	14-27
Review Questions	14-28
Exercises	14-29

Chapter 15
Geometric Construction and Editing Tools

Geometric Constructions	15-2
Starting Up AutoCAD® 2013	15-3
Geometric Construction - CAD Method	15-4
• Bisection of a Line or Arc	15-4
• Bisection of an Angle	15-7
• Transfer of an Angle	15-9
• Dividing a Given Line into a Number of Equal Parts	15-13
• Circle through Three Points	15-15
• Line Tangent to a Circle from a Given Point	15-16
• Circle of a Given Radius Tangent to Two Given Lines	15-17
The *Gasket* Design	15-20
Drawing Units Display Setup	15-21
GRID and *SNAP* Intervals Setup	15-22
Using the *LINE* Command	15-23
Object Snap Toolbar	15-25
Using the *EXTEND* Command	15-28
Using the *TRIM* Command	15-29
Creating a *TTR Circle*	15-30
Using the *FILLET* Command	15-31
Converting Objects into a *Polyline*	15-32
Using the *OFFSET* Command	15-33
Using the Area Inquiry Tool to Measure Area and Perimeter	15-34
Using the *EXPLODE* Command	15-36
Create another *FILLET*	15-36
Saving the CAD file	15-37
Exit AutoCAD	15-37
Review Questions	15-38
Exercises	15-39

Chapter 16
Orthographic Views in Multiview Drawings

Introduction	16-2
The LOCATOR Design	16-2
The *Locator* Part	16-3
Starting Up AutoCAD® 2013	16-3
Layers Setup	16-4
Drawing *Construction Lines*	16-5
Using the *OFFSET* Command	16-5
Set Layer *Object* as the Current Layer	16-7
Using the *Running Object Snaps*	16-7
Creating *Object Lines*	16-9
Turn *OFF* the Construction Lines	16-10

Adding More Objects in the Front View	16-10
AutoCAD's AutoSnap ™ and AutoTrack ™ Features	16-11
Adding More Objects in the Top View	16-13
Drawing Using the *Miter Line* Method	16-17
More *Layers Setup*	16-19
Top View to Side View Projection	16-20
Completing the Front View	16-22
Object Information Using the List Command	16-24
Object Information Using the Properties Command	16-25
Review Questions	16-26
Exercises	16-27

Chapter 17
Basic Dimensioning and Notes

Introduction	17-2
The Bracket Design	17-2
Starting Up AutoCAD® 2013	17-3
Layers Setup	17-4
The Bracket Design	17-5
Drawing Construction Lines	17-6
Using the *OFFSET* Command	17-6
Set Layer *Object_Lines* as the *Current Layer*	17-8
Creating Object Lines	17-8
Creating Hidden Lines	17-9
Creating Center Lines	17-10
Turn *OFF* the Construction Lines	17-10
Using the *FILLET* Command	17-11
Saving the Completed CAD Design	17-12
Accessing the Dimensioning Commands	17-13
The *Dimension Toolbar*	17-14
Using *Dimension Style Manager*	17-14
Dimensions Nomenclature and Basics	17-15
Using the *Center Mark* Command	17-18
Adding *Linear* Dimensions	17-19
Adding *Angular* Dimensions	17-20
Adding *Radius* and *Diameter* Dimensions	17-21
Using the *SINGLE LINE TEXT* Command	17-22
Adding Special Characters	17-23
Saving the Design	17-24
A Special Note on Layers Containing Dimensions	17-24
Review Questions	17-25
Exercises	17-26

Autodesk Inventor 2013
Tutorial

*Parametric Modeling
Fundamentals*

Chapter 1
Introduction – Getting Started

Learning Objectives

- **Development of Computer Geometric Modeling**
- **Feature-Based Parametric Modeling**
- **Startup Options and Units Setup**
- **Autodesk Inventor Screen Layout**
- **User Interface & Mouse Buttons**
- **Autodesk Inventor On-Line Help**

Introduction

The rapid changes in the field of **Computer Aided Engineering** (CAE) have brought exciting advances in the engineering community. Recent advances have made the long-sought goal of **concurrent engineering** closer to a reality. CAE has become the core of concurrent engineering and is aimed at reducing design time, producing prototypes faster, and achieving higher product quality. *Autodesk Inventor* is an integrated package of mechanical computer aided engineering software tools developed by *Autodesk, Inc*. *Autodesk Inventor* is a tool that facilitates a concurrent engineering approach to the design and stress-analysis of mechanical engineering products. The computer models can also be used by manufacturing equipment such as machining centers, lathes, mills, or rapid prototyping machines to manufacture the product. In this text, we will be dealing only with the solid modeling modules used for part design and part drawings.

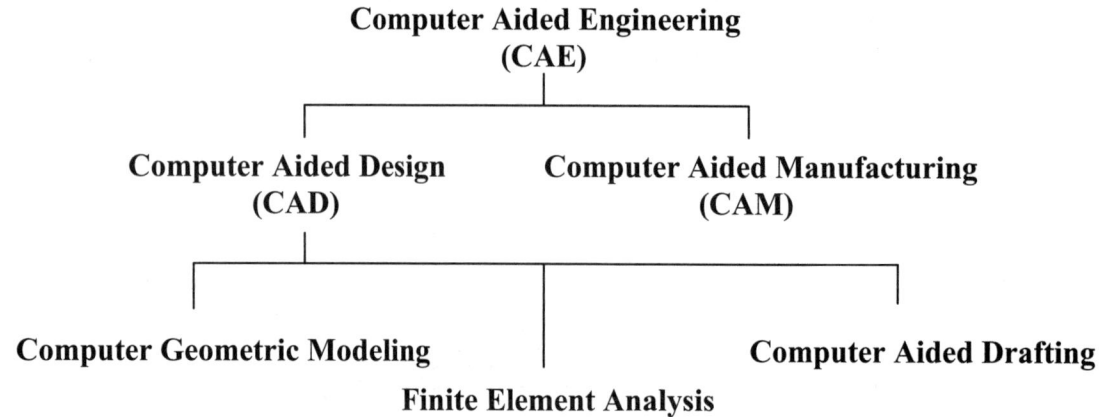

Development of Computer Geometric Modeling

Computer geometric modeling is a relatively new technology, and its rapid expansion in the last fifty years is truly amazing. Computer-modeling technology has advanced along with the development of computer hardware. The first generation CAD programs, developed in the 1950s, were mostly non-interactive; CAD users were required to create program-codes to generate the desired two-dimensional (2D) geometric shapes. Initially, the development of CAD technology occurred mostly in academic research facilities. The Massachusetts Institute of Technology, Carnegie-Mellon University, and Cambridge University were the leading pioneers at that time. The interest in CAD technology spread quickly and several major industry companies, such as General Motors, Lockheed, McDonnell, IBM, and Ford Motor Co., participated in the development of interactive CAD programs in the 1960s. Usage of CAD systems was primarily in the automotive industry, aerospace industry, and government agencies that developed their own programs for their specific needs. The 1960s also marked the beginning of the development of finite element analysis methods for computer stress analysis and computer aided manufacturing for generating machine tool paths.

The 1970s are generally viewed as the years of the most significant progress in the development of computer hardware, namely the invention and development of **microprocessors**. With the improvement in computing power, new types of 3D CAD programs that were user-friendly and interactive became reality. CAD technology quickly expanded from very simple **computer aided drafting** to very complex **computer aided design**. The use of 2D and 3D wireframe modelers was accepted as the leading edge technology that could increase productivity in industry. The developments of surface modeling and solid modeling technologies were taking shape by the late 1970s, but the high cost of computer hardware and programming slowed the development of such technology. During this period, the available CAD systems all required room-sized mainframe computers that were extremely expensive.

In the 1980s, improvements in computer hardware brought the power of mainframes to the desktop at less cost and with more accessibility to the general public. By the mid-1980s, CAD technology had become the main focus of a variety of manufacturing industries and was very competitive with traditional design/drafting methods. It was during this period of time that 3D solid modeling technology had major advancements, which boosted the usage of CAE technology in industry.

The introduction of the *feature-based parametric solid modeling* approach, at the end of the 1980s, elevated CAD/CAM/CAE technology to a new level. In the 1990s, CAD programs evolved into powerful design/manufacturing/management tools. CAD technology has come a long way, and during these years of development, modeling schemes progressed from two-dimensional (2D) wireframe to three-dimensional (3D) wireframe, to surface modeling, to solid modeling and, finally, to feature-based parametric solid modeling.

The first generation CAD packages were simply 2D **computer aided drafting** programs, basically the electronic equivalents of the drafting board. For typical models, the use of this type of program would require that several views of the objects be created individually as they would be on the drafting board. The 3D designs remained in the designer's mind, not in the computer database. Mental translations of 3D objects to 2D views are required throughout the use of these packages. Although such systems have some advantages over traditional board drafting, they are still tedious and labor intensive. The need for the development of 3D modelers came quite naturally, given the limitations of the 2D drafting packages.

The development of three-dimensional modeling schemes started with three-dimensional (3D) wireframes. Wireframe models are models consisting of points and edges, which are straight lines connecting between appropriate points. The edges of wireframe models are used, similar to lines in 2D drawings, to represent transitions of surfaces and features. The use of lines and points is also a very economical way to represent 3D designs.

The development of the 3D wireframe modeler was a major leap in the area of computer geometric modeling. The computer database in the 3D wireframe modeler contains the locations of all the points in space coordinates, and it is typically sufficient to create just one model rather than multiple views of the same model. This single 3D model can then be viewed from any direction as needed. Most 3D wireframe modelers allow the user to create projected lines/edges of 3D wireframe models. In comparison to other types of 3D modelers, the 3D wireframe modelers require very little computing power and generally can be used to achieve reasonably good representations of 3D models. However, because surface definition is not part of a wireframe model, all wireframe images have the inherent problem of ambiguity. Two examples of such ambiguity are illustrated.

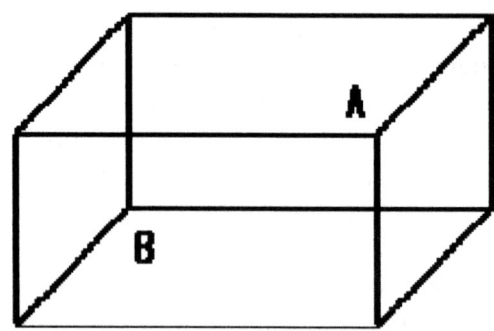

Wireframe Ambiguity: Which corner is in front, A or B?

A non-realizable object: Wireframe models contain no surface definitions.

Surface modeling is the logical development in computer geometry modeling to follow the 3D wireframe modeling scheme by organizing and grouping edges that define polygonal surfaces. Surface modeling describes the part's surfaces but not its interiors. Designers are still required to interactively examine surface models to insure that the various surfaces on a model are contiguous throughout. Many of the concepts used in 3D wireframe and surface modelers are incorporated in the solid modeling scheme, but it is solid modeling that offers the most advantages as a design tool.

In the solid modeling presentation scheme, the solid definitions include nodes, edges, and surfaces, and it is a complete and unambiguous mathematical representation of a precisely enclosed and filled volume. Unlike the surface modeling method, solid modelers start with a solid or use topology rules to guarantee that all of the surfaces are stitched together properly. Two predominant methods for representing solid models are **constructive solid geometry** (CSG) representation and **boundary representation** (B-rep).

The CSG representation method can be defined as the combination of 3D solid primitives. What constitutes a "primitive" varies somewhat with the software but typically includes a rectangular prism, a cylinder, a cone, a wedge, and a sphere. Most solid modelers also allow the user to define additional primitives, which are shapes typically formed by the basic shapes. The underlying concept of the CSG representation method is very straightforward; we simply **add** or **subtract** one primitive from another. The CSG approach is also known as the machinist's approach, as it can be used to simulate the manufacturing procedures for creating the 3D object.

In the B-rep representation method, objects are represented in terms of their spatial boundaries. This method defines the points, edges, and surfaces of a volume, and/or issues commands that sweep or rotate a defined face into a third dimension to form a solid. The object is then made up of the unions of these surfaces that completely and precisely enclose a volume.

By the 1980s, a new paradigm called *concurrent engineering* had emerged. With concurrent engineering, designers, design engineers, analysts, manufacturing engineers, and management engineers all work together closely right from the initial stages of the design. In this way, all aspects of the design can be evaluated and any potential problems can be identified right from the start and throughout the design process. Using the principles of concurrent engineering, a new type of computer modeling technique appeared. The technique is known as the *feature-based parametric modeling technique*. The key advantage of the *feature-based parametric modeling technique* is its capability to produce very flexible designs. Changes can be made easily and design alternatives can be evaluated with minimum effort. Various software packages offer different approaches to feature-based parametric modeling, yet the end result is a flexible design defined by its design variables and parametric features.

Feature-Based Parametric Modeling

One of the key elements in the *Autodesk Inventor* solid modeling software is its use of the **feature-based parametric modeling technique**. The feature-based parametric modeling approach has elevated solid modeling technology to the level of a very powerful design tool. Parametric modeling automates the design and revision procedures by the use of parametric features. Parametric features control the model geometry by the use of design variables. The word ***parametric*** means that the geometric definitions of the design, such as dimensions, can be varied at any time during the design process. Features are predefined parts or construction tools for which users define the key parameters. A part is described as a sequence of engineering features, which can be modified and/or changed at any time. The concept of parametric features makes modeling more closely match the actual design-manufacturing process than the mathematics of a solid modeling program. In parametric modeling, models and drawings are updated automatically when the design is refined.

Parametric modeling offers many benefits:

- **We begin with simple, conceptual models with minimal detail; this approach conforms to the design philosophy of "shape before size."**

- **Geometric constraints, dimensional constraints, and relational parametric equations can be used to capture design intent.**

- **The ability to update an entire system, including parts, assemblies and drawings after changing one parameter of complex designs.**

- **We can quickly explore and evaluate different design variations and alternatives to determine the best design.**

- **Existing design data can be reused to create new designs.**

- **Quick design turn-around.**

One of the key features of *Autodesk Inventor* is the use of an assembly-centric paradigm, which enables users to concentrate on the design without depending on the associated parameters or constraints. Users can specify how parts fit together and the *Autodesk Inventor assembly-based fit function* automatically determines the parts' sizes and positions. This unique approach is known as the **Direct Adaptive Assembly approach**, which defines part relationships directly with no order dependency.

The *Adaptive Assembly approach* is a unique design methodology that can only be found in *Autodesk Inventor*. The goal of this methodology is to improve the design process and allows you, the designer, to **Design the Way You Think**.

Getting Started with *Autodesk Inventor*

- *Autodesk Inventor* is composed of several application software modules (these modules are called *applications*), all sharing a common database. In this text, the main concentration is placed on the solid modeling modules used for part design. The general procedures required in creating solid models, engineering drawings, and assemblies are illustrated.

How to start *Autodesk Inventor* depends on the type of workstation and the particular software configuration you are using. With most *Windows* systems, you may select **Autodesk Inventor** on the *Start* menu or select the **Autodesk Inventor** icon on the desktop. Consult your instructor or technical support personnel if you have difficulty starting the software. The program takes a while to load, so be patient.

The tutorials in this text are based on the assumption that you are using *Autodesk Inventor's* default settings. If your system has been customized for other uses, contact your technical support personnel to restore the default software configuration.

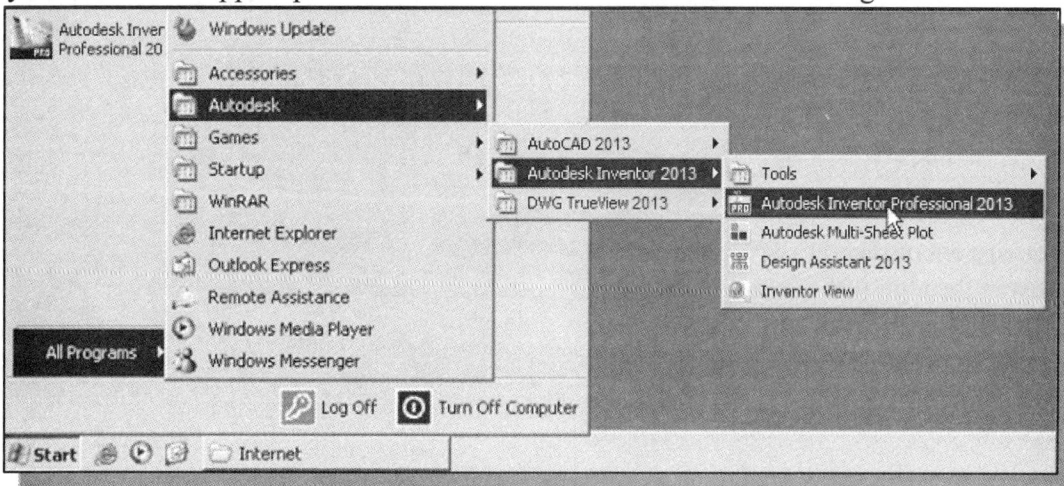

The Screen Layout and Getting Started Toolbar

Once the program is loaded into the memory, the *Inventor* window appears on the screen with the *Get Started* toolbar options activated.

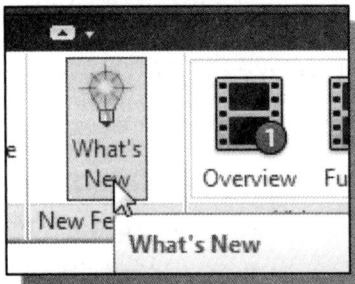

❖ Note that the *Get Started* toolbar contains helpful information in regards to using the *Inventor* software. For example, clicking the **What's New** option will bring up the *Internet Browser*, which contains the list of new features that are included in this release of *Autodesk Inventor*.

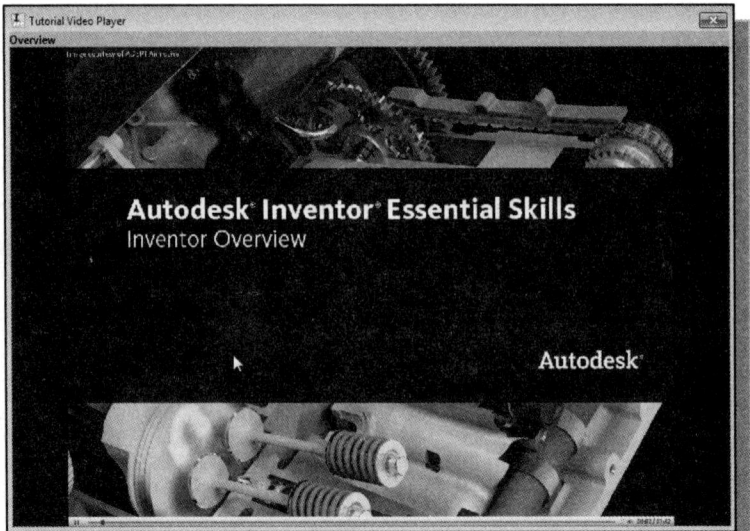

❖ You are encouraged to browse through the general introduction available in the *Videos and Tutorials* section.

The New File Dialog Box and Units Setup

When starting a new CAD file, the first thing we should do is to choose the units we would like to use. We will use the English (feet and inches) setting for this example.

- Select the **New** icon with a single click of the left-mouse-button in the *Launch* toolbar.

❖ Note that the New option allows us to start a new modeling task, which can be creating a new model or several other modeling tasks.

- Select the **English** tab in the *New File* dialog box as shown. Note the default tab contains the file options which are based on the default units chosen during installation.

- Select the **Standard(in).ipt** icon as shown. The different icons are templates for the different modeling tasks. The **idw** file type stands for drawing file, the **iam** file type stands for assembly file, and the **ipt** file type stands for part file. The **ipn** file type stands for assembly presentation.

- Click **Create** in the *Create New File* dialog box to accept the selected settings.

The *Default Autodesk Inventor* Screen Layout

The default *Autodesk Inventor* drawing screen contains the *pull-down* menus, the *Standard* toolbar, the *Features* toolbar, the *Sketch* toolbar, the *drawing* area, the *browser* area, and the *Status Bar*. A line of quick text appears next to the icon as you move the *mouse cursor* over different icons. You may resize the *Autodesk Inventor* drawing window by clicking and dragging the edges of the window, or relocate the window by clicking and dragging the window title area.

- The **Ribbon** is a new feature in *Autodesk Inventor* since the *2011 release*; the *Ribbon* is composed of a series of tool panels, which are organized into tabs labeled by task. The *Ribbon* provides a compact palette of all of the tools necessary to accomplish the different modeling tasks. The drop-down arrow next to any icon indicates additional commands are available on the expanded panel; access the expanded panel by clicking on the drop-down arrow.

- **Application Menu**

The *Application* menu at the upper left corner of the main window contains tools for all file-related operations, such as Open, Save, Export, etc.

- **Quick Access Toolbar**

The *Quick Access* toolbar at the top of the *Inventor* window allows us quick access to file-related commands and to Undo/Redo the last operations.

- **Ribbon Tabs**

The *Ribbon* is composed of a series of tool panels, which are organized into tabs labeled by task. The assortments of tool panels can be accessed by clicking on the tabs.

- **Online Help Panel**

The *Help* options panel provides us with multiple options to access on-line help for *Autodesk Inventor*. The **Online Help system** provides general help information, such as command options and command references.

- **2D Sketch Toolbar**

The *Create* toolbar provides tools for creating the different types of 3D features, such as Extrude, Revolve, Sweep, etc.

- **Graphics Window**

The *graphics window* is the area where models and drawings are displayed.

- **Message and Status Bar**

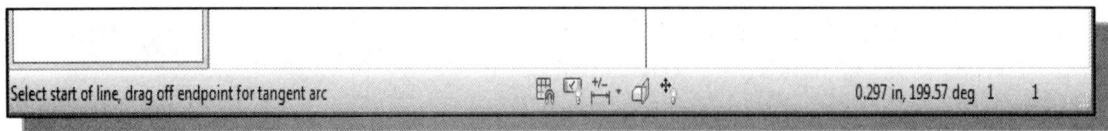

The *Message and Status Bar* area shows a single-line help when the cursor is on top of an icon. This area also displays information pertinent to the active operation. For example, in the figure above, the coordinates and length information of a line are displayed while the *Line* command is activated.

Mouse Buttons

Autodesk Inventor utilizes the mouse buttons extensively. In learning *Autodesk Inventor*'s interactive environment, it is important to understand the basic functions of the mouse buttons. It is highly recommended that you use a mouse or a tablet with *Autodesk Inventor* since the package uses the buttons for various functions.

- **Left mouse button**
  The **left-mouse-button** is used for most operations, such as selecting menus and icons, or picking graphic entities. One click of the button is used to select icons, menus and form entries, and to pick graphic items.

- **Right mouse button**
  The **right-mouse-button** is used to bring up additional available options. The software also utilizes the **right-mouse-button** as the same as the **ENTER** key, and is often used to accept the default setting to a prompt or to end a process.

- **Middle mouse button/wheel**
  The middle mouse button/wheel can be used to **Pan** (hold down the wheel button and drag the mouse) or **Zoom** (turn the wheel) realtime.

[Esc] – Canceling Commands

The [**Esc**] key is used to cancel a command in *Autodesk Inventor*. The [**Esc**] key is located near the top-left corner of the keyboard. Sometimes, it may be necessary to press the [**Esc**] key twice to cancel a command; it depends on where we are in the command sequence. For some commands, the [**Esc**] key is used to exit the command.

Autodesk Inventor Help System

❖ Several types of help are available at any time during an *Autodesk Inventor* session. *Autodesk Inventor* provides many help functions, such as:

- Use the **Help** button near the upper right corner of the *Inventor* window.

- Help quick-key: Press the [**F1**] key to access the ***Inventor Help* system**.

- Use the ***Info Center*** to get information on a specific topic.

- Use the ***Autodesk Exchange*** to access information on the Autodesk community website.

Data Management using Inventor Project files

With *Autodesk Inventor*, it is quite feasible to create designs without any regard to using the *Autodesk Inventor* data management system. Data management becomes critical for projects involving complex designs, especially when multiple team members are involved, or when we are working on integrating multiple design projects, or when it is necessary to share files among the design projects. *Autodesk Inventor* provides a fairly flexible data management system. It allows one person to use the basic option to help manage the locations of the different design files, or a team of designers can use the data management system to manage their projects stored on a networked computer system.

The *Autodesk Inventor* data management system organizes files based on **projects**. Each project is identified with a main folder that can contain files and folders associated to the design. In *Autodesk Inventor*, a *project* file (.ipj) defines the locations of all files associated with the project, including templates and library files.

The *Autodesk Inventor* data management system uses two types of projects:
➢ **Single-user Project**
➢ **Autodesk Vault Project** (installation of *Autodesk Vault* software is required)

The ***single-user project*** is for simpler projects where all project files are located on the same computer. The ***Autodesk Vault project*** is more suitable for projects requiring multiple users using a networked computer system.

- Click on the **Get Started** tab, with the left-mouse-button, in the *Ribbon* toolbar.

❖ Note the **Get Started** tab is the default panel displayed during startup.

- Click on the **Projects** icon with a single click of the left-mouse-button in the *Launch* toolbar.

❖ The **Projects Editor** appears on the screen. Note that several options are available to access the *Editor*; it can also be accessed through the **Open file** command.

❖ In the *Projects Editor*: the **Default** project is available.

The **Default** project is automatically active by default; and the *default project* does not define any location for files. In other words, the data management system is not used. Using the *default project*, designs can still be created and modified, and any model file can be opened and saved anywhere without regard to project and file management.

Setup of a New Inventor Project

- In this section, we will create a new *Inventor* project for the chapters of this book, using the *Inventor* built-in **Single User Project** option. Note that it is also feasible to create a separate project for each chapter.

    1. Click **New** to begin the setup of a new *project file*.

2. The *Inventor project wizard* appears on the screen; select the **New Single User Project** option as shown.

3. Click **Next** to proceed with the next setup option.

4. In the *Project File Name* input box, enter **Parametric-Modeling** as the name of the new project.

5. In the *Project Folder* input box, note the default folder location, such as **C:\Users\Docuements\Inventor-Data\Parametric Modeling** is displayed; choose a preferred folder name as the folder name of the new project.

6. Click **Finish** to proceed with the creation of the new project.

7. A warning message appears on the screen, indicating the specified folder does not exist. Click **OK** to create the folder.

8. A second warning message appears on the screen, indicating that the newly created project cannot be made active since an *Inventor* file is open. Click **OK** to close the message dialog box.

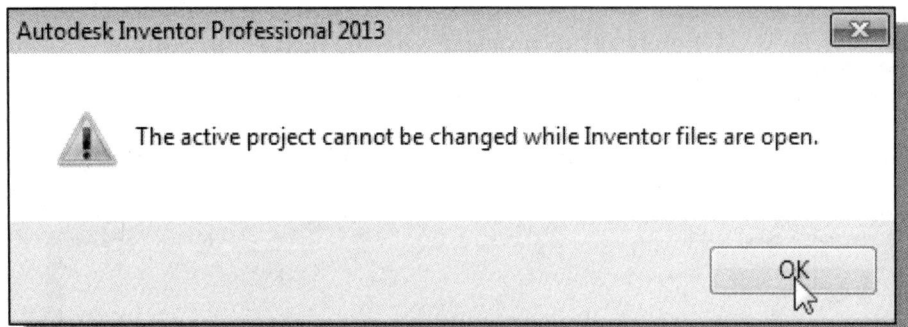

- The new project has been created and its name appears in the project list area as shown in the figure.

9. Click **Done** to exit the *Inventor Projects Editor* option.

The Content of the Inventor Project File

➢ An *Inventor* project file is actually a text file in .xml format with an .ipj extension. The file specifies the paths to the folder containing the files in the project. To assure that links between files work properly, it is advised to add the locations for folders to the project file before working on model files.

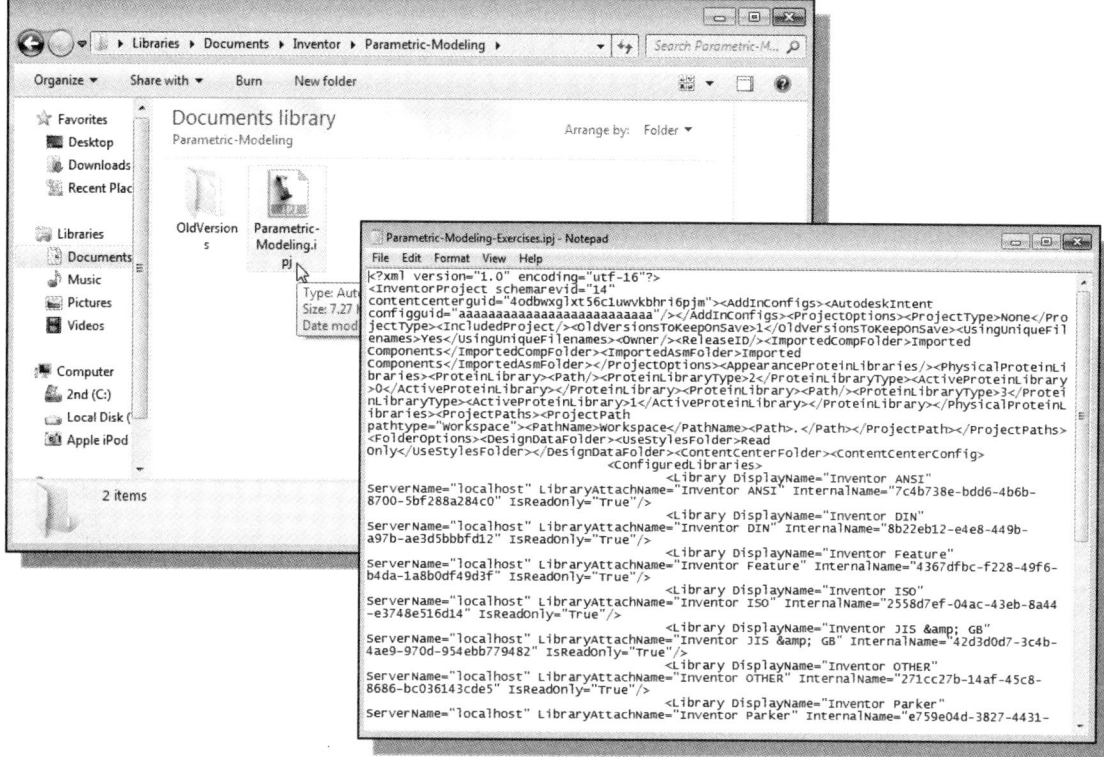

Leaving Autodesk Inventor

➢ To leave the *Application* menu, use the left-mouse-button and click on **Exit Inventor** from the pull-down menu.

Notes:

Chapter 2
Parametric Modeling Fundamentals

Learning Objectives

- ♦ Create Simple Extruded Solid Models
- ♦ Understand the Basic Parametric Modeling Procedure
- ♦ Create 2-D Sketches
- ♦ Understand the "Shape before Size" Design Approach
- ♦ Use the Dynamic Viewing Commands
- ♦ Create and Edit Parametric Dimensions

Introduction

The **feature-based parametric modeling** technique enables the designer to incorporate the original **design intent** into the construction of the model. The word *parametric* means the geometric definitions of the design, such as dimensions, can be varied at any time in the design process. Parametric modeling is accomplished by identifying and creating the key features of the design with the aid of computer software. The design variables, described in the sketches and described as parametric relations, can then be used to quickly modify/update the design.

In *Autodesk Inventor*, the parametric part modeling process involves the following steps:

1. **Create a rough two-dimensional sketch of the basic shape of the base feature of the design.**

2. **Apply/modify constraints and dimensions to the two-dimensional sketch.**

3. **Extrude, revolve, or sweep the parametric two-dimensional sketch to create the base solid feature of the design.**

4. **Add additional parametric features by identifying feature relations and complete the design.**

5. **Perform analyses on the computer model and refine the design as needed.**

6. **Create the desired drawing views to document the design.**

The approach of creating two-dimensional sketches of the three-dimensional features is an effective way to construct solid models. Many designs are in fact the same shape in one direction. Computer input and output devices we use today are largely two-dimensional in nature, which makes this modeling technique quite practical. This method also conforms to the design process that helps the designer with conceptual design along with the capability to capture the ***design intent***. Most engineers and designers can relate to the experience of making rough sketches on restaurant napkins to convey conceptual design ideas. *Autodesk Inventor* provides many powerful modeling and design-tools, and there are many different approaches to accomplishing modeling tasks. The basic principle of **feature-based modeling** is to build models by adding simple features one at a time. In this chapter, the general parametric part modeling procedure is illustrated; a very simple solid model with extruded features is used to introduce the *Autodesk Inventor* user interface. The display viewing functions and the basic two-dimensional sketching tools are also demonstrated.

The *Adjuster* Design

Starting *Autodesk Inventor*

1. Select the **Autodesk Inventor** option on the *Start* menu or select the **Autodesk Inventor** icon on the desktop to start *Autodesk Inventor*. The *Autodesk Inventor* main window will appear on the screen.

2. Select the **Projects** icon with a single click of the left-mouse-button.

3. In the *Projects List*, **double-click** on the ***Parametric-Modeling-Exercises*** project name to activate the project as shown.

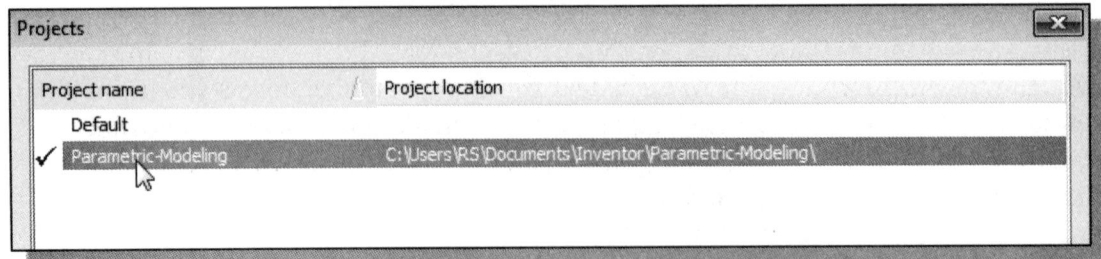

- Note that *Autodesk Inventor* will keep this activated project as the default project until another project is activated.

4. Click **Done** to accept the setting and end the *Projects Editor*.

5. Select the **New File** icon with a single click of the left-mouse-button.

- Notice the ***Parametric-Modeling*** project name is displayed as the active project.

6. Select the **English** tab as shown below. When starting a new CAD file, the first thing we should do is choose the units we would like to use. We will use the English setting (inches) for this example.

7. Select the **Standard(in).ipt** icon as shown.

8. Pick **Create** in the *New File* dialog box to accept the selected settings.

Parametric Modeling Fundamentals   2-5

The default *Autodesk Inventor* screen layout

The default *Autodesk Inventor* drawing screen contains the *pull-down* menus, the *Standard* toolbar, the *Features* toolbar, the *Sketch* toolbar, the *drawing* area, the *browser* area, and the *Status Bar*. A line of quick text appears next to the icon as you move the *mouse cursor* over different icons. You may resize the *Autodesk Inventor* drawing window by clicking and dragging the edges of the window, or relocate the window by clicking dragging the window title area.

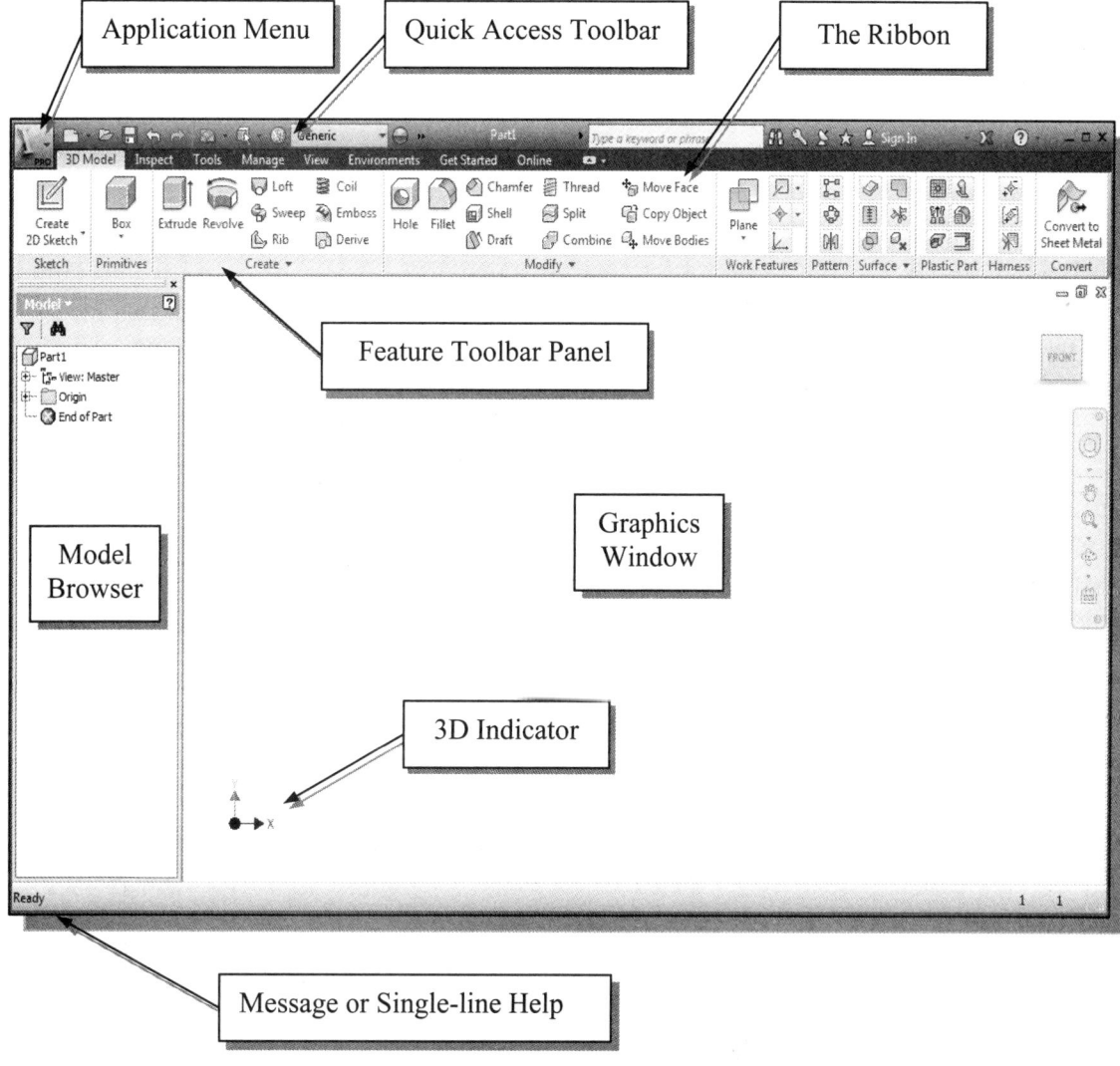

- The **Ribbon** is a new feature in *Autodesk Inventor* since the 2011 release. The *Ribbon* is composed of a series of tool panels, which are organized into tabs labeled by task. The *Ribbon* provides a compact palette of all of the tools necessary to accomplish the different modeling tasks. The drop-down arrow next to any icon indicates additional commands are available on the expanded panel; access the expanded panel by clicking on the drop-down arrow.

Sketch plane – It is an XY monitor, but an XYZ World

Design modeling software is becoming more powerful and user friendly, yet the system still does only what the user tells it to do. When using a geometric modeler, we therefore need to have a good understanding of what its inherent limitations are.

In most 3D geometric modelers, 3D objects are located and defined in what is usually called **world space** or **global space**. Although a number of different coordinate systems can be used to create and manipulate objects in a 3D modeling system, the objects are typically defined and stored using the world space. The world space is usually a **3D Cartesian coordinate system** that the user cannot change or manipulate.

In engineering designs, models can be very complex, and it would be tedious and confusing if only the world coordinate system were available. Practical 3D modeling systems allow the user to define **Local Coordinate Systems (LCS)** or **User Coordinate Systems (UCS)** relative to the world coordinate system. Once a local coordinate system is defined, we can then create geometry in terms of this more convenient system.

Although objects are created and stored in 3D space coordinates, most of the geometric entities can be referenced using 2D Cartesian coordinate systems. Typical input devices such as a mouse or digitizer are two-dimensional by nature; the movement of the input device is interpreted by the system in a planar sense. The same limitation is true of common output devices, such as CRT displays and plotters. The modeling software performs a series of three-dimensional to two-dimensional transformations to correctly project 3D objects onto the 2D display plane.

The *Autodesk Inventor **sketching plane*** is a special construction approach that enables the planar nature of the 2D input devices to be directly mapped into the 3D coordinate system. The *sketching plane* is a local coordinate system that can be aligned to an existing face of a part, or a reference plane.

Think of the sketching plane as the surface on which we can sketch the 2D sections of the parts. It is similar to a piece of paper, a white board, or a chalkboard that can be attached to any planar surface. The first sketch we create is usually drawn on one of the established datum planes. Subsequent sketches/features can then be created on sketching planes that are aligned to existing **planar faces of the solid part** or **datum planes.**

1. Activate the **Create 2D Sketch** icon with a single click of the left-mouse-button.

2. Move the cursor over the edge of the *XY Plane* in the graphics area. When the *XY Plane* is highlighted, click once with the **left-mouse-button** to select the *Plane* as the sketch plane for the new sketch.

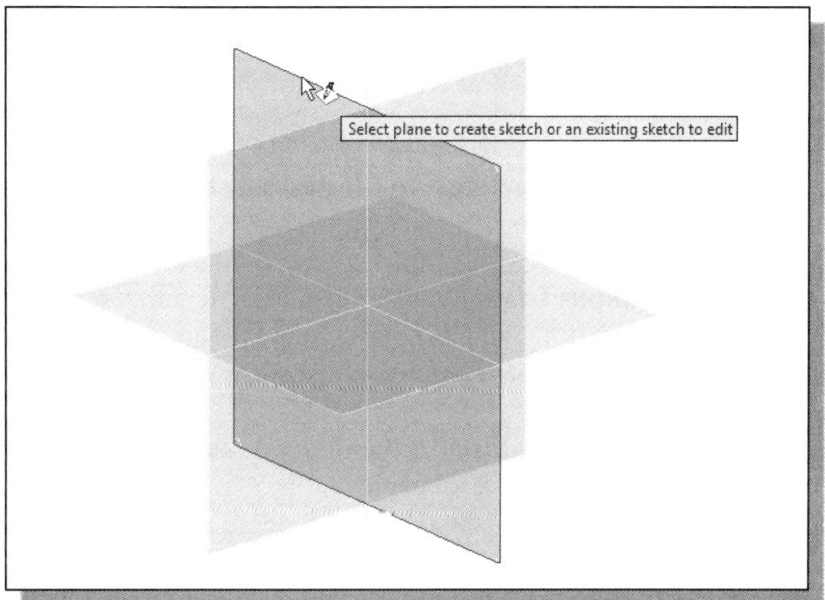

- The *sketching plane* is a reference location where two-dimensional sketches are created. Note that the *sketching plane* can be any planar part surface or datum plane.

3. Confirm the main *Ribbon* area is switched to the **Sketch** toolbars; this indicates we have entered the 2D Sketching mode.

Creating Rough Sketches

Quite often during the early design stage, the shape of a design may not have any precise dimensions. Most conventional CAD systems require the user to input the precise lengths and locations of all geometric entities defining the design, which are not available during the early design stage. With *parametric modeling,* we can use the computer to elaborate and formulate the design idea further during the initial design stage. With *Autodesk Inventor,* we can use the computer as an electronic sketchpad to help us concentrate on the formulation of forms and shapes for the design. This approach is the main advantage of *parametric modeling* over conventional solid-modeling techniques.

As the name implies, a ***rough sketch*** is not precise at all. When sketching, we simply sketch the geometry so that it closely resembles the desired shape. Precise scale or lengths are not needed. *Autodesk Inventor* provides many tools to assist us in finalizing sketches. For example, geometric entities such as horizontal and vertical lines are set automatically. However, if the rough sketches are poor, it will require much more work to generate the desired parametric sketches. Here are some general guidelines for creating sketches in *Autodesk Inventor*:

- **Create a sketch that is proportional to the desired shape.** Concentrate on the shapes and forms of the design.

- **Keep the sketches simple.** Leave out small geometry features such as fillets, rounds and chamfers. They can easily be placed using the **Fillet** and **Chamfer** commands after the parametric sketches have been established.

- **Exaggerate the geometric features of the desired shape.** For example, if the desired angle is 85 degrees, create an angle that is 50 or 60 degrees. Otherwise, *Autodesk Inventor* might assume the intended angle to be a 90-degree angle.

- **Draw the geometry so that it does not overlap.** The geometry should eventually form a closed region. *Self-intersecting* geometry shapes are not allowed.

- **The sketched geometric entities should form a closed region.** To create a solid feature, such as an extruded solid, a closed region is required so that the extruded solid forms a 3D volume.

- ➢ **Note:** The concepts and principles involved in *parametric modeling* are very different, and sometimes they are totally opposite, to those of conventional computer aided drafting. In order to understand and fully utilize *Autodesk Inventor's* functionality, it will be helpful to take a *Zen* approach to learning the topics presented in this text: **Have an open mind and temporarily forget your experiences using conventional Computer Aided Drafting systems.**

Parametric Modeling Fundamentals   2-9

Step 1: Creating a Rough Sketch

> The *Sketch* toolbar provides tools for creating the basic geometry that can be used to create features and parts.

1. Move the graphics cursor to the **Line** icon in the *Sketch* toolbar. A *Help-tip box* appears next to the cursor and a brief description of the command is displayed at the bottom of the drawing screen: "*Creates Straight line segments and tangent arcs.*"

2. Select the icon by clicking once with the **left-mouse-button**; this will activate the Line command. *Autodesk Inventor* expects us to identify the starting location of a straight line.

Graphics Cursors

> Notice the cursor changes from an arrow to a crosshair when graphical input is expected.

1. Left-click a starting point for the shape, roughly just below the center of the graphics window.

2. As you move the graphics cursor, you will see a digital readout next to the cursor and also in the *Status Bar* area at the bottom of the window. The readout gives you the cursor location, the line length, and the angle of the line measured from horizontal. Move the cursor around and you will notice different symbols appear at different locations.

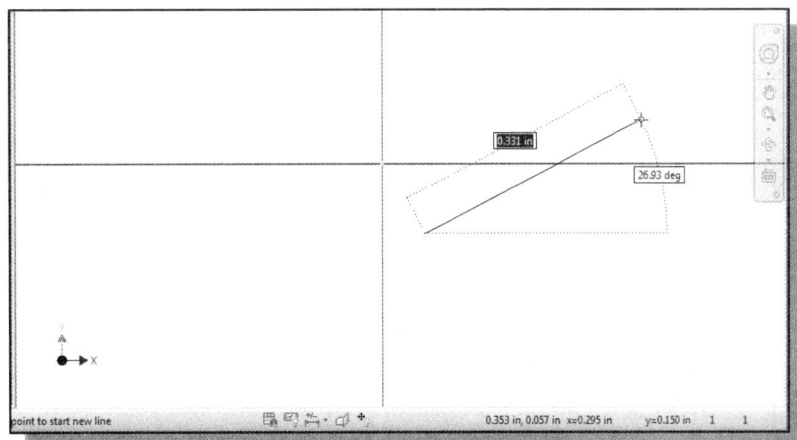

> The readout displayed next to the cursor is called the ***Dynamic Input***. This option is part of the **Heads-Up Display** option that is new in *Inventor*. *Dynamic Input* can be used for entering precise values, but its usage is limited in *parametric modeling*.

3. Move the graphics cursor toward the right side of the graphics window and create a horizontal line as shown below (**Point 2**). Notice the geometric constraint symbol, a short horizontal line indicating the geometric property, is displayed.

Geometric Constraint Symbols

Autodesk Inventor displays different visual clues, or symbols, to show you alignments, perpendicularities, tangencies, etc. These constraints are used to capture the *design intent* by creating constraints where they are recognized. *Autodesk Inventor* displays the governing geometric rules as models are built. To prevent constraints from forming, hold down the [**Ctrl**] key while creating an individual sketch curve. For example, while sketching line segments with the Line command, endpoints are joined with a Coincident *constraint*, but when the [**Ctrl**] key is pressed and held, the inferred constraint will not be created.

‖	**Vertical**	indicates a line is vertical
=	**Horizontal**	indicates a line is horizontal
- - -	**Dashed line**	indicates the alignment is to the center point or endpoint of an entity
∥	**Parallel**	indicates a line is parallel to other entities
⊥	**Perpendicular**	indicates a line is perpendicular to other entities
◠	**Coincident**	indicates the cursor is at the endpoint of an entity
⊚	**Concentric**	indicates the cursor is at the center of an entity
⊙	**Tangent**	indicates the cursor is at tangency points to curves

1. Complete the sketch as shown below, creating a closed region ending at the starting point (**Point 1**). Do not be overly concerned with the actual size of the sketch. Note that all line segments are sketched horizontally or vertically.

2. Inside the graphics window, click once with the **right-mouse-button** to display the option menu. Select Done [Esc] in the popup menu, or hit the [**Esc**] key once, to end the Sketch Line command.

Step 2: Apply/Modify Constraints and Dimensions

➢ As the sketch is made, *Autodesk Inventor* automatically applies some of the geometric constraints (such as horizontal, parallel, and perpendicular) to the sketched geometry. We can continue to modify the geometry, apply additional constraints, and/or define the size of the existing geometry. In this example, we will illustrate adding dimensions to describe the sketched entities.

1. Move the cursor to the *Constrain* toolbar area; it is the toolbar next to the *2D Draw* toolbar. Note the first icon in this toolbar is the General Dimension icon. The Dimension command is generally known as **Smart Dimensioning** in parametric modeling.

2-12   Parametric Modeling with Autodesk Inventor

2. Move the cursor on top of the **Dimension** icon. The **Smart Dimensioning** command allows us to quickly create and modify dimensions. Left-click once on the icon to activate the **Dimension** command.

3. The message "*Select Geometry to Dimension*" is displayed in the *Status Bar* area at the bottom of the *Inventor* window. Select the bottom horizontal line by left-clicking once on the line.

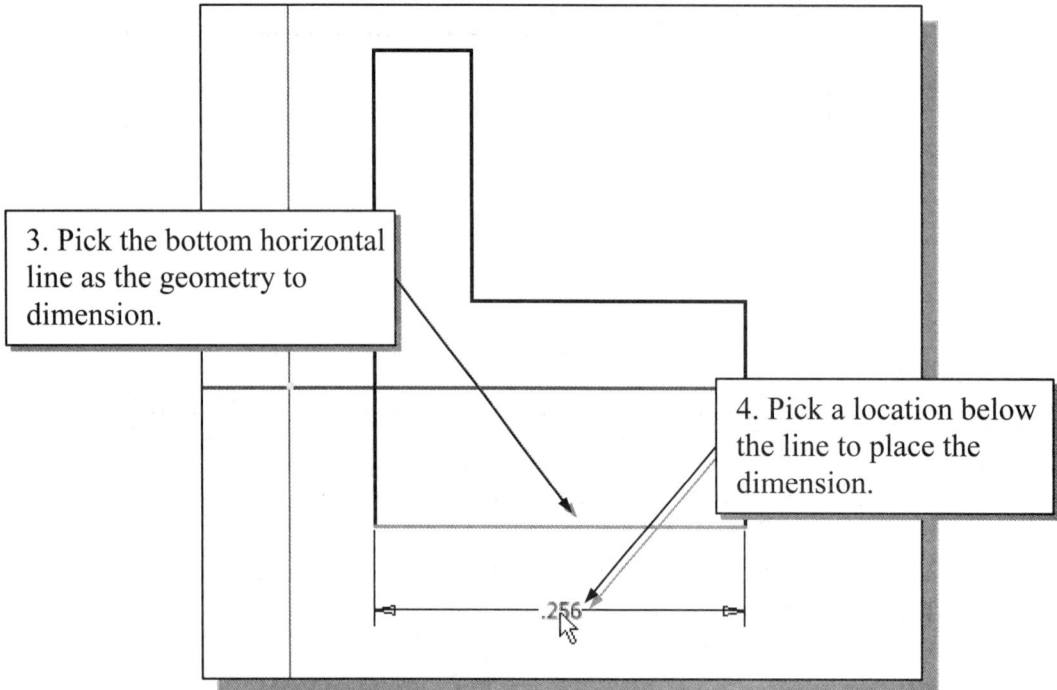

3. Pick the bottom horizontal line as the geometry to dimension.

4. Pick a location below the line to place the dimension.

4. Move the graphics cursor below the selected line and left-click to place the dimension. (Note that the value displayed on your screen might be different than what is shown in the figure above.)

5. The message "*Select Geometry to Dimension*" is displayed in the *Status Bar* area, at the bottom of the *Inventor* window. Select the lower right-vertical line.

6. Pick a location toward the right of the sketch to place the dimension.

7. Accept the default value by clicking on the Accept button as shown.

❖ The **General Dimension** command will create a length dimension if a single line is selected.

8. The message "*Select Geometry to Dimension*" is displayed in the *Status Bar* area, located at the bottom of the *Inventor* window. Select the top-horizontal line as shown below.

9. Select the bottom-horizontal line as shown below.

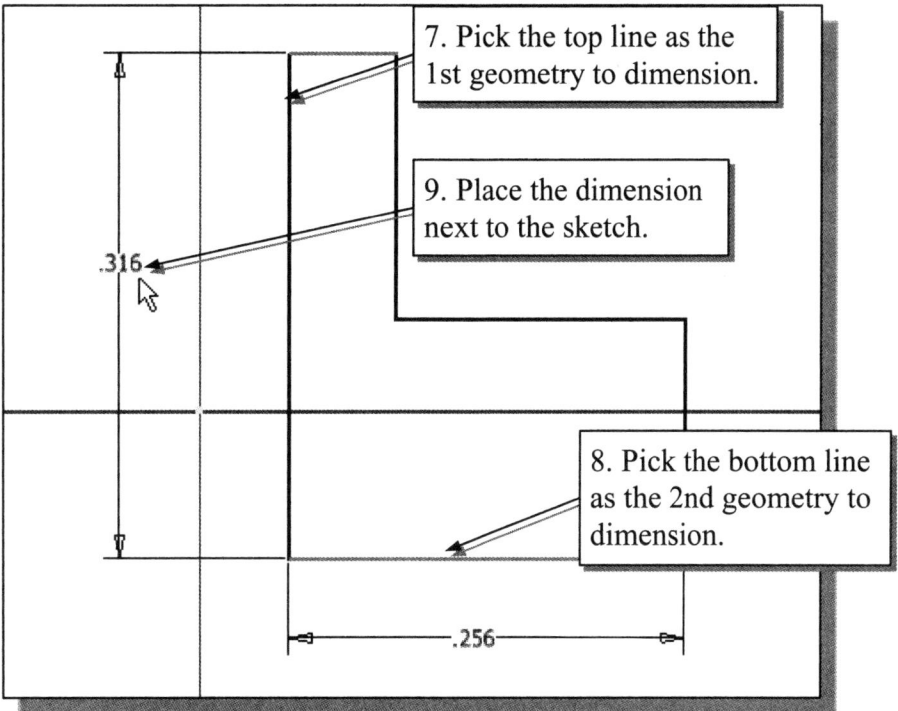

10. Pick a location to the left of the sketch to place the dimension.

❖ When two parallel lines are selected, the General Dimension command will create a dimension measuring the distance between them.

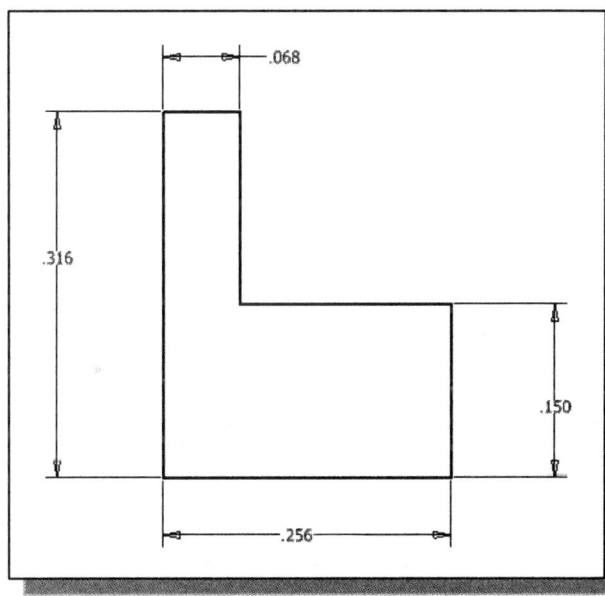

11. On you own, repeat the above steps and create additional dimensions (accepting the default values created by Inventor) so that the sketch appears as shown.

Dynamic Viewing Functions – *Zoom* and *Pan*

- *Autodesk Inventor* provides a special user interface called *Dynamic Viewing* that enables convenient viewing of the entities in the graphics window.

1. Click on the **Zoom** icon, located in the *Navigation* bar as shown.

2. Move the cursor near the center of the graphics window.

3. Inside the graphics window, **press and hold down the left-mouse-button**, then move downward to enlarge the current display scale factor.

4. Press the [**Esc**] key once to exit the Zoom command.

5. Click on the **Pan** icon, located above the Zoom command in the *Navigation* bar. The icon is the picture of a hand.

➤ The Pan command enables us to move the view to a different position. This function acts as if you are using a video camera.

6. On your own, use the Zoom and Pan options to reposition the sketch near the center of the screen.

Modifying the Dimensions of the Sketch

1. Select the dimension that is to the bottom of the sketch by **double-clicking** on the dimension text.

   1. Select this dimension to modify.

2. In the *Edit Dimension* window, the current length of the line is displayed. Enter **2.5** to set the length of the line.

3. Click on the **Accept** icon to accept the entered value.

➤ *Autodesk Inventor* will now update the profile with the new dimension value.

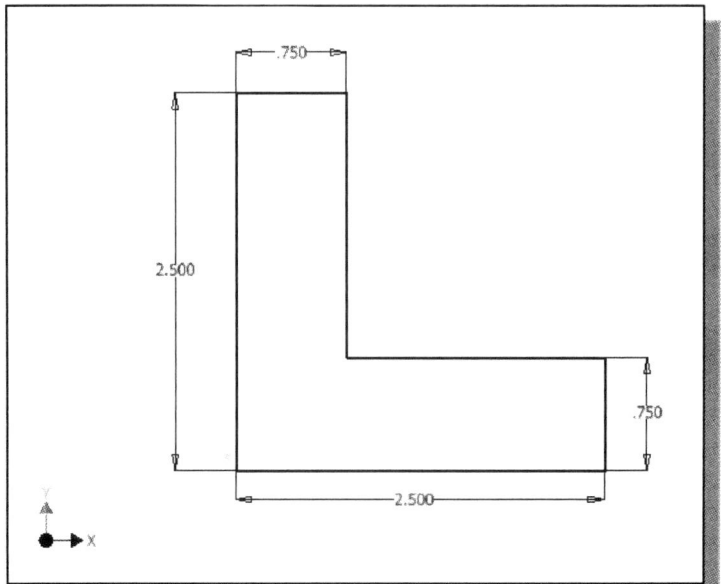

4. On you own, repeat the above steps and adjust the dimensions so that the sketch appears as shown.

5. In the *Ribbon* toolbar, click once with the **left-mouse-button** to select **Finish Sketch** in the *Ribbon* area to end the Sketch option.

Step 3: Completing the Base Solid Feature

Now that the 2D sketch is completed, we will proceed to the next step: create a 3D part from the 2D profile. Extruding a 2D profile is one of the common methods that can be used to create 3D parts. We can extrude planar faces along a path. We can also specify a height value and a tapered angle. In *Autodesk Inventor*, each face has a positive side and a negative side, the current face we're working on is set as the default positive side. This positive side identifies the positive extrusion direction and it is referred to as the face's ***normal***.

1. In the 3D Model tab, select the **Extrude** command by clicking the left-mouse-button on the icon as shown.

2. In the *Extrude* edit box, enter **2.5** as the extrusion distance. Notice that the sketch region is automatically selected as the extrusion profile.

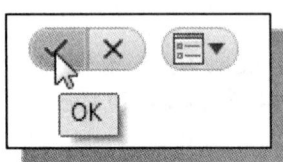

3. Click on the **OK** button to proceed with creating the 3D part.

> Note that all dimensions disappeared from the screen. All parametric definitions are stored in the ***Autodesk Inventor* database** and any of the parametric definitions can be re-displayed and edited at any time.

Isometric View

❖ *Autodesk Inventor* provides many ways to display views of the three-dimensional design. Several options are available that allow us to quickly view the design to track the overall effect of any changes being made to the model. We will first orient the model to display in the *isometric view*, by using the pull-down menu.

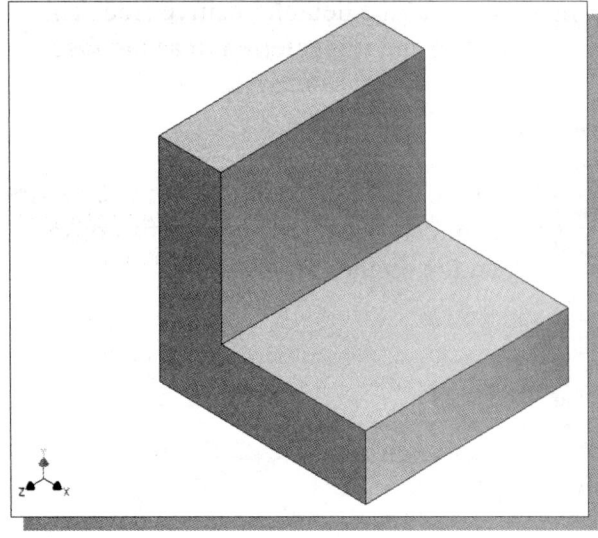

1. Hit the function key **[F6]** once to automatically adjust the display and also reset the display to the *isometric* view.

❖ Note that most of the view-related commands can be accessed in the **ViewCube** and/or the *Navigation* bar located to the right side of the graphics window.

Dynamic Rotation of the 3D Block – *Free Orbit*

The **Free Orbit** command allows us to:
- Orbit a part or assembly in the graphics window. Rotation can be around the center mark, free in all directions, or around the X/Y-axes in the *3D-Orbit* display.
- Reposition the part or assembly in the graphics window.
- Display isometric or standard orthographic views of a part or assembly.
- The **Free Orbit** tool is accessible while other tools are active. *Autodesk Inventor* remembers the last used mode when you exit the **Orbit** command.

1. Click on the **Free Orbit** icon in the *Navigation* bar.

> The *3D Orbit* display is a circular rim with four handles and a center mark. *3D Orbit* enables us to manipulate the view of 3D objects by clicking and dragging with the left-mouse-button:

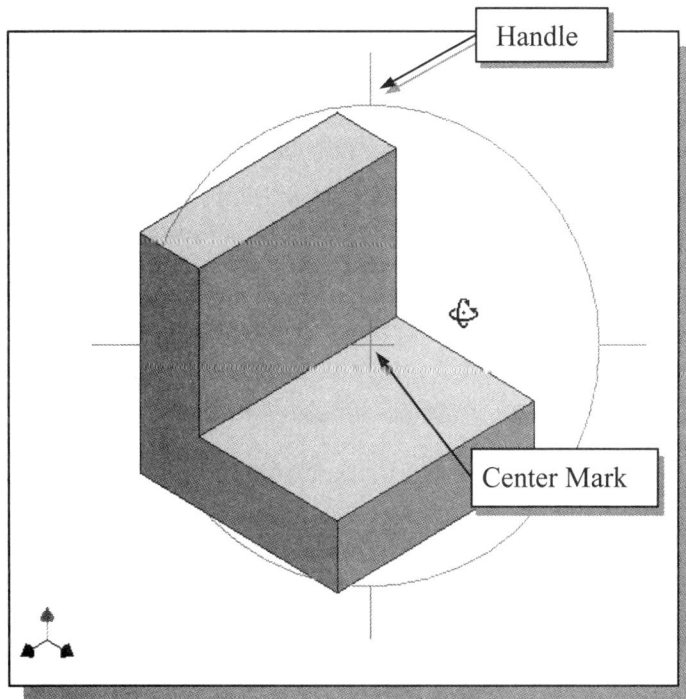

- Drag with the left-mouse-button near the center for free rotation.

- Drag on the handles to orbit around the horizontal or vertical axes.

- Drag on the rim to orbit about an axis that is perpendicular to the displayed view.

- Single left-mouse-click to align the center mark of the view.

2. Inside the *circular rim*, press down the left-mouse-button and drag in an arbitrary direction; the **3D Orbit** command allows us to freely orbit the solid model.

3. Move the cursor near the circular rim and notice the cursor symbol changes to a single circle. Drag with the left-mouse-button to orbit about an axis that is perpendicular to the displayed view.

4. Single left-mouse-click near the top-handle to align the selected location to the center mark in the graphics window.

5. Activate the **Constrained Orbit** option by clicking on the associated icon as shown.

❖ *The Constrained Orbit can be used to rotate the model about axes in Model Space, equivalent to moving the eye position about the model in latitude and longitude.*

6. On your own, use the different options described in the above steps and familiarize yourself with both of the 3D Orbit commands. Reset the display to the *Isometric* view as shown in the above figure before continuing to the next section.

❖ Note that while in the 3D Orbit mode, a horizontal marker will be displayed next to the cursor if the cursor is away from the circular rim. This is the **exit marker**. Left-clicking once will allow you to exit the 3D Orbit command.

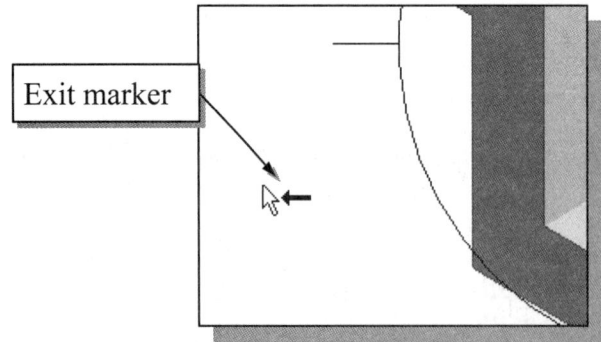

Parametric Modeling Fundamentals   2-19

Dynamic Viewing – Quick Keys

We can also use the function keys on the keyboard and the mouse to access the *Dynamic Viewing* functions.

❖ Panning – (1) F2 and the left-mouse-button

Hold the **F2** function key down, and drag with the left-mouse-button to pan the display. This allows you to reposition the display while maintaining the same scale factor of the display.

Pan

(2) Press and drag with the mouse wheel

Press and drag with the mouse wheel can also reposition the display.

❖ Zooming – (1) F3 and drag with the left-mouse-button

Hold the **F3** function key down, and drag with the left-mouse-button vertically on the screen to adjust the scale of the display. Moving upward will reduce the scale of the display, making the entities display smaller on the screen. Moving downward will magnify the scale of the display.

Zoom

(2) Turning the mouse wheel

Turning the mouse wheel can also adjust the scale of the display. Turning forward will reduce the scale of the display, making the entities display smaller on the screen. Turning backward will magnify the scale of the display.

❖ **3D Dynamic Rotation – Shift and the middle-mouse-button**

Hold the **Shift** key down and drag with the middle-mouse-button to orbit the display. Note that the 3D dynamic rotation can also be activated using the **F4** function key and the left-mouse-button.

Dynamic Rotation   Shift + ⇐ MOUSE ⇒ (↑↓)

Viewing Tools – Standard Toolbar

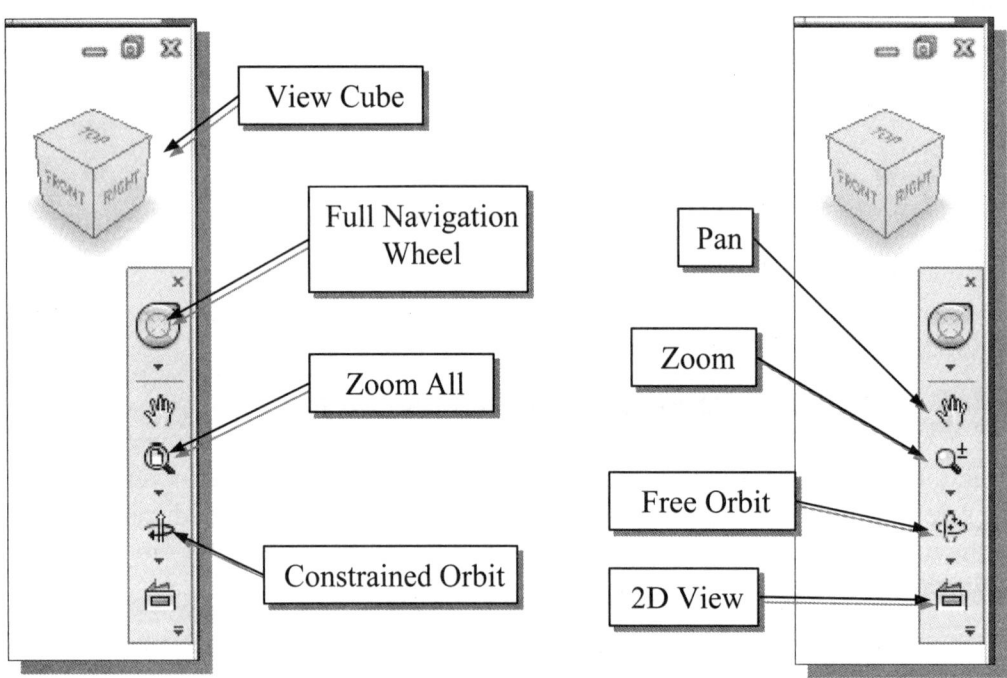

Zoom All – Adjusts the view so that all items on the screen fit inside the graphics window.

Zoom Window – Use the cursor to define a region for the view; the defined region is zoomed to fill the graphics window.

Zoom – Moving upward will reduce the scale of the display, making the entities display smaller on the screen. Moving downward will magnify the scale of the display.

Pan – This allows you to reposition the display while maintaining the same scale factor of the display

Zoom Selected – In a part or assembly, zooms the selected edge, feature, line, or other element to fill the graphics window. You can select the element either before or after clicking the Zoom button. (Not used in drawings.)

Orbit – In a part or assembly, adds an orbit symbol and cursor to the view. You can orbit the view planar to the screen around the center mark, around a horizontal or vertical axis, or around the X and Y axes. (Not used in drawings.)

2D View – In a part or assembly, zooms and orbits the model to display the selected element planar to the screen or a selected edge or line horizontal to the screen. (Not used in drawings.)

View Cube – The ViewCube is a 3D navigation tool that appears, by default, when you enter *Inventor*. The ViewCube is a clickable interface which allows you to switch between standard and isometric views.

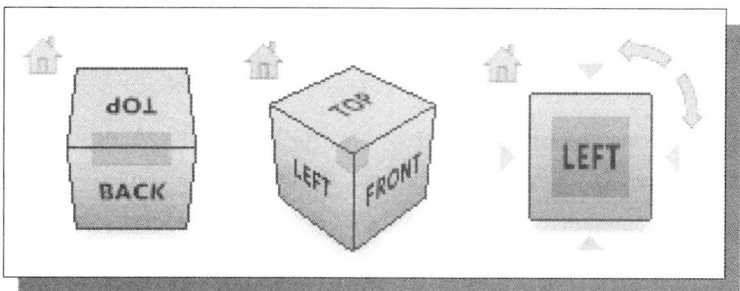

Once the ViewCube is displayed, it is shown in one of the corners of the graphics window over the model in an inactive state. The ViewCube also provides visual feedback about the current viewpoint of the model as view changes occur. When the cursor is positioned over the ViewCube, it becomes active and allows you to switch to one of the available preset views, roll the current view, or change to the Home view of the model.

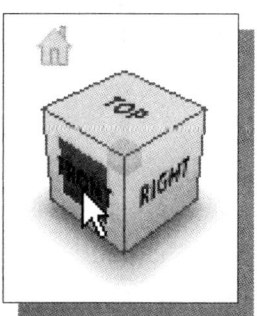

1. Move the cursor over the ViewCube and notice the different sides of the ViewCube become highlighted and can be activated.

2. Single left-mouse-click when the front side is activated as shown. The current view is set to view the front side.

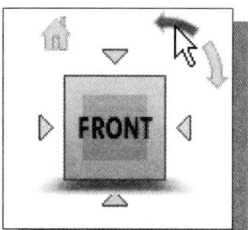

3. Move the cursor over the counter-clockwise arrow of the ViewCube and notice the orbit option becomes highlighted.

4. Single left-mouse-click to activate the counter-clockwise option as shown. The current view is orbited 90 degrees; we are still viewing the front side.

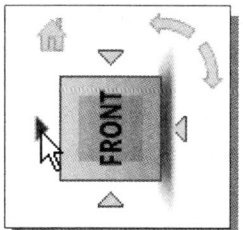

5. Move the cursor over the left arrow of the ViewCube and notice the orbit option becomes highlighted.

6. Single left-mouse-click to activate the left arrow option as shown. The current view is now set to view the top side.

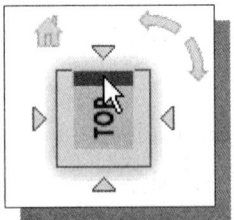

7. Move the cursor over the top edge of the ViewCube and notice the roll option becomes highlighted.

8. Single left-mouse-click to activate the roll option as shown. The view will be adjusted to roll 45 degrees.

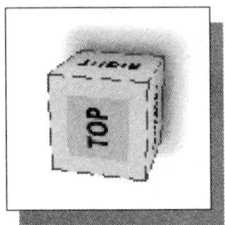

9. Move the cursor over the ViewCube and drag with the left-mouse-button to activate the **Free Rotation** option.

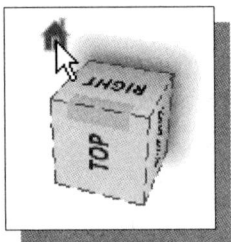

10. Move the cursor over the home icon of the ViewCube and notice the Home View option becomes highlighted.

11. Single left-mouse-click to activate the **Home View** option as shown. The view will be adjusted back to the default *isometric view*.

Full Navigation Wheel – The Navigation Wheel contains tracking menus that are divided into different sections known as wedges. Each wedge on a wheel represents a single navigation tool. You can pan, zoom, or manipulate the current view of a model in different ways. The 3D Navigation Wheel and 2D Navigation Wheel (mostly used in the 2D drawing mode) have some or all of the following options:

Zoom – Adjusts the magnification of the view.
Center – Centers the view based on the position of the cursor over the wheel.
Rewind – Restores the previous view.
Forward – Increases the magnification of the view.
Orbit – Allows 3D free rotation with the left-mouse-button.
Pan – Allows panning by dragging with the left-mouse-button.
Up/Down – Allows panning with the use of a scroll control.
Walk – Allows *walking*, with linear motion perpendicular to the screen, through the model space.
Look – Allows rotation of the current view vertically and horizontally

3D Full Navigation Wheel   2D Full Navigation Wheel

Parametric Modeling Fundamentals   2-23

1. Activate the **Full Navigation Wheel,** by clicking on the icon as shown.

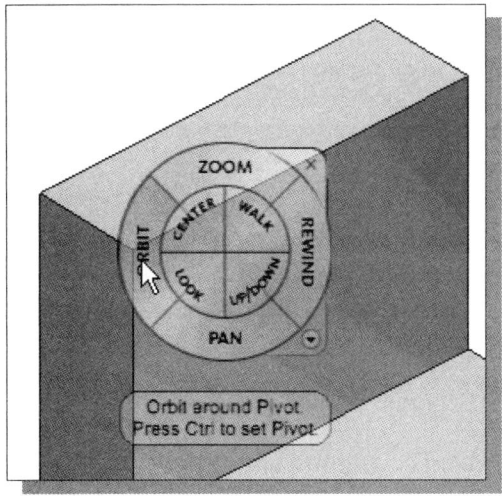

2. Move the cursor in the graphics window and notice the **Full Navigation Wheel** menu follows the cursor on the screen.

3. Move the cursor on the Orbit option to highlight the option.

4. Click and drag with the left-mouse-button to activate the **Free Rotation** option.

5. Drag with the left-mouse-button and notice the **ViewCube** also reflects the model orientation.

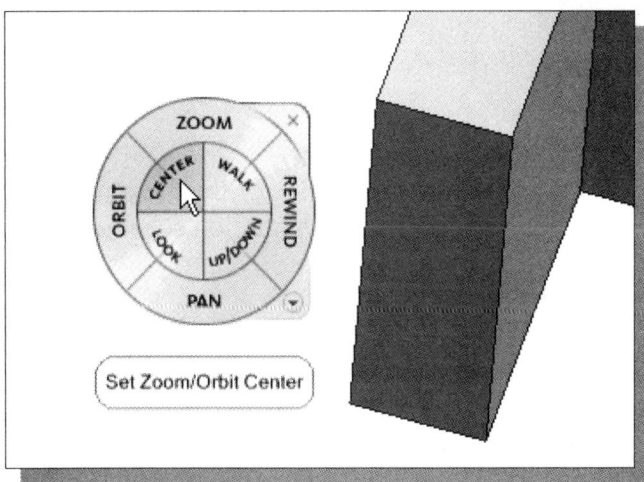

6. Move the cursor to the left side of the model and click the **Center** option as shown. The display is adjusted so the selected point is the new **Zoom/Orbit** center.

7. On your own, experiment with the other available options.

Display Modes

- The **Visual Style** in the *View* tab has ten display-modes; ranging from very realistic renderings of the model to very artistic representations of the model. The more commonly used modes are as follows:

❖ **Realistic Shaded Solid:**

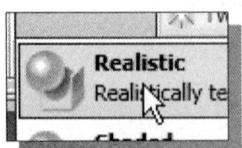

The *Realistic Shaded Solid* display mode generates a high quality shaded image of the 3D object.

❖ **Standard Shaded Solid:**

The *Standard Shaded Solid* display option generates a shaded image of the 3D object that requires fewer computer resources compared to the realistic rendering.

❖ **Wireframe Image:**

The *Wireframe Image* display option allows the display of the 3D objects using the basic wireframe representation scheme.

❖ **Wireframe with Hidden-Edge Display:**

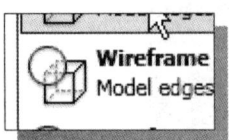

The **Wireframe with Hidden-Edge Display** option can be used to generate an image of the 3D object with all the back lines hidden.

Orthographic vs. Perspective

- Besides the three basic display modes, we can also choose orthographic view or perspective view of the display. Click on the icon next to the display mode button on the *Standard* toolbar, as shown in the figure.

❖ **Orthographic**
The first icon allows the display of the 3D object using the parallel edges representation scheme.

❖ **Perspective**
The second icon allows the display of the 3D object using the perspective, nonparallel edges, and representation scheme.

Disable the Heads-Up Display Option

- The **Heads-Up Display** option in *Inventor* provides mainly the **Dynamic Input** function, which can be quite useful for 2D drafting activities. For example, in the use of a 2D drafting CAD system, most of the dimensions of the design would have been determined by the documentation stage. However, in *parametric modeling*, the usage of the *Dynamic Input* option is quite limited, as this approach does not conform to the "**shape before size**" design philosophy.

1. Select the **Tools** tab in the *Ribbon* as shown.

2. Select **Application Options** in the options toolbar as shown.

3. Pick the **Sketch** tab to display the sketch related settings.

4. In the *Heads-Up Display* section, turn **OFF** the *Enable Heads-Up Display* option as shown.

5. On your own, examine the other sketch settings that are available; switch **On** the *Grid lines* in the *Display* section.

6. Click **OK** to accept the settings.

Step 4-1: Adding an Extruded Feature

1. Activate the *Model* tab and select the **Create 2D Sketch** command by left-clicking once on the icon.

2. In the *Status Bar* area, the message: "*Select face, workplane, sketch or sketch geometry*" is displayed. *Autodesk Inventor* expects us to identify a planar surface where the 2D sketch of the next feature is to be created. Move the graphics cursor on the 3D part and notice that *Autodesk Inventor* will automatically highlight feasible planes and surfaces as the cursor is on top of the different surfaces. Pick the top horizontal face of the 3D solid object.

2. Pick the top face of the solid model.

➢ Note that the sketch plane is aligned to the selected face. *Autodesk Inventor* automatically establishes a User-Coordinate-System (UCS), and records its location with respect to the part on which it was created.

• Next, we will create and profile another sketch, a rectangle, which will be used to create another extrusion feature that will be added to the existing solid object.

1. Select the **Line** command by clicking once with the **left-mouse-button** on the icon in the *Sketch* toolbar.

2. Create a sketch with segments perpendicular/parallel to the existing edges of the solid model as shown below.

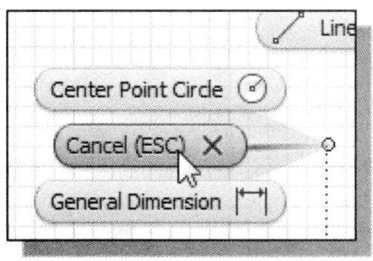

3. Inside the graphics window, click once with the **right-mouse-button** to display the option menu. Select **Cancel (ESC)** in the popup menu to end the Line command.

4. Select the **General Dimension** command in the *Sketch* toolbar. The General Dimension command allows us to quickly create and modify dimensions. Left-click once on the icon to activate the General Dimension command.

5. The message "*Select Geometry to Dimension*" is displayed in the *Status Bar* area, at the bottom of the *Inventor* window. Create the four dimensions to describe the size of the sketch as shown in the figure.

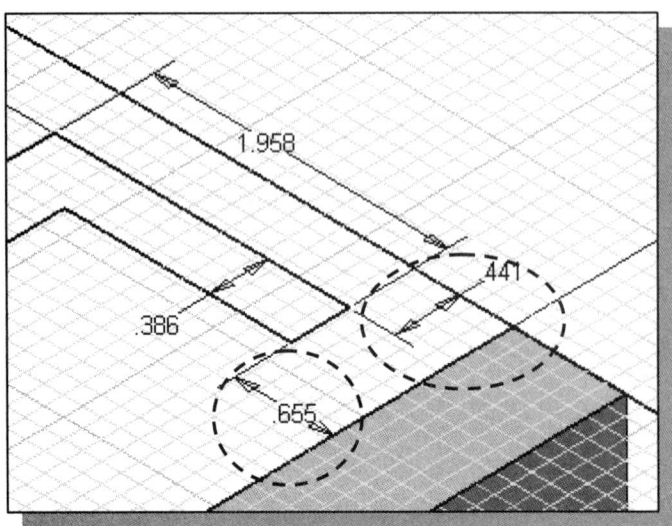

6. Create the two location dimensions to describe the position of the sketch relative to the top corner of the solid model as shown.

7. On your own, modify the two location dimensions to **0.0** and adjust the size dimensions as shown in the figure below.

8. Inside the graphics window, click once with the **right-mouse-button** to display the option menu. Select **OK** in the popup menu to end the General Dimension command.

9. Inside the graphics window, click once with the **right-mouse-button** to display the option menu. Select **Finish Sketch** in the popup menu to end the Sketch option.

10. In the *Part Features* toolbar (the toolbar that is located to the left side of the graphics window), select the **Extrude** command by releasing the left-mouse-button on the icon.

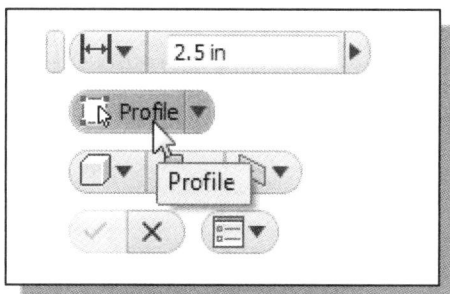

11. In the *Extrude* popup control, the **Profile** option is activated; *Autodesk Inventor* expects us to identify the profile to be extruded.

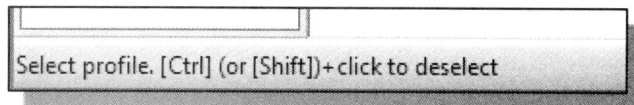

12. Move the cursor inside the rectangle we just created and left-click once to select the region as the profile to be extruded.

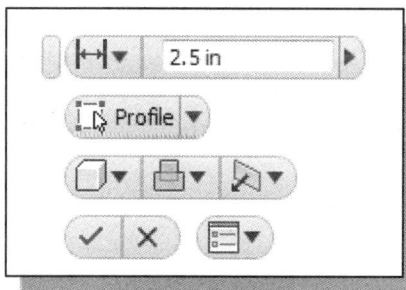

13. In the *Extrude* popup window, enter **2.5** as the extrude distance as shown.

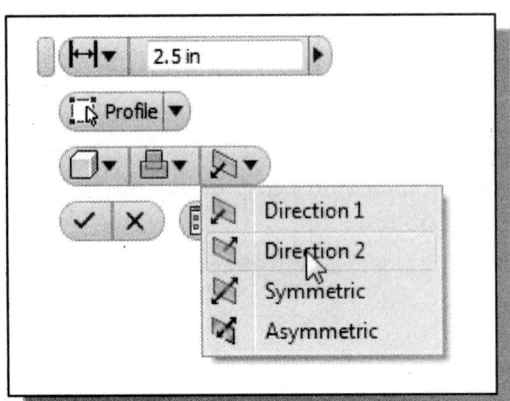

14. Click on the **direction 2 icon** to set the extrusion direction downward as shown.

15. Click on the **OK** button to proceed with creating the extruded feature.

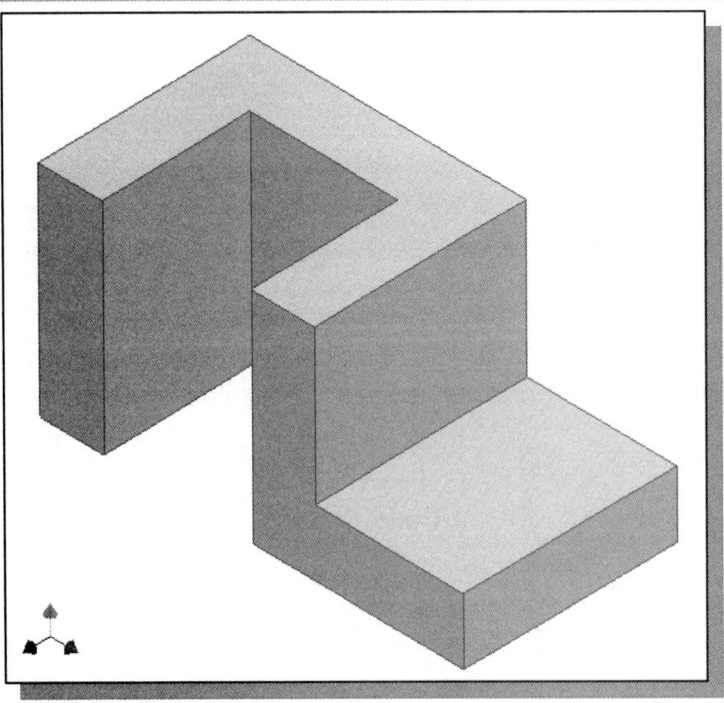

Step 4-2: Adding a Cut Feature

- Next, we will create and profile a circle, which will be used to create a **cut** feature that will be added to the existing solid object.

1. In the *Sketch* toolbar select the **Create 2D Sketch** command by left-clicking once on the icon.

2. In the *Status Bar* area, the message: "*Select face, workplane, sketch or sketch geometry.*" is displayed. *Autodesk Inventor* expects us to identify a planar surface where the 2D sketch of the next feature is to be created. Pick the top horizontal face of the 3D solid model as shown.

> Note that the sketch plane is aligned to the selected face. *Autodesk Inventor* automatically establishes a User-Coordinate-System (UCS), and records its location with respect to the part on which it was created.

3. Select the **Center point circle** command by clicking once with the **left-mouse-button** on the icon in the *Sketch* toolbar.

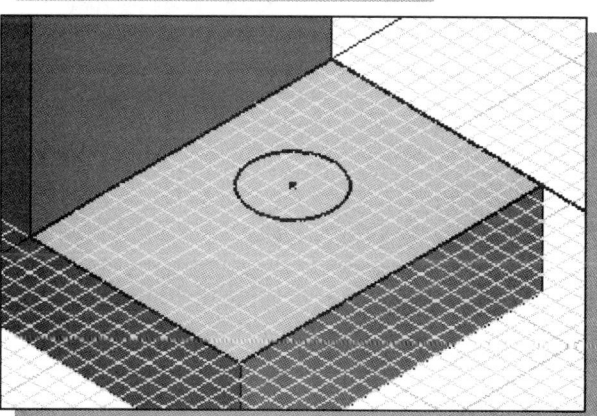

4. Create a circle of arbitrary size on the top face of the solid model as shown.

5. On your own, create and modify the dimensions of the sketch as shown in the figure.

6. Inside the graphics window, click once with the **right-mouse-button** to display the option menu. Select **OK** in the popup menu to end the General Dimension command.

7. Inside the graphics window, click once with the **right-mouse-button** to display the option menu. Select **Finish Sketch** in the popup menu to end the Sketch option.

8. In the *Part Features* toolbar (the toolbar that is located to the left side of the graphics window), select the **Extrude** command by releasing the left-mouse-button on the icon.

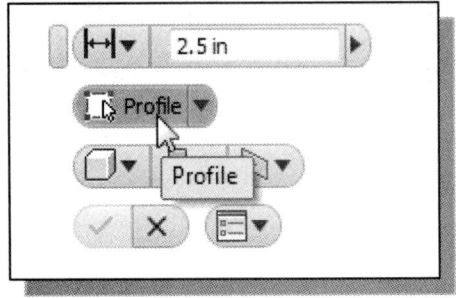

9. In the *Extrude* popup control, the **Profile** button is pressed down; *Autodesk Inventor* expects us to identify the profile to be extruded.

Parametric Modeling Fundamentals   2-33

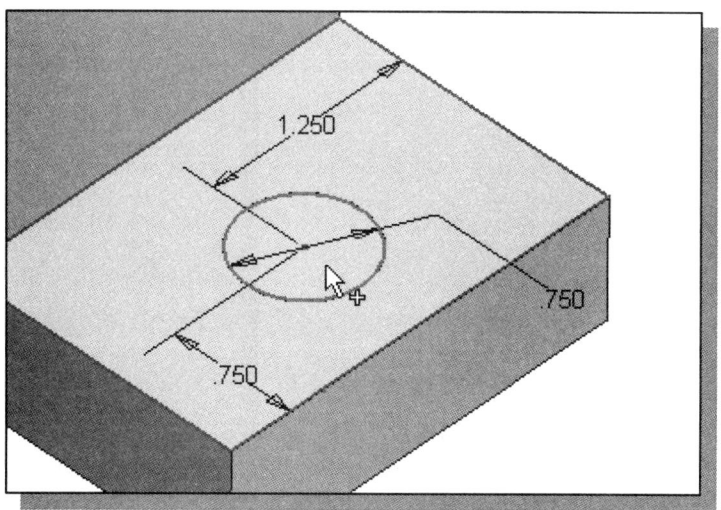

10. Click on the inside of the sketched circle as shown.

11. Select the **CUT** option in the *feature option* list, to set the extrusion operation to *Cut*.

12. Set the *Extents* option to **Through All** as shown. The *All* option instructs the software to calculate the extrusion distance and assures the created feature will always cut through the full length of the model.

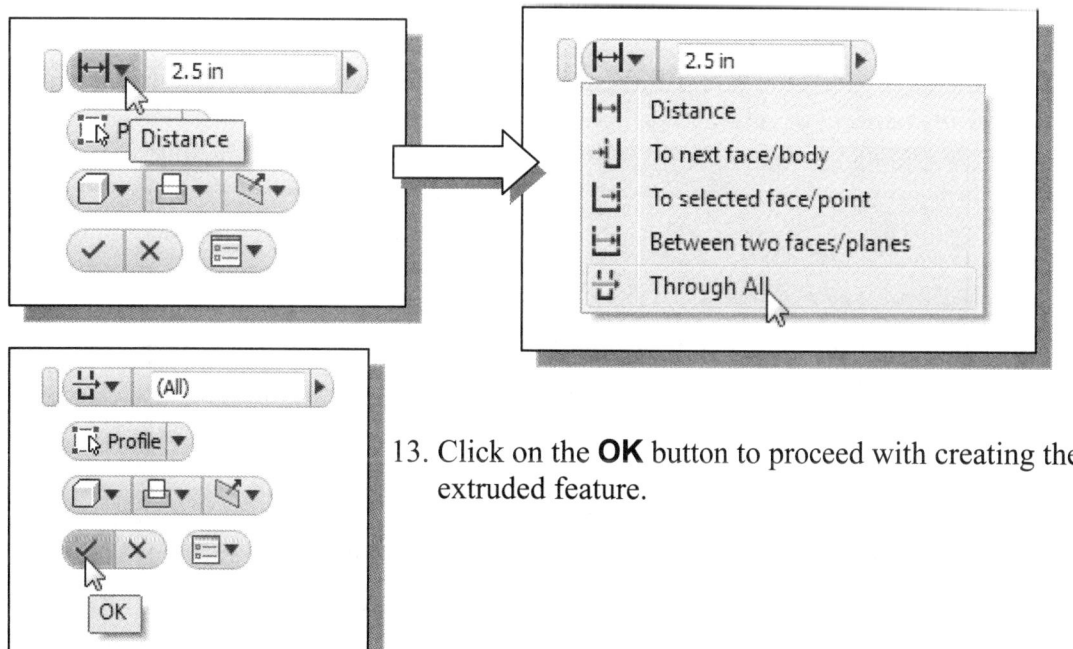

13. Click on the **OK** button to proceed with creating the extruded feature.

Save the Model

1. Select **Save** in the *Quick Access* toolbar, or you can also use the "**Ctrl-S**" combination (hold down the "Ctrl" key and hit the "S" key once) to save the part.

2. In the *Save As* dialog box, **right-mouse-click** once in the *list area* to bring up the *option menu*.

Parametric Modeling Fundamentals   2-35

3. In the *option list*, select **New** as shown.

4. In the second *option list*, select **Folder** to create a subfolder.

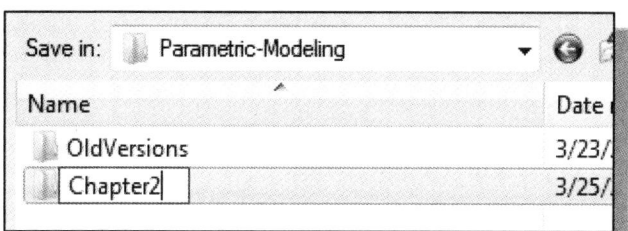

5. Enter **Chapter2** as the new folder name as shown.

6. **Double-click** on the Chapter2 folder to open it.

7. In the *file name* editor box, enter **Adjuster** as the file name.

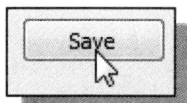 8. Click on the **Save** button to save the file.

❖ You should form a habit of saving your work periodically, just in case something goes wrong while you are working on it. In general, you should save your work at an interval of every 15 to 20 minutes. You should also save before making any major modifications to the model.

Questions: (Time: 20 minutes)

1. What is the first thing we should set up in *Autodesk Inventor* when creating a new model?

2. Describe the general *parametric modeling* procedure.

3. Describe the general guidelines in creating *Rough Sketches*.

4. What is the main difference between a rough sketch and a *profile*?

5. List two of the geometric constraint symbols used by *Autodesk Inventor*.

6. What was the first feature we created in this lesson?

7. How many solid features were created in the tutorial?

8. How do we control the size of a feature in parametric modeling?

9. Which command was used to create the last cut feature in the tutorial? How many dimensions do we need to fully describe the cut feature?

10. List and describe three differences between parametric modeling and traditional 2D Computer Aided Drafting techniques.

Exercises: Create and save the exercises in the Chapter2 folder.
(Time: 90 minutes. All dimensions are in inches.)

1. **Inclined Support** (Thickness: **.5**)

2. **Spacer Plate** (Thickness: **.125**)

3. **Positioning Stop**

4. **Guide Block**

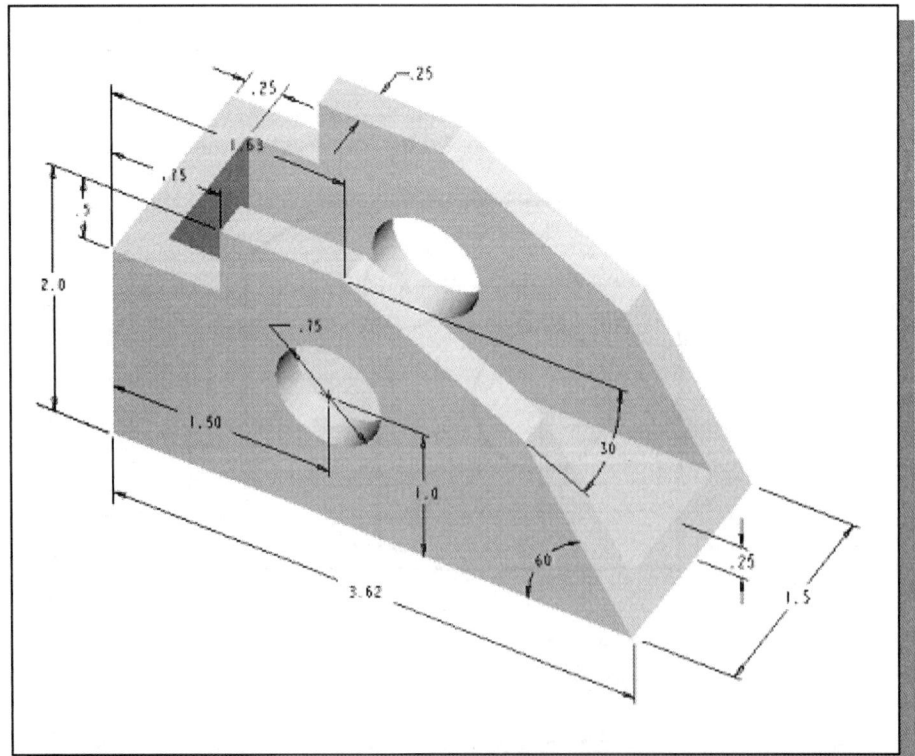

Chapter 3
Constructive Solid Geometry Concepts

Learning Objectives

- **Understand Constructive Solid Geometry Concepts**
- **Create a Binary Tree**
- **Understand the Basic Boolean Operations**
- **Setup GRID and SNAP Intervals**
- **Understand the Importance of Order of Features**
- **Create Placed Features**
- **Use the Different Extrusion Options**

Introduction

In the 1980s, one of the main advancements in **solid modeling** was the development of the **Constructive Solid Geometry** (CSG) method. CSG describes the solid model as combinations of basic three-dimensional shapes (**primitive solids**). The basic primitive solid set typically includes: Rectangular-prism (Block), Cylinder, Cone, Sphere, and Torus (Tube). Two solid objects can be combined into one object in various ways using operations known as **Boolean operations**. There are three basic Boolean operations: **JOIN (Union)**, **CUT (Difference)**, and **INTERSECT**. The *JOIN* operation combines the two volumes included in the different solids into a single solid. The *CUT* operation subtracts the volume of one solid object from the other solid object. The *INTERSECT* operation keeps only the volume common to both solid objects. The CSG method is also known as the **Machinist's Approach**, as the method is parallel to machine shop practices.

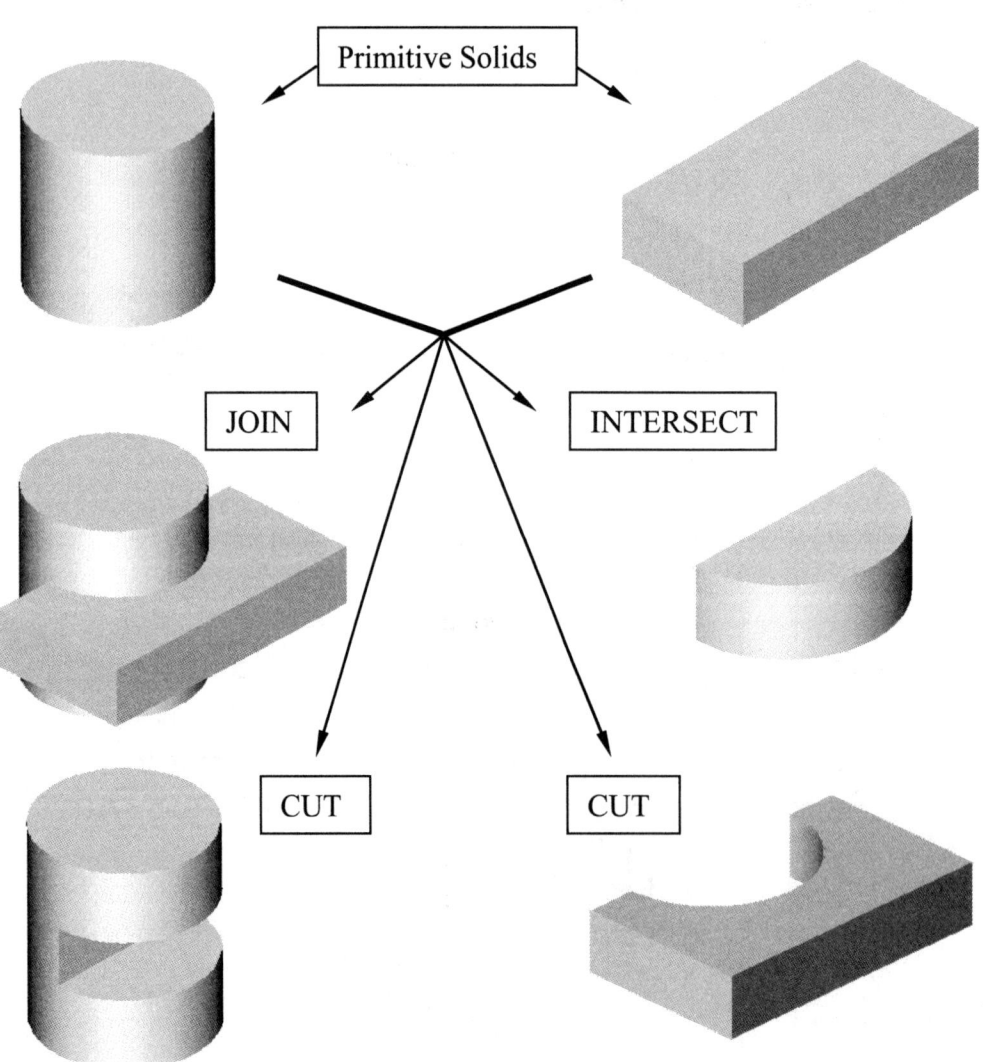

Binary Tree

The CSG is also referred to as the method used to store a solid model in the database. The resulting solid can be easily represented by what is called a **binary tree**. In a binary tree, the terminal branches (leaves) are the various primitives that are linked together to make the final solid object (the root). The binary tree is an effective way to keep track of the *history* of the resulting solid. By keeping track of the history, the solid model can be re-built by re-linking through the binary tree. This provides a convenient way to modify the model. We can make modifications at the appropriate links in the binary tree and re-link the rest of the history tree without building a new model.

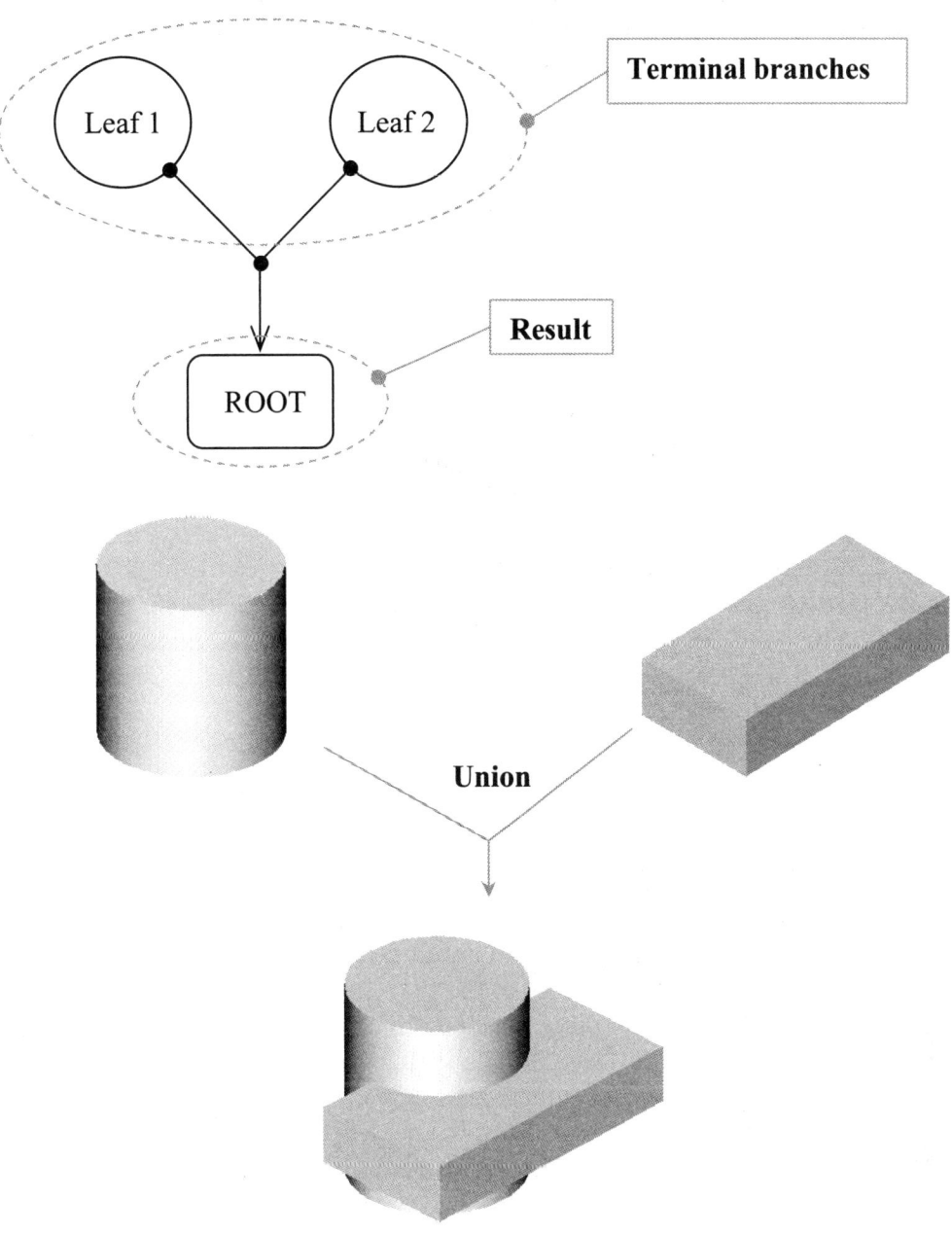

The *Locator* Design

The CSG concept is one of the important building blocks for feature-based modeling. In *Autodesk Inventor*, the CSG concept can be used as a planning tool to determine the number of features that are needed to construct the model. It is also a good practice to create features that are parallel to the manufacturing process required for the design. With parametric modeling, we are no longer limited to using only the predefined basic solid shapes. In fact, any solid features we create in *Autodesk Inventor* are used as primitive solids; parametric modeling allows us to maintain full control of the design variables that are used to describe the features. In this lesson, a more in-depth look at the parametric modeling procedure is presented. The equivalent CSG operation for each feature is also illustrated.

➢ Before going through the tutorial, on your own, make a sketch of a CSG binary tree of the **Locator** design using only two basic types of primitive solids: cylinder and rectangular prism. In your sketch, how many *Boolean operations* will be required to create the model? What is your choice of the first primitive solid to use, and why? Take a few minutes to consider these questions and do the preliminary planning by sketching on a piece of paper. Compare the sketch you make to the CSG binary tree steps shown on page 3-6. Note that there are many different possibilities in combining the basic primitive solids to form the solid model. Even for the simplest design, it is possible to take several different approaches to creating the same solid model.

Modeling Strategy – CSG Binary Tree

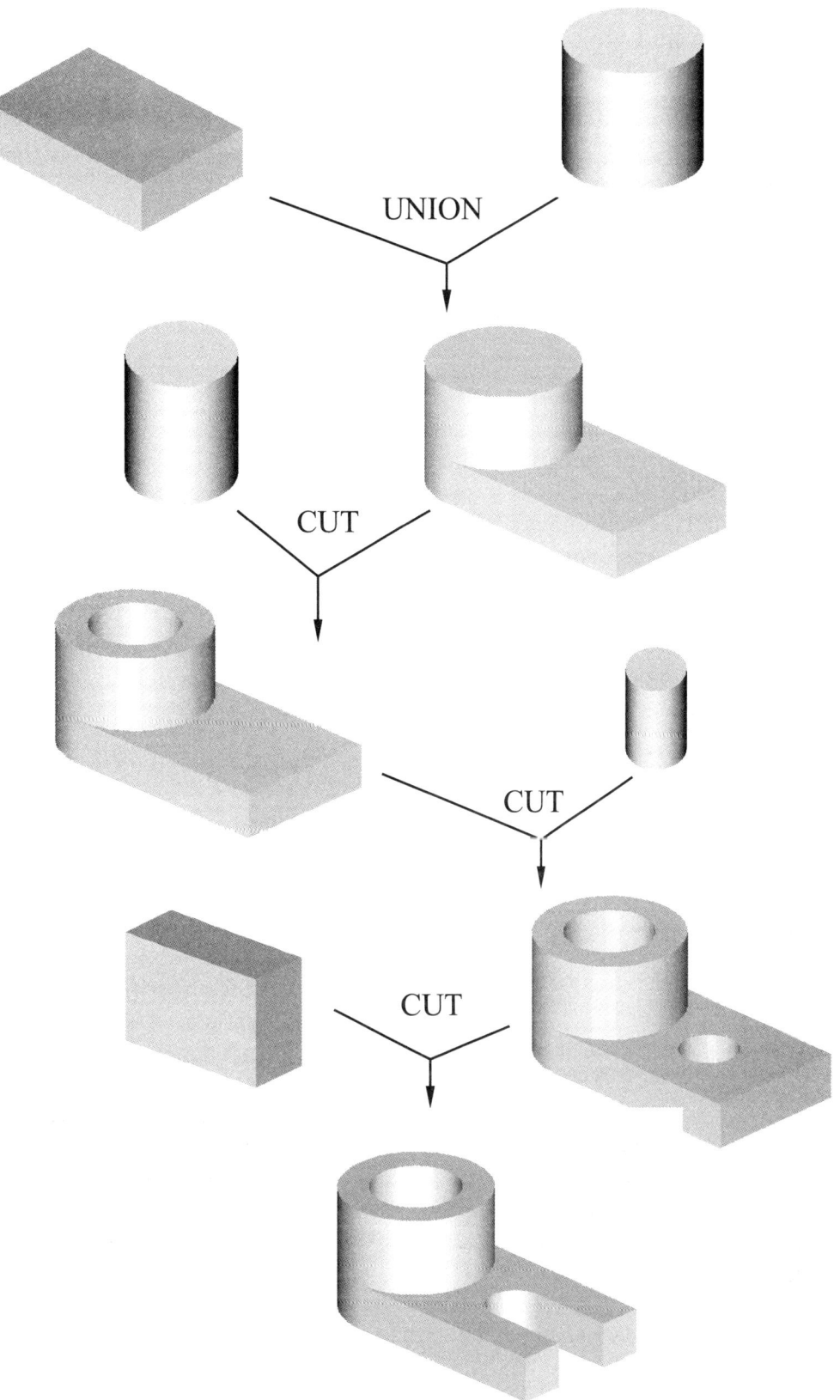

Starting Autodesk Inventor

1. Select the **Autodesk Inventor** option on the *Start* menu or select the **Autodesk Inventor** icon on the desktop to start *Autodesk Inventor*. The *Autodesk Inventor* main window will appear on the screen.

2. Select the **New File** icon with a single click of the left-mouse-button in the *Launch* toolbar.

❖ Every object we construct in a CAD system is measured in units. We should determine the value of the units within the CAD system before creating the first geometric entities. For example, in one model, a unit might equal one millimeter of the real-world object; in another model, a unit might equal an inch. In *Autodesk Inventor*, the **Choose Template** option is used to control how *Autodesk Inventor* interprets the coordinate and angle entries.

3. Select the **Metric** tab as shown below. We will use the millimeter (mm) setting for this example.

4. In the *New File – Part Template* area, select the **Standard(mm).ipt** icon as shown.

5. Confirm the *Parametric-Modeling* project is activated; note the **Projects** button is available to view/modify the active project.

6. Pick **Create** in the *Startup* dialog box to accept the selected settings.

Base Feature

In *parametric modeling*, the first solid feature is called the **base feature**, which usually is the primary shape of the model. Depending upon the design intent, additional features are added to the base feature.

Some of the considerations involved in selecting the base feature are:

- **Design intent** – Determine the functionality of the design; identify the feature that is central to the design.

- **Order of features** – Choose the feature that is the logical base in terms of the order of features in the design.

- **Ease of making modifications** – Select a base feature that is more stable and is less likely to be changed.

1. Activate the **Create 2D Sketch** icon with a single click of the left-mouse-button.

2. Move the cursor over the edge of the *Front Plane* in the graphics area. When the *XY Plane* is highlighted, click once with the **left-mouse-button** to select the *Plane* as the sketch plane for the new sketch.

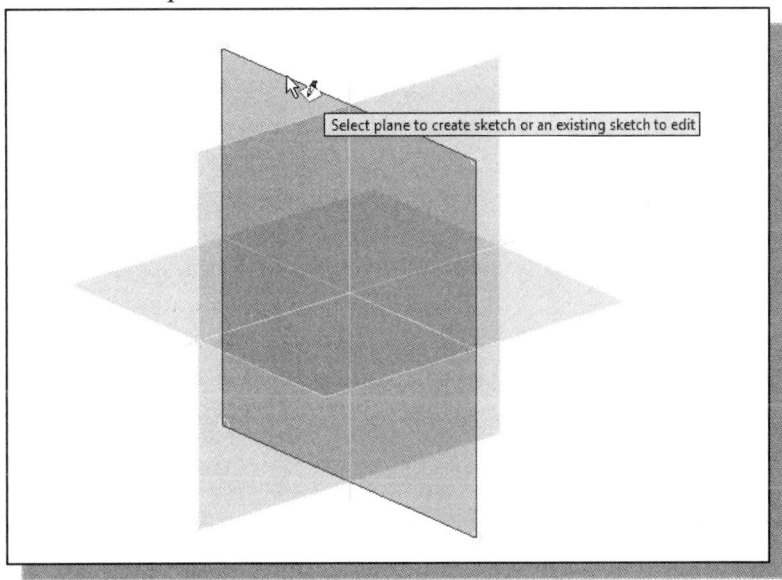

GRID Intervals Setup

1. In the *Ribbon* toolbar panel, select
   [Tools] → **[Document Settings]**

2. In the *Document Settings* dialog box, click on the **Sketch** tab as shown in the below figure.

3. In the *Document Settings* dialog box, set the *X* and *Y Snap Spacing* to **5 mm**.

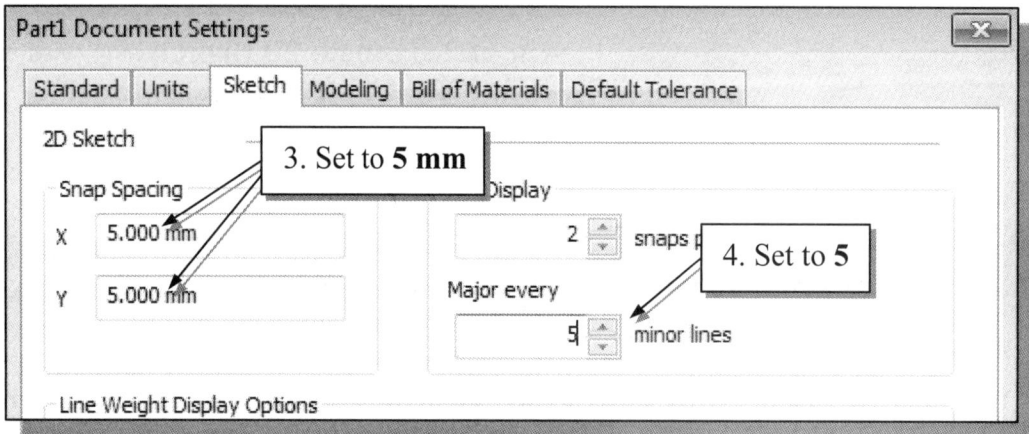

4. Change *Grid Display* to display one *major line* every **5** *minor lines*.

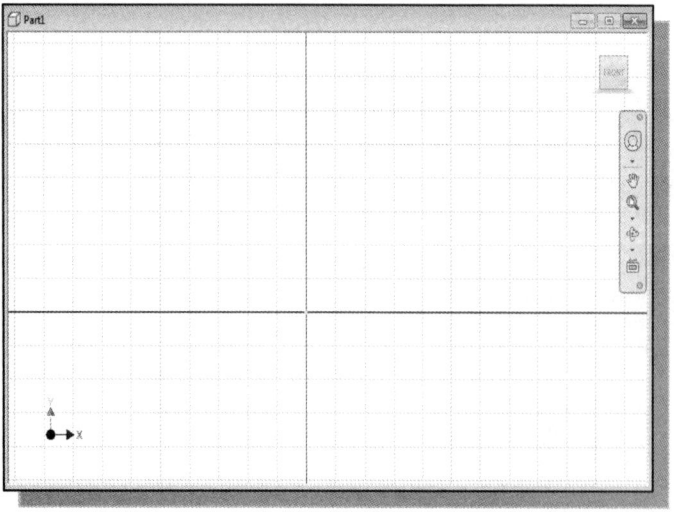

5. Pick **OK** to exit the *Sketch Settings* dialog box.

➢ Note that the above *Snap Spacing* settings actually set the grid spacing in *Autodesk Inventor*. Although the **Snap to grid** option is also available in *Autodesk Inventor*, its usage in parametric modeling is not recommended.

➢ On your own, use the dynamic Zoom function to view the grid setup.

➤ A rectangular block will be created first as the base feature of the **Locator** design.

1. Switch to *Sketch* toolbars and select the **Two point rectangle** command by clicking once with the **left-mouse-button**.

2. Create a rectangle of arbitrary size by selecting two locations on the screen as shown below.

3. Inside the graphics window, click once with the right-mouse-button to bring up the option menu.

4. Select **OK** to end the Rectangle command.

5. Activate the **General Dimension** command by clicking once with the left-mouse-button. The General Dimension command allows us to quickly create and modify dimensions.

6. Inside the graphics window, click once with the right-mouse-button to bring up the option menu and click **Edit Dimension** to turn **OFF** the editing option while creating dimensions.

7. The message "*Select Geometry to Dimension*" is displayed in the *Status Bar* area at the bottom of the *Inventor* window. Select the bottom horizontal line by left-clicking once on the line.

6. Select the bottom horizontal line as the geometry to dimension.

7. Pick a location below the line to place the dimension.

8. Move the graphics cursor below the selected line and left-click to place the dimension. (Note that the value displayed on your screen might be different than what is shown in the above figure.)

9. On your own, create a vertical size dimension of the sketched rectangle as shown.

10. Inside the graphics window, click once with the right-mouse-button to bring up the option menu and click **OK** to end the *Dimension* command.

Model Dimensions Format

1. In the *Ribbon* tabs, select
   [Tools] → **[Document Settings]**

2. In the *Document Settings* dialog box, set the *Modeling Dimension Display* to **Display as value** as shown in the figure.

3. Also set the precision to *no digits* after the decimal point for both the linear dimension and angular dimension displays as shown in the above figure.

4. Pick **OK** to exit the *Document Settings* dialog box.

Modifying the Dimensions of the Sketch

1. Select the height dimension that is to the right side of the sketch by *double-clicking* with the left-mouse-button on the dimension text.

2. In the *Edit Dimension* window, the current length of the line is displayed. Enter **50** to set the selected length of the sketch to 50 millimeters.

3. Click on the **Accept** icon to accept the entered value.

➢ *Autodesk Inventor* will now update the profile with the new dimension value.

4. On you own, repeat the above steps and adjust the dimensions so that the sketch appears as shown below. Also **exit** the Dimension command.

Repositioning Dimensions

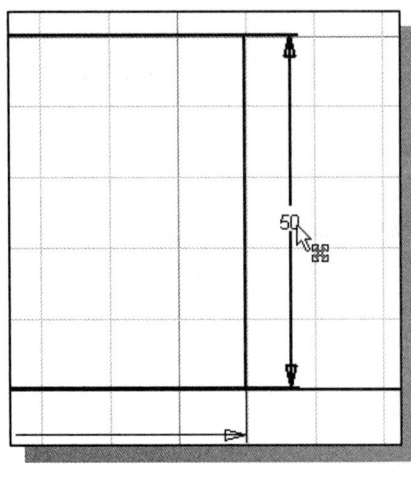

1. Move the cursor near the vertical dimension; note that the dimension is highlighted. Move the cursor slowly until a small marker appears next to the cursor, as shown in the figure.

2. Drag with the left-mouse-button to reposition the selected dimension.

3. Repeat the above steps to reposition the horizontal dimension.

Using the Measure Tools

- *Autodesk Inventor* also provides several measuring tools that allow us to measure area, perimeter and additional information of the constructed 2D sketches.

1. In the *Tools* pull-down menu, left-mouse-click once on the **Measure Distance** option as shown.

- Note that **other** measurement options are also available in the toolbar.

2. Click on the top edge of the rectangle as shown.

3. The associated length measurement of the selected geometry is displayed in the *Length* dialog box as shown.

4. Click the [**X**] icon to exit the Measure Length command.

5. In the *Tools* pull-down menu, left-mouse-click once on the **Measure Area** option as shown.

6. Click on one of the sides of the rectangle as shown.

7. The associated area of the selected geometry is calculated and displayed in the *Area* dialog box as shown.

8. Click the [**X**] icon to exit the **Measure Area** command.

9. In the *Tools* pull-down menu, left-mouse-click once on the **Measure Loop** option as shown.

10. Click on one of the sides of the rectangle as shown.

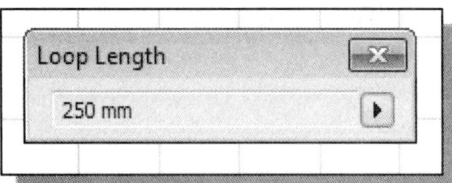

11. The associated perimeter information is shown in the *Loop Length* dialog box as shown.

12. Click the [**X**] icon to exit the **Measure Loop** command.

13. In the *Measure* toolbar, left-mouse-click once on the down arrow to display the option list and click **Region Properties** option as shown.

Constructive Solid Geometry Concepts   3-15

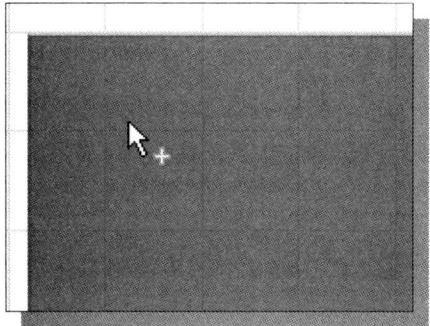

14. Click on the inside of the rectangle; notice the region is highlighted as the cursor is moved inside the rectangle, as shown.

15. In the *Region Properties* dialog box, click on the **Calculate** button to perform the calculations of the associated geometry information.

❖ In the *Region Properties* dialog box, the detailed region properties are calculated and displayed, including the *Area Moments of Inertia*, *Area* and *Perimeter*.

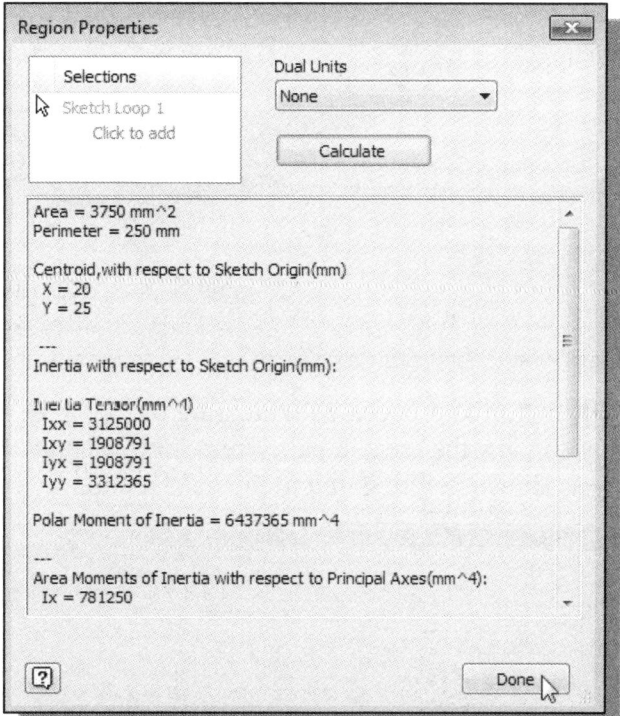

16. Click **Done** to exit the **Region Properties** command.

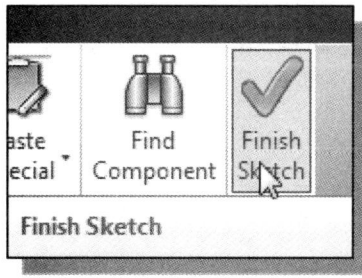

17. Select **Finish Sketch** in the *Ribbon* to end the Sketch option.

Completing the Base Solid Feature

1. In the *Part Features* toolbar (the toolbar that is located to the left side of the graphics window), select the **Extrude** command by releasing the left-mouse-button on the icon.

2. In the *Extrude* popup window, enter **15** as the extrusion distance. Notice that the sketch region is automatically selected as the extrusion profile.

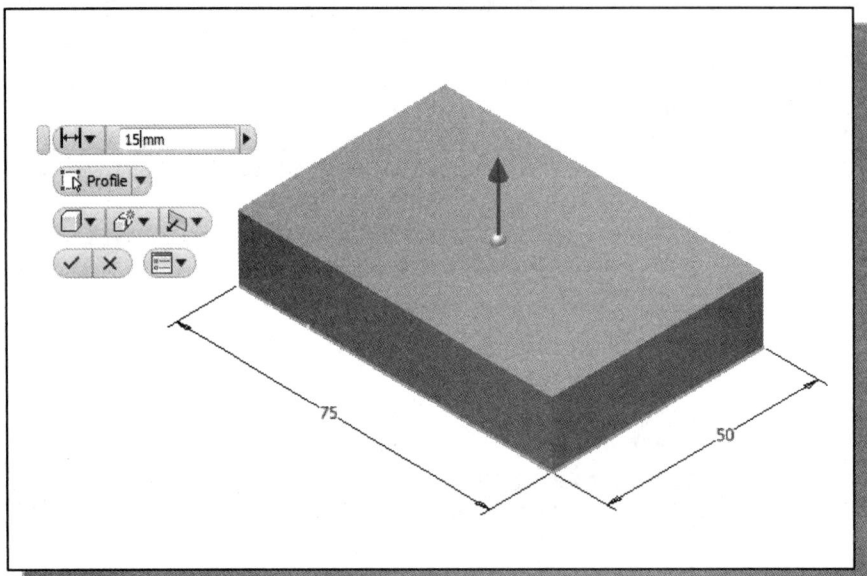

3. Click on the **OK** button to proceed with creating the 3D part. Use the *Dynamic Viewing* options to view the created part. Press **F6** to change the display to the isometric view as shown before going to the next section.

Creating the Next Solid Feature

1. In the *Sketch* toolbar select the **Create 2D Sketch** command by left-clicking once on the icon.

2. In the *Status Bar* area, the message: "*Select face, workplane, sketch or sketch geometry*" is displayed. *Autodesk Inventor* expects us to identify a planar surface where the 2D sketch of the next feature is to be created. Move the graphics cursor on the 3D part and notice that *Autodesk Inventor* will automatically highlight feasible planes and surfaces as the cursor is on top of the different surfaces.

3. Use the **ViewCube** to display the bottom face of the solid model as shown below.

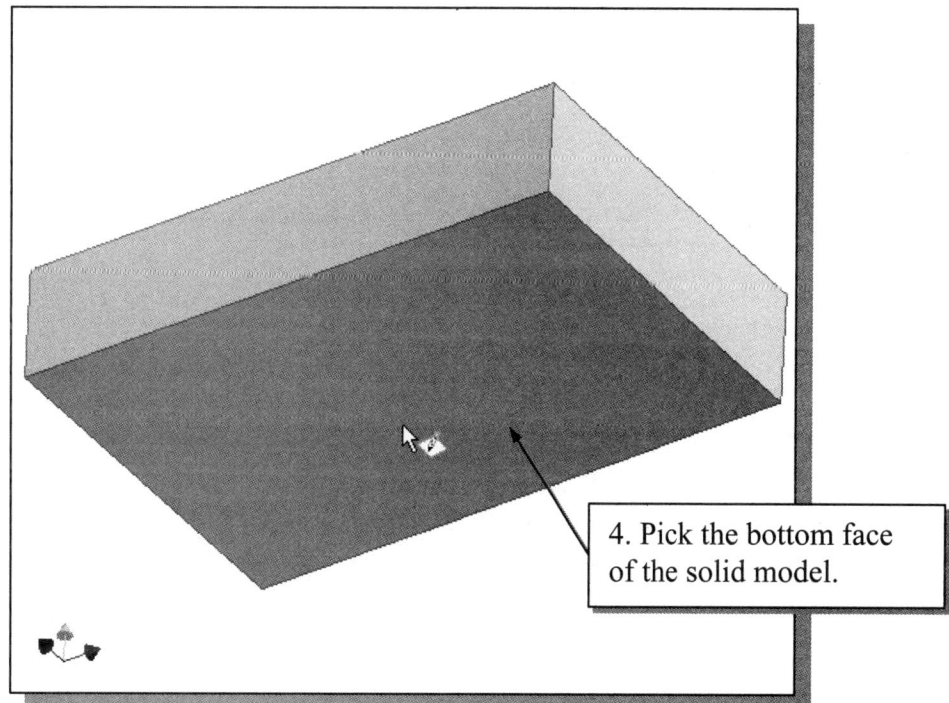

4. Pick the bottom face of the solid model.

4. Pick the bottom face of the 3D model as the sketching plane.

> Note that the sketching plane is aligned to the selected face. *Autodesk Inventor* automatically establishes a User-Coordinate-System (UCS) and records its location with respect to the part on which it was created.

5. Select the **Center point circle** command by clicking once with the left-mouse-button on the icon in the *Sketch* toolbar.

➢ We will align the center of the circle to the midpoint of the base feature.

6. Inside the graphics window, click once with the right-mouse-button to bring up the option menu and choose the snap to **Midpoint** option.

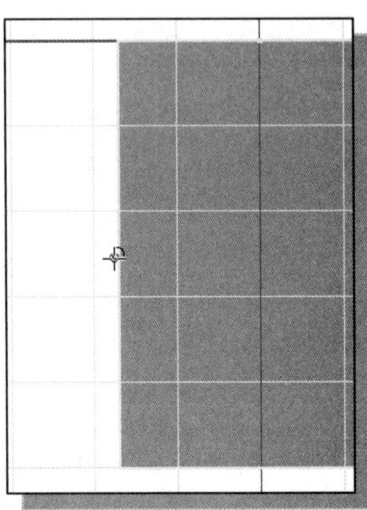

7. Select the left edge of the base feature to align the center point of the new circle.

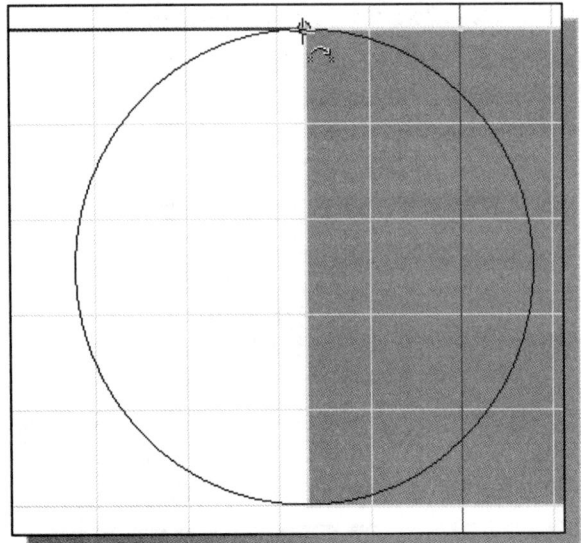

8. Select the top corner of the base feature to create a circle as shown in the figure.

9. Inside the graphics window, click once with the right-mouse-button to display the option menu. Select **OK** to end the Circle command.

10. In the *Ribbon* toolbar, click once with the **left-mouse-button** to select **Finish Sketch** in the popup menu to end the Sketch mode.

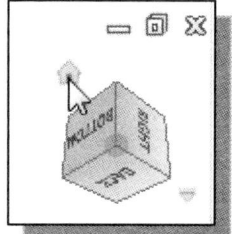

11. Press the function key **F6** once or select **Home View** in the **ViewCube** to change the display to the isometric view as shown.

12. In the *Create Features* toolbar (the toolbar that is located to the right side of the *Sketch* toolbar in the *Ribbon*), select the **Extrude** command by releasing the left-mouse-button on the icon.

13. In the *Extrude* popup control, the **Profile** button is pressed down; *Autodesk Inventor* expects us to identify the profile to be extruded. Move the cursor inside the circle we just created and left-click once to select the region as the profile to be extruded.

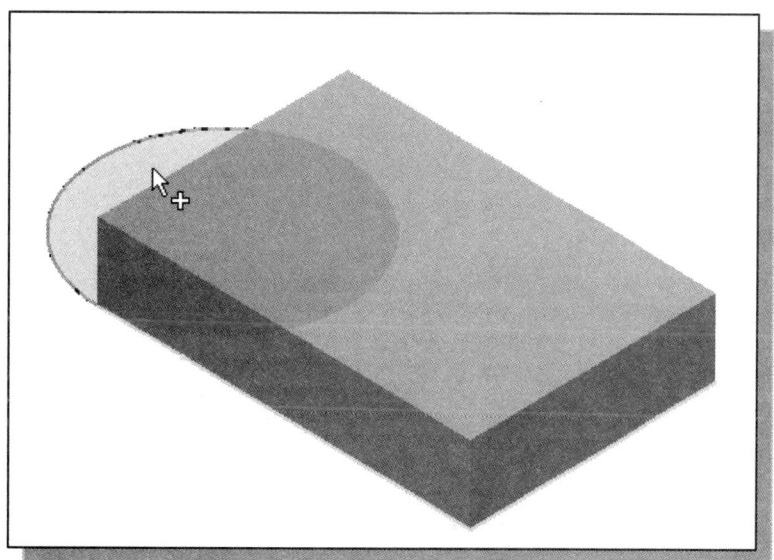

14. In the *Extrude* popup control, enter **40** as the blind extrusion distance as shown below. Set the solid operation to **Join**. Click on the **Direction 2** button to reverse the direction of extrusion (upward) as shown below.

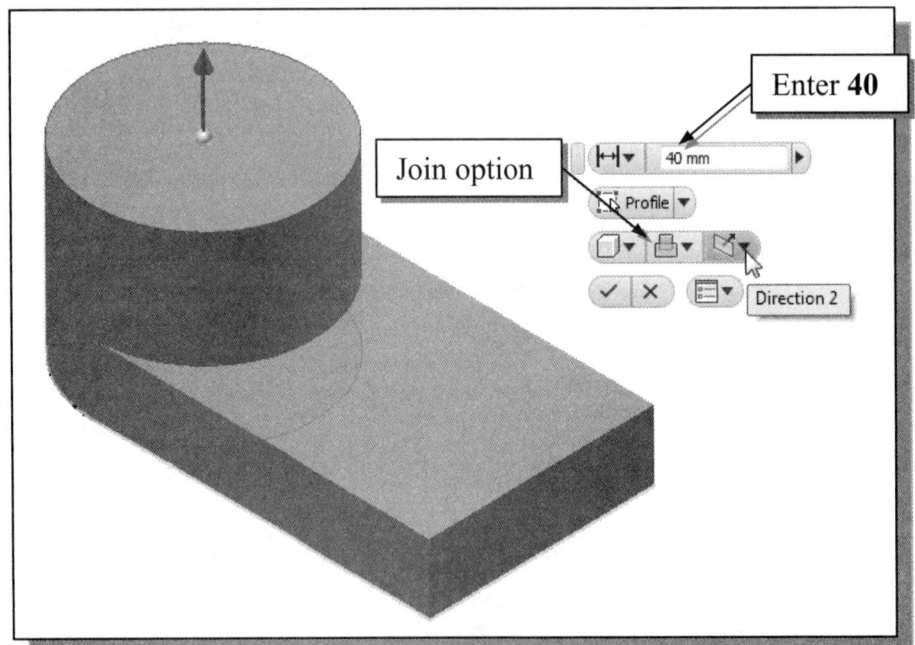

➤ Note that most of the settings can also be set through the icons displayed on the screen.

15. Click on the **OK** button to proceed with the *Join* operation.

- The two features are joined together into one solid part; the *CSG-Union* operation was performed.

Constructive Solid Geometry Concepts 3-21

Creating a CUT Feature

- We will create a circular cut as the next solid feature of the design. We will align the sketch plane to the top of the last cylinder feature.

1. In the *Sketch* toolbar select the **Create 2D Sketch** command by left-clicking once on the icon.

2. Pick the top face of the cylinder as shown.

2. Pick the top face to align the sketch.

3. Select the **Center point circle** command by clicking once with the **left-mouse-button** on the icon in the *Sketch* toolbar.

4. Select the **Center** point of the top face of the 3D model as shown.

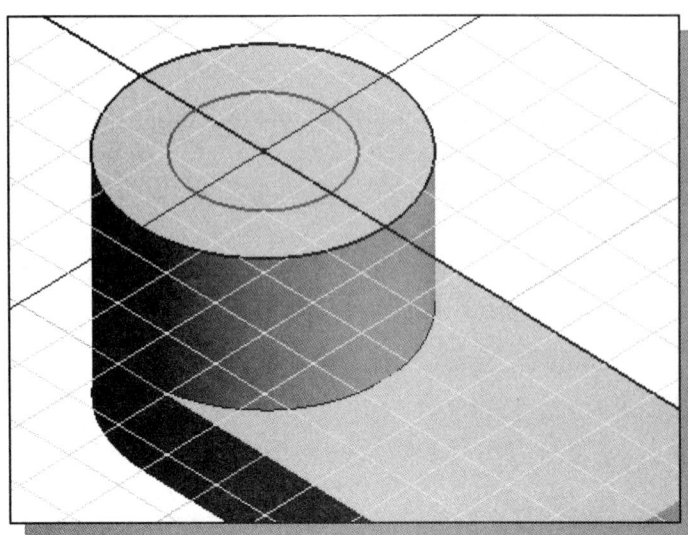

5. Sketch a circle of arbitrary size inside the top face of the cylinder as shown below.

6. Use the right-mouse-button to display the option menu and select **OK** in the popup menu to end the Circle command.

7. Inside the graphics window, click once with the **right-mouse-button** to display the option menu. Select the **General Dimension** option in the popup menu.

8. Create a dimension to describe the size of the circle and set it to **30mm**.

9. Inside the graphics window, click once with the right-mouse-button to display the option menu. Select **OK** in the popup menu to end the Dimension command.

10. Inside the graphics window, click once with the right-mouse-button to display the option menu. Select **Finish 2D Sketch** in the popup menu to end the Sketch option.

Constructive Solid Geometry Concepts   3-23

11. In the *Part Features* toolbar (the toolbar that is located to the left side of the graphics window), select the **Extrude** command by releasing the left-mouse-button on the icon.

12. In the *Extrude* popup window, the **Profile** button is pressed down; *Autodesk Inventor* expects us to identify the profile to be extruded. Move the cursor **inside** the **circle** we just created and left-click once to select the inside region as the profile to be extruded.

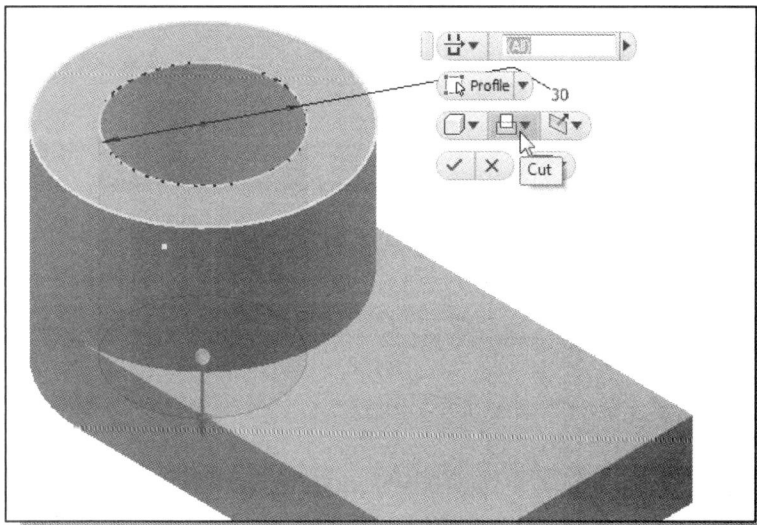

13. In the *Extrusion* popup window, set the operation option to **Cut**. Select **Through All** as the *Extents* option, as shown below. Confirm the arrowhead points downward.

14. Click on the **OK** button to proceed with the *Cut* operation.

- The circular volume is removed from the solid model; the *CSG-Cut* operation resulted in a single solid.

Creating a PLACED FEATURE

- In *Autodesk Inventor*, there are two types of geometric features: **placed features** and **sketched features**. The last cut feature we created is a *sketched feature*, where we created a rough sketch and performed an extrusion operation. We can also create a hole feature, which is a placed feature. A *placed feature* is a feature that does not need a sketch and can be created automatically. Holes, fillets, chamfers, and shells are all placed features.

1. In the *Part Features* toolbar (the toolbar that is located to the left side of the graphics window), select the **Hole** command by releasing the left-mouse-button on the icon.

2. In the *Hole* window, notice the **Face** button is pressed down.

3. Pick a location inside the horizontal surface of the base feature as shown.

4. Enter **20 mm** as the diameter of the hole as shown. **Do Not** click the OK button yet.

Constructive Solid Geometry Concepts 3-25

5. Pick the **right-edge** of the top face of the base feature as shown. This will be used as the first reference for placing the hole on the plane.

6. Enter **30** mm as the distance as shown.

7. Pick the **adjacent edge** of the top face as shown. This will be used as the second reference for placing the hole on the plane.

8. Enter **25** mm as the distance as shown.

9. In *Holes* dialog box, set the *Termination* option to **Through All**.

10. Click on the **OK** button to proceed with the *Hole* feature.

- The circular volume is removed from the solid model; the *CSG-Cut* operation resulted in a single solid.

Creating a Rectangular Cut Feature

- Next create a rectangular cut as the last solid feature of the *Locator*.

1. In the *Sketch* toolbar select the **Create 2D Sketch** command by left-clicking once on the icon.

2. Pick the right face of the base feature as shown.

3. Select the **Two point rectangle** command by clicking once with the left-mouse-button on the icon in the *Sketch* toolbar.

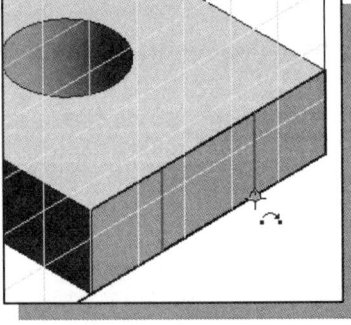

4. Create a rectangle that is aligned to the top and bottom edges of the base feature as shown.

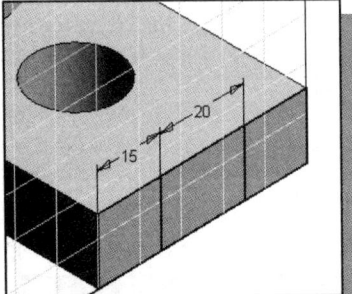

5. On your own, create and modify the two dimensions as shown.

6. Select **Finish Sketch** in the *Ribbon* toolbar to end the Sketch option.

Constructive Solid Geometry Concepts   3-27

7. In the *Create Features* toolbar (the toolbar that is located to the right side of the *Sketch* toolbar in the *Ribbon*), select the **Extrude** command by releasing the left-mouse-button on the icon.

8. In the *Extrude* popup window, the **Profile** button is pressed down; *Autodesk Inventor* expects us to identify the profile to be extruded. Move the cursor inside the rectangle we just created and left-click once to select the region as the profile to be extruded.

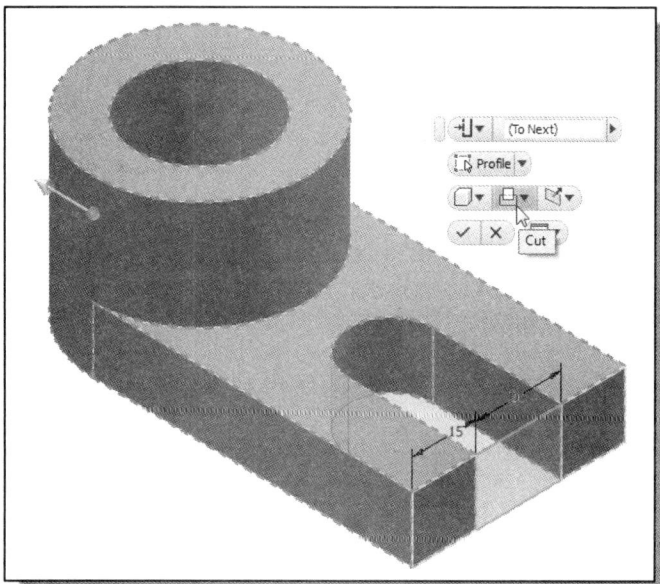

9. In the *Extrude* popup window, set the operation option to **Cut**. Select **To Next** as the *Extents* option as shown. Set the arrowhead points toward the center of the solid model.

10. Click on the **OK** button to create the *Cut* feature and complete the design.

Save the Model

1. Select **Save** in the *Quick Access Toolbar*, or you can also use the "**Ctrl-S**" combination (hold down the "Ctrl" key and hit the "S" key once) to save the part.

2. Switch to the **Parametric Modeling** *folder* if it is not the current folder.

3. In the *Save As* dialog box, **right-mouse-click** once in the *list area* to bring up the *option menu*.

4. In the *option list*, select **New** as shown.

5. In the second *option list*, select **Folder** to create a subfolder.

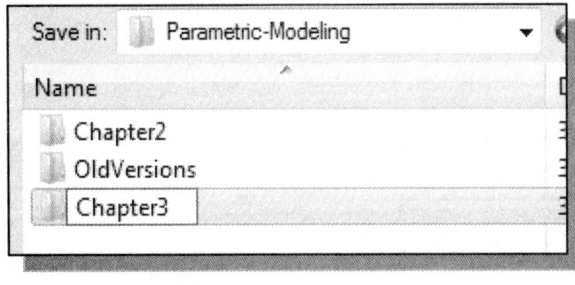

6. Enter **Chapter3** as the new folder name as shown.

7. **Double-click** on the Chapter3 folder to open it.

8. In the *file name* editor box, enter **Locator** as the file name.

9. Click on the **Save** button to save the file.

Questions: (Time: 20 minutes)

1. List and describe three basic *Boolean operations* commonly used in computer geometric modeling software?

2. What is a *primitive solid*?

3. What does *CSG* stand for?

4. Which *Boolean operation* keeps only the volume common to the two solid objects?

5. What is the main difference between a *CUT feature* and a *HOLE feature* in *Autodesk Inventor*?

6. Create the following 2D Sketch and measure the associated area and perimeter.

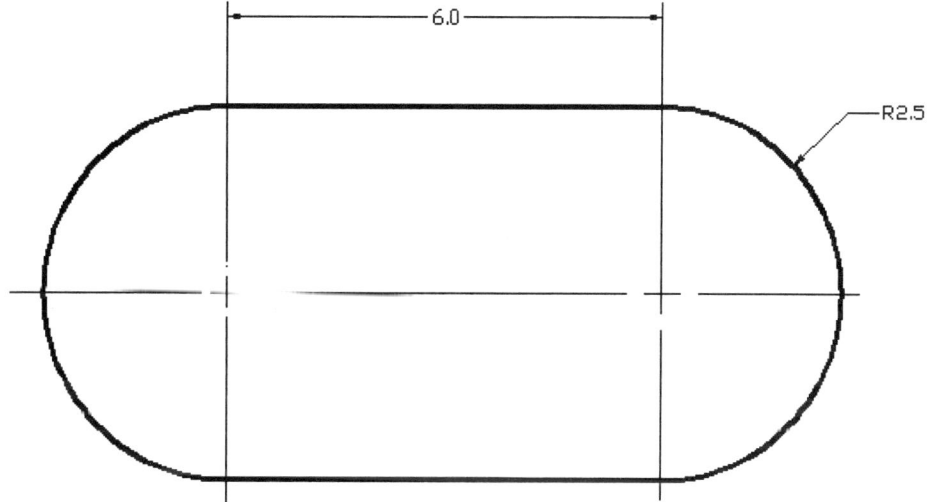

7. Using the CSG concepts, create *Binary Tree* sketches showing the steps you plan to use to create the two models shown on the next page:

Exercises: Create and save the exercises in the Chapter3 folder.
(Time: 90 minutes. All dimensions are in inches.)

1. **L-Bracket**

2. **Coupling Base**

3. **Indexing Guide**

4. **Transfer Fork**

Notes:

Chapter 4
Model History Tree

Learning Objectives

- **Understand Feature Interactions**
- **Use the Part Browser**
- **Modify and Update Feature Dimensions**
- **Perform History-Based Part Modifications**
- **Change the Names of Created Features**
- **Implement Basic Design Changes**

Introduction

In *Autodesk Inventor*, the **design intents** are embedded into features in the **history tree**. The structure of the model history tree resembles that of a **CSG binary tree**. A CSG binary tree contains only *Boolean relations*, while the ***Autodesk Inventor* history tree** contains all features, including *Boolean relations*. A history tree is a sequential record of the features used to create the part. This history tree contains the construction steps, plus the rules defining the design intent of each construction operation. In a history tree, each time a new modeling event is created previously defined features can be used to define information such as size, location, and orientation. It is therefore important to think about your modeling strategy before you start creating anything. It is important, but also difficult, to plan ahead for all possible design changes that might occur. This approach in modeling is a major difference of **FEATURE-BASED CAD SOFTWARE**, such as *Autodesk Inventor*, from previous generation CAD systems.

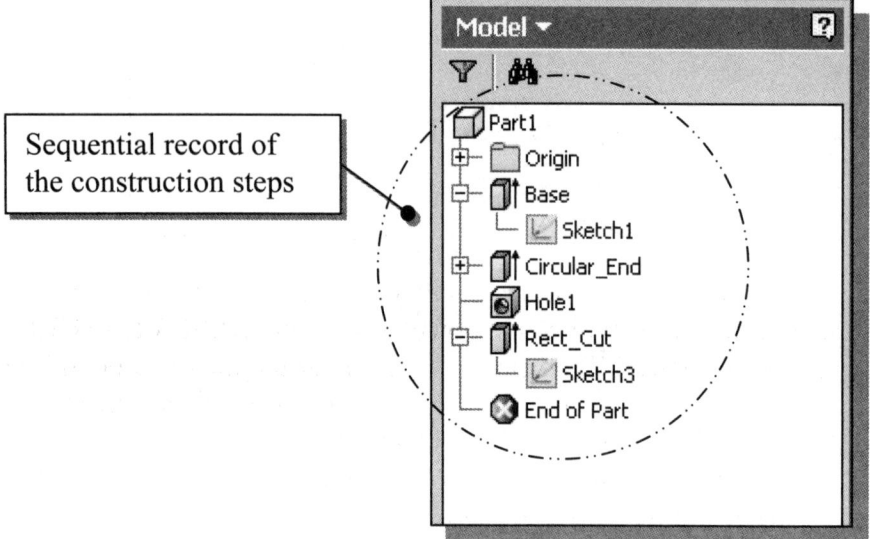

Sequential record of the construction steps

Feature-based parametric modeling is a cumulative process. Every time a new feature is added, a new result is created and the feature is also added to the history tree. The database also includes parameters of features that were used to define them. All of this happens automatically as features are created and manipulated. At this point, it is important to understand that all of this information is retained, and modifications are done based on the same input information.

In *Autodesk Inventor*, the history tree gives information about modeling order and other information about the feature. Part modifications can be accomplished by accessing the features in the history tree. It is therefore important to understand and utilize the feature history tree to modify designs. *Autodesk Inventor* remembers the history of a part, including all the rules that were used to create it, so that changes can be made to any operation that was performed to create the part. In *Autodesk Inventor*, to modify a feature, we access the feature by selecting the feature in the ***browser*** window.

The *Saddle Bracket* Design

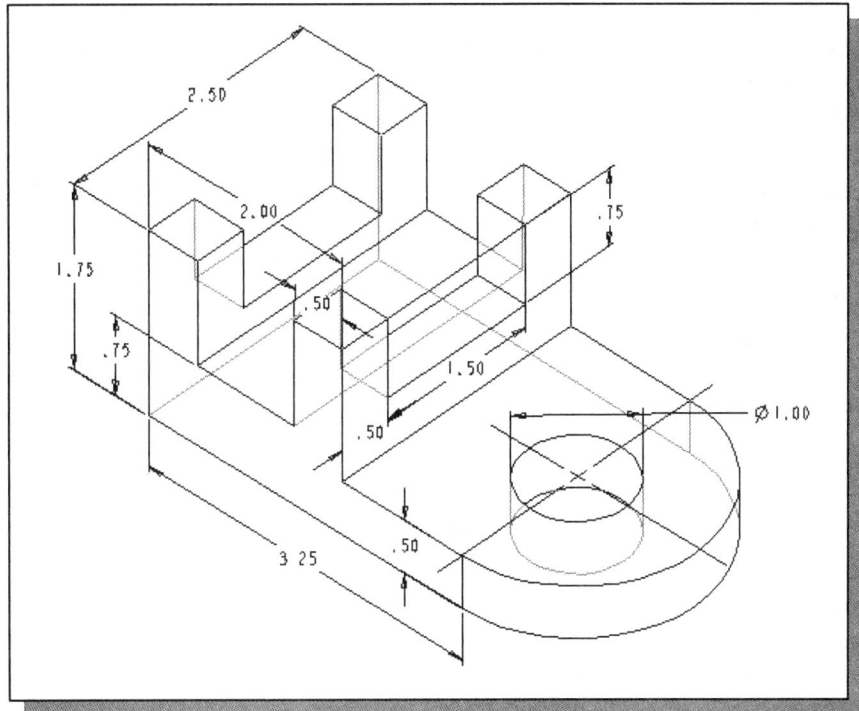

❖ Based on your knowledge of *Autodesk Inventor* so far, how many features would you use to create the design? Which feature would you choose as the **BASE FEATURE**, the first solid feature, of the model? What is your choice in arranging the order of the features? Would you organize the features differently if additional fillets were to be added in the design? Take a few minutes to consider these questions and do preliminary planning by sketching on a piece of paper. You are also encouraged to create the model on your own prior to following through the tutorial.

Starting *Autodesk Inventor*

1. Select the **Autodesk Inventor** option on the *Start* menu or select the **Autodesk Inventor** icon on the desktop to start *Autodesk Inventor*. The *Autodesk Inventor* main window will appear on the screen.

2. Once the program is loaded into memory, select the **New File** icon with a single click of the left-mouse-button in the *Launch* toolbar.

3. Select the **English** tab and in the *Part template* area, select **Standard(in).ipt**.

4. Click **Create** in the *New File* dialog box to accept the selected settings to start a new model.

Modeling Strategy

The *Autodesk Inventor Browser*

- In the *Autodesk Inventor* screen layout, the **browser** is located to the left of the graphics window. *Autodesk Inventor* can be used for part modeling, assembly modeling, part drawings, and assembly presentation. The *browser* window provides a visual structure of the features, constraints, and attributes that are used to create the part, assembly, or scene. The *browser* also provides right-click menu access for tasks associated specifically with the part or feature, and it is the primary focus for executing many of the *Autodesk Inventor* commands.

- The first item displayed in the *browser* is the name of the part, which is also the file name. By default, the name "Part1" is used when we first started *Autodesk Inventor*. The *browser* can also be used to modify parts and assemblies by moving, deleting, or renaming items within the hierarchy. Any changes made in the *browser* directly affect the part or assembly and the results of the modifications are displayed on the screen instantly. The *browser* also reports any problems and conflicts during the modification and updating procedure.

Creating the Base Feature

1. Move the graphics cursor to the **Line** icon in the *2D Sketch* toolbar. A *Help-tip box* appears next to the cursor and a brief description of the command is displayed at the bottom of the drawing screen: "*Creates Straight line segments and tangent arcs.*" Click once with the left-mouse-button to select the command.

2. Move the cursor over the edge of the *XY Plane* in the graphics area. When the *XY Plane* is highlighted, click once with the **left-mouse-button** to select the *Plane* as the sketch plane for the new sketch.

3. Select the **Line** icon by clicking once with the left-mouse-button; this will activate the Line command.

4. On your own, create and adjust the geometry by adding and modifying dimensions as shown below.

5. Inside the graphics window, click once with the right-mouse-button to display the option menu. Select **Finish 2D Sketch** in the popup menu to end the Sketch option.

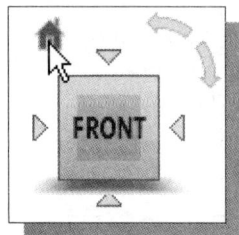

6. On your own, use the dynamic viewing functions to view the sketch. Click the home view icon to change the display to the *isometric* view.

7. In the *model create* toolbar, select the **Extrude** command by releasing the left-mouse-button on the icon.

8. In the *Distance* option box, enter **2.5** as the total extrusion distance.

9. In the *Extrude* popup window, left-click once on the **Symmetric** icon. The **Symmetric** option allows us to extrude in both directions of the sketched profile.

10. Click on the **OK** button to accept the settings and create the base feature.

➢ On your own, use the *Dynamic Viewing* functions to view the 3D model. Also notice the extrusion feature is added to the *Model Tree* in the *browser* area.

Adding the Second Solid Feature

1. In the *Sketch* toolbar select the **Create 2D Sketch** command by left-clicking once on the icon.

2. In the *Status Bar* area, the message: "*Select face, workplane, sketch or sketch geometry.*" is displayed. Move the graphics cursor on the 3D part and notice that *Autodesk Inventor* will automatically highlight feasible planes and surfaces as the cursor is on top of the different surfaces. Move the cursor inside the upper horizontal face of the 3D object as shown below.

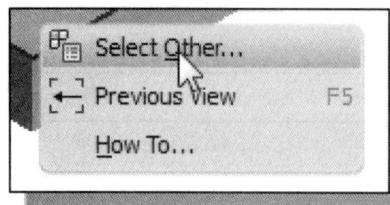

3. Click once with the **right-mouse-button** to bring up the option menu and select **Select Other** to switch to the next feasible choice.

4. On your own, click on the down arrow to examine all possible surface selections.

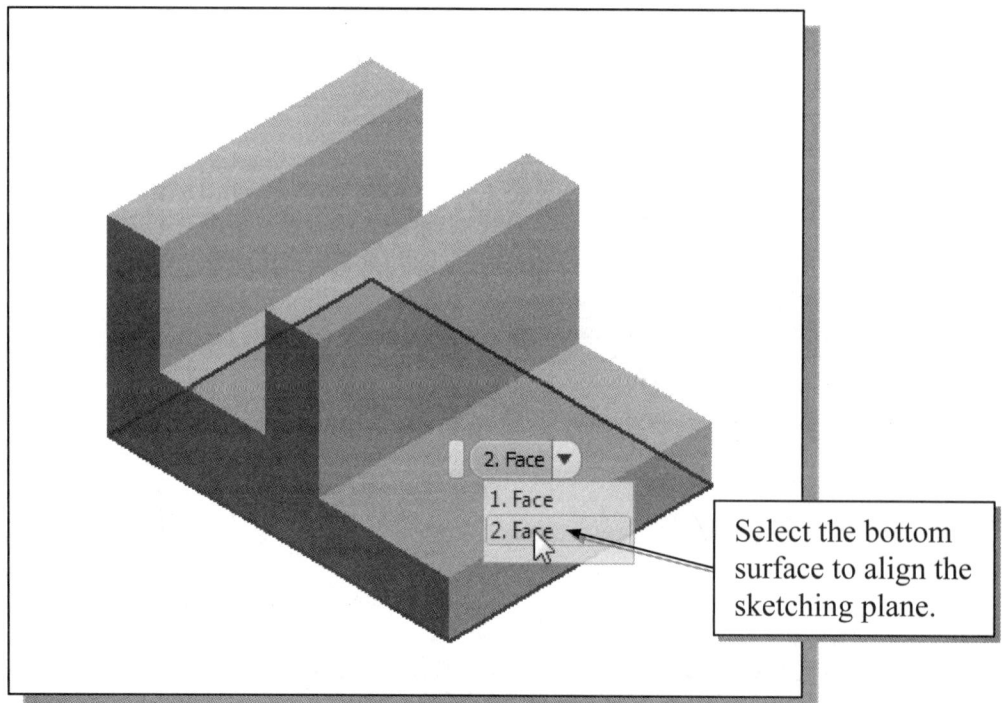

Select the bottom surface to align the sketching plane.

5. Select the **bottom horizontal face** of the solid model when it is highlighted as shown in the above figure.

Creating a 2D Sketch

1. Select the **Center point circle** command by clicking once with the left-mouse-button on the icon in the *Sketch* toolbar.

> We will align the center of the circle to the midpoint of the base feature.

2. On your own, use the snap to midpoint option to pick the midpoint of the edge when the midpoint is displayed with a GREEN color as shown in the figure.

3. Select the front corner of the base feature to create a circle as shown below.

4. Inside the graphics window, click once with the right-mouse-button to display the option menu. Select **OK** in the popup menu to end the Circle command.

5. Inside the graphics window, click once with the right-mouse-button to display the option menu. Select **Finish Sketch** in the popup menu to end the Sketch option.

6. In the *Part Features* toolbar (the toolbar that is located to the left side of the graphics window), select the **Extrude** command by releasing the left-mouse-button on the icon.

7. Click inside the **circle** we just created and left-click once to select the region as the **profile** to be extruded.

8. In the *Extrude* popup control, set the operation option to **Join.**

9. Also set the *Extents* option to **To Selected Face** as shown below.

10. Select the top face of the base feature as the termination surface for the extrusion.

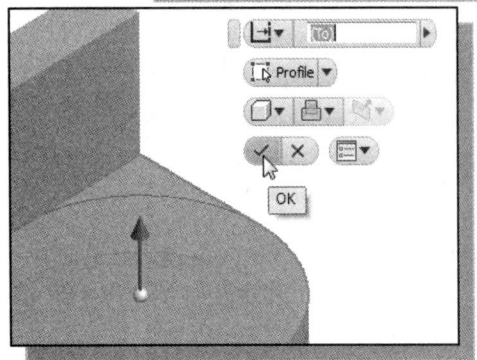

11. Click on the **OK** button to proceed with the *Join* operation.

Renaming the Part Features

♦ Currently, our model contains two extruded features. The feature is highlighted in the display area when we select the feature in the *browser* window. Each time a new feature is created, the feature is also displayed in the *Model Tree* window. By default, *Autodesk Inventor* will use generic names for part features. However, when we begin to deal with parts with a large number of features, it will be much easier to identify the features using more meaningful names. Two methods can be used to rename the features: 1. **Clicking** twice on the name of the feature and 2. Using the **Properties** option. In this example, the use of the first method is illustrated.

1. Select the first extruded feature in the *model browser* area by left-clicking once on the name of the feature, **Extrusion1**. Notice the selected feature is highlighted in the graphics window.

2. Left-mouse-click on the feature name again to enter the *Edit* mode as shown.

3. Enter **Base** as the new name for the first extruded feature.

4. On your own, rename the second extruded feature to **Circular_End**.

Adjusting the Width of the Base Feature

❖ One of the main advantages of parametric modeling is the ease of performing part modifications at any time in the design process. Part modifications can be done through accessing the features in the history tree. *Autodesk Inventor* remembers the history of a part, including all the rules that were used to create it, so that changes can be made to any operation that was performed to create the part. For our *Saddle Bracket* design, we will reduce the size of the base feature from 3.25 inches to 3.0 inches, and the extrusion distance to 2.0 inches.

1. Select the first extruded feature, **Base**, in the *browser* area. Notice the selected feature is highlighted in the graphics window.

2. Inside the *browser* area, **right-mouse-click** on the first extruded feature to bring up the option menu and select the **Show Dimensions** option in the pop-up menu.

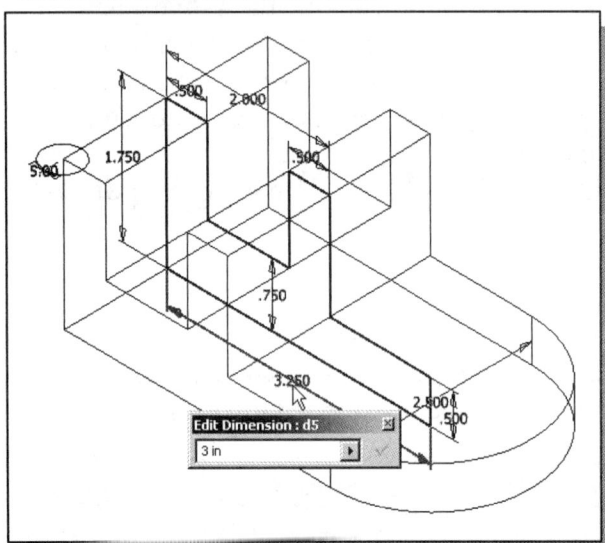

3. All dimensions used to create the **Base** feature are displayed on the screen. Select the overall width of the **Base** feature, the **3.25** dimension value, by double-clicking on the dimension text as shown.

4. Enter **3.0** in the *Edit Dimension* window.

5. On your own, repeat the above steps and modify the extruded distance from **2.5** to **2.0**.

6. Click **Local Update** in the *Quick Access Toolbar*.

➢ Note that *Autodesk Inventor* updates the model by re-linking all elements used to create the model. Any problems or conflicts that occur will also be displayed during the updating process.

Adding a Placed Feature

1. In the *Part Features* toolbar (the toolbar that is located to the left side of the graphics window), select the **Hole** command by releasing the left-mouse-button on the icon.

2. In the *Hole* dialog box, choose **Concentric** in the placement option as shown.

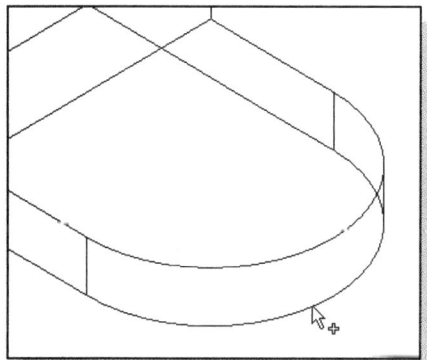

3. Pick the bottom plane of the solid model as the placement plane as shown.

4. Pick the top arc to use as the *concentric reference*.

5. Set the hole diameter to **0.75 in** as shown.

6. Set the termination option to **Through All** as shown.

7. Click **OK** to accept the settings and create the *Hole* feature.

Creating a Rectangular Cut Feature

1. In the *Sketch* toolbar select the **Create 2D Sketch** command by left-clicking once on the icon.

2. Pick the **vertical face** of the solid as shown. (Note the alignment of the origin of the sketch plane.)

> On your own, create a rectangular cut (**1.0 x 0.75**) feature (**To Next** option) as shown and rename the feature to **Rect_Cut**.

History-Based Part Modifications

- *Autodesk Inventor* uses the *history-based part modification* approach, which enables us to make modifications to the appropriate features and re-link the rest of the history tree without having to reconstruct the model from scratch. We can think of it as going back in time and modifying some aspects of the modeling steps used to create the part. We can modify any feature that we have created. As an example, we will adjust the depth of the rectangular cutout.

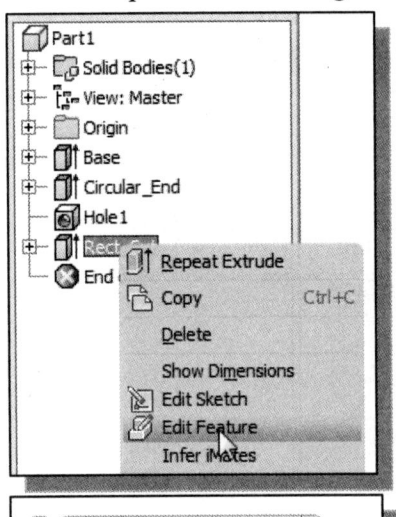

1. In the *browser* window, select the last cut feature, **Rect_Cut**, by left-clicking once on the name of the feature.

2. In the *browser* window, right-mouse-click once on the **Rect_Cut** feature.

3. Select **Edit Feature** in the pop-up menu. Notice the *Extrude* dialog box appears on the screen.

4. In the *Extrude* dialog box, set the termination *Extents* to the **Through All** option.

5. Click on the **OK** button to accept the settings.

- As can been seen, the history-based modification approach is very straightforward and it only took a few seconds to adjust the cut feature to the **Through All** option.

A Design Change

❖ Engineering designs usually go through many revisions and changes. *Autodesk Inventor* provides an assortment of tools to handle design changes quickly and effectively. We will demonstrate some of the tools available by changing the **Base** feature of the design.

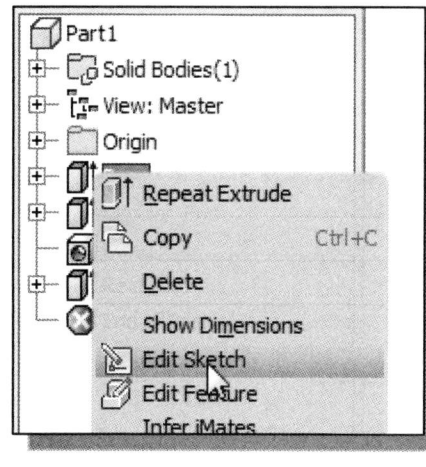

1. In the *browser* window, select the **Base** feature by left-clicking once on the name of the feature.

2. In the *browser*, right-mouse-click once on the **Base** feature to bring up the option menu; then pick **Edit Sketch** in the pop-up menu.

3. Click **Home** to reset the display to *Isometric*.

❖ *Autodesk Inventor* will now display the original 2D sketch of the selected feature in the graphics window. We have literally gone back to the point where we first created the 2D sketch. Notice the feature being modified is also highlighted in the desktop *browser*.

4. Click on the **Look At** icon in the *Standard* toolbar area.

  • The **Look At** command automatically aligns the *sketch plane* of a selected entity to the screen.

5. Select any line segment of the 2D sketch to reset the display to align to the 2D sketch.

6. Select the **Fillet** command in the *2D Sketch* toolbar.

7. In the graphics window, enter **0.25** as the new radius of the fillet.

8. Select the two edges as shown to create the fillet.

7. Pick these two edges to create the fillet.

- Note that the fillet is created automatically with the dimension attached. The attached dimension can also be modified through the history tree.

9. Click on the [**X**] icon in the *2D Fillet* window to end the Fillet command.

10. Select **Finish Sketch** in the *Ribbon* toolbar to end the Sketch option.

❖ In a typical design process, the initial design will undergo many analyses, testing, and reviews. The *history-based part modification* approach is an extremely powerful tool that enables us to quickly update the design. At the same time, it is quite clear that PLANNING AHEAD is also important in doing feature-based modeling.

11. In the *Standard* toolbar, click **Save** and save the model as *Saddle_Bracket.ipt*. (On your own, create the Chapter4 folder.)

Assigning and Calculating the Associated Physical Properties

❖ *Autodesk Inventor* models have properties called **iProperties**. The *iProperties* can be used to create reports, and update assembly bills of materials, drawing parts lists, and other information. With *iProperties*, we can also set and calculate physical properties for a part or assembly using the material library. This allows us to examine the physical properties of the model, such as weight or center of gravity.

1. In the *browser*, **right-mouse-click** once on the *part name* to bring up the option menu; then pick **iProperties** in the *pop-up* menu.

2. On your own, look at the different information listed in the *iProperties* dialog box.

3. Click on the **Physical** tab; this is the page that contains the physical properties of the selected model.

- Note that the *Material* option is not assigned, and none of the physical properties are shown.

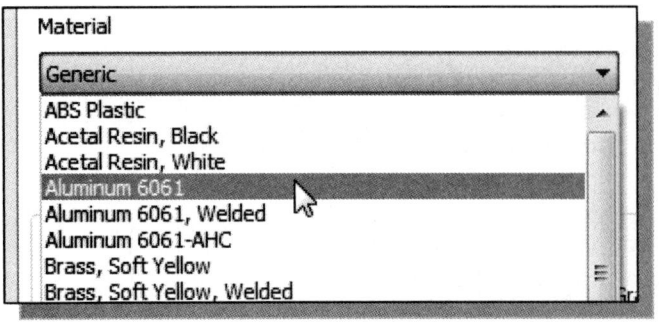

4. Click the down-arrow in the *Material* option to display the material list, and select **Aluminum-6061** as shown.

❖ Note the *General Properties* area now has the *Mass*, *Area*, *Volume* and the *Center of Gravity* information of the model, based on the density of the selected material.

5. Click on the **Global** button to display the *Mass Moments Inertial* of the design.

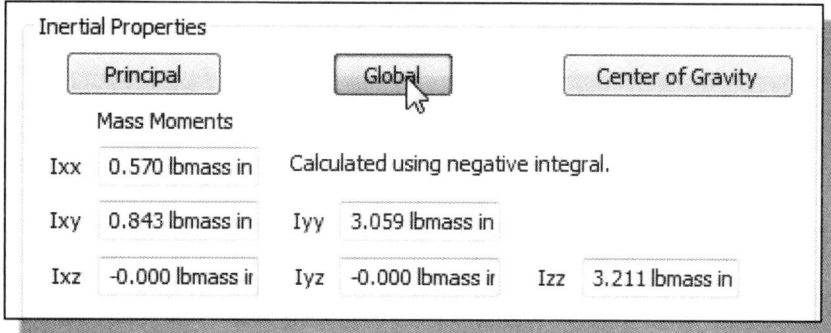

6. On your own, select **Cast Iron** as the *Material* type and compare the differences in using the different materials.

❖ Also note the default display of the model is set to using the *Material* assigned. Selecting a different material type will change the display of the model.

Questions: (Time: 30 minutes)

1. What are stored in the *Autodesk Inventor History Tree*?

2. When extruding, what is the difference between *Distance* and *Through All*?

3. Describe the *history-based part modification* approach.

4. What determines how a model reacts when other features in the model change?

5. Describe the steps to rename existing features.

6. Describe two methods available in *Autodesk Inventor* to *modify the dimension values* of parametric sketches.

7. Create *History Tree sketches* showing the steps you plan to use to create the two models shown on the next page:

Ex.1)

Ex.2)

Exercises: Create and save the exercises in the Chapter4 folder.
(Time: 90 minutes. All dimensions are in inches.)

1. **Latch Clip** (thickness: **0.25** inches. Material: **Cast Iron**. Mass and Volume =?)

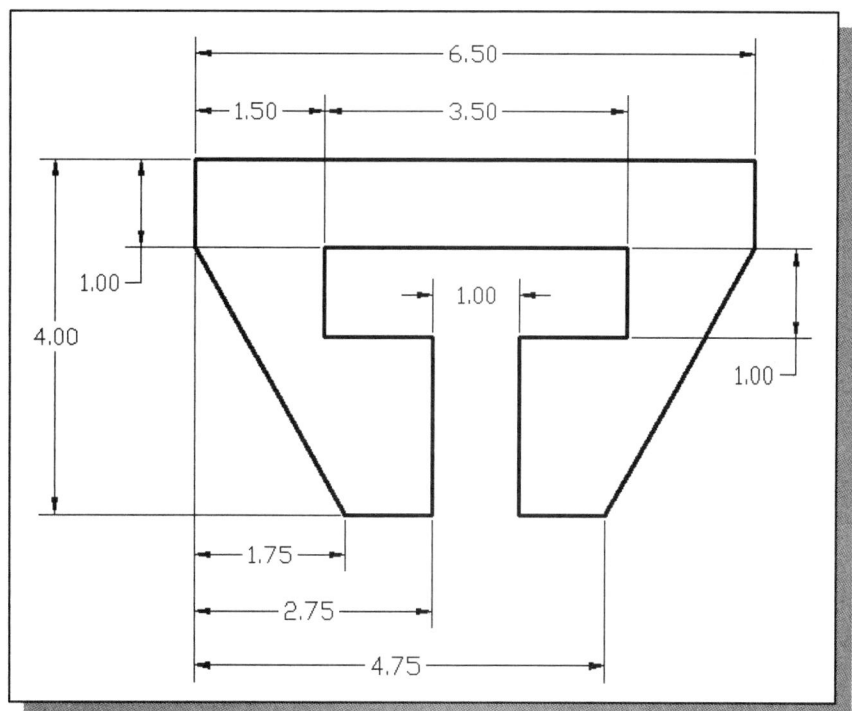

2. **Guide Plate** (thickness: **0.25** inches. Boss height **0.125** inches.)

3. **Swivel Yoke** (Material: **Aluminum-6061**. Weight and Volume =?)

4. **Hanger Jaw**

5-1

Chapter 5
Parametric Constraints Fundamentals

Learning Objectives

- **Create Parametric Relations**
- **Use Dimensional Variables**
- **Display, Add, and Delete Geometric Constraints**
- **Understand and Apply Different Geometric Constraints**
- **Display and Modify Parametric Relations**
- **Create Fully Constrained Sketches**

CONSTRAINTS and RELATIONS

A primary and essential difference between parametric modeling and previous generation computer modeling is that parametric modeling captures the *design intent*. In the previous lessons, we have seen that the design philosophy of *"shape before size"* is implemented through the use of *Autodesk Inventor's* Profile and Dimension commands. In performing geometric constructions, dimensional values are necessary to describe the **SIZE** and **LOCATION** of constructed geometric entities. Besides using dimensions to define the geometry, we can also apply geometric rules to control geometric entities. More importantly, *Autodesk Inventor* can capture design intent through the use of **geometric constraints**, **dimensional constraints**, and **parametric relations**. In *Autodesk Inventor*, there are two types of constraints: **geometric constraints** and **dimensional constraints**. For part modeling in *Autodesk Inventor*, constraints are applied to *2D sketches*. **Geometric constraints** are **geometric restrictions** that can be applied to geometric entities; for example, *horizontal, parallel, perpendicular*, and *tangent* are commonly used *geometric constraints* in parametric modeling. **Dimensional constraints** are used to describe the SIZE and LOCATION of individual geometric shapes. One should also realize that depending upon the way the constraints are applied, the same results can be accomplished by applying different constraints to the geometric entities. In *Autodesk Inventor*, **parametric relations** are user-defined mathematical equations composed of dimensional variables and/or *design variables*. In parametric modeling, features are made of geometric entities with both relations and constraints describing individual design intent. In this lesson, we will discuss the fundamentals of parametric relations and geometric constraints.

Create a *Simple Triangular Plate* Design

> In parametric modeling, **geometric properties** such as *horizontal, parallel, perpendicular*, and *tangent* can be applied to geometric entities automatically or manually. By carefully applying proper **geometric constraints**, very intelligent models can be created. This concept is illustrated by the following example.

Fully Constrained Geometry

In *Autodesk Inventor*, as we create 2D sketches, geometric constraints such as *horizontal* and *parallel* are automatically added to the sketched geometry. In most cases, additional constraints and dimensions are needed to fully describe the sketched geometry beyond the geometric constraints added by the system. Although we can use *Autodesk Inventor* to build partially constrained or totally unconstrained solid models, the models may behave unpredictably as changes are made. In most cases, it is important to consider the design intent and to add proper constraints to geometric entities. In the following sections, a simple triangle is used to illustrate the different tools that are available in *Autodesk Inventor* to create/modify geometric and dimensional constraints.

Starting *Autodesk Inventor*

1. Select the **Autodesk Inventor** option on the *Start* menu or select the **Autodesk Inventor** icon on the desktop to start *Autodesk Inventor*. The *Autodesk Inventor* main window will appear on the screen. Once the program is loaded into memory, the *Startup* dialog box appears at the center of the screen.

2. Select the **New** icon with a single click of the left-mouse-button in the *Launch* toolbar as shown.

3. Select the **English** tab and in the *Part template* area, select **Standard(in).ipt**.

4. Click **Create** in the *New File* dialog box to accept the selected settings to start a new model.

5. Click once with the left-mouse-button to select the **Create 2D Sketch** command.

6. Click once with the **left-mouse-button** to select the *XY Plane* as the sketch plane for the new sketch.

7. Click the **Line** icon in the *Sketch* toolbar to activate the command. A *Help-tip box* appears next to the cursor, and a brief description of the command is displayed at the bottom of the drawing screen: *"Creates Straight line segments and tangent arcs."*

8. Create a triangle of arbitrary size positioned near the lower left corner of the screen as shown below. (Note that the base of the triangle is horizontal.)

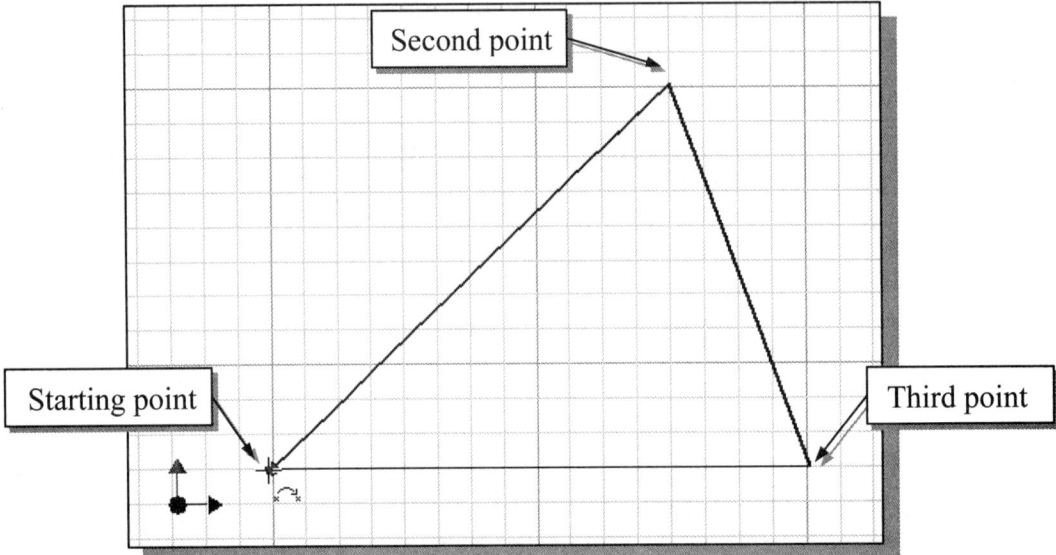

Displaying Existing Constraints

1. Select the **Show Constraints** command in the *Constrain* toolbar. This icon allows us to display constraints that are already applied to the 2D profiles. Left-click once on the icon to activate **Show Constraints**.

➢ In *parametric modeling*, constraints are typically applied as geometric entities are created. *Autodesk Inventor* will attempt to add proper constraints to the geometric entities based on the way the entities were created. Constraints are displayed as symbols next to the entities as they are created. The current profile consists of three line entities, three straight lines. The horizontal line has a **Horizontal** *constraint* applied to it.

Parametric Constraints Fundamentals 5-5

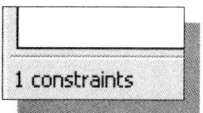

2. Move the cursor on top of the horizontal line and notice the number of constraints applied is displayed in the message area.

3. Click on the **Pin** icon, the last icon in the *active constraint box*, to lock the display of the *Active Constraints* at its current location.

4. On your own, move the cursor on top of the other two lines and notice no additional constraints exist on the other two entities.

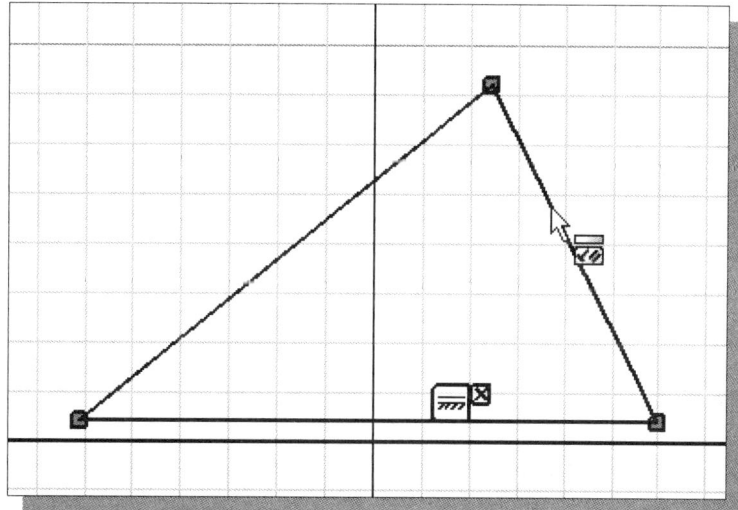

5. Move the cursor on top of the constraints displayed and notice the highlighted endpoint/line indicating the location/entities where the constraints are applied.

6. Click on the **X** icons, the last icon in the active constraint box, to unlock and turn off the display of the constraints.

7. Inside the graphics window, right-mouse-click to bring up the option menu and select **OK** to end the Show Constraints command.

Applying Geometric/Dimensional Constraints

- In *Autodesk Inventor*, twelve types of constraints are available for 2D sketches.

 Coincident constraint: Constrains two points together or one point to a curve.

 Colinear constraint: Causes two lines or ellipse axes to lie along the same line.

 Concentric constraint: Constrains two arcs, circles, or ellipses to the same center point.

 Fixed location constraint: Constrains points or curves to a fixed location relative to the sketch coordinate system.

 Parallel constraint: Causes selected lines or ellipse axes to lie parallel to one another.

 Perpendicular constraint: Causes selected curves or ellipse axes to lie at right angles to one another.

 Horizontal constraint: Causes lines, ellipse axes, or pairs of points to lie parallel to the X-axis of the sketch coordinate system.

 Vertical constraint: Causes lines, ellipse axes, or pairs of points to lie parallel to the Y-axis of the sketch coordinate system.

 Tangent constraint: Constrains two curves to be tangent to one another.

 Smooth (G2) constraint: Creates a curvature continuous (G2) condition between a spline and a line, arc, or spline.

 Symmetric constraint: Constrains lines or curves to become symmetrically constrained about a selected line.

 Equal constraint: Selected arcs/circles constrained to the same radius or selected lines to the same length.

Parametric Constraints Fundamentals 5-7

1. Select the **General Dimension** command in the *Sketch* toolbar. The General Dimension command allows us to quickly create and modify dimensions. Left-click once on the icon to activate the General Dimension command.

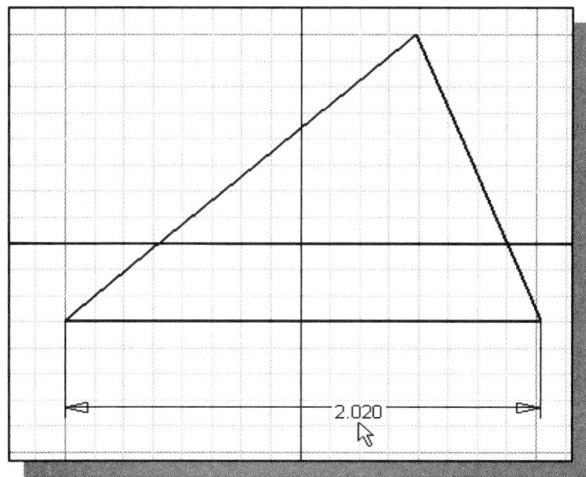

2. On your own, create the dimension as shown in the figure below. (Note that the displayed value might be different on your screen.)

❖ Note *Inventor* identifies the need for additional dimensions at the bottom of the screen.

3. Move the cursor on top of the different **Constraint** icons. A *Help-tip box* appears next to the cursor and a brief description of the command is displayed at the bottom of the drawing screen as the cursor is moved over the different icons.

4. Click on the **Fix** constraint icon to activate the command.

5. Pick the **lower right corner** of the triangle to make the corner a fixed point.

6. On your own, use the **Show Constraints** command to confirm the Fix constraint is properly applied.

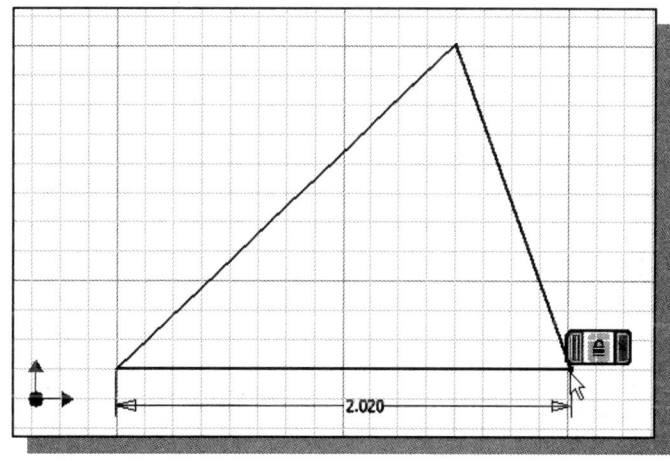

> Geometric constraints can be used to control the direction in which changes can occur. For example, in the current design we are adding a horizontal dimension to control the length of the horizontal line. If the length of the line is modified to a greater value, *Autodesk Inventor* will lengthen the line toward the left side. This is due to the fact that the Fix constraint will restrict any horizontal movement of the horizontal line toward the right side.

7. Select the **General Dimension** command in the *2D Sketch* toolbar.

8. Click on the dimension text to open the *Edit Dimension* window.

9. Enter a value that is greater than the displayed value to observe the effects of the modification. (For example, the dimension value is 2.02, so enter **3.0** in the text box area.)

10. On your own, use the **Undo** command to reset the dimension value to the previous value.

11. Select the **Vertical** constraint icon in the *2D Constraints* toolbar.

12. Pick the inclined line on the right to make the line vertical as shown in the figure below.

13. Hit the [**Esc**] key once to end the Vertical Constraint command.

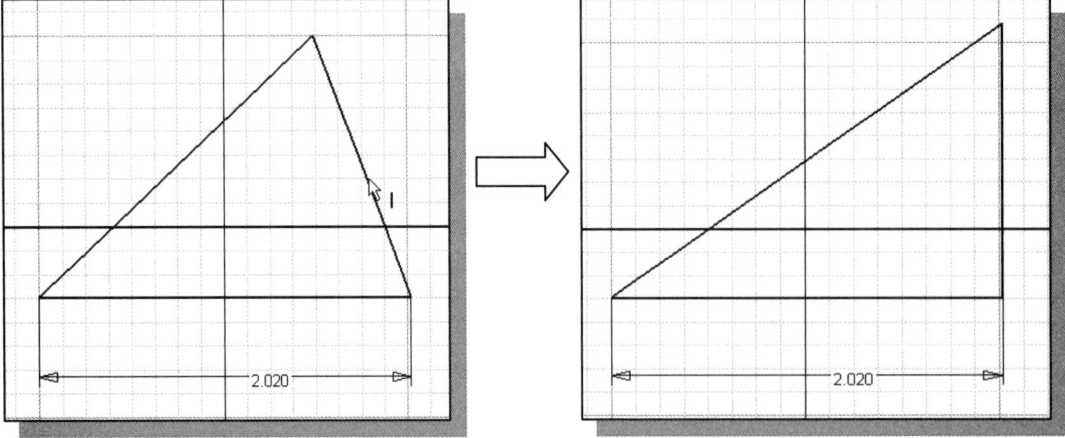

> One should think of the constraints and dimensions as defining elements of the geometric entities. How many more constraints or dimensions will be necessary to fully constrain the sketched geometry? Which constraints or dimensions would you use to fully describe the sketched geometry?

14. Inside the graphics window, click once with the **right-mouse-button** to display the option menu. Select **Show All Constraints** in the popup menu to show all the applied constraints. (Note that function key **F8** can also be used to activate this command.)

15. Move the cursor on top of the top corner of the triangle. (Note the display of the two Coincident constraints at the top corner.)

16. Drag the top corner of the triangle and note that the corner can be moved to a new location. Release the mouse button at a new location and notice the corner is adjusted only in an upward or downward direction. Note that the two adjacent lines are automatically adjusted to the new location.

17. On your own, experiment with dragging the other corners to new locations.

- The three constraints that are applied to the geometry provide a full description for the location of the two lower corners of the triangle. The Vertical constraint, along with the Fix constraint at the lower right corner, does not fully describe the location of the top corner of the triangle. We will need to add additional information, such as the length of the vertical line or an angle dimension.

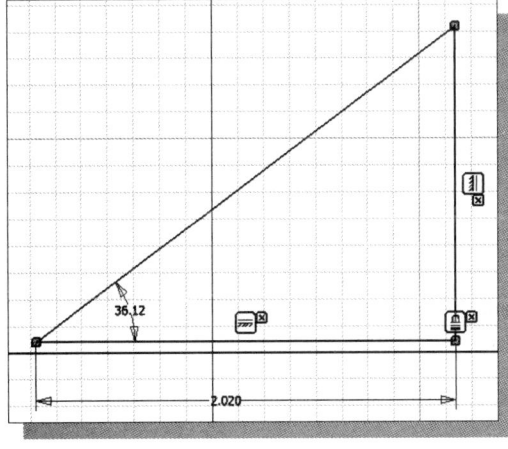

18. On your own, add an angle dimension to the left corner of the triangle.

19. Press the [**Esc**] key once to exit the General Dimension command.

20. On your own, modify the angle to **45°** and then experiment with dragging the top corner of the triangle.

- Note the sketched geometry is fully constrained with the added dimension.

Over-Constraining and Driven Dimensions

- We can use *Autodesk Inventor* to build partially constrained or totally unconstrained solid models. In most cases, these types of models may behave unpredictably as changes are made. However, *Autodesk Inventor* will not let us over-constrain a sketch; additional dimensions can still be added to the sketch, but they are used as references only. These additional dimensions are called **driven dimensions**. *Driven dimensions* do not constrain the sketch; they only reflect the values of the dimensioned geometry. They are enclosed in parentheses to distinguish them from normal (parametric) dimensions. A *driven dimension* can be converted to a normal dimension only if another dimension or geometric constraint is removed.

1. Select the **General Dimension** command in the *Sketch* toolbar.

2. Select the **vertical line**.

3. Pick a location that is to the right side of the triangle to place the dimension text.

4. A warning dialog box appears on the screen stating that the dimension we are trying to create will over-constrain the sketch. Click on the **Accept** button to proceed with the creation of a driven dimension.

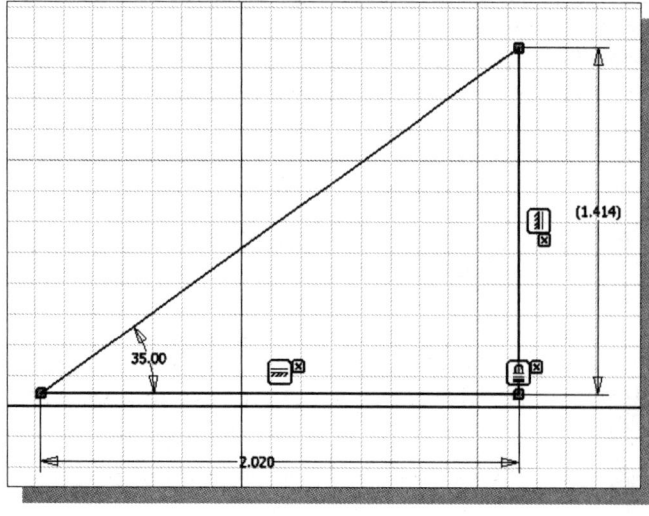

5. On your own, modify the angle dimension to **35°** and observe the changes of the 2D sketch and the driven dimension.

❖ Note *Inventor* has indicated the sketch is **Fully Constrained**.

Deleting Existing Constraints

1. On your own, display all the active constraints if they are not already displayed. (Hint: Use the **Show Constraints** command in the *Sketch* toolbar or **Show All Constraints** in the option menu.)

2. Move the cursor on top of the **Fix** constraint icon and **right-mouse-click** once to bring up the option menu.

3. Select **Delete** to remove the Fix constraint that is applied to the lower right corner of the triangle.

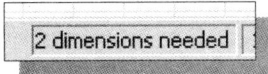

❖ Note the removal of the **Fix** constraint has caused the need for **two additional dimensions**.

4. Drag the top corner of the triangle and note that the entire triangle is free to move in all directions. Drag the corner toward the top right corner of the graphics window as shown in the above figure. Release the mouse button to move the triangle to the new location.

5. On your own, experiment with dragging the other corners and/or the three line segments to new locations on the screen.

❖ **Dimensional constraints** are used to describe the SIZE and LOCATION of individual geometric shapes. **Geometric constraints** are **geometric restrictions** that can be applied to geometric entities. The constraints applied to the triangle are sufficient to maintain its size and shape, but the geometry can be moved around; its location definition isn't complete.

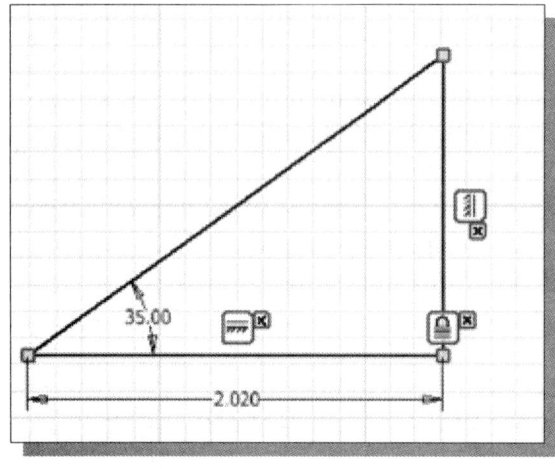

6. On your own, reapply the **Fix** constraint to the lower right corner of the triangle and delete the reference dimension.

7. Delete the extra reference dimension and confirm the same constraints and dimensions are applied on your sketch as shown.

❖ Note that the sketch is fully constrained.

8. Click on the **Display/Hide Constraints** button in the status toolbar to hide all the constraints.

Using the Auto Dimension Command

➢ In *Autodesk Inventor*, the **Auto Dimension** command can be used to assist in creating a fully constrained sketch. **Fully constrained** sketches can be updated more predictably as design changes are implemented. The general procedure for applying dimensions to sketches is to use the **General Dimension** command to add the more critical dimensions, and then use the **Auto Dimension** command to add the additional dimensions/constraints to fully constrain the sketch. The Auto Dimension command can also be used to apply the missing dimensions that are needed. It is also important to realize that different sets of dimensions and geometric constraints can be applied to the same sketch to accomplish a fully constrained geometry.

1. Click on the **Auto Dimension** icon in the *2D Sketch* panel.

❖ Note that *Autodesk Inventor* confirms that the sketch is fully constrained with the message "*0 Dimensions Required.*"

2. Click **Done** to exit the Auto Dimension command.

Parametric Constraints Fundamentals   5-13

3. Select the **Center point circle** command by clicking once with the left-mouse-button on the icon in the *Sketch* toolbar.

4. On your own, create a circle of arbitrary size inside the triangle as shown below.

5. Click on the **Auto Dimension** icon in the *2D Sketch* panel.

❖ Note that *Autodesk Inventor* confirms that the sketch is not fully constrained and "*3 Dimensions Required*" to fully constrain the circle. What are the dimensions and/or constraints that can be applied to fully constrain the circle?

6. Click **Done** to exit the Auto Dimension command.

7. Click on the **Tangent** constraint icon in the *Sketch* toolbar.

8. Pick the circle by left-mouse-clicking once on the geometry.

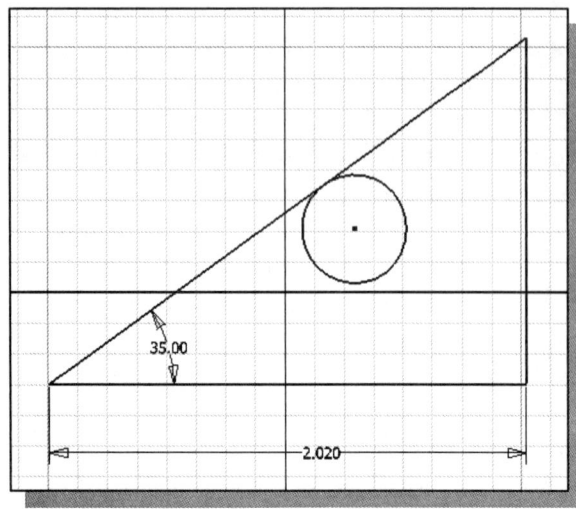

9. Pick the inclined line. The sketched geometry is adjusted as shown.

10. Inside the graphics window, click once with the right-mouse-button to display the option menu. Select **OK** in the popup menu to end the **Tangent** command.

- How many more constraints or dimensions do you think will be necessary to fully constrain the circle? Which constraints or dimensions would you use to fully constrain the geometry?

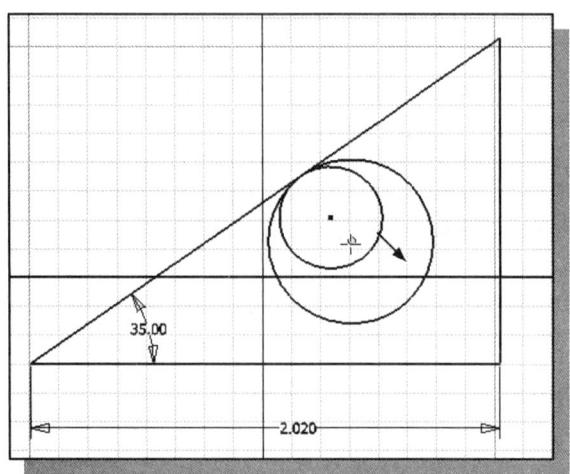

11. Move the cursor on top of the right side of the circle, and then drag the circle toward the right edge of the graphics window. Notice the size of the circle is adjusted while the system maintains the **Tangent** constraint.

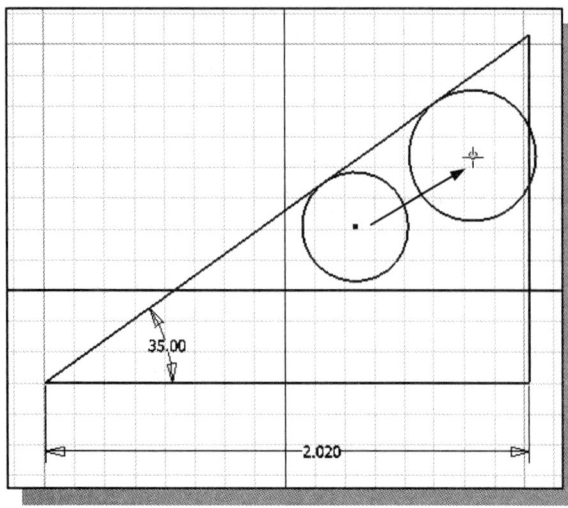

12. Drag the center of the circle toward the upper right direction. Notice the **Tangent** constraint is always maintained by the system.

➢ On your own, experiment with adding additional constraints and/or dimensions to fully constrain the sketched geometry. Use the **Undo** command to undo any changes before proceeding to the next section.

Parametric Constraints Fundamentals   5-15

13. Inside the graphics window, click once with the **right-mouse-button** to display the option menu. Select **Create Constraint → Coincident** in the popup menus.

- The option menu is a quick way to access many of the commonly used commands in *Autodesk Inventor*.

14. Pick the vertical line.

15. Pick the center of the circle to align the center of the circle and the vertical line.

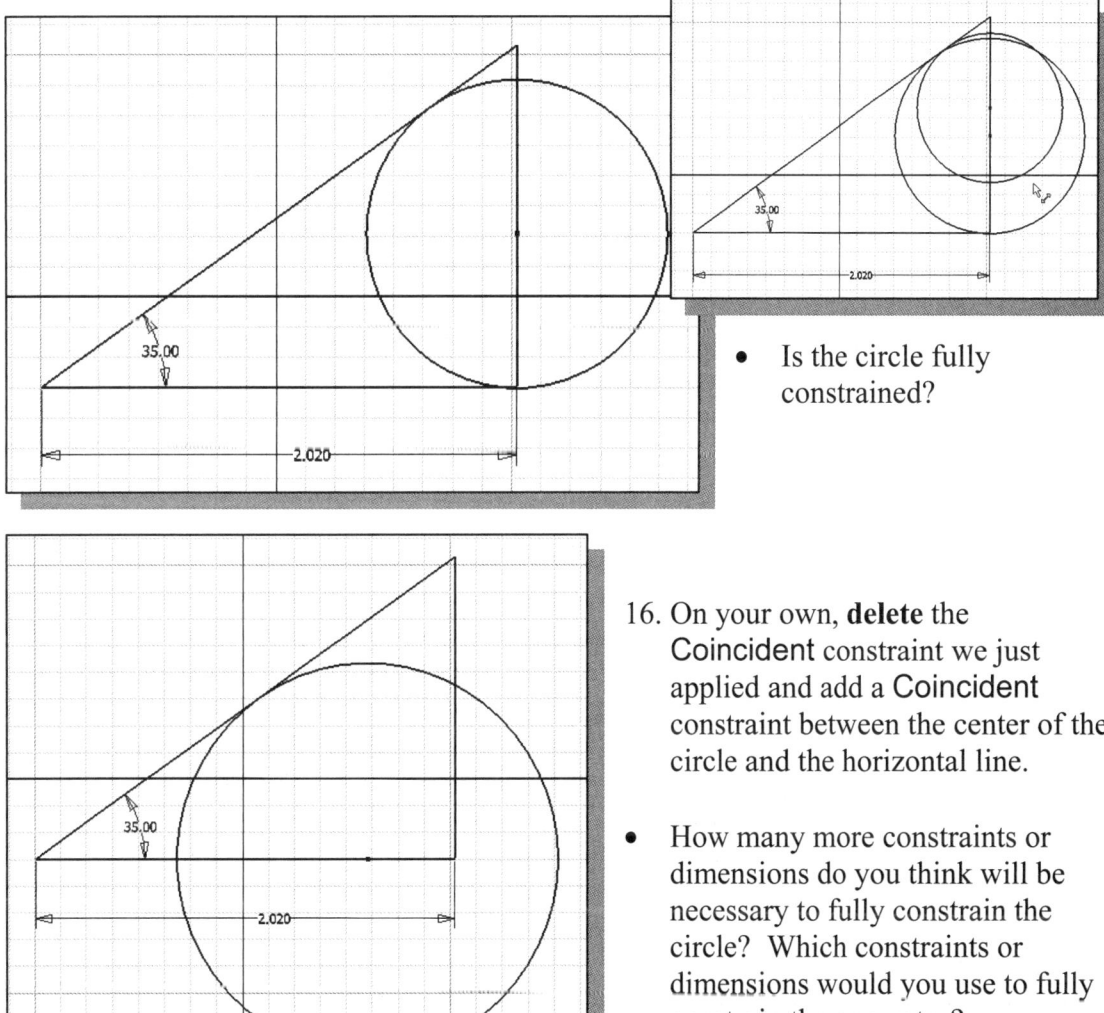

- Is the circle fully constrained?

16. On your own, **delete** the Coincident constraint we just applied and add a Coincident constraint between the center of the circle and the horizontal line.

- How many more constraints or dimensions do you think will be necessary to fully constrain the circle? Which constraints or dimensions would you use to fully constrain the geometry?

❖ The application of different constraints affects the geometry differently. The design intent is maintained in the CAD model's database and thus allows us to create very intelligent CAD models that can be modified/revised fairly easily. On your own, experiment and observe the results of applying different constraints to the triangle. For example: (1) adding another **Fix** constraint to the top corner of the triangle; (2) deleting the horizontal dimension and adding another **Fix** constraint to the left corner of the triangle; and (3) adding another **Tangent** constraint and adding the size dimension to the circle.

17. On your own, modify the 2D sketch as shown below.

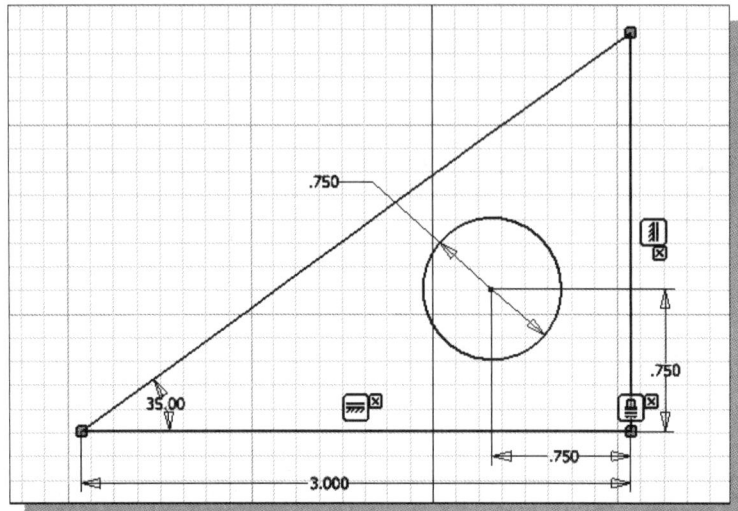

➢ On your own, use the **Extrude** command and create a 3D solid model with a plate thickness of **0.25**. Also experiment with modifying the parametric relations and dimensions through the *part browser*.

Constraint and Sketch Settings

- Select **Application Options** in the **Tools** pull-down menu. Click on the **Sketch** tab to display and/or modify the constraint settings. On your own, adjust the settings and experiment with the effects of the different settings.

❖ Confirm the *Snap to grid* option is set to **OFF** before proceeding to the next section.

Parametric Relations

- In parametric modeling, dimensions are design parameters that are used to control the sizes and locations of geometric features. Dimensions are more than just values; they can also be used as feature control variables. This concept is illustrated by the following example.

1. Start a new drawing by left-clicking once on the **New → Part** icon in the *Standard* toolbar.

- Another graphics window appears on the screen. We can switch between the two models by clicking on the different graphics windows.

2. Click once with the left-mouse-button to select the **Create 2D Sketch** command.

3. Click once with the **left-mouse-button** to select the *XY Plane* as the sketch plane for the new sketch.

4. Select the **Two point rectangle** command by clicking once with the left-mouse-button on the icon in the *Sketch* toolbar.

5. Create a rectangle of arbitrary size positioned near the center of the screen.

6. Select the **Center point circle** command by clicking once with the left-mouse-button on the icon in the *Sketch* toolbar.

7. Create a **circle** of arbitrary size inside the rectangle as shown.

8. Select the **General Dimension** command in the *Sketch* toolbar.

9. On your own, create and adjust the geometry by modifying the dimensions as shown below. (Note: Add a **Fix** constraint at one of the corners to fully constrain the sketch.)

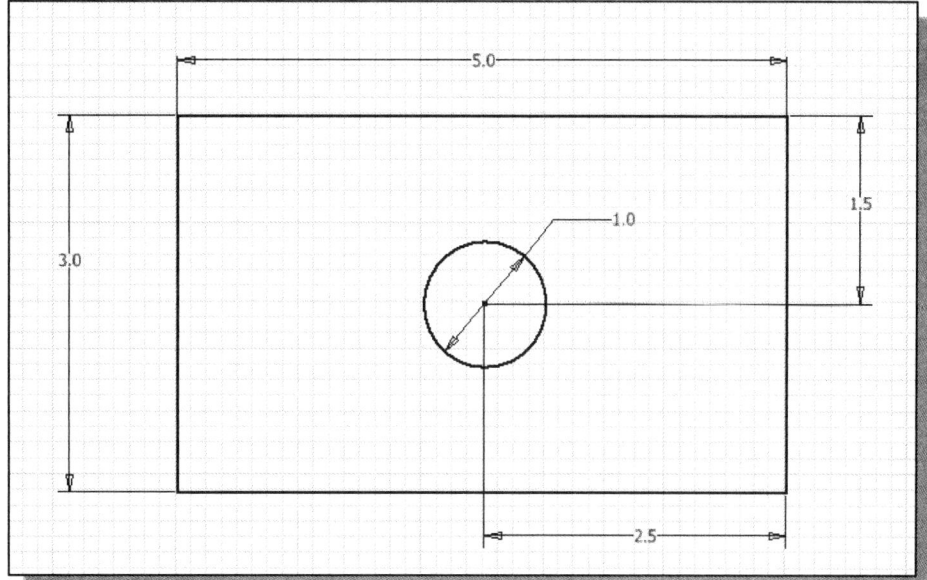

- On your own, change the overall width of the rectangle to **6.0** and the overall height of the rectangle to **3.6** and observe the location of the circle in relation to the edges of the rectangle. Adjust the dimensions back to **5.0** and **3.0** as shown in the above figure before continuing.

Dimensional Values and Dimensional Variables

Initially in *Autodesk Inventor*, values are used to create different geometric entities. The text created by the Dimension command also reflects the actual location or size of the entity. Each dimension is also assigned a name that allows the dimension to be used as a control variable. The default format is "dxx," where the "xx" is a number that *Autodesk Inventor* increments automatically each time a new dimension is added.

Let us look at our current design, which represents a plate with a hole at the center. The dimensional values describe the size and/or location of the plate and the hole. If a modification is required to change the width of the plate, the location of the hole will remain the same as described by the two location dimensional values. This is okay if that is the design intent. On the other hand, the *design intent* may require (1) keeping the hole at the center of the plate and (2) maintaining the size of the hole to be one-third of the height of the plate. We will establish a set of parametric relations using the dimensional variables to capture the design intent described in statements (1) and (2) above.

1. Left-click once on the **General Dimension** icon to activate the General Dimension command.

2. Click on the **width dimension** of the rectangle to display the *Edit Dimension* window.

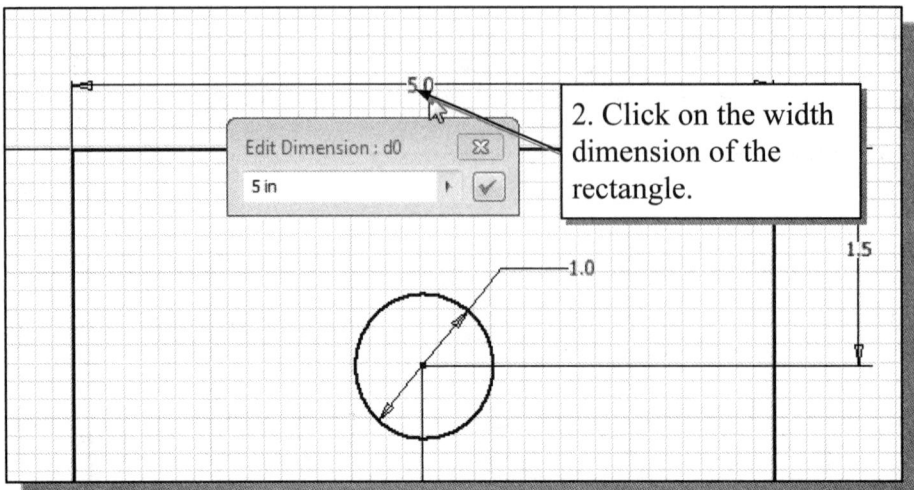

2. Click on the width dimension of the rectangle.

- Notice the *variable name* **d0** is displayed in the title area of the *Edit Dimension* window and also in the cursor box when the cursor is moved near the text box.

3. Click on the *check mark* button to close the *Edit Dimension* window.

Parametric Equations

- Each time we add a dimension to a model, that value is established as a parameter for the model. We can use parameters in equations to set the values of other parameters.

    1. Click on the **horizontal location dimension** of the circle to display the *Edit Dimension* window.

1. Edit this dimension.

2. Click on the width dimension of the rectangle **d0** (value of **5.0**). Notice the variable name is automatically entered in the *Edit Dimension* window.

3. In the *Edit Dimension* window, enter **/2** to set the horizontal location dimension of the circle to be one-half of the width of the rectangle.

4. Click on the **check mark** button to close the *Edit Dimension* window.

❖ Notice, the derived dimension values are displayed with **fx** in front of the numbers. The parametric relations we entered are used to control the location of the circle; the location is based on the height and width of the rectangle.

5. On your own, repeat the above steps and set the vertical location dimension to one-half of the height of the rectangle.

Viewing the Established Parameters and Relations

1. In the *Manage* toolbar select the **Parameters** command by left-clicking once on the icon. The *Parameters* popup window appears.

- The **Parameters** command can be used to display all dimensions used to define the model. We can also create additional parameters as design variables, which are called ***user parameters***.

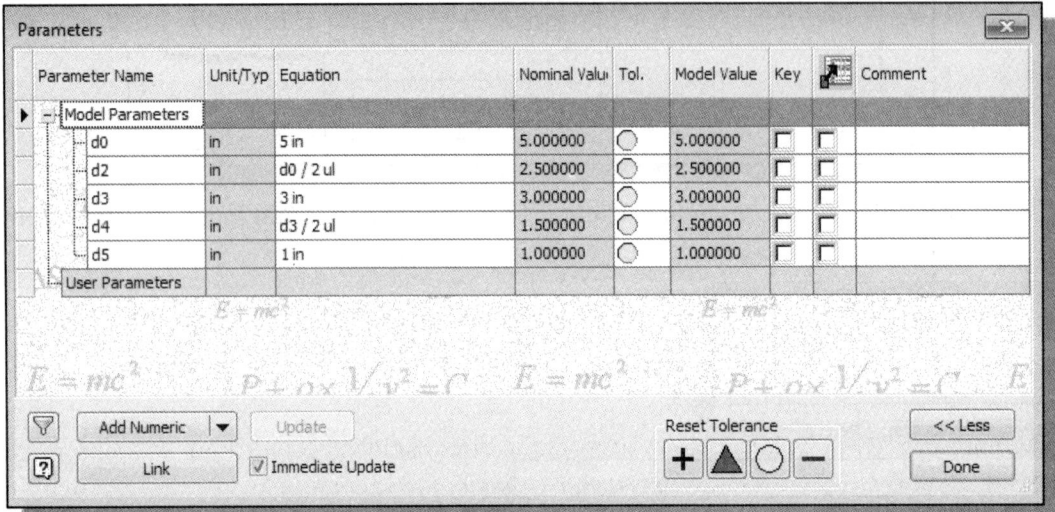

2. Click on the **1.0** value in the equation section of the *Parameters* window. Enter **d3/3** as the parametric relation to set the size of the circle to be one-third of the height of the rectangle as shown below.

3. Click on the **Done** button to accept the settings.

4. On your own, change the dimensions of the rectangle to **6.0 x 3.6** and observe the changes to the location and size of the circle. (Hint: Double-click the dimension text to bring up the *Edit Dimension* window.)

❖ *Autodesk Inventor* automatically adjusts the dimensions of the design, and the parametric relations we entered are also applied and maintained. The dimensional constraints are used to control the size and location of the hole. The design intent, previously expressed by statements (1) and (2) at the beginning of this section, is now embedded into the model.

➢ On your own, use the **Extrude** command and create a 3D solid model with a plate thickness of **0.25**. Also, experiment with modifying the parametric relations and dimensions through the *part browser*.

Saving the Model File

1. Select **Save** in the *Standard* toolbar. We can also use the "**Ctrl-S**" combination (press down the "Ctrl" key and hit the "S" key once) to save the part.

2. In the popup window, enter **Plate** as the name of the file.

3. Click on the **SAVE** button to save the file.

Using the Measure Tools

- Besides using the measure tools to get geometric information at the 2D level, the measure tools can also be used on 3D models.

1. In the *Tools* pull-down menu, left-mouse-click once on the **Measure Distance** option as shown.

   - Note that Region Properties is not available at the 3D level.

2. Click on the top edge of the rectangular plate as shown.

3. The associated length measurement of the selected geometry is displayed in the *Length* dialog box as shown.

4. Click on the **triangular icon** in the *Measure Distance* dialog box to display the available options.

5. Choose [**Dual Unit**] → [**Millimeter**] to also display the measurement in mm.

6. On your own, set the precision to show 3 decimal places as shown.

7. Click the **top-right corner** of the 3D model as shown.

❖ Notice the information regarding the selected point is displayed in the *Measure Distance* box. The absolute position of the point is displayed. (Note the displayed numbers may be different on your screen.)

8. Select the front left bottom corner as the second location for the Measure Length command. The distance in between the two selected objects is calculated.

9. Set the display option to **Wireframe Display** by clicking the associated icon in the *Display* toolbar as shown.

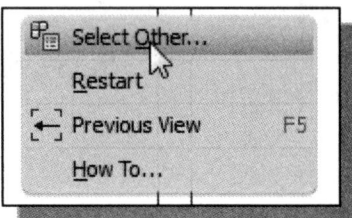

10. Use the **Select other** option and select the left vertical plane by clicking on the selection arrows.

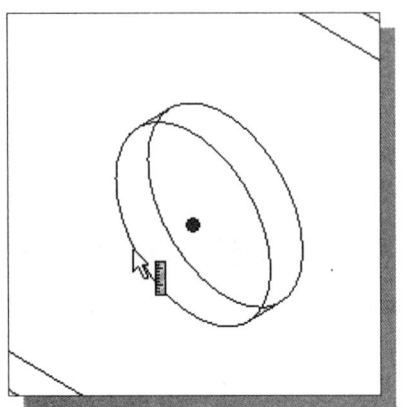

11. Select the circular hole in the front face; notice the center point is highlighted (the actual point used for the calculation) as shown.

❖ Different types of entities can be selected and the measurements are calculated accordingly.

Parametric Constraints Fundamentals 5-27

12. On your own, switch to the **Measure Area** option as shown.

13. Click on the front face of the plate model to display the area of the selected surface.

14. Note that we can also select cylindrical surfaces; select the cylindrical surface as shown.

15. On your own, experiment with the different **measure tools** available.

Questions: (Time: 30 minutes)

1. What is the difference between *dimensional* constraints and *geometric* constraints?

2. How can we confirm that a sketch is fully constrained?

3. How do we distinguish between derived dimensions and regular dimensions on the screen?

4. Describe the procedure to Display/Edit user-defined equations.

5. List and describe three different geometric constraints available in *Autodesk Inventor*.

6. Does *Autodesk Inventor* allow us to build partially constrained or totally unconstrained solid models? What are the advantages and disadvantages of building these types of models?

7. How do we display and examine the existing constraints that are applied to the sketched entities?

8. Describe the advantages of using parametric equations.

9. Can we delete an applied constraint? How?

10. Create the following 2D Sketch and measure the associated area and perimeter.

11. Describe the purpose and usage of the Auto Dimension command.

Exercises: Create and save the exercises in the Chapter5 folder.
    (Time: 90 minutes.)
(Create and establish three parametric relations for each of the following designs.)

1. **Swivel Base** (Dimensions are in millimeters. Base thickness: **10 mm.** Boss: **5 mm.**)

2. **C-Clip** (Dimensions are in inches. Plate thickness: **0.25 inches**.)

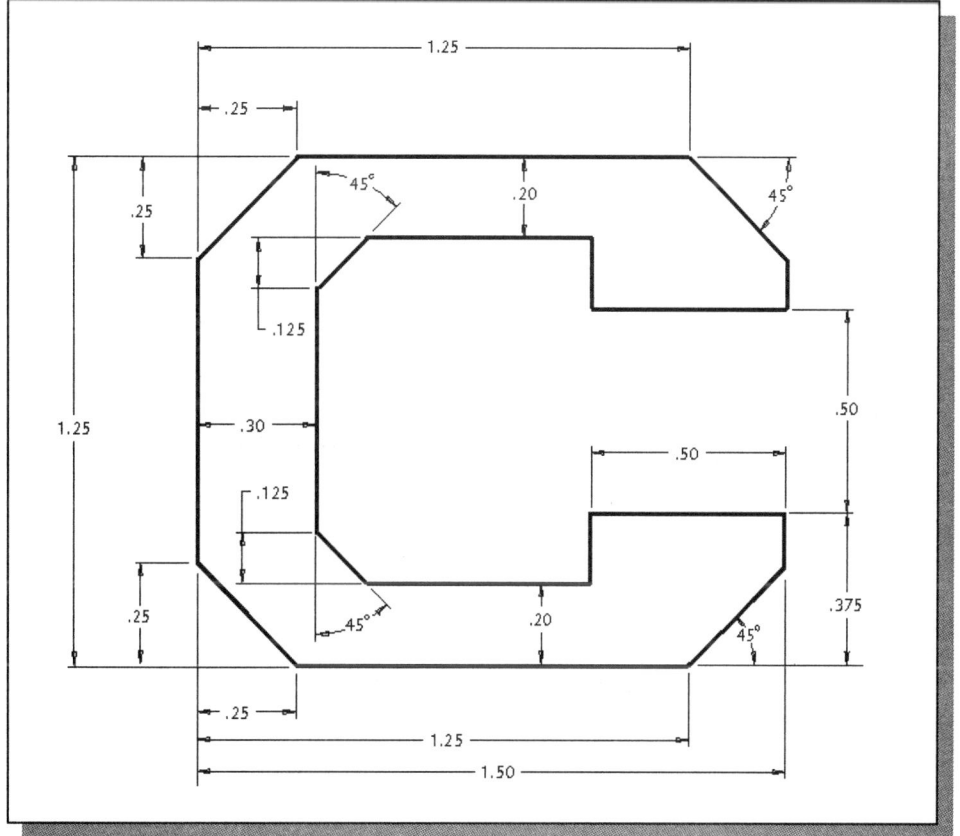

3. **Wedge Block** (Dimensions are in inches)

4. **Hinge Guide** (Dimensions are in inches.)

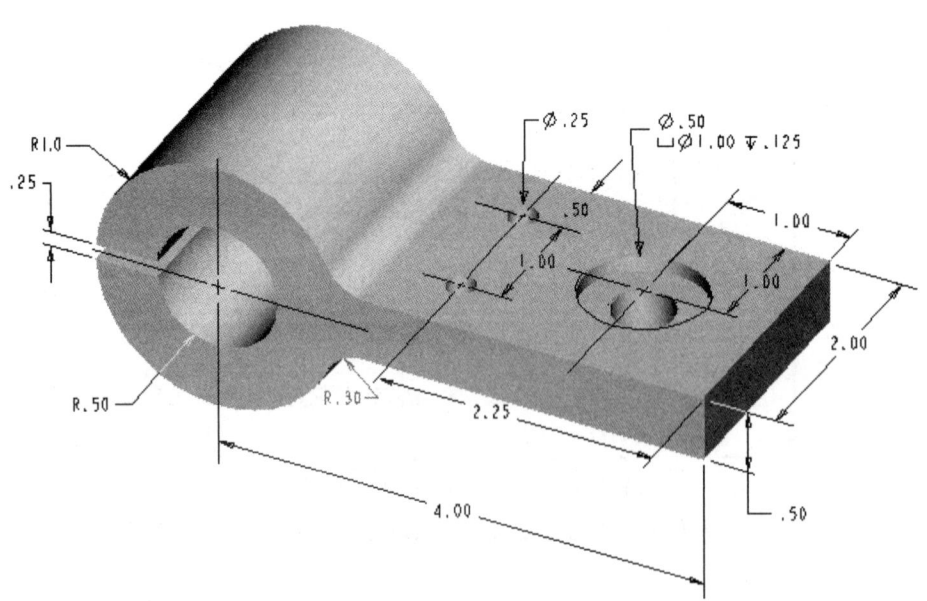

Chapter 6
Geometric Construction Tools

Learning Objectives

- **Applying Geometry Constraints**
- **Use the Trim/Extend Command**
- **Use the Offset Command**
- **Understand the Profile Sketch Approach**
- **Create Projected Geometry**
- **Understanding and Using Reference Geometry**
- **Edit with Click and Drag**
- **Using the Auto Dimension Command**

Introduction

The main characteristics of solid modeling are the accuracy and completeness of the geometric database of the three-dimensional objects. However, working in three-dimensional space using input and output devices that are largely two-dimensional in nature is potentially tedious and confusing. *Autodesk Inventor* provides an assortment of two-dimensional construction tools to make the creation of wireframe geometry easier and more efficient. *Autodesk Inventor* includes two types of wireframe geometry: **curves** and **profiles**. Curves are basic geometric entities such as lines, arcs, etc. Profiles are a group of curves used to define a boundary. A *profile* is a closed region and can contain other closed regions. Profiles are commonly used to create extruded and revolved features. An *invalid profile* consists of self-intersecting curves or open regions. In this lesson, the basic geometric construction tools, such as Trim and Extend, are used to create profiles. The *Autodesk Inventor's **profile sketch*** approach to creating profiles is also introduced. Mastering the geometric construction tools along with the application of proper constraints and parametric relations is the true essence of *parametric modeling*.

The *Gasket* Design

❖ Based on your knowledge of *Autodesk Inventor* so far, how would you create this design? What is the most difficult geometry involved in the design? Take a few minutes to consider a modeling strategy and do preliminary planning by sketching on a piece of paper. You are also encouraged to create the design on your own prior to following through the tutorial.

Modeling Strategy

Starting *Autodesk Inventor*

1. Select the **Autodesk Inventor** option on the *Start* menu or select the **Autodesk Inventor** icon on the desktop to start *Autodesk Inventor*. The *Autodesk Inventor* main window will appear on the screen.

2. Select the **New File** icon with a single click of the left-mouse-button in the *Launch* toolbar.

3. Select the **Metric** tab as shown. We will use the millimeter (mm) setting for this design.

4. In the *New File* dialog box, use the scroll bar on the right and select the **Standard(mm).ipt** icon as shown.

5. Click **Create** in the *New File* dialog box to accept the selected settings to start a new model.

6. Click once with the left-mouse-button to select the **Create 2D Sketch** command. Click once with the **left-mouse-button** to select the *XY Plane* as the sketch plane for the new sketch.

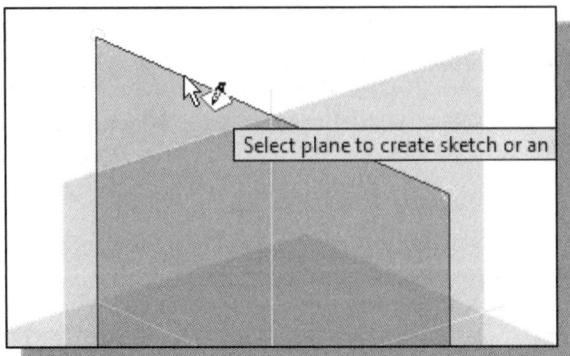

Create a 2D Sketch

1. Click on the **Line** icon in the *Sketch* toolbar.

2. Create a sketch as shown in the figure below. Start the sketch from the top right corner. The line segments are all parallel and/or perpendicular to each other. We will intentionally make the line segments of arbitrary length, as it is quite common during the design stage that not all of the shapes and forms are determined.

3. Inside the graphics window, right-mouse-click to bring up the option menu, and select **Done** to end the Line command.

4. Select the **Center point circle** command by clicking once with the left-mouse-button on the icon in the *2D Sketch* panel.

5. Pick a location that is above the bottom horizontal line as the center location of the circle.

6. Move the cursor toward the right and create a circle of arbitrary size, by clicking once with the left-mouse-button.

7. Click on the **Line** icon in the *2D Sketch* panel.

8. Move the cursor near the upper portion of the circle and pick a location on the circle when the Coincident constraint symbol is displayed.

Geometric Construction Tools 6-7

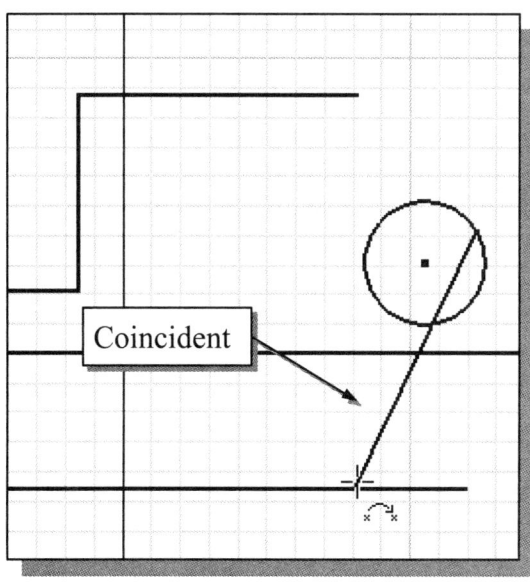

9. For the other end of the line, select a location that is on the lower horizontal line and about one-third from the right endpoint. Notice the **Coincident** constraint symbol is displayed when the cursor is on the horizontal line.

10. Inside the graphics window, right-mouse-click to bring up the option menu and select **OK** to end the Line command.

Edit the Sketch by Dragging the Sketched Entities

❖ In *Autodesk Inventor*, we can click and drag any under-constrained curve or point in the sketch to change the size or shape of the sketched profile. As illustrated in the previous chapter, this option can be used to identify under-constrained entities. This *Editing by Dragging* method is also an effective visual approach that allows designers to quickly make changes.

1. Move the cursor on the lower left vertical edge of the sketch. Click and drag the edge to a new location that is toward the right side of the sketch.

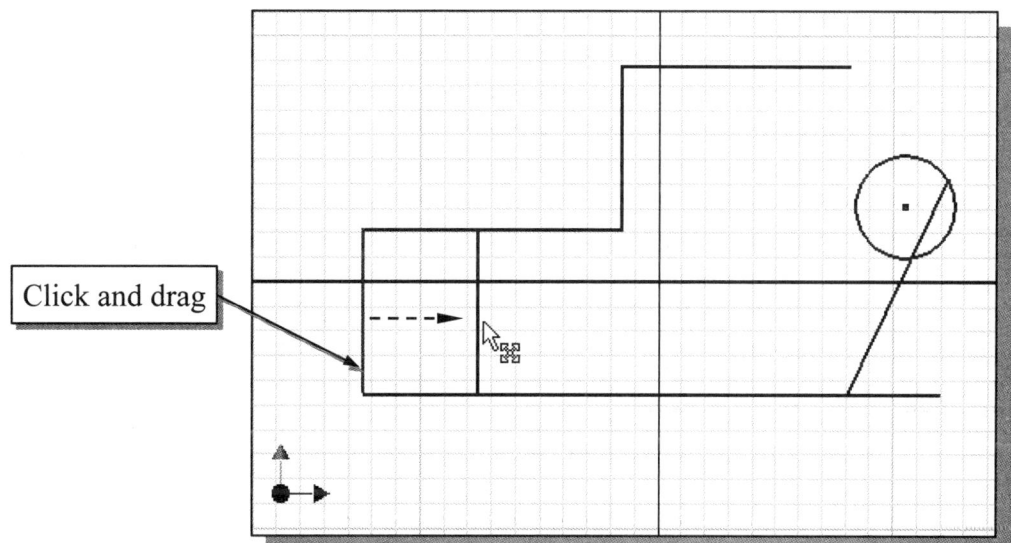

❖ Note that we can only drag the vertical edge horizontally; the connections to the two horizontal lines are maintained while we are moving the geometry.

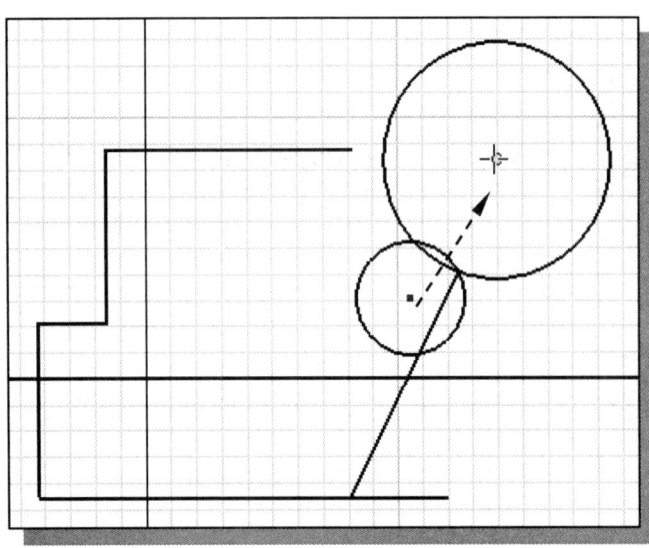

2. Click and drag the center point of the circle to a new location.

❖ Note that as we adjust the size and the location of the circle, the connection to the inclined line is maintained.

3. Click and drag the lower endpoint of the inclined line to a new location.

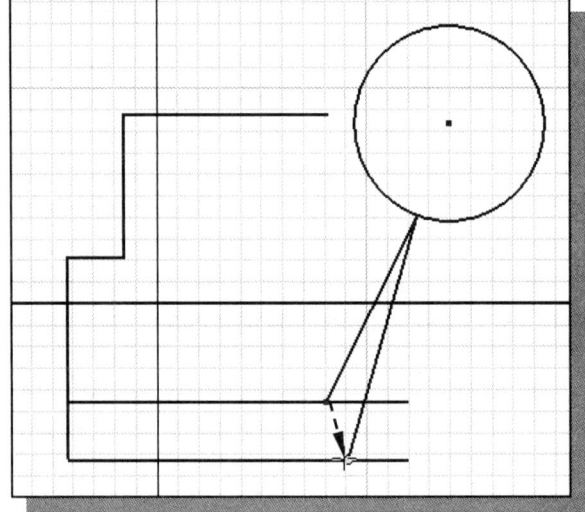

❖ Note that as we adjust the size and the location of the inclined line the location of the bottom horizontal edge is also adjusted.

➢ Note that several changes occur as we adjust the size and the location of the inclined line. The location of the bottom horizontal line and the length of the vertical line are adjusted accordingly.

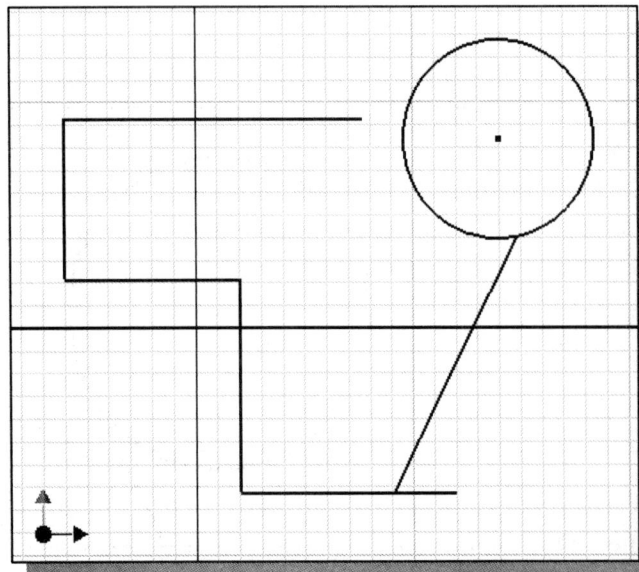

4. On your own, adjust the sketch so that the shape of the sketch appears roughly as shown.

❖ The *Editing by Dragging* method is an effective approach that allows designers to explore and experiment with different design concepts.

Add Additional Constraints

1. Choose **General Dimension** in the *2D Sketch* panel.

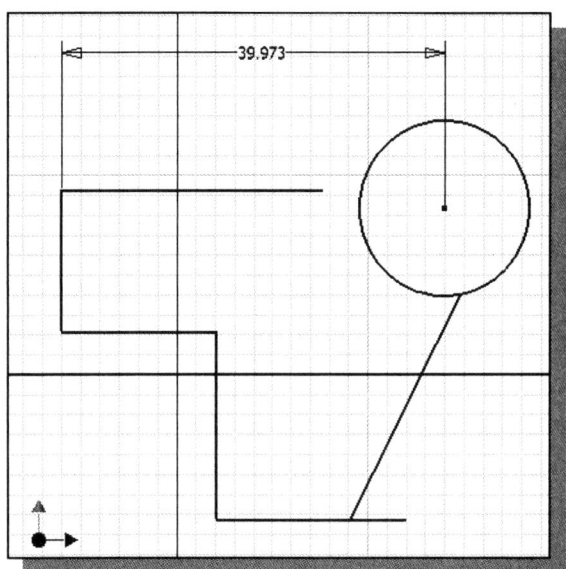

2. Add the horizontal location dimension, from the top left vertical edge to the center of the circle as shown. (Do not be overly concerned with the dimensional value; we are still working on creating a *rough sketch*.)

3. Click on the **Tangent** constraint icon in the *2D Sketch* panel.

4. Pick the inclined line by left-mouse-clicking once on the geometry.

5. Pick the circle. The sketched geometry is adjusted as shown below.

6. Inside the graphics window, right-mouse-click to bring up the option menu.

7. In the option menu, select **OK** to end the Tangent command.

8. Click and drag the circle to a new location.

❖ Note that the dimension we added now restricts the horizontal movement of the center of the circle. The tangent relation to the inclined line is maintained.

Use the Trim and Extend Commands

➢ In the following sections, we will illustrate using the Trim and Extend commands to complete the desired 2D profile.

❖ The **Trim** and **Extend** commands can be used to shorten/lengthen an object so that it ends precisely at a boundary. As a general rule, *Autodesk Inventor* will try to clean up sketches by forming a closed region sketch. Also note that while we are in either **Trim** or **Extend**, we can press the [**Shift**] key to switch to the opposite operation.

1. Choose **Extend** in the *Modify toolbar* panel. The message "*Extend curves*" is displayed in the prompt area.

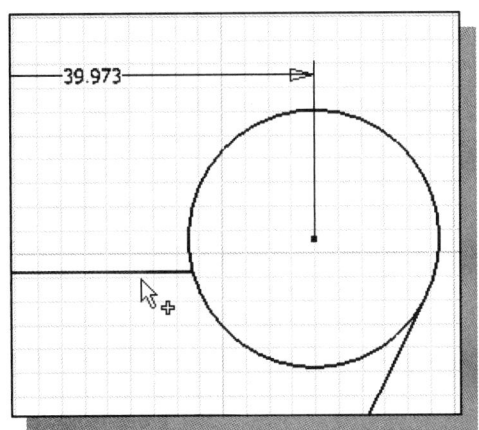

2. We will first extend the top horizontal line to the circle. Move the cursor near the right hand endpoint of the top horizontal line. *Autodesk Inventor* will automatically display the possible result of the selection.

3. Next, we will trim the bottom horizontal line to the inclined line. The **Trim** operation can be activated by selecting the Trim icon in the *2D Sketch* panel or by pressing down the [**Shift**] key while we are in the Extend command. Move the cursor near the right hand endpoint of the bottom horizontal line and select the line and press down the [**Shift**] key. *Autodesk Inventor* will display a dashed line indicating the portion of the line that will be trimmed.

3. Press down the [**Shift**] key and move the cursor near the right end of the line.

4. Left-mouse-click once on the line to perform the **Trim** operation.

5. On your own, create the vertical location dimension as shown below.

6. Adjust the dimension to **0.0** so that the horizontal line and the center of the circle are aligned horizontally.

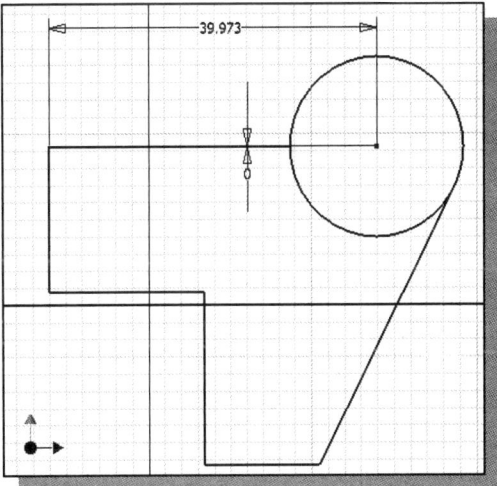

7. On your own, create the **height dimension** to the left and use the **Show Constraints** command to examine the applied constraints. Confirm that a **Perpendicular constraint** is applied to the horizontal and vertical lines as shown.

A perpendicular constraint is applied to the horizontal line and the vertical line.

The Auto Dimension Command

➤ In *Autodesk Inventor*, we can use the **Auto Dimension** command to assist in creating a fully constrained sketch. Fully constrained sketches can be updated more predictably as design changes are implemented. The general procedure for applying dimensions to sketches is to use the **General Dimension** command to add the desired key dimensions, and then use the **Auto Dimension** command as a quick way to calculate all other sketch dimensions necessary. *Autodesk Inventor* remembers which dimensions were added by the user and which were calculated by the system, so that automatic dimensions do not replace the desired dimensions.

1. Click on the **Auto Dimension** icon in the *2D Sketch* panel.

- Note that 6 dimensions are needed to fully constrain the sketch, as indicated in the *Status Bar*.

Geometric Construction Tools   6-13

2. The *Auto Dimension* dialog box appears on the screen. Confirm that the **Dimensions** and **Constraints** options are switched *ON* as shown.

3. Click on the **Apply** button to proceed with the Auto Dimension command.

➢ Note that the system automatically calculates additional dimensions for all created geometric entities. Note that the dimensions created by the **Auto Dimension** command can also be **Removed**; this option will remove the dimensions created by the command, but maintain the dimensions created by the user.

4. Click on the **Remove** button to undo the dimensions created by the *Auto Dimension* command.

➢ Note the **Remove** option only removes the dimensions created by the **Auto Dimension** command.

5. On your own, **trim** the circle and add the additional dimensions as shown.

6. Note the display in the *Status Bar* indicates two additional dimensions are still needed to fully constrain the sketch.

Create Fillets and Completing the Sketch

1. Click on the **Fillet** icon in the *2D Sketch* panel.

2. The *2D Fillet* radius dialog box appears on the screen. Use the default radius value and click on the top horizontal line and the arc to create a fillet as shown.

3. On your own, create the three additional fillets as shown in the below figure. Note that the **Equal** constraint is activated and all rounds and fillets are created with the constraint.

4. Click on the [**X**] icon to close the *2D Fillet* dialog box and end the **Fillet** command.

Fully Constrained Geometry

1. Click on the **Fix** constraint icon in the *2D Sketch Panel*.

2. Apply the **Fix** constraint to the center of the arc as shown below.

➢ Note that the sketch is now fully constrained.

3. Click on the **Auto Dimension** icon in the *2D Sketch* panel.

➢ Note that the system automatically recalculates if any additional dimension is needed for all created geometric entities. The applied **Fix** constraint provided the previously missing location dimensions for the created sketches.

4. Click **Done** to exit the Auto Dimension command.

5. On your own, complete the sketch and change the dimensions to the desired values as shown below. (Hint: Change the larger values first.)

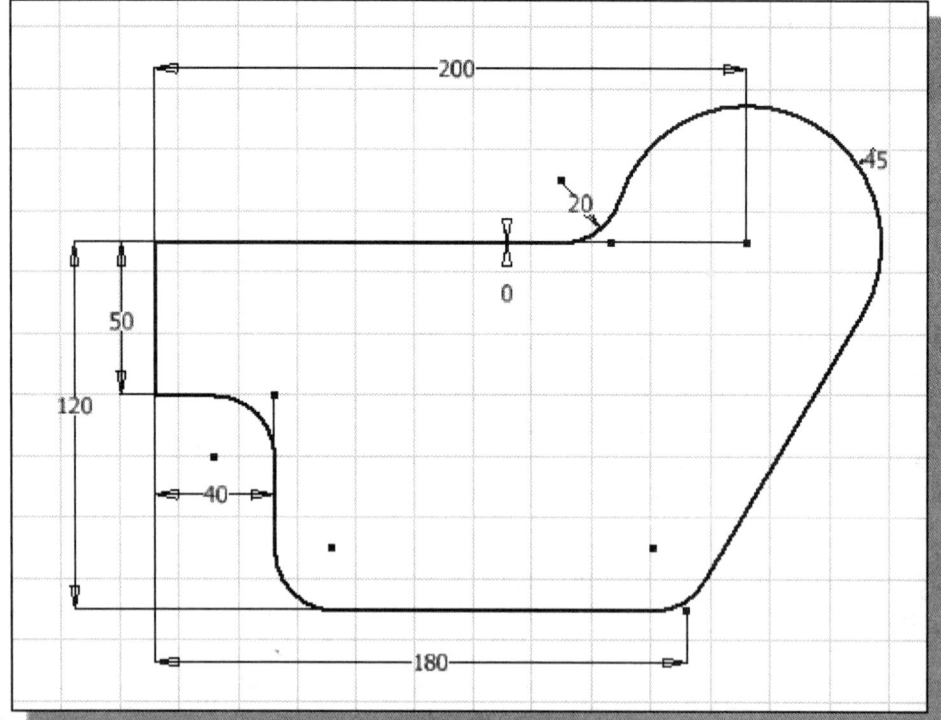

❖ Note that by applying proper geometric and dimensional constraints to the sketched geometry; a *constraint network* is created that assures the geometry shape behaves predictably as changes are made.

Profile Sketch

❖ In *Autodesk Inventor*, *profiles* are closed regions that are defined from sketches. Profiles are used as cross sections to create solid features. For example, **Extrude**, **Revolve**, **Sweep**, **Loft**, and **Coil** operations all require the definition of at least a single profile. The sketches used to define a profile can contain additional geometry since the additional geometry entities are consumed when the feature is created. To create a profile we can create single or multiple closed regions, or we can select existing solid edges to form closed regions. A profile cannot contain self-intersecting geometry; regions selected in a single operation form a single profile. As a general rule, we should dimension and constrain profiles to prevent them from unpredictable size and shape changes. *Autodesk Inventor* does allow us to create under-constrained or non-constrained profiles; the dimensions and/or constraints can be added/edited later.

1. In the *Part Features* toolbar, select the **Extrude** command by left-mouse-clicking once on the icon.

❖ Note that *Autodesk Inventor* automatically highlights the closed region of the sketch. The defining geometry now forms the **profile** required for the *Extrude* operation.

2. In the *Extrude* dialog box, enter **5 mm** as the extrusion distance as shown.

3. Click on the **OK** button to accept the settings and create the solid feature.

❖ Note that all the sketched geometry entities and dimensions are consumed and have disappeared from the screen when the feature is created.

Redefine the Sketch and Profile

- Engineering designs usually go through many revisions and changes. *Autodesk Inventor* provides an assortment of tools to handle design changes quickly and effectively. We will demonstrate some of the tools available by changing the base feature of the design. The profile used to create the extrusion is selected from the sketched geometry entities. In *Autodesk Inventor*, any profile can be edited and/or redefined at any time. It is this type of functionality in parametric solid modeling software that provides designers with greater flexibility and the ease to experiment with different design considerations.

1. In the *browser*, **right-mouse-click** once on the **Extrusion1** feature to bring up the option menu, and then pick **Edit Sketch** in the pop-up menu.

Geometric Construction Tools   6-19

2. On your own, create a circle and a rectangle of arbitrary sizes, positioned as shown in the figure below. We will intentionally under-constrain the new sketch to illustrate the flexibility of the system.

3. Inside the graphics window, click once with the right-mouse-button to display the option menu. Select **Finish 2D Sketch** in the popup menu to end the Sketch option.

➢ Note that, at this point, the solid model remains the same as before. We will next redefine the profile used for the base feature.

4. In the *browser*, right-mouse-click once on the Extrusion1 feature to bring up the option menu, and then pick **Edit Feature** in the pop-up menu.

❖ *Autodesk Inventor* will now display the 2D sketch of the selected feature in the graphics window. We have literally gone back in time to the point where we defined the extrusion feature.

5. Click on the **Look At** icon in the *Standard* toolbar area.

• The **Look At** command automatically aligns the *sketch plane* of a selected entity to the screen.

6. Select any line segment of the 2D sketch.

7. Click on the **Zoom All** icon in the *Standard* toolbar.

➢ We have literally gone back to the point where we first defined the 2D profile. The original sketch and the new sketch we just created are wireframe entities recorded by the system as belonging to the same **SKETCH**; but only the **PROFILED** entities are used to create the feature.

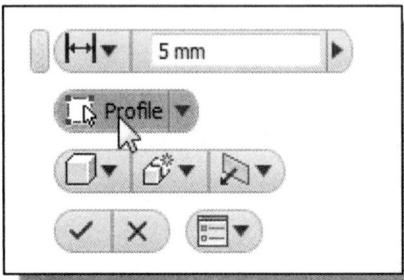

8. In the *Extrude* control panel, click on the **Profile** button to edit/redefine the 2D profile.

9. The geometry entities used to define the profile are highlighted as shown in the figure above. To **deselect**, move the cursor inside the **highlighted** region, press the [**Ctrl**] key or [**Shift**] key and left-mouse-click once.

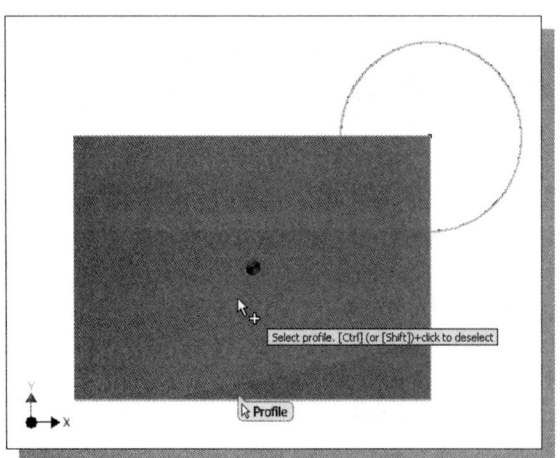

10. Click inside the rectangle of the sketch on the right side of the graphics window.

➢ *Autodesk Inventor* automatically selects the geometry entities that form a closed region to define the profile.

11. Click inside the circle to complete the profile definition as shown in the figure below.

12. In the *Extrude* control panel, click on the **OK** button to accept the settings and update the solid feature.

- The feature is recreated using the newly sketched geometric entities, which are under-constrained and with no dimensions. The profile is created with extra wireframe entities by selecting multiple regions. The extra geometry entities can be used as construction geometry to help in defining the profile. This approach encourages engineering content over drafting technique, which is one of the key features of *Autodesk Inventor* over other solid modeling software.

13. On your own, repeat the above steps and reset the profile back to the original gasket sketch.

Create an OFFSET Cut Feature

➤ To complete the design, we will create a cutout feature by using the **Offset** command. First, we will set up the sketching plane to align with the front face of the 3D model.

1. In the *Sketch* toolbar select the **Create 2D Sketch** command by left-clicking once on the icon.

2. In the *Status Bar* area, the message: "*Select face, workplane, sketch or sketch geometry.*" is displayed. Select the **front face** of the 3D model in the graphics window.

3. Click on the **Offset** icon in the *2D Sketch* panel.

4. Select any edge of the **front face** of the 3D model. *Autodesk Inventor* will automatically select all of the connecting geometry to form a closed region.

5. Move the cursor toward the center of the selected region and notice an offset copy of the outline is displayed.

6. Left-mouse-click once to create the offset profile as shown.

Geometric Construction Tools   6-23

7. On your own, use the **General Dimension** command to create the offset dimension as shown in the figure below.

8. Modify the offset dimension to **15 mm** as shown in the figure to the right.

9. Inside the graphics window, click once with the right-mouse-button to display the option menu. Select **OK** in the popup menu to end the General Dimension command.

10. Inside the graphics window, click once with the right-mouse-button to display the option menu. Select **Finish Sketch** in the popup menu to end the Sketch option.

11. In the *Part Features* toolbar (the toolbar that is located to the left side of the graphics window), select the **Extrude** command by releasing the left-mouse-button on the icon.

12. Select the **inside region** of the offset geometry as the profile for the extrusion.

13. Inside the *Extrude* dialog box, select the **Cut** operation, set the *Extents* to **All** and set the direction of the cutout as shown in the figure below.

14. In the *Extrude* dialog box, click on the **OK** button to accept the settings and create the solid feature.

> The offset geometry is associated with the original geometry. On your own, adjust the overall height of the design to **150 millimeters** and confirm that the offset geometry is adjusted accordingly.

Questions: (Time: 25 minutes)

1. What are the two types of wireframe geometry available in *Autodesk Inventor*?

2. Can we create a profile with extra 2D geometry entities?

3. How do we access the *Autodesk Inventor's* **Edit Sketch** option?

4. How do we create a *profile* in *Autodesk Inventor*?

5. Can we build a profile that consists of self-intersecting curves?

6. Describe the procedure to create a copy of a sketched 2D wireframe geometry?

7. Can we create additional entities in a 2D sketch, without using them at all?

8. How do we align the *sketch plane* of a selected entity to the screen?

9. Describe the steps we used to switch existing profiles in the tutorial?

10. Describe the advantages of using the **Offset** command vs. creating a separate sketch.

Exercises: Create and save the exercises in the Chapter6 folder.
(Time: 90 minutes.)

1. **V-slide Plate** (Dimensions are in inches. Plate Thickness: **0.25**)

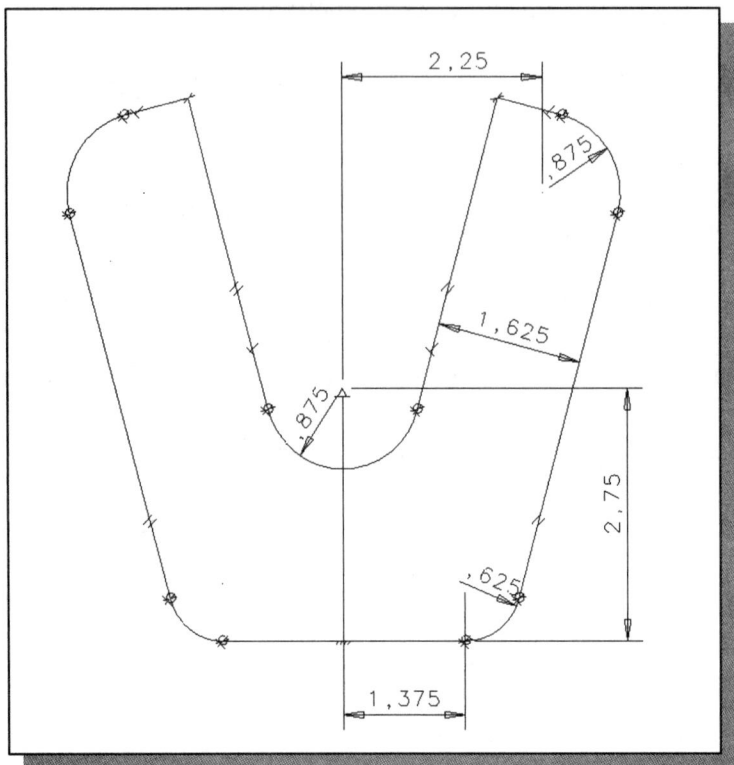

2. **Shaft Support** (Dimensions are in millimeters.)

3. **Tube Mount** (Dimensions are in inches.)

4. **Anchor Base** (Dimensions are in inches.)

Notes:

Chapter 7
Parent/Child Relationships and the BORN Technique

Learning Objectives

- **Understand the Concept and Usage of the BORN Technique**
- **Understand the Importance of Parent/Child Relations in Features**
- **Use the Suppress Feature Option**
- **Resolve Undesired Feature Interactions**

Introduction

The parent/child relationship is one of the most powerful aspects of *parametric modeling*. In *Autodesk Inventor*, each time a new modeling event is created, previously defined features can be used to define information such as size, location, and orientation. The referenced features become **PARENT** features to the new feature, and the new feature is called the **CHILD** feature. The parent/child relationships determine how a model reacts when other features in the model change, thus capturing design intent. It is crucial to keep track of these parent/child relations. Any modification to a parent feature can change one or more of its children.

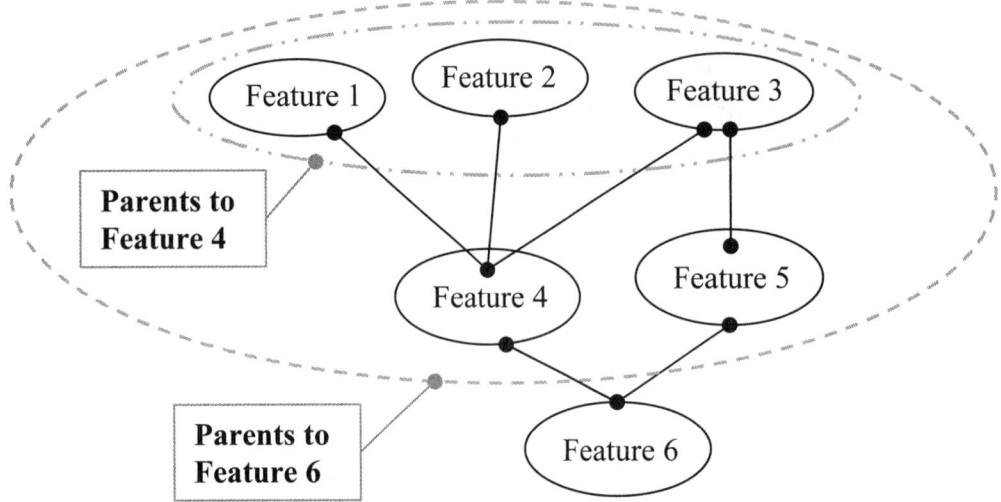

Parent/child relationships can be created *implicitly* or *explicitly*; implicit relationships are implied by the feature creation method and explicit relationships are entered manually by the user. In the previous chapters, we first select a sketching plane before creating a 2D profile. The selected surface becomes a parent of the new feature. If the sketching plane is moved, the child feature will move with it. As one might expect, parent/child relationships can become quite complicated when the features begin to accumulate. It is therefore important to think about modeling strategy before we start to create anything. The main consideration is to try to plan ahead for possible design changes that might occur which would be affected by the existing parent/child relationships. Parametric modeling software, such as Autodesk Inventor, also allows us to adjust feature properties so that any feature conflicts can be quickly resolved.

The BORN Technique

In *parametric modeling*, the **base feature** (the *first solid feature* of the solid model) is the center of all features and is considered the key feature of the design. All subsequent features are built by referencing the first feature. Much emphasis is placed on the selection of the *base feature*.

A more advanced technique of creating solid models is what is known as the "**Base Orphan Reference Node**" (**BORN**) technique. The basic concept of the BORN technique is to use a *Cartesian coordinate system* as the first feature prior to creating any solid features. With the *Cartesian coordinate system* established, we then have three mutually perpendicular datum planes (namely the *XY*, *YZ*, and *ZX planes*), three datum axes and a datum point, available to use as sketching planes. The three datum planes can also be used as references for dimensions and geometric constructions. Using this technique, the first node in the history tree is called an "orphan," meaning that it has no history to be replayed. The technique of using the reference geometry in this "base node" is therefore called the "Base Orphan Reference Node" (BORN) technique.

Autodesk Inventor automatically establishes a set of reference geometry when we start a new part, namely a *Cartesian coordinate system* with three work planes, three work axes, and a work point. All subsequent solid features can then use the coordinate system and/or reference geometry as sketching planes. The *base feature* is still important, but the *base feature* is no longer the ONLY choice for creating subsequent solid features. This approach provides us with more options while we are creating parametric solid models. More importantly, this approach provides greater flexibility for part modifications and design changes. This approach is also very useful in creating assembly models, which will be illustrated in the later chapters of this text.

The *U-Bracket* Design

> Based on your knowledge of *Inventor* so far, how many features would you use to create the model? Which feature would you choose as the **base feature**? What is your choice for arranging the order of the features? Would you organize the features differently if the rectangular cut at the center is changed to a circular shape (Radius: 1.25 inch)?

Sketch Plane Settings

1. Select the *Autodesk Inventor* option on the *Start* menu or select the *Autodesk Inventor* icon on the desktop to start *Autodesk Inventor*. The *Autodesk Inventor* main window will appear on the screen.

2. Select **Application Options** in the **Tools** pull-down menu.

   - The **Application Options** menu allows us to set behavioral options, such as *color*, *file locations*, etc.

3. Click on the **Part** tab to display and/or modify the default sketch plane settings.

   - Note the option to setup the sketch plane is available to be used during new part creation. Confirm the **No new sketch** option is set as shown.

4. Click on the **Sketch** tab to examine/modify the default sketching settings.

5. Turn **OFF** the *Snap to grid* and *Look at sketch plane on sketch creation* options.

6. Click on the **OK** button to accept the setting.

- Note that the new settings will take effect when a new part file is created.

7. Click on the **New** icon in the *Standard* toolbar and, on your own, open a new *English* units **standard (in) part** file.

Apply the BORN Technique

1. In the *Part Browser* window, click on the [+] symbol in front of the ***Origin*** feature to display more information on the feature.

❖ In the *Part Browser* window, notice a new part name appeared with seven work features established. The seven work features include three *workplanes*, three *work axes*, and a *work point*. By default, the three workplanes and work axes are aligned to the **world coordinate system** and the work point is aligned to the *origin* of the **world coordinate system**.

2. Inside the *browser* window, move the cursor on top of the third work plane, the **XY Plane**. Notice a rectangle, representing the work-plane, appears in the graphics window.

3. Inside the *browser* window, click once with the right-mouse-button on XY Plane to display the option menu. Click on **Visibility** to toggle on the display of the plane.

4. On your own, repeat the above steps and toggle *ON* the display of all of the *workplanes*, *work axes*, and the *center point* on the screen.

5. On your own, use the *Dynamic Viewing* options (ViewCube, 3D Orbit, Zoom and Pan) to view the default work features.

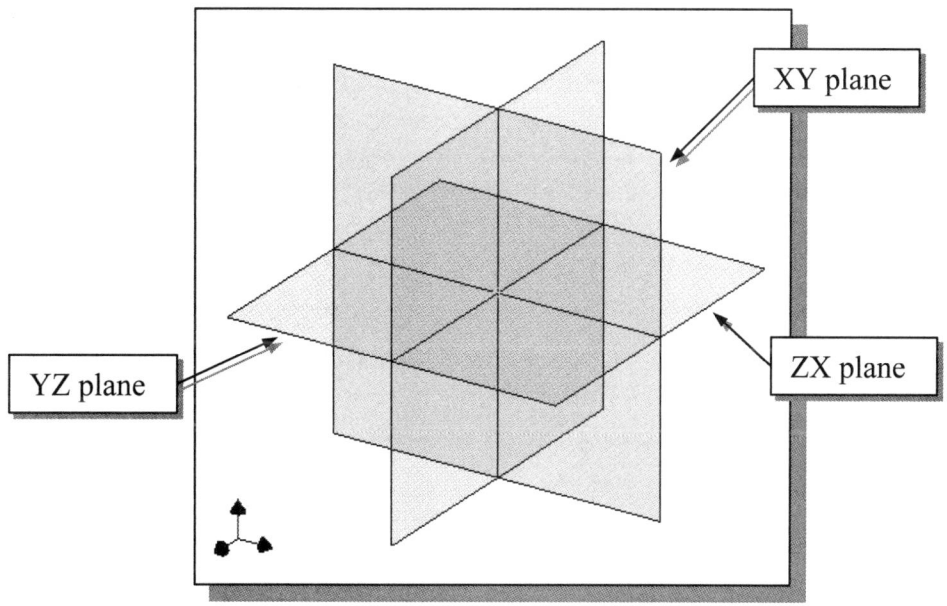

❖ By default, the basic set of workplanes is aligned to the world coordinate system; the workplanes are the first features of the part. We can now proceed to create solid features referencing the three mutually perpendicular datum planes.

6. In the *Sketch* toolbar select the **Create 2D Sketch** command by left-clicking once on the icon.

7. In the *Status Bar* area, the message: "*Select face, workplane, sketch or sketch geometry.*" is displayed. *Autodesk Inventor* expects us to identify a planar surface where the 2D sketch of the next feature is to be created. Move the graphics cursor on top of the **XZ Plane**, inside the *browser* window as shown, and notice that *Autodesk Inventor* will automatically highlight the corresponding plane in the graphics window. Left-click once to select the XZ Plane as the sketching plane.

❖ *Autodesk Inventor* allows us to identify and select features in the graphics window as well as in the *browser* window.

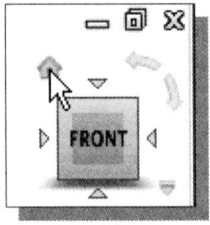

8. Single left-mouse-click to activate the **Home View** option as shown. The view will be adjusted back to the default *isometric view*.

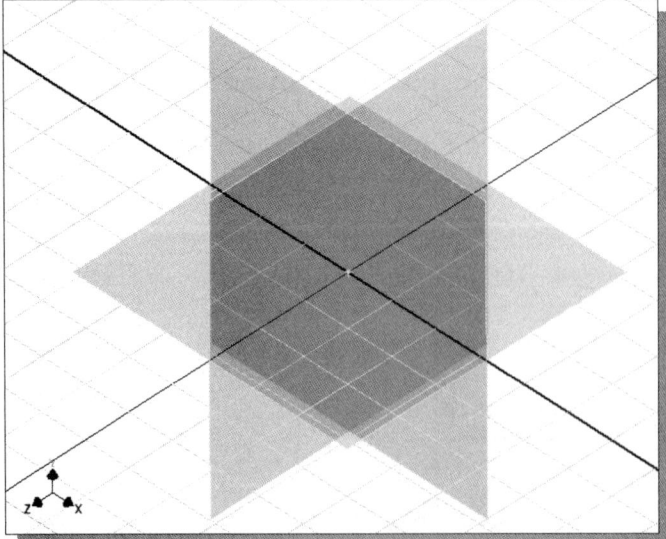

➢ Note the alignment of the sketch plane to the XZ plane as shown.

Create the 2D Sketch for the Base Feature

1. Select the **Two point rectangle** command by clicking once with the **left-mouse-button** on the icon in the *Draw* toolbar.

2. Create a rectangle surrounding the *center point* as shown below. (Note: Do not align the center of the rectangle to the origin.)

3. Select the **Center point circle** command by clicking once with the left-mouse-button on the icon in the *Draw* toolbar.

❖ We will align the center of the circle to the midpoint of the short edge of the rectangle.

4. Move the cursor along the shorter edge of the rectangle and pick the midpoint of the edge when the midpoint is displayed with a GREEN color.

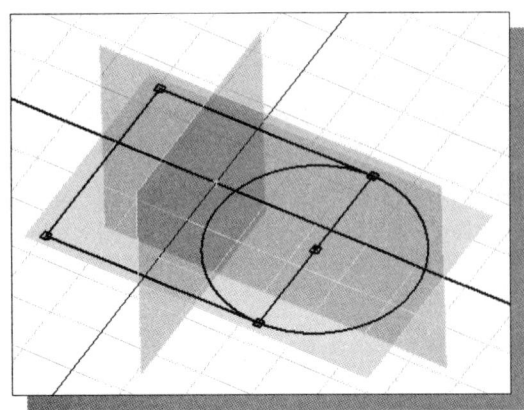

5. Select a neighboring corner of the rectangle to create a circle as shown below.

6. On your own, create a smaller circle sharing the same center point location as shown.

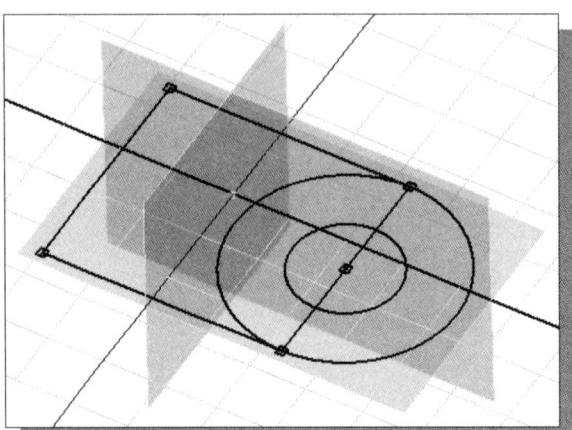

7. On your own, repeat the above steps and create two additional circles on the other side of the rectangle.

8. Inside the graphics window, click once with the right-mouse-button to display the option menu. Select **OK** in the popup menu to end the **Circle** command.

9. Choose **Trim** in the *Modify* panel. The message "*Trim curves*" is displayed in the prompt area.

10. On your own, trim the rectangle and the two outer circles so that the sketch appears as shown.

11. Move the cursor on top of the **General Dimension** icon. The General Dimension command allows us to quickly create and modify dimensions. Left-click once on the icon to activate the General Dimension command.

12. On your own, create the dimensions to fully constrain the sketch as shown. (Do not be overly concerned with the actual numbers displayed; the dimensions will be adjusted shortly.)

13. Click on the **Auto Dimension** icon in the *Constrain* panel.

14. Confirm the 2D sketch is fully constrained as shown in the figure. (Click the **Apply/Remove** buttons if necessary.)

15. Choose **General Dimension** in the *Constrain* panel.

16. On your own, adjust the dimensions as shown in the figure.

17. Inside the graphics window, click once with the right-mouse-button to display the option menu. Select **OK** in the popup menu to end the General Dimension command.

18. In the *Ribbon toolbar* area, select **Finish Sketch** in the popup menu to end the Sketch option.

Create the First Extrude Feature

1. In the *Create* toolbar, select the **Extrude** command by clicking once with the left-mouse-button on the icon.

2. Select the inside region of the sketch to define the profile of the extrusion as shown.

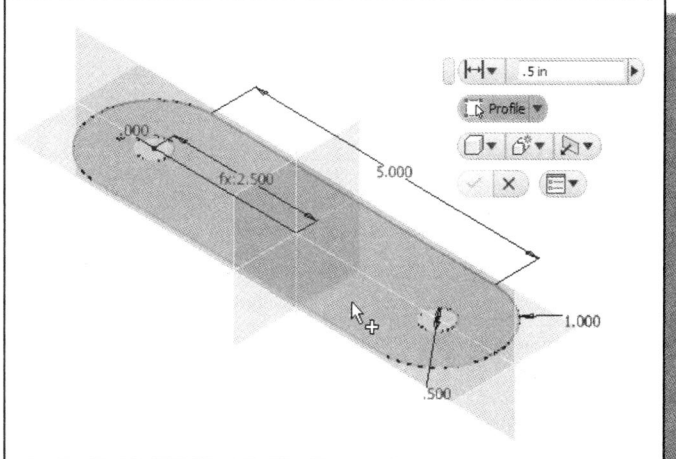

3. In the *Distance* option box, enter **0.5** as the extrusion distance.

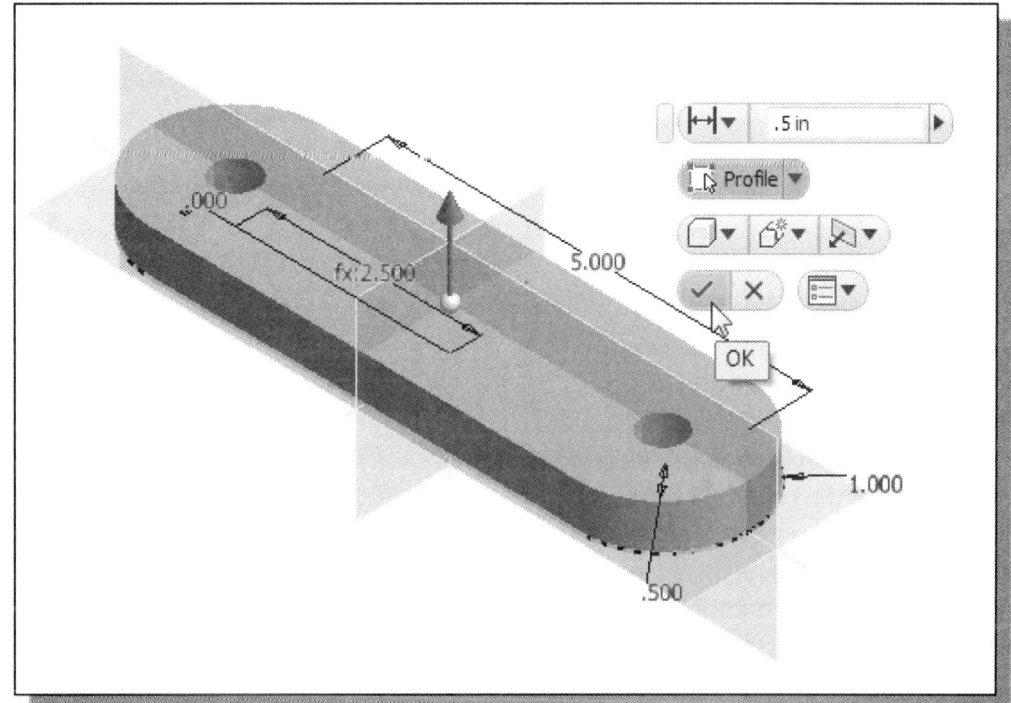

4. In the *Extrude* popup control, click on the **OK** button to create the base feature.

The Implied Parent/Child Relationships

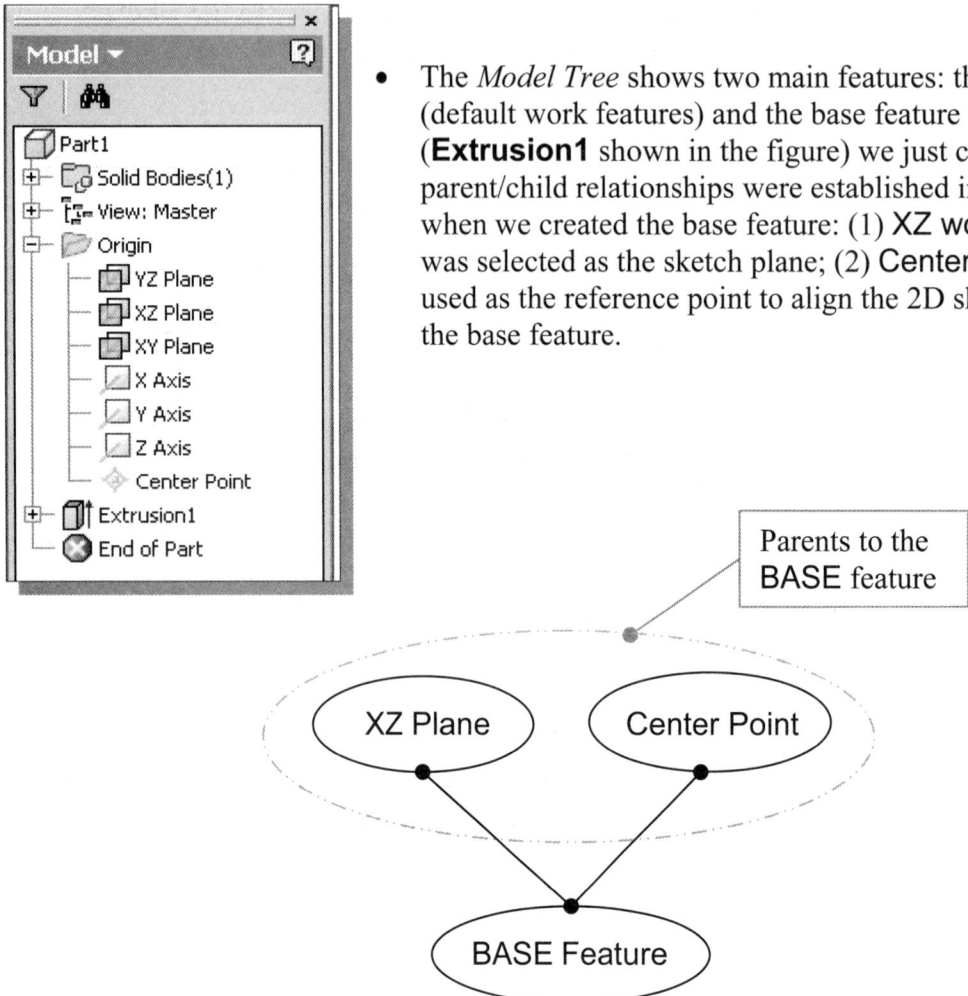

- The *Model Tree* shows two main features: the **Origin** (default work features) and the base feature (**Extrusion1** shown in the figure) we just created. The parent/child relationships were established implicitly when we created the base feature: (1) XZ workplane was selected as the sketch plane; (2) Center Point was used as the reference point to align the 2D sketch of the base feature.

Create the Second Solid Feature

- For the next solid feature, we will create the top section of the design. Note that the center of the base feature is aligned to the Center Point of the default work features. This was done intentionally so that additional solid features can be created referencing the default work features. For the second solid feature, the XY workplane will be used as the sketch plane.

Parent/Child Relationships and the BORN Technique 7-13

1. In the *Sketch* toolbar select the **Create 2D Sketch** command by left-clicking once on the icon.

2. In the *Status Bar* area, the message: "*Select face, work plane, sketch or sketch geometry.*" is displayed. Pick the **XY Plane** by clicking the work plane name inside the *browser* as shown.

3. Select the **View** tab in the *Ribbon* panel as shown.

4. Select **Wireframe** display mode under the *Visual Style* icon as shown.

5. Select the **Sketch** tab in the *Ribbon*.

6. Select the **Center point arc** command by clicking once with the left-mouse-button on the icon in the *icon stack* as shown.

7. Pick the **center point**, watch for the Green dot for alignment, as the center location of the new arc.

8. On your own, create a semi-circle of arbitrary size, with both endpoints aligned to the X-axis, as shown below.

9. Move the cursor on top of the **General Dimension** icon. Left-click once on the icon to activate the General Dimension command.

10. On your own, create and adjust the radius of the arc to **1.75**.

11. Select the **Line** command in the *Draw* toolbar.

12. Create a line connecting the two endpoints of the arc as shown in the figure below. (Hint: Use the **Coincident** constraint to help align the 2D sketch.)

13. Inside the graphics window, click once with the right-mouse-button to display the option menu. Select **Finish 2D Sketch** in the popup menu to end the Sketch option.

14. In the *Create Features* toolbar, select the **Extrude** command by clicking once with the left-mouse-button on the icon.

15. Select the inside region of the sketched arc-line curves as the profile to be extruded.

16. In the *Extrude* dialog box, set to the **Symmetric** option.

17. In the *Distance* value box, set the extrusion distance to **2.5**.

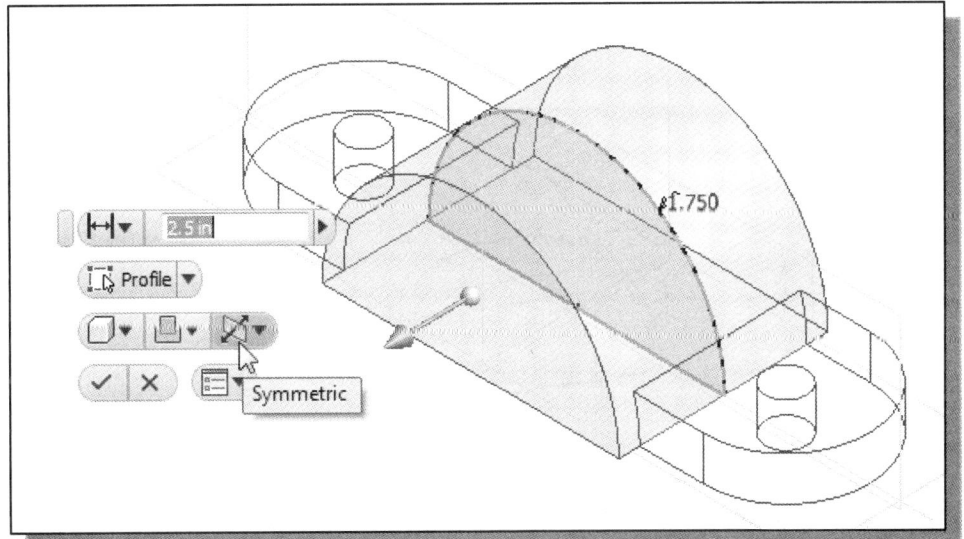

18. Click on the **OK** button to proceed with the Extrude operation.

Create the First Cut Feature

- A rectangular cut will be created as the next solid feature.

1. In the *Sketch* toolbar select the **Create 2D Sketch** command by left-clicking once on the icon.

2. In the *Status Bar* area, the message: "*Select face, workplane, sketch or sketch geometry*" is displayed. Pick the front vertical face of the solid model shown.

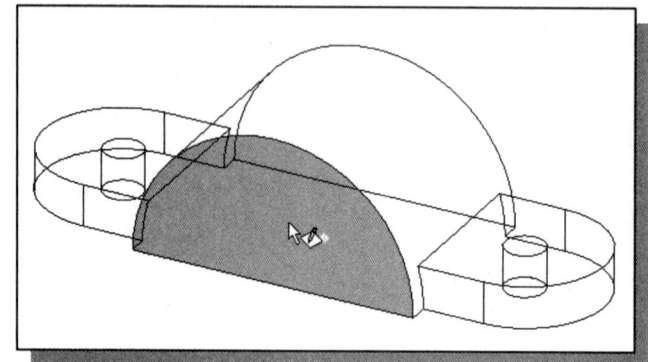

3. On your own, create a rectangle and apply the dimensions as shown below. (Hint: Use the **Center Point** to assure the alignment of the 2D sketch.)

4. On your own, use the **Extrude** command and create a cutout that cuts through the entire 3D solid model as shown.

The Second Cut Feature

1. In the Model Tree area, select all of the **Datum Planes, Datum Axes** and the **Center Point** while holding down the [**SHIFT**] key.

2. *Right-mouse-click* on any of the selected items to display the option menu and turn **OFF** the visibility of the selected items as shown.

3. In the *Sketch* toolbar select the **Create 2D Sketch** command by left-clicking once on the icon.

4. In the *Status Bar* area, the message: "*Select face, work plane, sketch or sketch geometry*" is displayed. Select the horizontal face of the last cut feature as the *sketching plane*.

5. In the *Standard* toolbar area, click on the **Look At** button.

6. Select one of the edges of the highlighted sketching plane.

7. Select the **Center point circle** command by clicking once with the left-mouse-button on the icon in the *Draw* panel.

8. Pick the **center point**, located at the center of the part, to align the center of the new circle.

9. On your own, create a circle of arbitrary size.

10. On your own, add the size dimension of the circle and set the dimension to **0.25**.

11. Inside the graphics window, click once with the right-mouse-button to display the option menu. Select **Finish 2D Sketch** in the popup menu to end the Sketch option.

12. In the *Create Features* toolbar, select the **Extrude** command by clicking once with the left-mouse-button on the icon.

13. Select the inside region of the sketched circle as the profile to be extruded.

14. In the *Extrude* control panel, set to the **Cut - All** option.

15. Click on the **OK** button to proceed with creating the cut feature.

Examine the Parent/Child Relationships

1. On your own, rename the feature names to: **Base**, **MainBody**, **Rect_Cut** and **Center_Drill** as shown in the figure.

❖ The *Model Tree* window now contains seven items: the *Origin* (default work features) and four solid features. All of the parent/child relationships were established implicitly as we created the solid features. As more features are created, it becomes much more difficult to make a sketch showing all the parent/child relationships involved in the model. On the other hand, it is not really necessary to have a detailed picture showing all the relationships among the features. In using a feature-based modeler, the main emphasis is to consider the interactions that exist between the **immediate features**. Treat each feature as a unit by itself, and be clear on the parent/child relationships for each feature. Thinking in terms of *features* is what distinguishes *feature-based modeling* and the previous generation solid modeling techniques. Let us take a look at the last feature we created, the **Center_Drill** feature. What are the parent/child relationships associated with this feature? (1) Since this is the last feature we created, it is not a parent feature to any other features. (2) Since we used one of the surfaces of the rectangular cutout as the sketching plane, the **Rect_Cut** feature is a parent feature to the **Center_Drill** feature. (3) We also used the Origin as a reference point to align the center; therefore, the *Origin* is also a parent to the **Center_Drill** feature.

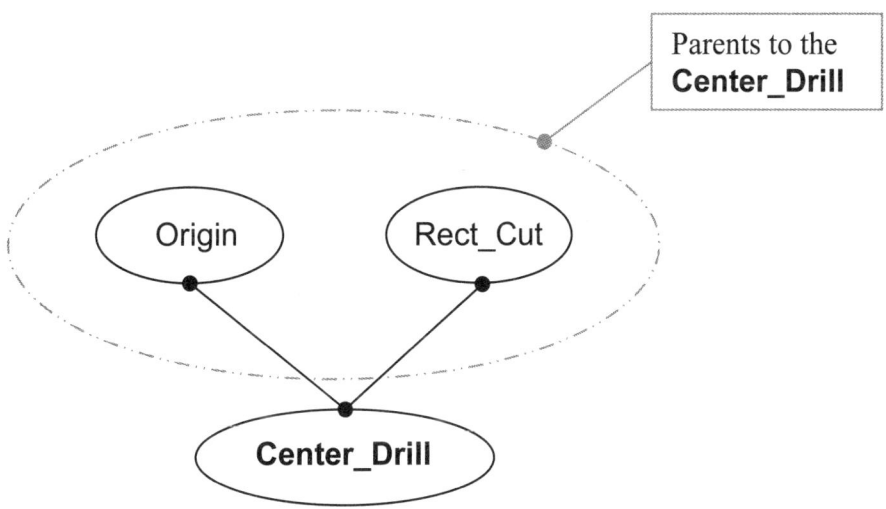

Modify a Parent Dimension

❖ Any changes to the parent features will affect the child feature. For example, if we modify the height of the **Rect_Cut** feature from 1.0 to 0.75, the depth of the child feature (**Center_Drill** feature) will be affected.

1. In the *Model Tree* window, move the cursor on top of **Rect_Cut** and click once with the right-mouse-button to bring up the option menu.

2. In the option menu, select **Show Dimensions**.

3. Select the height dimension (1.0) by double-clicking on the dimension.

4. Enter **0.75** as the new height dimension as shown.

5. Click on the **Update** button in the *Quick Access Toolbar* area to proceed with updating the solid model.

➤ Note that the position of the **Center_Drill** feature is also adjusted as the placement plane is lowered. The drill-hole still goes through the main body of the *U-Bracket* design. The parent/child relationship assures the intent of the design is maintained.

6. On your own, adjust the height of the **Rect_Cut** feature back to **1.0** inch before proceeding to the next section.

A Design Change

> Engineering designs usually go through many revisions and changes. For example, a design change may call for a circular cutout instead of the current rectangular cutout feature in our model. *Autodesk Inventor* provides an assortment of tools to handle design changes quickly and effectively. In the following sections, we will demonstrate some of the more advanced tools available in *Autodesk Inventor*, which allow us to perform the modification of changing the rectangular cutout (2.0 × 1.0 inch) to a circular cutout (radius: 1.25 inch).

❖ Based on your knowledge of *Autodesk Inventor* so far, how would you accomplish this modification? What other approaches can you think of that are also feasible? Of the approaches you came up with, which one is the easiest to do and which is the most flexible? If this design change was anticipated right at the beginning of the design process, what would be your choice in arranging the order of the features? You are encouraged to perform the modifications prior to following through the rest of the tutorial.

Feature Suppression

❖ With *Autodesk Inventor*, we can take several different approaches to accomplish this modification. We could (1) create a new model, or (2) change the shape of the existing cut feature using the **Redefine** command, or (3) perform **feature suppression** on the rectangular cut feature and add a circular cut feature. The third approach offers the most flexibility and requires the least amount of editing to the existing geometry. **Feature suppression** is a method that enables us to disable a feature while retaining the complete feature information; the feature can be reactivated at any time. Prior to adding the new cut feature, we will first suppress the rectangular cut feature.

1. Move the cursor inside the *Model Tree* window. Click once with the right-mouse-button on top of **Rect_Cut** to bring up the option menu.

2. Pick **Suppress** in the pop-up menu.

❖ We have literally *gone back in time*. The Rect_Cut and Center_Drill features have disappeared in the display area. The child feature cannot exist without its parent(s), and any modification to the parent (Rect_Cut) influences the child (Center_Drill).

3. Move the cursor inside the *Model Tree* window. Click once with the right-mouse-button on top of **Center_Drill** to bring up the option menu.

4. Pick **Unsuppress Features** in the pop-up menu.

➢ In the display area and the *Model Tree* window, both the **Rect_Cut** feature and the **Center_Drill** feature are re-activated. The child feature cannot exist without its parent(s); the parent (Rect_Cut) must be activated to enable the child (Center_Drill).

A Different Approach to the CENTER_DRILL Feature

❖ The main advantage of using the BORN technique is to provide greater flexibility for part modifications and design changes. In this case, the Center_Drill feature can be placed on the XZ workplane and therefore not be linked to the Rect_Cut feature.

1. Move the cursor inside the *Model Tree* window. Click once with the **right-mouse-button** on top of **Center_Drill** to bring up the option menu.

2. Pick **Delete** in the pop-up menu.

3. In the *Delete Features* window, confirm the **consumed sketches and features** option is switched *ON*.

4. Click **OK** to proceed with the Delete command.

5. In the *Sketch* toolbar select the **Create 2D Sketch** command by left-clicking once on the icon.

6. In the *Status Bar* area, the message: "*Select face, workplane, sketch or sketch geometry*" is displayed. Pick the **XZ workplane** in the *Model Tree* window as shown below.

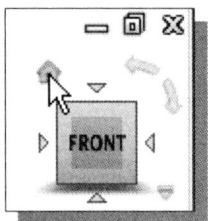

7. Inside the graphics area, single left-mouse-click to activate the **Home View** option as shown. The view will be adjusted back to the default *isometric view*.

➢ Note the alignment of the sketch plane to the XZ plane as shown.

8. Select the **Center point circle** command by clicking once with the left-mouse-button on the icon in the *Draw* panel.

9. Pick the center point to align the center of the new circle. Select another location to create a circle of arbitrary size.

10. On your own, add the size dimension of the circle and set the dimension to **0.25**.

11. On your own, complete the extrude cut feature.

Suppress the Rect_Cut Feature

❖ Now the **Center_Drill** feature is no longer a child of the **Rect_Cut** feature, any changes to the **Rect_Cut** feature do not affect the **Center_Drill** feature.

1. Move the cursor inside the *Model Tree* window. Click once with the right-mouse-button on top of **Rect_Cut** to bring up the option menu.

2. Pick **Suppress Features** in the pop-up menu.

❖ The **Rect_Cut** feature is now disabled without affecting the *new* **Center_Drill** feature.

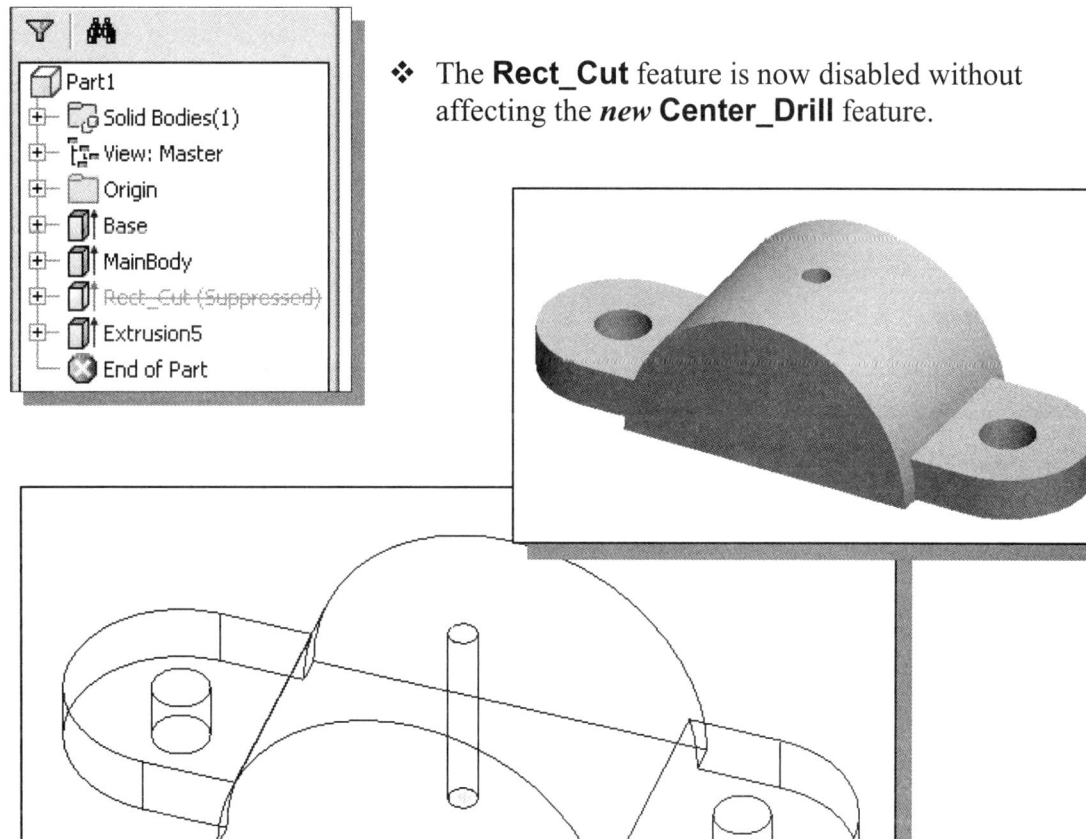

Create a Circular Cut Feature

1. In the *Sketch* toolbar select the **Create 2D Sketch** command by left-clicking once on the icon.

2. In the *Status Bar* area, the message: "*Select face, work plane, sketch or sketch geometry*" is displayed. Pick the **XY workplane** in the *Model Tree* window as shown below.

3. Activate the **View** tab in the *Ribbon* panel as shown.

4. Select **Wireframe** display mode under the *Visual Style* icon as shown.

5. Select the **Center point circle** command by clicking once with the left-mouse-button on the icon in the *Draw* panel.

6. Pick the center point to align the center of the new circle.

Parent/Child Relationships and the BORN Technique   7-27

7. On your own, create a circle of arbitrary size.

8. On your own, create the size dimension of the circle and set the dimension to **2.5** as shown in the figure.

9. On your own, complete the **cut** feature using the **Symmetric -All** command.

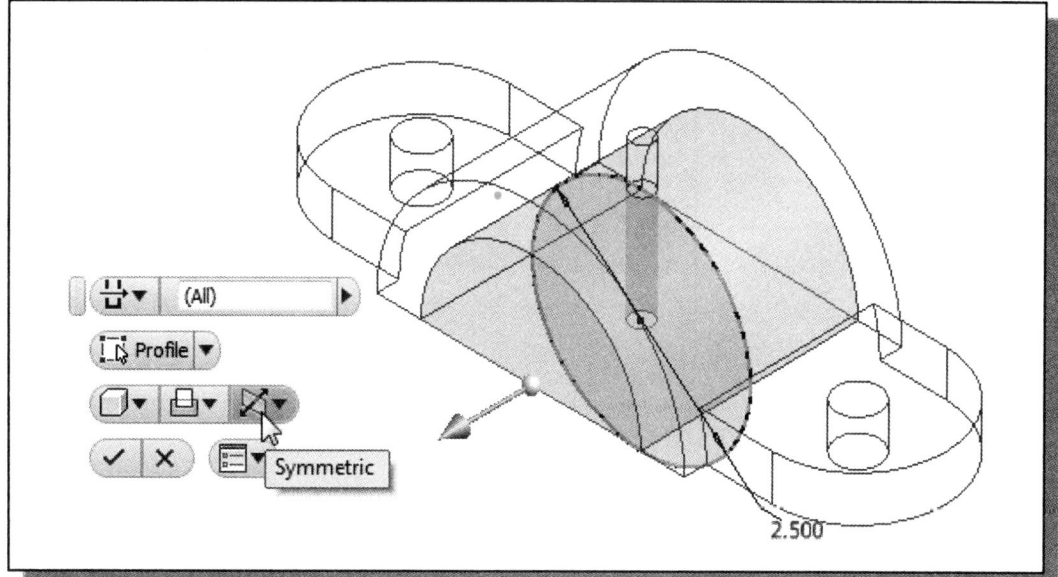

❖ Note that the parents of the Circular_Cut feature are the XY Plane and the Center Point.

➢ On your own, save the model as **U-Bracket**; this model will be used again in the next chapter.

A Flexible Design Approach

In a typical design process, the initial design will undergo many analyses, testing, reviews and revisions. *Autodesk Inventor* allows the users to quickly make changes and explore different options of the initial design throughout the design process.

The model we constructed in this chapter contains two distinct design options. The *feature-based parametric modeling* approach enables us to quickly explore design alternatives and we can include different design ideas into the same model. With parametric modeling, designers can concentrate on improving the design, and the design process becomes quicker and more effortless. The key to successfully using parametric modeling as a design tool lies in understanding and properly controlling the interactions of features, especially the parent/child relations.

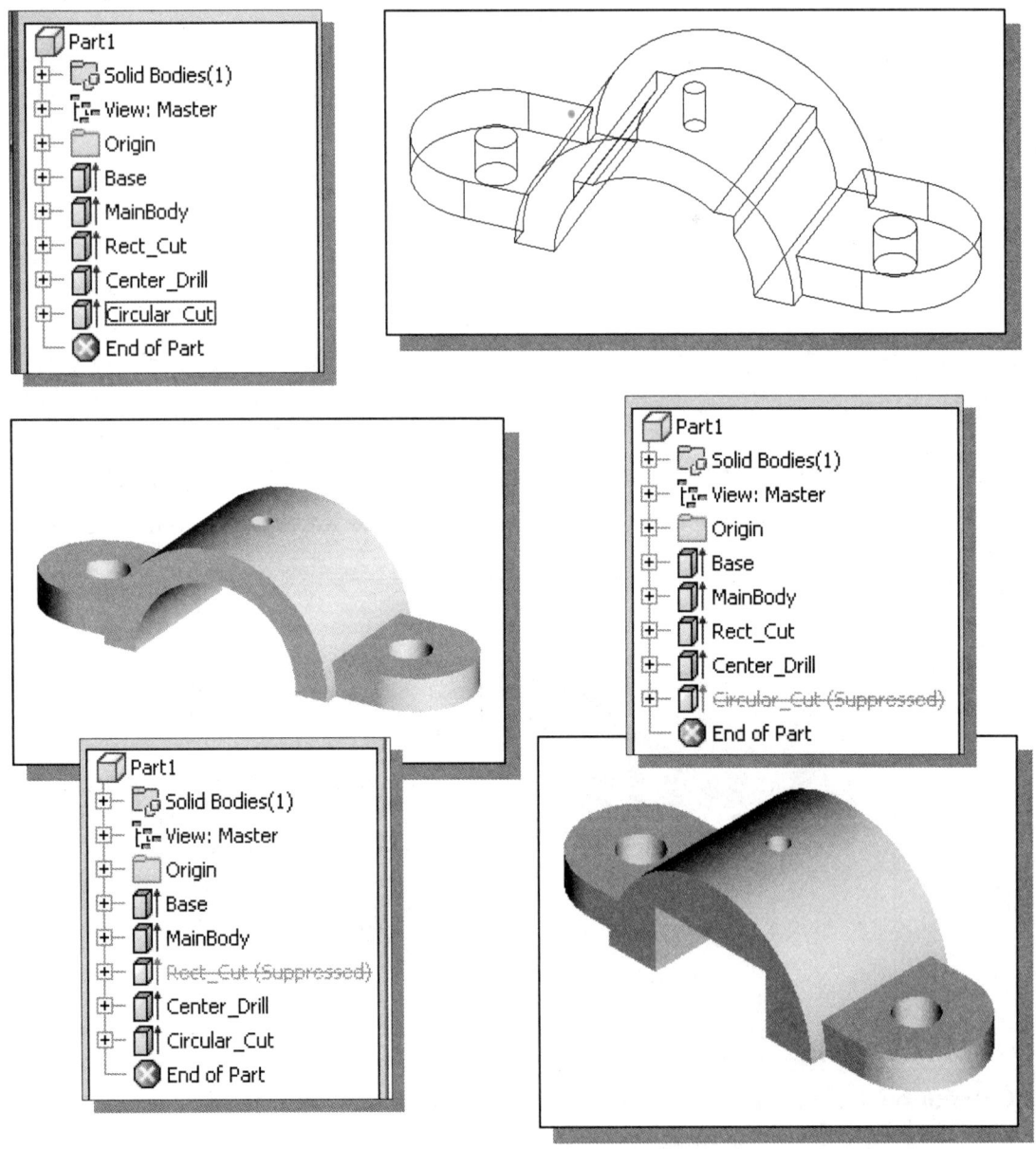

View and Edit Material Properties

❖ The *Inventor Material Library* provides many commonly used materials. The material properties listed in the *Material Library* can be edited and new materials can be added.

1. In the **Tools** tab, click **Material** as shown.

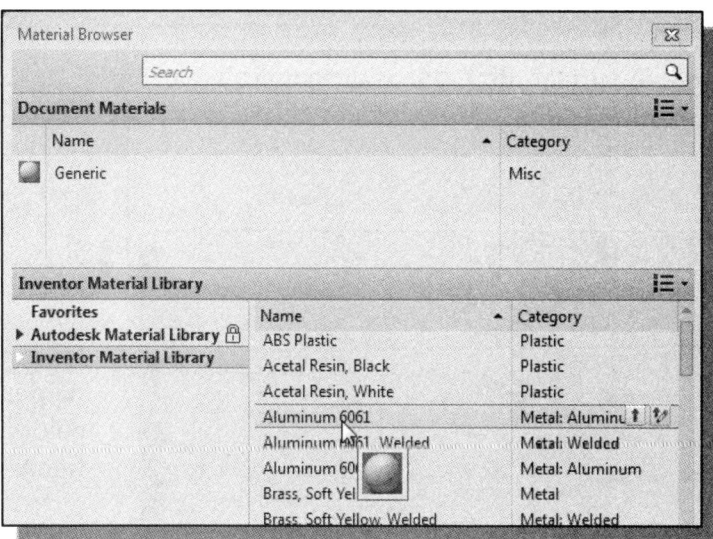

2. In the Inventor Material library group, select **Aluminum-6061**.

3. Click the **Add Material to document and display in editor** icon as shown.

4. Click on the **Physical Aspect** button to view the associated material properties.

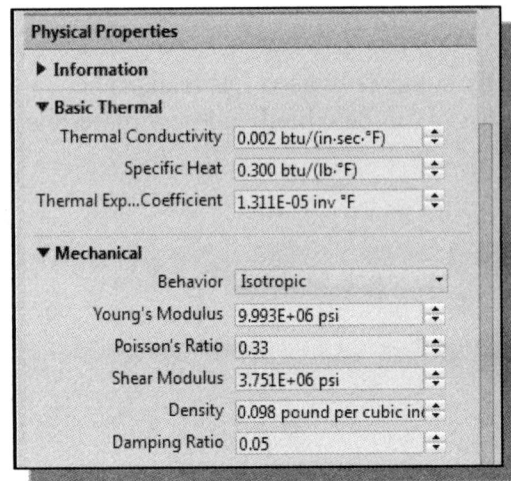

5. Expand the Mechanical properties list as shown.

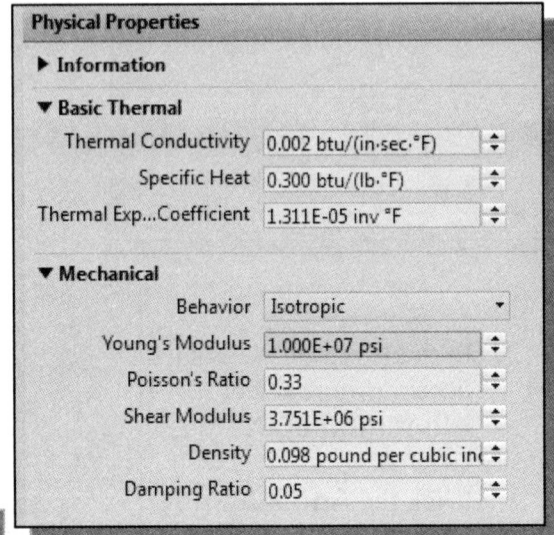

6. Enter **.0E7 psi** as the new value for *Young's Modulus*.

7. On your own, edit the material **Appearance - Glossiness** to **50** and color to **light Green** as shown in the figure.

8. Click **OK** to accept the changes and close the editor.

9. Click **Close** to exit the **Material Browser**.

- Note the new material setting is assigned to the model.

Questions: (Time: 25 minutes)

1. Why is it important to consider the parent/child relationships between features?

2. Describe the procedure to **suppress** a *feature*.

3. What is the basic concept of the BORN technique?

4. What happens to a feature when it is suppressed?

5. How do you identify a suppressed feature in a model?

6. What is the main advantage of using the BORN technique?

7. Create sketches showing the steps you plan to use to create the models shown on the next page:

Exercises: Create and save the exercises in the Chapter7 folder.
(Time: 90 minutes, All dimensions are in inches.)

1. **Shaft Guide** (Material: **Cast Iron**)

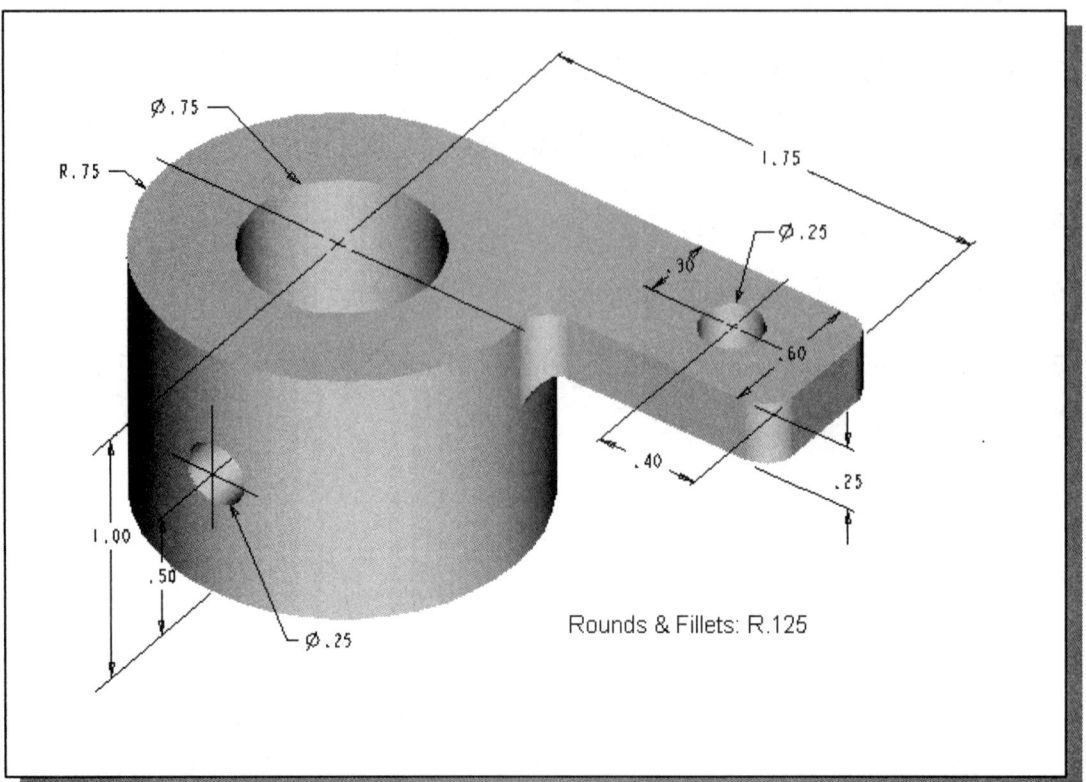

Rounds & Fillets: R.125

2. **Angle Bracket** (Material: **Carbon Steel**)

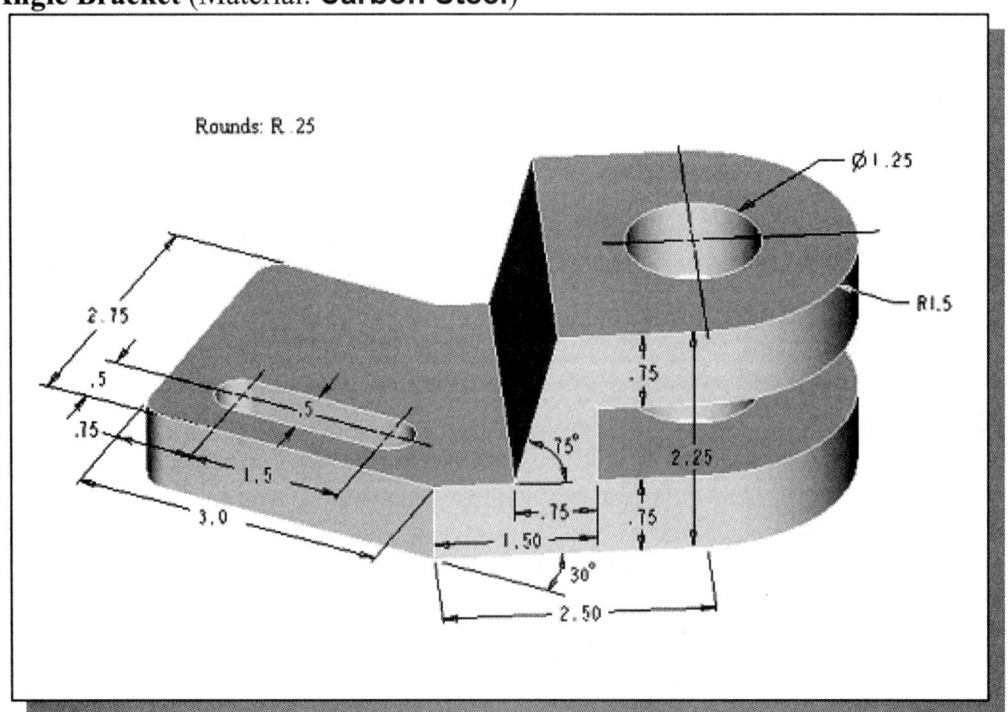

3. **Connecting Rod** (Material: **Carbon Steel**)

4. **Tube Hanger**

Notes:

Chapter 8
Part Drawings and 3D Annotations

Learning Objectives

- **Create Drawing Layouts from Solid Models**
- **Understand Associative Functionality**
- **Using the Default Borders and Title Block in the Layout Mode**
- **Arrange and Manage 2D Views in Drawing Mode**
- **Display and Hide Feature Dimensions**
- **Create Reference Dimensions**
- **Create 3D Annotations in Isometric Views**

Drawings from Parts and Associative Functionality

With the software/hardware improvements in solid modeling, the importance of two-dimensional drawings is decreasing. Drafting is considered one of the downstream applications of using solid models. In many production facilities, solid models are used to generate machine tool paths for *computer numerical control* (CNC) machines. Solid models are also used in *rapid prototyping* to create 3D physical models out of plastic resins, powdered metal, etc. Ideally, the solid model database should be used directly to generate the final product. However, the majority of applications in most production facilities still require the use of two-dimensional drawings. Using the solid model as the starting point for a design, solid modeling tools can easily create all the necessary two-dimensional views. In this sense, solid modeling tools are making the process of creating two-dimensional drawings more efficient and effective.

Autodesk Inventor provides associative functionality in the different *Autodesk Inventor* modes. This functionality allows us to change the design at any level, and the system reflects it at all levels automatically. For example, a solid model can be modified in the *Part Modeling Mode* and the system automatically reflects that change in the *Drawing Mode*. We can also modify a feature dimension in the *Drawing Mode*, and the system automatically updates the solid model in all modes.

In this lesson, the general procedure of creating multi-view drawings is illustrated. The *U_Bracket* design from last chapter is used to demonstrate the associative functionality between the model and drawing views. The procedure to create 3D annotations on isometric views is also demonstrated.

Starting *Autodesk Inventor*

1. Select the **Autodesk Inventor** option on the *Start* menu or select the **Autodesk Inventor** icon on the desktop to start *Autodesk Inventor*. The *Autodesk Inventor* main window will appear on the screen.

2. Once the program is loaded into memory, select the **Open File** option as shown.

3. In the *File name* list box, select the **U-Bracket.ipt** file. (Use the **Projects** option to locate the file if the wrong project is displayed in the *Project File* box.)

4. Click on the **Open** button to accept the selected settings.

Drawing Mode – 2D Paper Space

> *Autodesk Inventor* allows us to generate 2D engineering drawings from solid models so that we can plot the drawings to any exact scale on paper. An engineering drawing is a tool that can be used to communicate engineering ideas/designs to manufacturing, purchasing, service, and other departments. Until now we have been working in ***model space*** to create our design in ***full size***. We can arrange our design on a two-dimensional sheet of paper so that the plotted hardcopy is exactly what we want. This two-dimensional sheet of paper is known as ***paper space*** in *AutoCAD* and *Autodesk Inventor*. We can place borders and title blocks, objects that are less critical to our design, on *paper space*. In general, each company uses a set of standards for drawing content, based on the type of product and also on established internal processes. The appearance of an engineering drawing varies depending on when, where, and for what purpose it is produced. However, the general procedure for creating an engineering drawing from a solid model is fairly well defined. In *Autodesk Inventor*, creation of 2D engineering drawings from solid models consists of four basic steps: drawing sheet formatting, creating/positioning views, annotations, and printing/plotting.

1. Click on the **drop-down arrow** next to the **New File** icon in the *Quick Access* toolbar area to display the available **New File** options.

2. Select **Drawing** from the option list.

➢ Note that a new graphics window appears on the screen. We can switch between the solid model and the drawing by clicking the corresponding tabs or graphics windows.

❖ In the graphics window, *Autodesk Inventor* displays a default drawing sheet that includes a title block. The drawing sheet is placed on the 2D paper space, and the title block also indicates the paper size being used.

➢ In the *browser* area, the Drawing1 icon is displayed at the top, which indicates that we have switched to ***Drawing Mode***. **Sheet1** is the current drawing sheet that is displayed in the graphics window.

Drawing Sheet Format

1. Choose the **Manage** tab in the *Ribbon* toolbar.

2. Click **Styles Editor** in the *Styles and Standards* toolbar as shown.

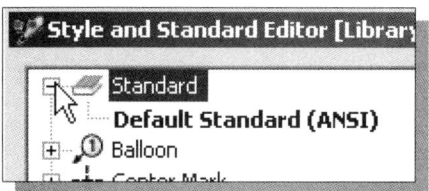

3. Click on the [+] sign in front of **Standard** to display the current active standard. Note that there can only be one **active standard** for each drawing.

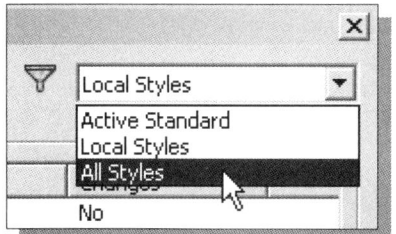

4. Set the *Filter Styles Setting* to display **All Styles**. Note that besides the default ANSI drafting standard, other standards, such as ISO, GB, BSI, DIN, and JIS, are also available.

5. Set the *Filter Styles Setting* to display **Active Standard** and note only the active standard is displayed.

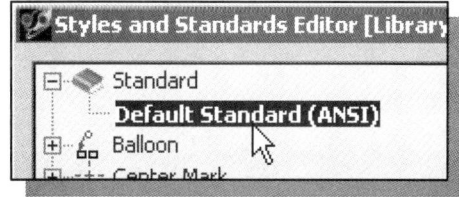

6. Click **Default Standard (ANSI)** to toggle the display of detailed settings for the current standard.

7. In the *View Preferences* page, confirm that the *Projection Type* is set to **Third Angle of projection**.

❖ Notice the different settings available in the *General* option window, such as the *Units* setting and the *Line Weight* setting.

8. Choose **Default (ANSI)** in the **Dimension** list as shown.

   ➢ Note that the default *Dimension Style* in *Inventor* is based on the ANSI Y14.5-1994 standard.

9. The **Units** tab contains the settings for linear/angular units. Note that the *Linear* units are set to **Decimal** and the *Precision* for linear dimensions is set to two digits after the decimal point.

10. Click on the **Text** tab to display and examine the settings for dimension text. Note that the default *Dimension Style*, DEFAULT-ANSI, cannot be modified. However, new *Dimension Styles* can be created and modified.

➢ On your own, display and examine the other *Settings* available.

11. Click on the **Done** button to exit the *Styles and Standards Editor* dialog box.

Using the Pre-defined Drawing Sheet Formats

1. Inside the *Drawing Browser* window, click on the [+] symbol in front of **Drawing Resources** to display the available options.

2. Click on the [+] symbol in front of **Sheet Formats** to display the available pre-defined sheet formats.

❖ Notice several pre-defined *sheet formats*, each with a different view configuration, are available in the *browser* window.

3. Inside the *browser* window, **double-click** on the **B size, 2 view** sheet format.

4. Click on the **OK** button to accept the default part file and generate the 2D views.

➢ The *U-Bracket* model is the only model opened. By default, all of the 2D drawings will be generated from this model file.

❖ We have created a B-size drawing of the *U-Bracket* model. *Autodesk Inventor* automatically generates and positions the front view and side view of the model inside the title block.

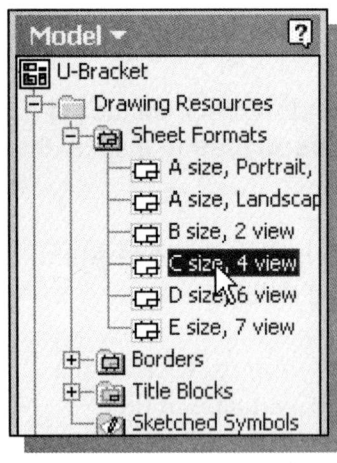

5. Inside the *browser* window, double-click on the **C size, 4 view** sheet format.

6. Click on the **OK** button to use the default part file, *U-Bracket.ipt*, to generate the 2D views.

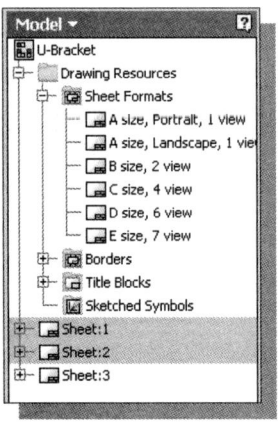

❖ Note that we have created three drawing sheets, displayed in the *Drawing Browser* window as **Sheet1, Sheet2**, and **Sheet3**. *Autodesk Inventor* allows us to create multiple 2D drawings from the same model file, which can be used for different purposes.

➤ In most cases, the pre-defined *sheet formats* can be used to quickly setup the views needed. However, it is also important to understand the concepts and principles involved in setting up the views. In the next sections, the procedures to set up drawing sheets and different types of views are illustrated.

Part Drawings and 3D Annotations   8-9

Delete, Activate, and Edit Drawing Sheets

1. Inside the *Drawing Browser* window, right-mouse-click on **Sheet3** to display the option menu.

2. Select **Delete Sheet** in the option menu to remove the Sheet3 drawing.

3. In the *warning window*, click on the **OK** button to proceed with deleting the drawing.

❖ Note that **Sheet3** is removed and **Sheet2** now becomes the active drawing sheet.

4. Inside the *Drawing Browser* window, right-mouse-click on **Sheet1** to display the option menu.

5. Select **Activate** in the option menu to set the Sheet1 drawing as the active drawing sheet.

6. Inside the *Drawing Browser* window, right-mouse-click on **Sheet1** to display the option menu.

7. Select **Edit Sheet** in the option menu to display the settings for the *Sheet1* drawing.

8. Set the sheet size to **B-size** and click on the **OK** button to exit the *Edit Sheet* dialog box.

Add a Base View

❖ In *Autodesk Inventor Drawing Mode*, the first drawing view we create is called a **base view**. A *base view* is the primary view in the drawing; other views can be derived from this view. When creating a *base view*, *Autodesk Inventor* allows us to specify the view to be shown. By default, *Autodesk Inventor* will treat the *world XY plane* as the front view of the solid model. Note that there can be more than one *base view* in a drawing.

1. Click on the **Base View** in the *Drawing Views* panel to create a base view.

2. In the *Drawing View* dialog box, confirm that the settings are set to **Front View** and **Hidden Line** as shown in the figure below. (**DO NOT** click on the **OK** button at this point.)

3. Move the cursor inside the graphics window and place the *base* view near the lower left corner of the graphics window as shown below. (If necessary, drag the *Create View* dialog box to another location on the screen.) Note that once the *base view* is placed, the *Drawing View* dialog box is closed automatically.

Create Projected Views

❖ In *Autodesk Inventor Drawing Mode*, **projected views** can be created with a first-angle or third-angle projection, depending on the drafting standard used for the drawing. We must have a base view before a projected view can be created. Projected views can be orthographic projections or isometric projections. Orthographic projections are aligned to the base view and inherit the base view's scale and display settings. Isometric projections are not aligned to the base view.

1. Notice the **Projected View** button in the *Drawing Views* panel is activated, this command allows us to create a projected view.

2. Move the cursor above the base view and select a location to position the projected side view of the model.

3. Move the cursor toward the upper right corner of the title block and select a location to position the isometric view of the model as shown below.

4. Inside the graphics window, right-mouse-click once to bring up the option menu.

5. Select **Create** to proceed with creating the two projected views.

Adjust the View Scale

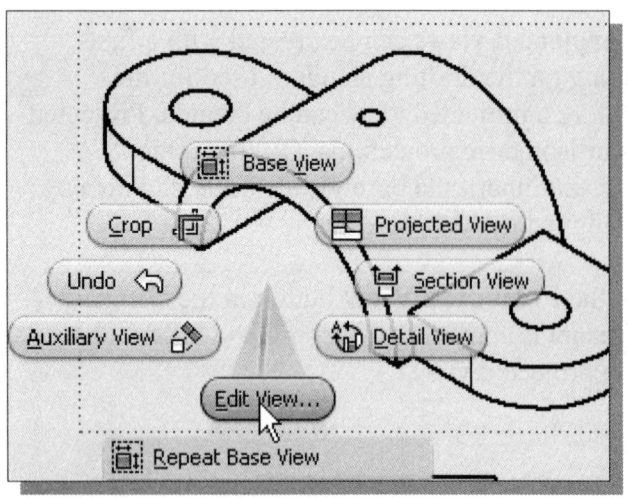

1. Move the cursor on top of the isometric view and watch for the box around the entire view indicating the view is selectable as shown in the figure. Right-mouse-click once to bring up the option menu.

2. Select **Edit View** in the option menu.

3. Inside the *Drawing View* dialog box set the *Scale* to **3:4** as shown in the figure.

4. Click on the **Display Options** tab and set the **Tangent Edges** option to *OFF* as shown.

5. Click on the **OK** button to accept the settings and proceed with updating the drawing views.

Repositioning Views

1. Move the cursor on top of the isometric view and watch for the **four-arrow Move symbol** as the cursor is near the border indicating the view can be dragged to a new location as shown in the figure.

2. Press and hold down the left-mouse-button and reposition the view to a new location.

3. On your own, reposition the views we have created so far. Note that the top view can be repositioned only in the vertical direction. The top view remains aligned to the base view, the front view.

> Note that in the *Drawing Browser* area, a hierarchy of the created views is displayed under **Sheet1**. The base view, **View1**, is listed as the first view created, with **View2** linked to it. The top view, **View2**, is projected from the base view, **View1**. The implied parent/child relationship is maintained by the system. Drawing views are associated with the model and the drawing sheets. As we create views from the base view, they are nested beneath the base view in the *browser*.

Display Feature Dimensions

- By default, feature dimensions are not displayed in 2D views in *Autodesk Inventor*. We can change the default settings while creating the views or switch on the display of the parametric dimensions using the option menu.

1. Select **Annotate** by left-clicking once in the *Ribbon* toolbar system.

2. Move the cursor on top of the *top* view of the model and watch for the box around the entire view indicating the view is selectable as shown in the figure.

3. Inside the graphics window, **right-mouse-click** once on the top view to bring up the option menu.

4. Select **Retrieve Dimensions** to display the parametric dimensions used to create the model.

5. In the *Retrieve Dimensions* dialog box, set the *Select Source* option to **Select Parts** as shown.

6. Move the *Retrieve Dimensions* dialog box, by pressing and dragging with the left-mouse button to the right side of the view.

7. Move the cursor to the *top* view and select the *U-Bracket* part as shown.

➢ All the dimensions used to create the part are now displayed in the selected view.

8. In the *Retrieve Dimensions* dialog box, switch on the **Select dimensions** option as shown.

➢ The system now expects us to select the dimensions to retrieve.

9. On your own, select the dimensions to retrieve by left-clicking once on the dimensions as shown. (Note that only selected dimensions are retrieved.)

10. Click on the **Apply** button to proceed with retrieving the selected dimensions.

11. In the *Retrieve Dimensions* dialog box, the **Select View** option is switched on as shown.

12. Select the *front* view.

13. On your own, retrieve the three dimensions as shown by using the **Select Dimensions** option.

14. Click on the **OK** button to end the Retrieve Dimensions command.

Repositioning and Hiding Feature Dimensions

1. Move the cursor on top of the width dimension text **5.00**, and watch for when the dimension text becomes highlighted with the four-arrow symbol indicating the dimension is selectable.

2. Reposition the dimension by using the left-mouse-button and drag the dimension text to a new location.

3. Move the cursor on top of the diameter dimension **0.5** and drag the grip point green dot associated with the dimension to reposition the dimension. Note that we can also drag on the dimension text, which only repositions the text.

4. On your own, reposition the dimensions displayed in the *top* view as shown in the figure below.

Part Drawings and 3D Annotations   8-17

5. Move the cursor on top of the radius dimension **R 1.75** and notice two green grip points appear. The grip points can be used to reposition the dimension.

6. Use the left-mouse-button and drag the grip point near the center of the view and notice the arrowhead is automatically adjusted to the inside, as shown in the figures below.

7. Move the cursor on top of the diameter dimension **2.50** and left-mouse-click once to select the dimension.

8. Right-mouse-click once on the dimension text to bring up the option menu.

9. Select **Delete** to remove the dimension from the display.

> Note that the feature dimension is deleted from the display, but the removed dimension still remains in the database. In other words, the feature dimension is turned off or is hidden. Any feature dimensions can be removed from the display just as they can be displayed.

Add Additional Dimensions – Reference Dimensions

- Besides displaying the **feature dimensions**, dimensions used to create the features, we can also add additional **reference dimensions** in the drawing. *Feature dimensions* are used to control the geometry, whereas *reference dimensions* are controlled by the existing geometry. In the drawing layout, therefore, we can **add** or **delete** *reference dimensions* but we can only *hide* the *feature dimensions*. One should try to use as many *feature dimensions* as possible and add *reference dimensions* only if necessary. It is also more effective to use *feature dimensions* in the drawing layout since they are created when the model was built. Note that additional *Drawing Mode* entities, such as lines and arcs, can be added to drawing views. Before *Drawing Mode* entities can be used in a reference dimension, they must be associated to a *drawing view*.

1. Click on the **General Dimension** button.

   ➢ Note the **General Dimension** command is similar to the **Smart Dimensioning** command in the *3D Modeling Mode*.

2. In the prompt area, the message "*Select first object:*" is displayed. Select the smaller arc of the front view.

3. Place the dimension text on the inside of the arc as shown in the above figure.

4. On your own, position the necessary dimensions for the design as shown in the figure.

   ➢ Note the extension lines can also be repositioned by dragging the associated grip points.

Part Drawings and 3D Annotations   8-19

Add Center Marks and Center Lines

1. Click on the **Center Mark** button in the *Drawing Annotation* window.

2. Click on the larger arc in the front view to add the center mark.

3. Inside the graphics window, click once with the right-mouse-button to display the option menu. Select **OK** in the popup menu to end the Center Mark command.

4. Select **Centerline Bisector** from the option list.

5. Click on the two hidden edges of one of the *drill* features of the front view as shown in the figure.

6. On your own, repeat the above step and create another centerline on the right side of the front view as shown.

7. Inside the graphics window, click once with the right-mouse-button to display the option menu. Select **Cancel [ESC]** in the popup menu to end the Centerline Bisector command.

8. On your own, repeat the above steps and create additional centerlines as shown in the figure below.

9. Inside the graphics window, click once with the right-mouse-button to display the option menu. Select **OK** in the popup menu to end the Centerline command.

10. Click on the right centerlines in the *top* view as shown.

11. Adjust the length of the horizontal centerline by dragging on one of the grip points as shown.

12. On your own, repeat the above steps and adjust the dimensions/centerlines as shown below.

13. Click on the **Save** icon in the *Standard* toolbar as shown.

Complete the Drawing Sheet

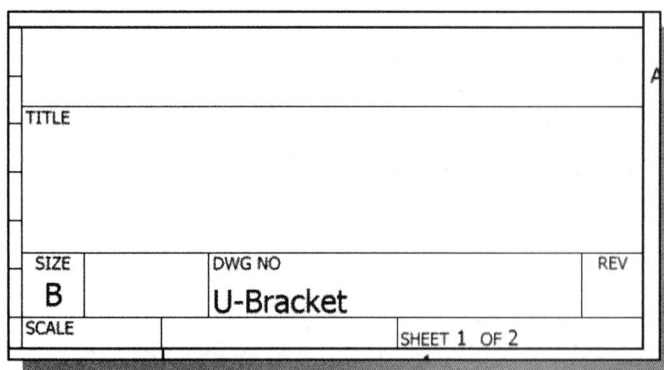

1. On your own, use the **Zoom** and the **Pan** commands to adjust the display as shown, this is so that we can complete the title block.

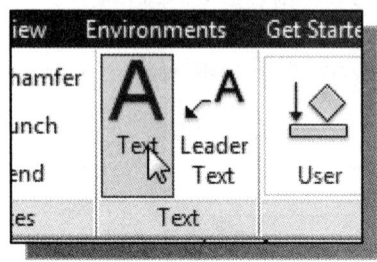

2. In the *Drawing Annotation* window, click on the **Text** button.

3. Pick a location that is inside the top block area as the location for the new text to be entered.

4. In the *Format Text* dialog box, enter the name of your organization. Also note the different settings available.

5. Click **OK** to proceed.

6. On your own, repeat the above steps and complete the title block.

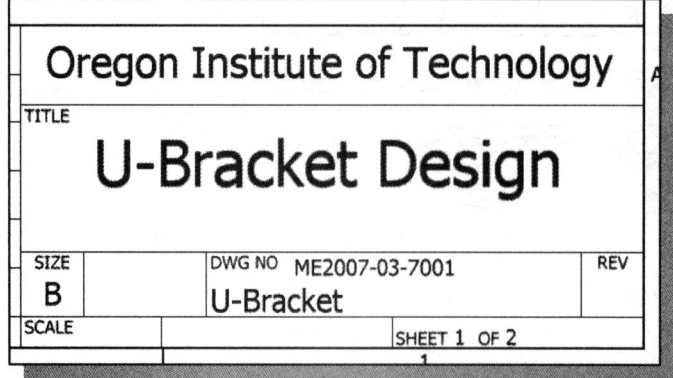

Associative Functionality – Modifying Feature Dimensions

- *Autodesk Inventor's associative functionality* allows us to change the design at any level, and the system reflects the changes at all levels automatically.

1. Click on the **U-Bracket** part window or tab to switch to the *Part Modeling Mode*.

2. In the *browser* window, right-click once on **Extrusion1** to bring up the option menu.

3. Select **Show Dimensions** in the popup option menu.

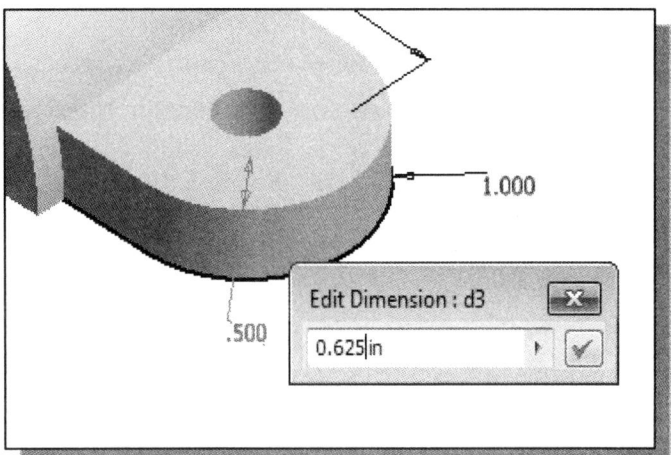

4. Double-click on one of the diameter dimensions (**0.50**) of the drill feature on the base feature as shown in the figure.

5. In the *Edit Dimension* dialog box, enter **0.625** as the new diameter dimension.

6. Click on the **check mark** button to accept the new setting.

7. On your own, adjust the diameter of the other drill feature to **0.625** as shown.

8. Click on the **Update** button in the *Standard* toolbar area to proceed with updating the solid model.

9. Click on the **U-Bracket** drawing graphics window or tab to switch to the *Paper Space*.

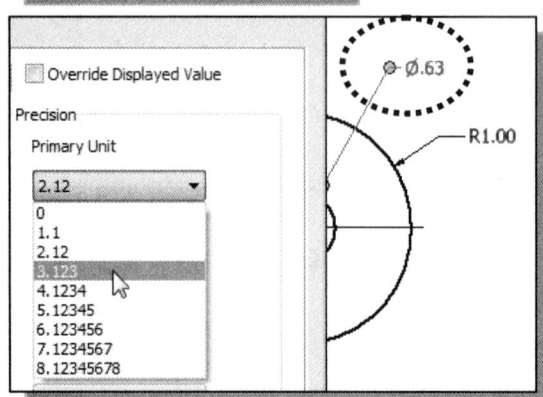

10. Inside the graphics window, double-click on the **0.63** dimension in the *top* view to bring up the *Dimension tolerance* dialog box.

11. Set the *Precision* option to **3 digits after the decimal point** as shown.

12. Inside the graphics window, right-click once on the **R 1.75** dimension in the *front* view to bring up the option menu.

13. Select **Edit Model Dimension** in the popup menu.

14. Change the dimension to **1.625**.

15. Click on the **check mark** button to accept the setting.

- Note the geometry of the cut feature is updated in all views automatically.

- On your own, switch to the *Part Modeling Mode* and confirm the design is updated as well.

- The completed multi-view drawing should appear as shown on the next page.

3D Annotations in Isometric Views

In *Inventor 2009*, a very exciting tool was introduced for documenting and communicating product designs. It can be used to apply **3D annotations** in isometric drawing views. This documentation approach provides the ability to create, manage, and deliver process-specific information without the need for 2D-based documentation. With this tool, the mental translation of 3D models to two-dimensional (2D) drawings for communicating information and then back to 3D models for manufacturing, is replaced by a simplified approach. The 3D annotation approach means faster and more precise product communication, which can improve the product development process.

1. Inside the *browser* window, double-click, with the left-mouse-button, on **Sheet2** to activate the second drawing sheet.

2. Move the cursor on top of the front view and click once with the **right-mouse-button** to bring up the option menu.

3. Select **Delete** in the option menu list as shown.

4. In the *Delete View* dialog box, click **OK** to accept the deletion of the selected view and any view projected from it. In this case, the side view will also be deleted.

5. Switch back to the Place Views toolbar as shown.

6. Click on the **Base View** in the *Drawing Views* panel to create a base view.

Part Drawings and 3D Annotations   8-27

7. In the *Drawing View* dialog box, confirm that the settings are set to **Iso Top Left** and **Hidden Line** as shown in the figure. (**DO NOT** click on the **OK** button at this point.)

8. Move the cursor inside the graphics window and place the *Iso* view near the left side of the graphics window.

9. On your own, repeat the above steps and place another view, **Iso Bottom Right**, on the right side as shown in the figure below.

10. Select **Annotate** by left-clicking once in the *Ribbon* toolbar area.

11. Click on the **Center Mark** button in the *Drawing Annotation* window.

12. Click on one of the circles in the *Iso-Top* view to add the center mark.

13. Inside the graphics window, click once with the right-mouse-button to display the option menu. Select **OK** in the popup menu to end the Centerline command.

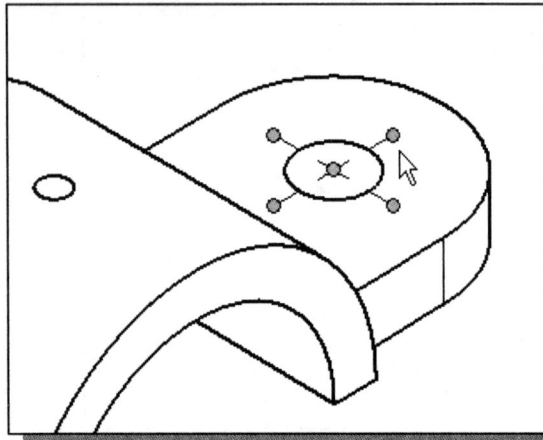

14. Click on the **centerlines** we just created as shown.

15. Adjust the length of the horizontal centerline by dragging on one of the **grip points**.

16. On your own, repeat the above steps and create the centerlines for the circle on the other side as shown in the figure below.

Part Drawings and 3D Annotations   8-29

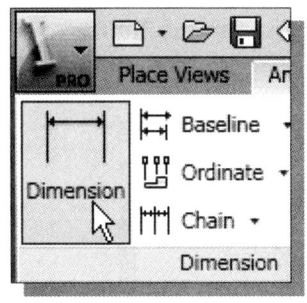

17. In the *Drawing Annotation* window, click on the **General Dimension** button.

> Note the **General Dimension** command in *Drawing Annotation* behaves similarly to the **Smart Dimensioning** command in the *3D Modeling Mode*. *Inventor* will automatically create the proper dimensions based on the selected geometry.

18. In the prompt area, the message "*Select first object:*" is displayed. Select the arc on the right side of the *Iso-Top* view as shown.

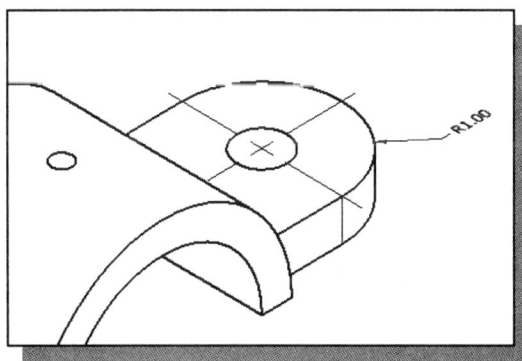

19. Position the dimension text next to the arc as shown in the figure.

> Note that the radius dimension is placed on the same plane of the arc. The 3D annotation command will automatically select the placement plane if the selected geometry lies on a specific plane.

20. Next, we will define the center to center distance of the two holes by selecting the two circles.

21. Place the dimension toward the front side of the model as shown in the figure below.

22. Use the **Centerline** command to create the horizontal centerline for the two arcs as shown in the figure below.

23. On your own, repeat the above steps and create the dimensions as shown.

24. On your own, repeat the above steps and create the centerlines and dimensions in the 2nd *isometric* view as shown.

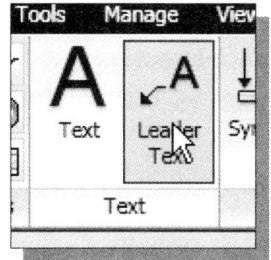

25. Click on the **Leader Text** command as shown. We will use this command to identify the size of the small drill hole at the center.

26. Select the small circle to attach an arrowhead to the circle.

27. Place the text toward the left side of the model as shown.

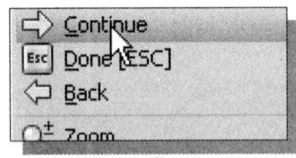

28. Right-mouse-click once to bring up the option menu and select **Continue** as shown.

29. In the *Format Text* dialog box, select the **Diameter** symbol from the list as shown.

30. Enter **.25** as the diameter value.

31. Click **OK** to create the leader text.

32. Double-click on the diameter **.63** dimension to bring up the *Edit Dimension* dialog box.

33. Click on the **Precision and Tolerance** tab.

34. Choose **3 digits** after the decimal points under the *Precision* list as shown.

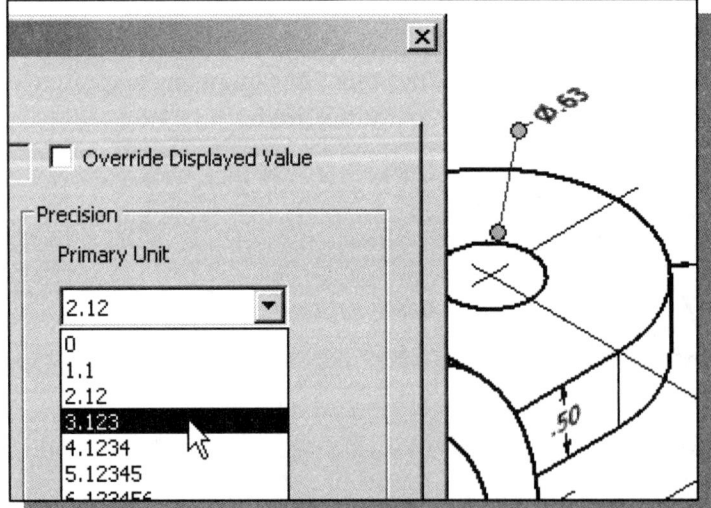

35. On your own, complete the drawing so that it appears as shown on the next page.

Questions: (Time: 25 minutes)

1. What does *Autodesk Inventor*'s *associative functionality* allow us to do?

2. How do we move a view on the *Drawing Sheet*?

3. How do we display feature/model dimensions in the drawing mode?

4. What is the difference between a *feature dimension* and a *reference dimension*?

5. How do we reposition dimensions?

6. What is a *base view*?

7. Can we delete a drawing view? How?

8. Can we adjust the length of centerlines in the drafting mode of Inventor? How?

9. Describe the purpose and usage of the **Leader Text** command.

10. Describe the advantages of using the *3D annotations in isometric drawing views* approach as a documentation tool that is available in Autodesk Inventor.

Exercises: Create the Solid models and the associated 2D drawings and save the exercises in the Chapter8 folder. (Time: 90 minutes)

1. **Slide Mount** (Dimensions are in inches.)

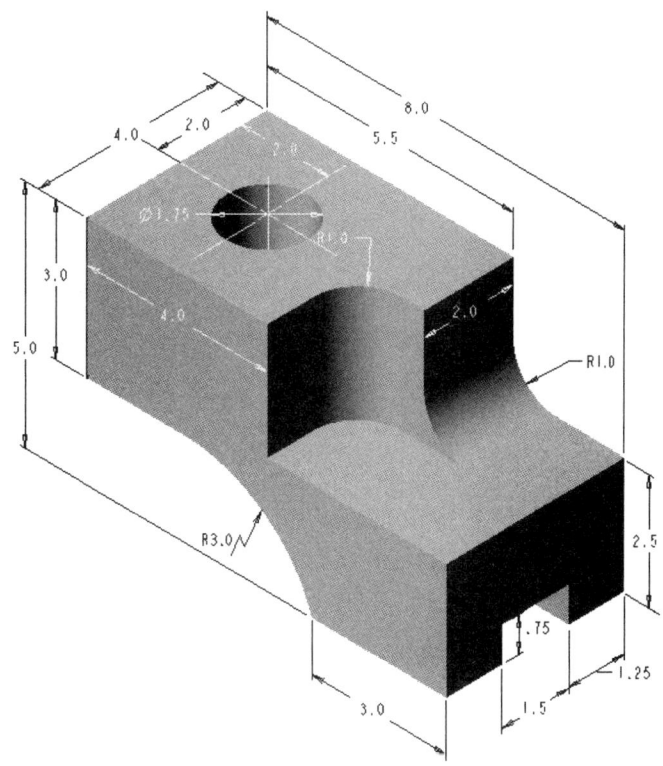

2. **Corner Stop** (Dimensions are in inches.)

3. **Switch Base** (Dimensions are in inches.)

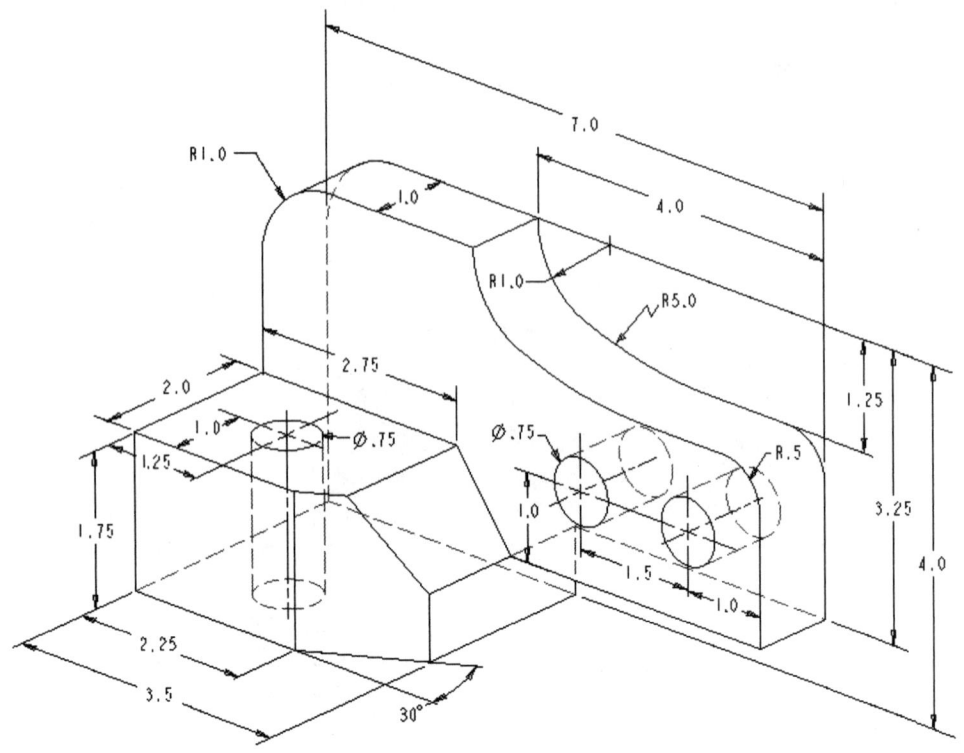

4. **Angle Support** (Dimensions are in inches)

Chapter 9
Symmetrical Features in Designs

Learning Objectives

- Create Revolved Features
- Use the Mirror Feature Command
- Create New Borders and Title Blocks
- Create Circular Patterns
- Create and Modify Linear Dimensions
- Use Autodesk Inventor's Associative Functionality
- Identify Symmetrical Features in Designs

Introduction

In parametric modeling, it is important to identify and determine the features that exist in the design. *Feature-based parametric modeling* enables us to build complex designs by working on smaller and simpler units. This approach simplifies the modeling process and allows us to concentrate on the characteristics of the design. Symmetry is an important characteristic that is often seen in designs. Symmetrical features can be easily accomplished by the assortment of tools that are available in feature-based modeling systems, such as *Autodesk Inventor*.

The modeling technique of extruding two-dimensional sketches along a straight line to form three-dimensional features, as illustrated in the previous chapters, is an effective way to construct solid models. For designs that involve cylindrical shapes, shapes that are symmetrical about an axis, revolving two-dimensional sketches about an axis can form the needed three-dimensional features. In solid modeling, this type of feature is called a ***revolved feature***.

In *Autodesk Inventor*, besides using the **Revolve** command to create revolved features, several options are also available to handle symmetrical features. For example, we can create multiple identical copies of symmetrical features with the **Feature Pattern** command, or create mirror images of models using the **Mirror Feature** command. We can also use *construction geometry* to assist the construction of more complex features. In this lesson, the construction and modeling techniques of these more advanced options are illustrated.

A Revolved Design: *PULLEY*

❖ Based on your knowledge of *Autodesk Inventor*, how many features would you use to create the design? Which feature would you choose as the **base feature** of the model? Identify the symmetrical features in the design and consider other possibilities in creating the design. You are encouraged to create the model on your own prior to following through the tutorial.

Modeling Strategy – A Revolved Design

Starting *Autodesk Inventor*

1. Select the **Autodesk Inventor** option on the *Start* menu or select the **Autodesk Inventor** icon on the desktop to start *Autodesk Inventor*. The *Autodesk Inventor* main window will appear on the screen.

2. Select the **New File** icon with a single click of the left-mouse-button in the *Launch* toolbar.

3. Select the **English** units set and in the *Part File* area, select **Standard(in).ipt**.

4. Click **Create** in the *New File* dialog box to start a new model.

Set Up the Display of the Sketch Plane

1. In the *Part Browser* window, click on the [**+**] symbol in front of the **Origin** feature to display more information on the feature.

❖ In the *browser* window, notice a new part name appeared with seven work features established. The seven work features include three *workplanes*, three *work axes* and a *work point*. By default, the three work planes and work axes are aligned to the **world coordinate system** and the work point is aligned to the *origin* of the **world coordinate system**.

2. Inside the *browser* window, select all of the work features by holding down the **[Shift]** key and click with the left-mouse-button.

3. Click the right-mouse-button on any of the work features to display the option menu. Click on **Visibility** to toggle *ON* the display of the plane.

Symmetrical Features in Designs   9-5

Creating the 2D Sketch for the Base feature

1. In the *Sketch* toolbar select the **Create 2D Sketch** command by left-clicking once on the icon.

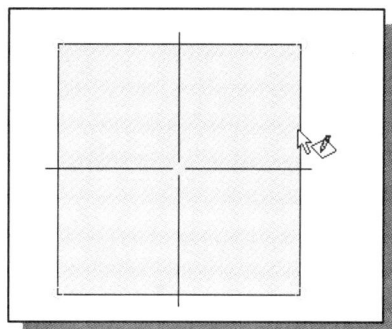

2. In the *Status Bar* area, the message: "*Select face, workplane, sketch or sketch geometry.*" is displayed. Select the **XY Plane** by clicking on any edges of the plane inside the graphics window, as shown.

3. Select the **Project Geometry** command in the *2D Sketch* panel. The Project Geometry command allows us to project existing features onto the active sketching plane. Left-click once on the icon to activate the Project Geometry command.

4. In the *Status Bar* area, the message: "*Select edge, vertex, work geometry or sketch geometry to project.*" is displayed. Inside the *browser* window, select the **X-axis** and **Y-axis** to project these entities onto the sketching plane.

5. Select the **Line** option in the *2D Sketch* panel. A *Help-tip box* appears next to the cursor and a brief description of the command is displayed at the bottom of the drawing screen: "*Creates Straight line segments and tangent arcs.*"

6. Create a closed-region sketch with the starting point aligned to the projected Y-axis as shown below. (Note that the *Pulley* design is symmetrical about a horizontal axis as well as a vertical axis, which allows us to simplify the 2D sketch as shown below.)

7. Select the **General Dimension** command in the *2D Sketch* panel.

8. Pick the **X-axis** as the first entity to dimension as shown in the figure below.

9. Select the **bottom horizontal line** as the second object to dimension.

10. Inside the graphics window, right-mouse-click to bring up the option menu and select **Linear Diameter**.

Symmetrical Features in Designs 9-7

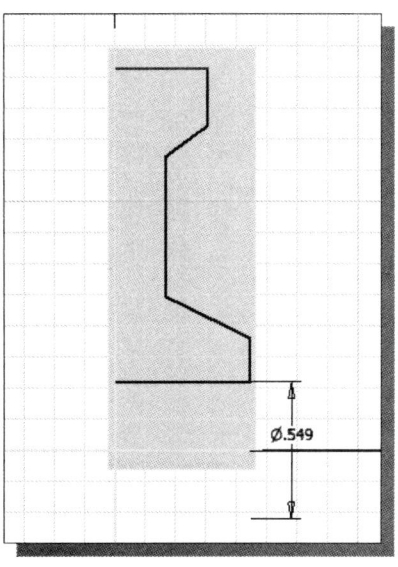

11. Place the dimension text to the right side of the sketch.

- **To create a dimension that will account for the symmetrical nature of the design: pick the axis of symmetry, pick the entity, select Linear Diameter in the option menu, and then place the dimension.**

12. Pick the projected **X-axis** as the first entity to dimension as shown in the figure below.

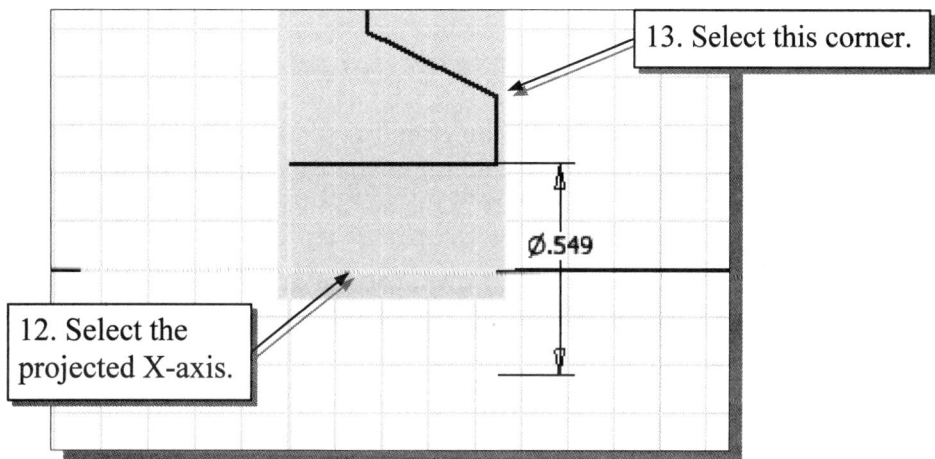

13. Select the **corner point** as the second object to dimension as shown in the above figure.

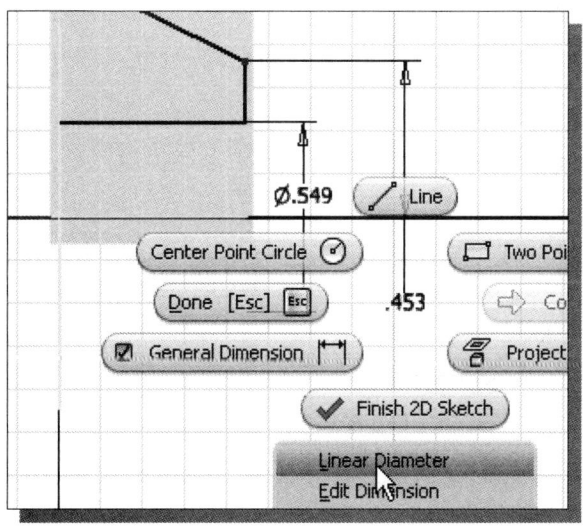

14. Inside the graphics window, right-mouse-click to bring up the option menu and select **Linear Diameter**.

15. Place the dimension text toward the right side of the sketch.

16. On your own, create and adjust the vertical size/location dimensions as shown below. (Hint: Modify the larger dimensions first.)

17. Inside the graphics window, click once with the right-mouse-button to display the option menu. Select **Finish Sketch** in the popup menu to end the Sketch option.

➢ On your own, use the **3D-Rotate** command to confirm the completed sketch and dimensions are on a 2D plane.

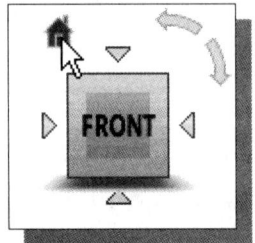

18. Select **Home View** in the ViewCube to adjust the display of the 2D sketch to the isometric view.

Create the Revolved Feature

1. In the *Create Feature* panel select the **Revolve** command by clicking the left-mouse-button on the icon.

2. In the *Revolve* dialog box, the **Axis** button is activated indicating *Autodesk Inventor* expects us to select the revolution axis for the revolved feature. Select **X-Axis** as the axis of rotation in the *browser* window as shown.

3. In the *Revolve* dialog box, confirm the termination *Extents* option is set to **Full** as shown.

4. Click on the **OK** button to accept the settings and create the revolved feature.

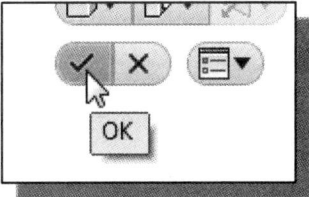

Mirroring Features

- In *Autodesk Inventor*, features can be mirrored to create and maintain complex symmetrical features. We can mirror a feature about a work plane or a specified surface. We can create a mirrored feature while maintaining the original parametric definitions, which can be quite useful in creating symmetrical features. For example, we can create one quadrant of a feature, and then mirror it twice to create a solid with four identical quadrants.

1. In the *Pattern* panel, select the **Mirror Feature** command by releasing the left-mouse-button on the icon.

2. In the *Mirror Pattern* dialog box, the **Features** button is activated. *Autodesk Inventor* expects us to select features to be mirrored. In the prompt area, the message "*Select feature to pattern*" is displayed. Select **any edge** of the 3D base feature.

3. Inside the graphics window, **right-mouse-click** to bring up the **option menu**.

4. Select **Continue** in the option list to proceede with the Mirror Feature command.

5. In the *Mirror Pattern* dialog box, the **Mirror Plane** button is activated. *Autodesk Inventor* expects us to select a planar surface about which to mirror. In the prompt area, the message "*Select plane to mirror about*" is displayed.

6. On your own, use the **ViewCube** or the **3D-Rotate** function key [**F4**] to dynamically rotate the solid model so that we are viewing the back surface as shown.

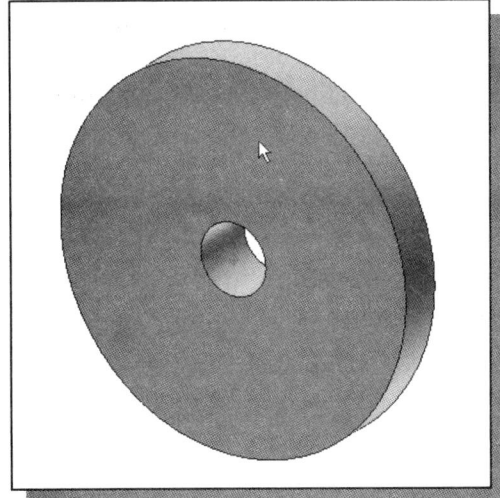

7. Select the surface as shown to the right as the planar surface about which to mirror.

8. Click on the **OK** button to accept the settings and create a mirrored feature.

9. On your own, use the **ViewCube** or the **3D-Rotate** function key [**F4**] to dynamically rotate the solid model and view the resulting solid.

 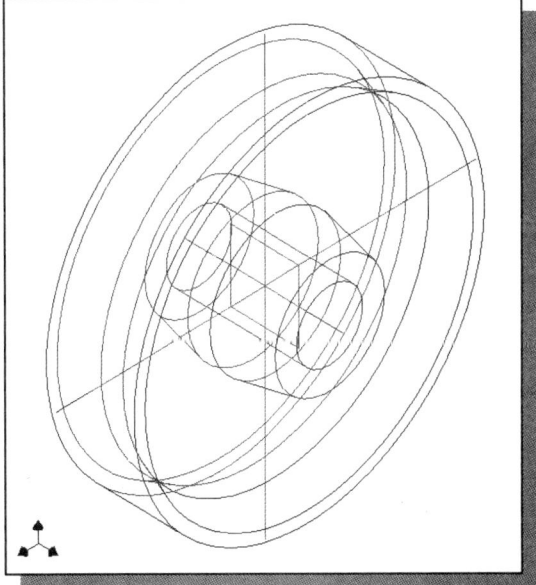

➤ Now is a good time to save the model (quick-key: [**Ctrl**] + [**S**]). It is a good habit to save your model periodically, just in case something might go wrong while you are working on it. You should also save the model after you have completed any major constructions.

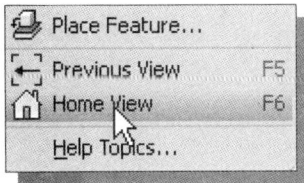

10. Inside the graphics window, right-mouse-click to bring up the option menu.

11. Select **Home View** in the option list to adjust the display of the 2D sketch on the screen.

Create a Pattern Leader Using Construction Geometry

- In *Autodesk Inventor*, we can also use **construction geometry** to help define, constrain, and dimension the required geometry. **Construction geometry** can be lines, arcs, and circles that are used to line up or define other geometry, but are not themselves used as the shape geometry of the model. When profiling the rough sketch, *Autodesk Inventor* will separate the construction geometry from the other entities and treat them as construction entities. Construction geometry can be dimensioned and constrained just like any other profile geometry. When the profile is turned into a 3D feature, the construction geometry remains in the sketch definition but does not show in the 3D model. Using construction geometry in profiles may mean fewer constraints and dimensions are needed to control the size and shape of geometric sketches. We will illustrate the use of the construction geometry to create a cut feature.

- The *Pulley* design requires the placement of five identical holes on the base solid. Instead of creating the five holes one at a time, we can simplify the creation of these holes by using the **Pattern** command, which allows us to create duplicate features. Prior to using the Pattern command, we will first create a *pattern leader*, which is a regular extruded feature.

1. In the *Sketch* toolbar select the **Create 2D Sketch** command by left-clicking once on the icon.

2. In the *Status Bar* area, the message: "*Select face, work plane, sketch or sketch geometry.*" is displayed. Pick the **YZ Plane**, inside the *browser* window, as shown.

3. Inside the graphics window, **right-mouse-click** to bring up the option menu.

4. Select **Project Geometry** in the option. The **Project Geometry** command allows us to project existing geometry to the active sketching plane.

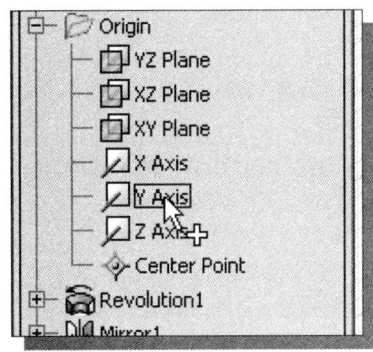

5. In the *Status Bar* area, the message: "*Select edge, vertex, work geometry or sketch geometry to project.*" is displayed. Inside the *browser* window, select the **Y-axis** and **Z-axis** to project these entities onto the sketching plane.

6. On your own, set the display to *wireframe* by clicking on the **Wireframe Display** icon in the *View* panel.

7. Select the **Center point circle** command by clicking once with the left-mouse-button on the icon in the *2D Sketch* panel.

8. Create a circle of arbitrary size as shown below.

9. In the *Standard* toolbar area, click on the **Look At** button.

10. Select the circle we just created to orient the display of the sketching plane on the screen.

11. Select the **Line** command in the *2D Sketch* panel. A brief description of the command is displayed at the bottom of the drawing screen: "*Creates Straight line segments and tangent arcs.*"

12. Set the *Style* option to **Construction** as shown.

13. Create a *construction line* by connecting from the center of the circle we just created to the projected center point (*origin*) at the center of the 3D model as shown below.

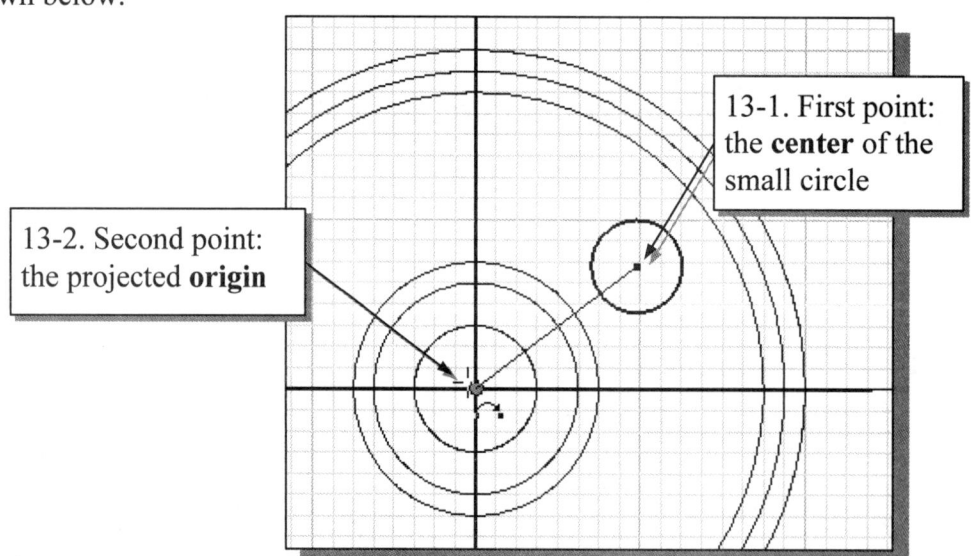

13-1. First point: the **center** of the small circle

13-2. Second point: the projected **origin**

14. Select the **General Dimension** command in the *Constrain* panel.

15. Pick the **horizontal axis** as the first entity to dimension as shown in the figure.

16. Select the **construction line** as the second object to dimension.

17. Place the dimension text to the right of the model as shown.

18. On your own, set the angle dimension to **30** as shown in the above figure.

➤ Note that the small circle moves as the location of the construction line is adjusted by the *angle dimension* we created.

19. Select the **Center point circle** command by clicking once with the left-mouse-button on the icon in the *Draw* panel.

20. Confirm the *Style* option is still set to **Construction**.

21. Create a *construction circle* by placing the center at the projected center point (***origin***).

22. Pick the **center** of the small circle to set the size of the construction circle as shown.

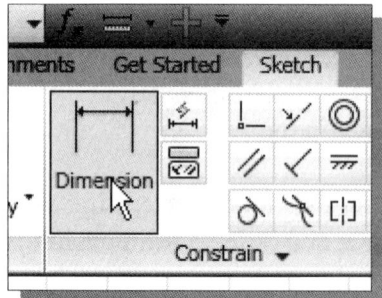

23. Select the **General Dimension** command in the *Constrain* panel.

24. On your own, create the two diameter dimensions, **.5** and **2.5**, as shown below.

25. Inside the graphics window, click once with the right-mouse-button to display the option menu. Select **Finish Sketch** in the popup menu to end the Sketch option.

26. In the *Create Features* panel select the **Extrude** command by releasing the left-mouse-button on the icon.

27. Pick the inside region of the circle to set up the profile of the extrusion.

28. Inside the *Extrude* dialog box, select the **Cut** operation for **Symmetric (both directions)**, and set the *Extents* to **All** as shown.

29. Click on the **OK** button to accept the settings and create the cut feature.

30. On your own, adjust the angle dimension applied to the construction line of the cut feature to **90** and observe the effect of the adjustment.

 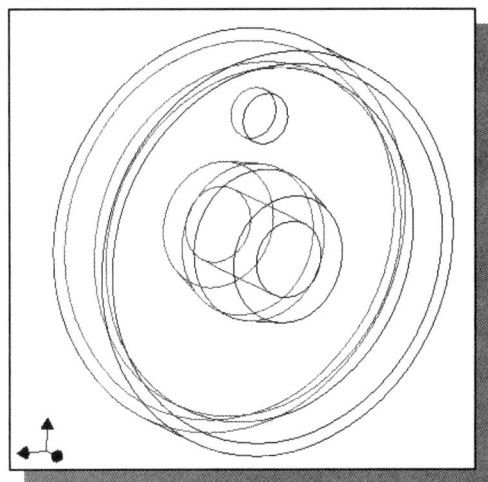

Circular Pattern

- In *Autodesk Inventor*, existing features can be easily duplicated. The **Pattern** command allows us to create both rectangular and polar arrays of features. The patterned features are parametrically linked to the original feature; any modifications to the original feature are also reflected in the arrayed features.

1. In the *Pattern Features* panel, select the **Circular Pattern** command by left-clicking once on the icon.

2. The message "*Select Feature to be arrayed:*" is displayed in the command prompt window. Select the **circular cut feature** when it is highlighted as shown.

3. Inside the graphics window, **right-mouse-click** to bring up the **option menu**.

4. Select **Continue** in the option list to proceed with the Circular Pattern command.

5. In the *Circular Pattern* dialog box, the **Rotation Axis** button is activated. *Autodesk Inventor* expects us to select an axis to pattern about. In the prompt area, the message "*Define the axis of revolution*" is displayed. Select the **X-Axis** in the *browser* window or in the graphics window.

6. In the *Circular Pattern* dialog box, enter **5** in the *Count* box and **360** in the *Angle* box as shown. (Note the different options available for the Circular Pattern command.)

7. Click on the **OK** button to accept the settings and create the *circular pattern*.

Examine the Design Parameters

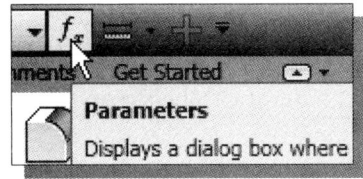

1. In the *Quick Access Toolbar* panel select the **Parameters** command by left-clicking once on the icon. The *Parameters* popup window appears.

2. Scroll down to the bottom of the list and locate the two dimensions used to create the circular pattern.

3. Click on the **Done** button to accept the settings.

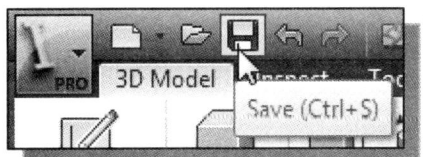

4. Select **Save** in the *Standard* toolbar; we can also use the "**Ctrl-S**" combination (press down the [Ctrl] key and hit the [S] key once) to save the part as *Pulley* in the **Chapter10** folder.

Drawing Mode – Defining a New Border and Title Block

1. Click on the **drop-down arrow** next to the **New File** button in the *Quick Access* toolbar area to display the available new file options.

2. Select **Drawing** from the drop-down list.

> Note that a new graphics window appears on the screen. We can switch between the solid model and the drawing by clicking the corresponding graphics window.

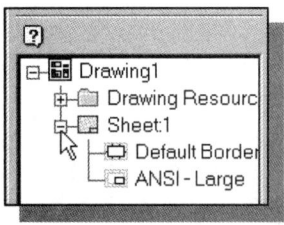

3. Inside the drawing *browser* window, click on the [**+**] symbol in front of **Sheet1** to display the settings.

4. On your own, **delete** the **Default Border** and the **ANSI** *title block*. (Hint: right-mouse-click on the names to bring up the option menu.)

5. Inside the drawing *browser* window, right-mouse-click on **Sheet1** to bring up the option menu.

6. Select **Edit Sheet** in the option list.

7. In the *Edit Sheet* dialog box, set the sheet size to **A** (8.5 × 11).

8. Confirm the page *Orientation* is set to **Landscape** and click on the **OK** button to accept the settings.

9. In the *Ribbon* toolbar panel, select **Manage → Define → Border**

10. On your own, create a rectangle (**7.75 × 10.25**) using the **Two Point Rectangle** command and the **General Dimension** command.

11. Inside the graphics window, **right-mouse-click** to bring up the option menu.

12. Select **Save Border** in the option list.

13. In the *Border* dialog box, enter **A-Size** as the new border name.

14. Click on the **Save** button to end the Define New Border command.

15. Inside the *browser* window, expand the **Drawing Resources** list by clicking on the [**+**] symbol.

16. **Double-click** on the **A-size** border, the border we just created, to place the border in the current drawing. Note that none of the dimensions used to construct the border are displayed.

17. In the Define Toolbar, select **[Define]** → **[Title Block]**

18. On your own, create a title block using the **Two Point Rectangle**, **Line**, **General Dimension**, and **Text** commands.

19. Inside the graphics window, right-mouse-click to bring up the option menu.

20. Select **Save Title Block** in the option list.

21. In the *Title Block* dialog box, enter **A-Horizontal** as the new title block name.

22. Click on the **Save** button to end the Define New Title Block command.

23. Inside the *browser* window, expand the **Title Blocks** list by clicking on the [**+**] symbol.

24. Double-click on the **A-Horizontal** title block, the title block we just created, to place it into the current drawing.

Create a Drawing Template

➢ In *Autodesk Inventor*, each new drawing is created from a template. During the installation of *Autodesk Inventor*, a default drafting standard was selected which sets the default template used to create drawings. We can use this template or another predefined template, modify one of the predefined templates, or create our own templates to enforce drafting standards and other conventions. Any drawing file can be used as a template; a drawing file becomes a template when it is saved in the *Templates* folder. Once the template is saved, we can create a new drawing file using the new template.

1. Select **Save Copy As Template** in the *Standard* toolbar, we will save the current drawing as a template file.

2. In the *Save As* dialog box, switch to the Inventor installation folder: **Inventor 2013** → **Templates** → **English** directory.

3. Enter **A-Size-H.idw** as the template filename.

4. Click on the **Save** button to create a drawing template file.

Create the Necessary Views

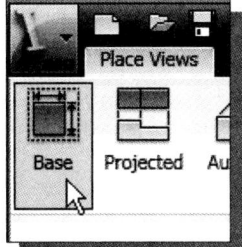

1. Click on **Base View** in the *Place Views* panel to create a base view.

2. In the *Drawing View* dialog box, set the scale to **3 : 4** and select the *left* view as shown in the figure below. (**DO NOT** click on the **OK** button.)

3. Move the cursor inside the graphics window and place the **base view** toward the left side of the border as shown. (If necessary, drag the *Drawing View* dialog box to another location on the screen.)

4. Right-mouse-click and choose **OK**.

5. Click on the **Section View** button in the *Create Views* panel to create a section view.

6. Click on the **base view** to select the view where the section line is to be created.

7. Inside the graphics window, align the cursor to the center of the base view and create the vertical cutting plane line as shown.

8. Inside the graphics window, right-mouse-click once to bring up the option menu.

9. Select **Continue** to proceed with the Section View command.

10. Inside the *Section View* dialog box, toggle *OFF* the **Label Visiblity** option as shown.

11. Set the *Display Style* to **Hidden Line Removed**, as shown in the above figure. (**DO NOT** click on the **OK** button.)

12. Next, *Autodesk Inventor* expects us to place the projected section. Select a location that is toward the right side of the base view as shown in the figure.

13. On your own, use the **Base View** option and create an *isometric* **view** (Iso Top Left – ¾ scale) of the design and place the view toward the right side of the section view as shown below.

Retrieve Dimensions – Features Option

1. Move the cursor on top of the *section* **view** of the model and watch for the box around the entire view indicating the view is selectable as shown in the figure.

2. Inside the graphics window, right-mouse-click once to bring up the option menu.

3. Select **Retrieve Dimensions** to display the parametric dimensions used to create the model.

4. In the *Retrieve Dimensions* dialog box, set the *Select Source* option to **Select Parts** as shown.

5. Move the cursor to the *section* **view** and select the top inside edge of the main body as shown.

➢ The dimensions used to create the revolved feature are now displayed in the section view.

6. Click on the **Select Dimensions** button to activate the command.

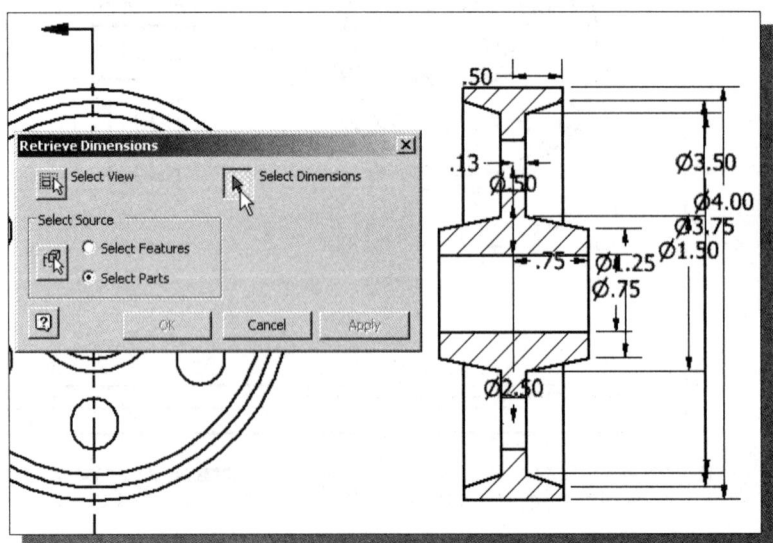

Symmetrical Features in Designs 9-27

7. On your own, select the desired **model dimensions** to be displayed.

 8. Click on the **Apply** button and notice the selected dimensions changed color indicating they have been retrieved.

9. Click on the **Cancel** button to end the Retrieve Dimensions command.

10. On your own, retrieve the model dimensions on the base view and adjust the positions of the dimensions as shown in the figure.

- On your own, use the **Save As** command and save the drawing as ***pulley.idw***.

Associative Functionality – A Design Change

- *Autodesk Inventor's associative functionality* allows us to change the design at any level, and the system reflects the changes at all levels automatically. We will illustrate the associative functionality by changing the circular pattern from five holes to six holes.

1. Inside the *Model Tree* window, below the VIEW1 list, right-click on the **Pulley.ipt** part name to bring up the option menu.

2. Select **Open** in the popup menu to switch to the associated solid model.

3. Inside the *Model Tree* window, right-click on the CircularPattern1 feature to bring up the option menu.

4. Select **Edit Feature** in the popup menu to bring up the associated feature option.

5. In the *Circular Pattern* dialog box, change the number to **6** as shown.

6. Click on the **OK** button to accept the setting.

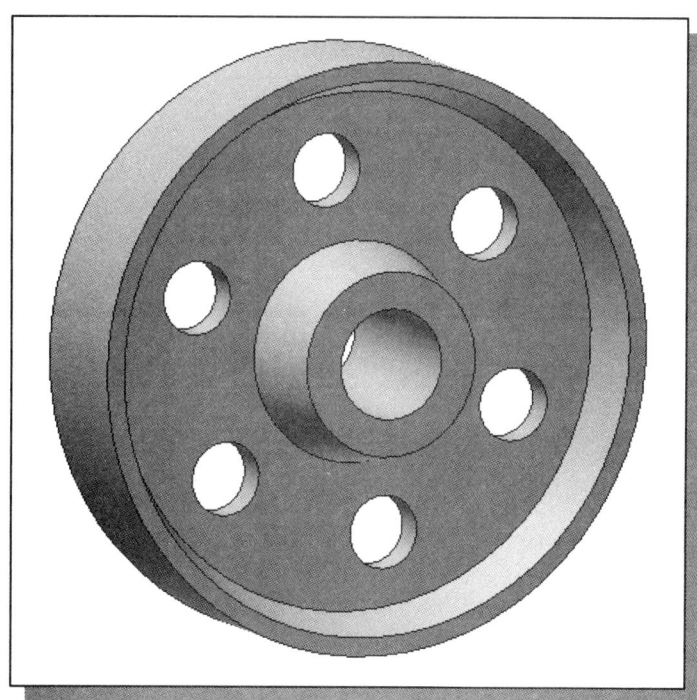

❖ The solid model is updated showing the 6 equally spaced holes as shown.

7. Switch back to the *Pulley* drawing and notice the drawing is also updated.

❖ Notice, in the *Pulley* drawing, the circular pattern is also updated automatically in all views.

Add Centerlines to the Pattern Feature

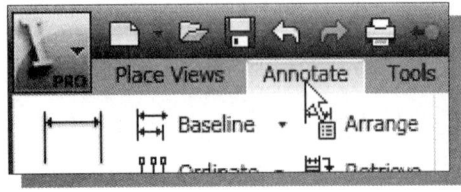

1. On your own, switch to the *Drawing Annotation* panel.

2. Select **Centered Pattern** from the symbol toolbar.

   ➢ The **Centered Pattern** option allows us to add centerlines to a patterned feature.

3. Inside the graphics window, click on any **circular edge** of the **base feature**.

4. Select any circular edge of the patterned feature.

4. Select any circular edge that is part of the **patterned feature**.

5. Continue to select the circular edges of the patterned features, in a **counterclockwise** manner, until all patterned items are selected. (Select the **first circle** again as the ending item.)

6. Inside the graphics window, **right-mouse-click** once to bring up the option menu.

7. Select **Create** to create the centerlines around the selected items.

8. Inside the graphics window, **right-mouse-click** once to bring up the option menu.

9. Select **Cancel [ESC]** to end the Centered Pattern command.

10. On your own, extend the segments of the centerlines so that they pass through the center of the base feature.

Complete the Drawing

1. On your own, use the **General Dimension** command to create the angle dimension as shown in the figure below.

2. For the diameter of the circular pattern, set the options so that the **Arrowheads Inside** option is switched *ON* and the **Single Dimension Line** option is switched *OFF*.

3. Select **Centerline Bisector** from the *Symbols* toolbar.

4. Inside the graphics window, click on the **top edge** of the 0.75 diameter hole as shown in the figure.

5. Inside the graphics window, click on the **bottom edge** of the 0.75 diameter hole as shown.

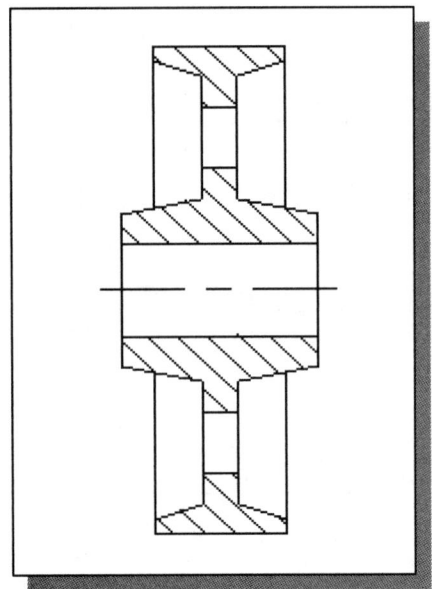

➢ Notice that a centerline is created through the center of the section view as shown in the figure.

6. Repeat the above step and create the centerlines through the other two holes.

7. On your own, complete the drawing and the title block so that the drawing appears as shown on the next page.

Symmetrical Features in Designs 9-33

Questions: (Time: 25 minutes)

1. List the different symmetrical features created in the *Pulley* design.

2. What are the advantages of using a *drawing template*?

3. Describe the steps required in using the **Mirror Feature** command.

4. Why is it important to identify symmetrical features in designs?

5. When and why should we use the **Pattern** option?

6. What are the required elements in order to generate a sectional view?

7. How do we create a *Linear Diameter dimension* for a revolved feature?

8. What is the difference between *construction geometry* and *normal geometry*?

9. List and describe the different centerline options available in the *Drawing Annotation* panel.

10. What is the main difference between a sectional view and a projected view?

Exercises: Create the Solid models and the associated 2D drawings and save the exercises in the Chapter10 folder. (Time: 90 minutes. All dimensions are in inches.)

1. **Shaft Support**

2. **Ratchet Plate** (thickness: 0.125 inch)

3. **Geneva Wheel**

4. **Support Mount**

Chapter 10
Assembly Modeling – Putting It All Together

Learning Objectives

- **Understand the Assembly Modeling Methodology**
- **Create Parts in the Assembly Modeler Mode**
- **Understand and Utilize Assembly Constraints**
- **Understand the Autodesk Inventor DOF Display**
- **Utilize the Autodesk Inventor Adaptive Design Approach**
- **Create Exploded Assemblies**

Introduction

In the previous lessons, we have gone over the fundamentals of creating basic parts and drawings. In this lesson, we will examine the assembly modeling functionality of *Autodesk Inventor*. We will start with a demonstration on how to create and modify assembly models. The main task in creating an assembly is establishing the assembly relationships between parts. To assemble parts into an assembly, we will need to consider the assembly relationships between parts. It is a good practice to assemble parts based on the way they would be assembled in the actual manufacturing process. We should also consider breaking down the assembly into smaller subassemblies, which helps the management of parts. In *Autodesk Inventor*, a subassembly is treated the same way as a single part during assembling. Many parallels exist between assembly modeling and part modeling in parametric modeling software such as *Autodesk Inventor*.

Autodesk Inventor provides full associative functionality in all design modules, including assemblies. When we change a part model, *Autodesk Inventor* will automatically reflect the changes in all assemblies that use the part. We can also modify a part in an assembly. **Bi-directional full associative functionality** is the main feature of parametric solid modeling software that allows us to increase productivity by reducing design cycle time.

One of the key features of *Autodesk Inventor* is the use of an assembly-centric paradigm, which enables users to concentrate on the design without depending on the associated parameters or constraints. Users can specify how parts fit together and the *Autodesk Inventor assembly-based fit function* automatically determines the parts' sizes and positions. This unique approach is known as the **Direct Adaptive Assembly** approach, which defines part relationships directly with no order dependency.

In this lesson, we will also illustrate the basic concept of *Autodesk Inventor*'s **Adaptive Design** approach. The key element in doing **Adaptive Design** is to *under-constrain* features or parts. The applied *assembly constraints* in the assembly modeler are used to control the sizes, shapes, and positions of **under-constrained** sketches, features, and parts. No equations are required and this approach is extremely flexible when performing modifications and changes to the design. We can modify adaptive assemblies at any point, in any order, regardless of how the parts were originally placed or constrained.

In *Autodesk Inventor*, features and parts can be made adaptive at any time during the creation or assembly. The features of a part can be defined as adaptive when they are created in the part file. When we place such a part in an assembly, the features will then resize and change shape based on the applied assembly constraints. We can make features and parts adaptive from either the part modeling or assembly modeling environments.

The *Adaptive Design approach* is a unique design methodology that can only be found in *Autodesk Inventor*. The goal of this methodology is to improve the design process and allows you, the designer, to ***design the way you think***.

Assembly Modeling Methodology

The *Autodesk Inventor* assembly modeler provides tools and functions that allow us to create 3D parametric assembly models. An assembly model is a 3D model with any combination of multiple part models. *Parametric assembly constraints* can be used to control relationships between parts in an assembly model.

Autodesk Inventor can work with any of the assembly modeling methodologies:

The Bottom Up Approach
The first step in the *bottom up* assembly modeling approach is to create the individual parts. The parts are then pulled together into an assembly. This approach is typically used for smaller projects with very few team members.

The Top Down Approach
The first step in the *top down* assembly modeling approach is to create the assembly model of the project. Initially, individual parts are represented by names or symbols. The details of the individual parts are added as the project gets further along. This approach is typically used for larger projects or during the conceptual design stage. Members of the project team can then concentrate on the particular section of the project to which he/she is assigned.

The Middle Out Approach
The *middle out* assembly modeling approach is a mixture of the bottom-up and top-down methods. This type of assembly model is usually constructed with most of the parts already created, and additional parts are designed and created using the assembly for construction information. Some requirements are known and some standard components are used, but new designs must also be produced to meet specific objectives. This combined strategy is a very flexible approach for creating assembly models.

The different assembly modeling approaches described above can be used as guidelines to manage design projects. Keep in mind that we can start modeling our assembly using one approach and then switch to a different approach without any problems.

In this lesson, the *bottom up* assembly modeling approach is illustrated. All of the parts (components) required to form the assembly are created first. *Autodesk Inventor's* assembly modeling tools allow us to create complex assemblies by using components that are created in part files or are placed in assembly files. A component can be a subassembly or a single part, where features and parts can be modified at any time. The sketches and profiles used to build part features can be fully or partially constrained. Partially constrained features may be adaptive, which means the size or shape of the associated parts are adjusted in an assembly when the parts are constrained to other parts. The basic concept and procedure of using the adaptive assembly approach is demonstrated in the tutorial.

The Shaft Support Assembly

Additional Parts

- Four parts are required for the assembly: (1) **Collar**, (2) **Bearing**, (3) **Base-Plate** and (4) **Cap-Screw**. On your own, create the four parts as shown below; save the models as separate part files: *Collar, Bearing, Base-Plate*, and *Cap-Screw*. (Place all parts in the **Chapter13** folder and close all part files or exit *Autodesk Inventor* after you have created the parts.)

(1) **Collar**

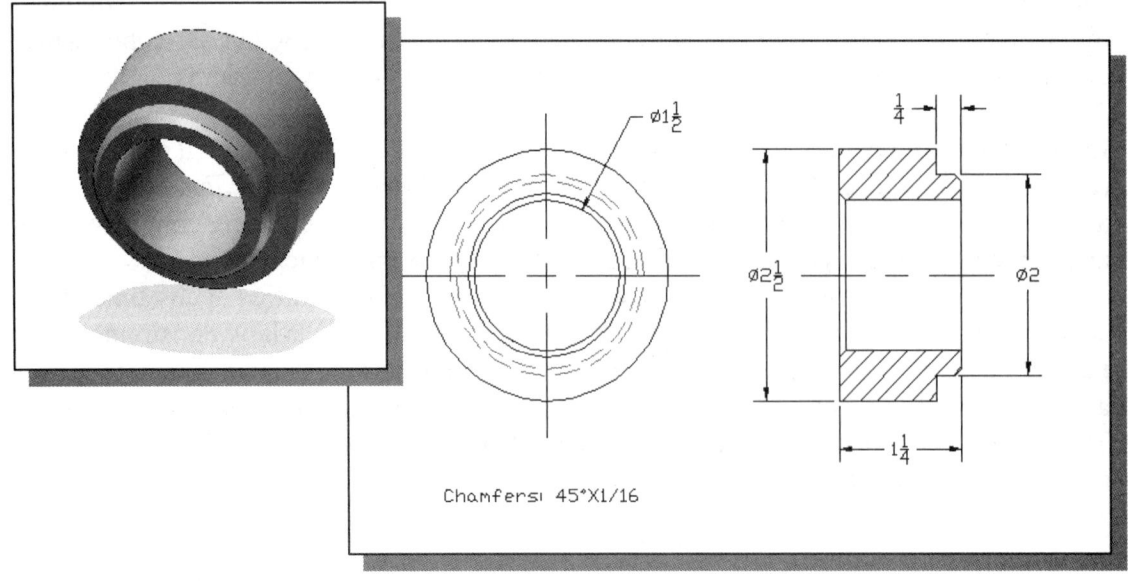

Chamfers: 45°X1/16

(2) **Bearing** (Construct the part with the datum origin aligned to the bottom center.)

(3) **Base-Plate** (Construct the part with the datum origin aligned to the bottom center of the large hole.)

(4) Cap-Screw

- *Autodesk Inventor* provides two options for creating threads: **Thread** and **Coil**. The **Thread** command does not create true 3D threads; a pre-defined thread image is applied on the selected surface, as shown in the figure. The **Coil** command can be used to create true threads, which contain complex three-dimensional curves and surfaces. You are encouraged to experiment with the **Coil** command and/or the **Thread** command to create threads.

- Hint: First create a revolved feature using the profile shown below.

Starting *Autodesk Inventor*

1. Select the **Autodesk Inventor** option on the *Start* menu or select the **Autodesk Inventor** icon on the desktop to start *Autodesk Inventor*. The *Autodesk Inventor* main window will appear on the screen.

2. Select the **New File** icon with a single click of the left-mouse-button in the *Launch* toolbar as shown.

3. Confirm the *Parametric-Modeling-Exercises* project is activated; note the **Projects** button is available to view/modify the active project.

4. Select the **English** tab and in the *Template* list, select **Standard(in).iam** (*Standard Inventor Assembly Model* template file).

5. Click on the **OK** button in the *New File* dialog box to accept the selected settings.

- In the *browser* window, **Assembly1** is displayed with a set of work planes, work axes and a work point. In most aspects, the usage of work planes, work axes and work point is very similar to that of the *Inventor Part Modeler*.

- Notice, in the *Ribbon* toolbar panels, several *component* options are available, such as **Place Component**, **Create Component** and **Place from Content Center**. As the names imply, we can use parts that have been created or create new parts within the *Inventor Assembly Modeler*.

Placing the First Component

- The first component placed in an assembly should be a fundamental part or subassembly. The first component in an assembly file sets the orientation of all subsequent parts and subassemblies. The origin of the first component is aligned to the origin of the assembly coordinates and the part is grounded (all degrees of freedom are removed). The rest of the assembly is built on the first component, the *base component*. In most cases, this *base component* should be one that is **not likely to be removed** and **preferably a non-moving part** in the design. Note that there is no distinction in an assembly between components; the first component we place is usually considered as the *base component* because it is usually a fundamental component to which others are constrained. We can change the base component to a different base component by placing a new base component, specifying it as grounded, and then re-constraining any components placed earlier, including the first component. For our project, we will use the ***Base-Plate*** as the base component in the assembly.

1. In the *Assembly* panel (the toolbar that is located to the left side of the graphics window) select the **Place Component** command by left-mouse-clicking the icon.

2. Select the ***Base-Plate*** (part file: ***Base-Plate.ipt***) in the list window.

3. Click on the **Open** button to retrieve the model.

4. By default, the first component is automatically aligned to the origin of the assembly coordinates. We can also place multiple copies of the same component. Right-mouse-click once to bring up the option menu and select **Done** to end the placement of the *Base-Plate* part.

Assembly Modeling – Putting It All Together   10-9

Placing the Second Component

➢ We will retrieve the *Bearing* part as the second component of the assembly model.

1. In the *Assembly* panel (the toolbar that is located to the left side of the graphics window) select the **Place Component** command by left-mouse-clicking the icon.

2. Select the **Bearing** design (part file: ***Bearing.ipt***) in the list window. And click on the **Open** button to retrieve the model.

3. Place the *Bearing* toward the upper right corner of the graphics window, as shown in the figure.

4. Inside the graphics window, right-mouse-click once to bring up the option menu and select **Done** to end the placement of the *Bearing* part.

- Inside the *browser* window, the retrieved parts are listed in their corresponding order. The **Pin** icon in front of the *Base-Plate* filename signifies the part is grounded and all ***six degrees of freedom*** are restricted. The number behind the filename is used to identify the number of copies of the same component in the assembly model.

Degrees of Freedom and Constraints

- Each component in an assembly has six **degrees of freedom** (**DOF**), or ways in which rigid 3D bodies can move: movement along the X, Y, and Z axes (translational freedom), plus rotation around the X, Y, and Z axes (rotational freedom). *Translational DOF*s allow the part to move in the direction of the specified vector. *Rotational DOF*s allow the part to turn about the specified axis.

> Select the **Degrees of Freedom** option in the **View** tab to display the DOF of the unconstrained component.

- In *Autodesk Inventor*, the degrees-of-freedom symbol shows the remaining degrees of freedom (both translational and rotational) for one or more components of the active assembly. When a component is fully constrained in an assembly, the component cannot move in any direction. The position of the component is fixed relative to other assembly components. All of its degrees of freedom are removed. When we place an assembly constraint between two selected components, they are positioned relative to one another. Movement is still possible in the unconstrained directions.

> It is usually a good idea to fully constrain components so that their behavior is predictable as changes are made to the assembly. Leaving some degrees of freedom open can sometimes help retain design flexibility. As a general rule, we should use only enough constraints to ensure predictable assembly behavior and avoid unnecessary complexity.

Assembly Constraints

- We are now ready to assemble the components together. We will start by placing assembly constraints on the **Bearing** and the **Base-Plate**.

To assemble components into an assembly, we need to establish the assembly relationships between components. It is a good practice to assemble components the way they would be assembled in the actual manufacturing process. **Assembly constraints** create a parent/child relationship that allows us to capture the design intent of the assembly. Because the component that we are placing actually becomes a child to the already assembled components, we must use caution when choosing constraint types and references to make sure they reflect the intent.

➢ Switch back to the *Assemble* panel; select the **Constrain** command by left-mouse-clicking once on the icon.

- The *Place Constraints* dialog box appears on the screen. Four types of assembly constraints are available.

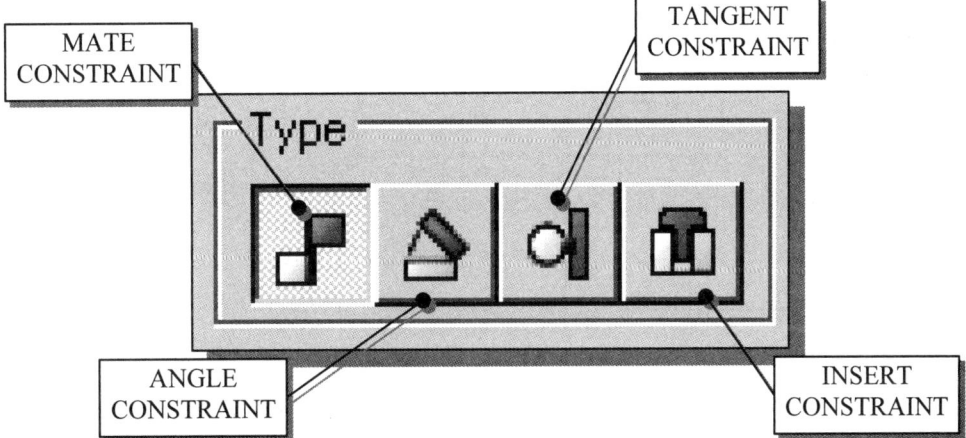

- Assembly models are created by applying proper *assembly constraints* to the individual components. The constraints are used to restrict the movement between parts. Constraints eliminate rigid body degrees of freedom (**DOF**). A 3D part has *six degrees of freedom* since the part can rotate and translate relative to the three coordinate axes. Each time we add a constraint between two parts; one or more DOF is eliminated. The movement of a fully constrained part is restricted in all directions. Four basic types of assembly constraints are available in *Autodesk Inventor*: **Mate, Angle, Tangent** and **Insert**. Each type of constraint removes different combinations of rigid body degrees of freedom. Note that it is possible to apply different constraints and achieve the same results.

- **Mate** – Constraint positions components face-to-face, or adjacent to one another, with faces flush. Removes one degree of linear translation and two degrees of angular rotation between planar surfaces. Selected surfaces point in opposite directions and can be **offset** by a specified distance. Mate constraint positions selected faces normal to one another, with faces coincident.

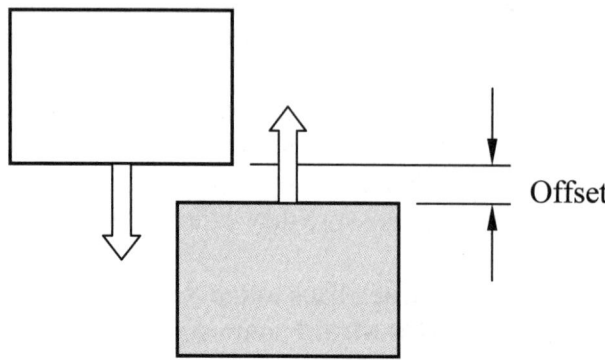

- **Flush** – Makes two planes coplanar with their faces aligned in the same direction. Selected surfaces point in the same direction and are offset by a specified distance. Flush constraint aligns components adjacent to one another with faces flush and positions selected faces, curves, or points so that they are aligned with surface normals pointing in the same direction. (Note that the Flush constraint is listed as a selectable option in the Mate constraint.)

- **Angle** – Creates an angular assembly constraint between parts, subassemblies, or assemblies. Selected surfaces point in the direction specified by the angle.

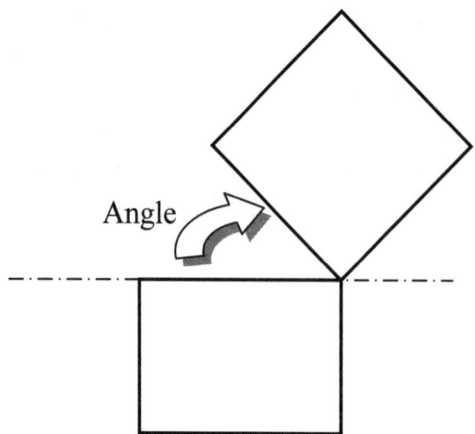

> **Tangent** – Aligns selected faces, planes, cylinders, spheres, and cones to contact at the point of tangency. Tangency may be on the inside or outside of a curve, depending on the selection of the direction of the surface normal. A Tangent constraint removes one degree of translational freedom.

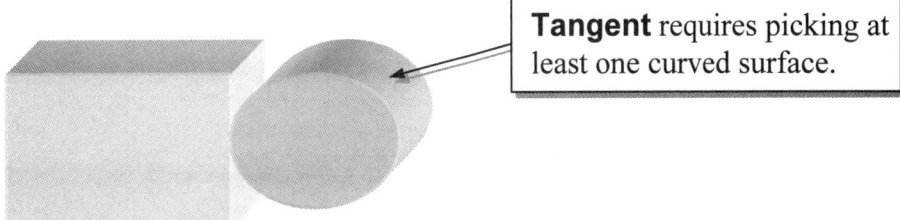

Tangent requires picking at least one curved surface.

> **Insert** – Aligns two circles, including their center axes and planes. Selected circular surfaces become co-axial. Insert constraint is a combination of a face-to-face Mate constraint between planar faces and a Mate constraint between the axes of the two components. A rotational degree of freedom remains open. The surfaces do not need to be full 360-degree circles. Selected surfaces can point in opposite directions or in the same direction and can be offset by a specified distance.

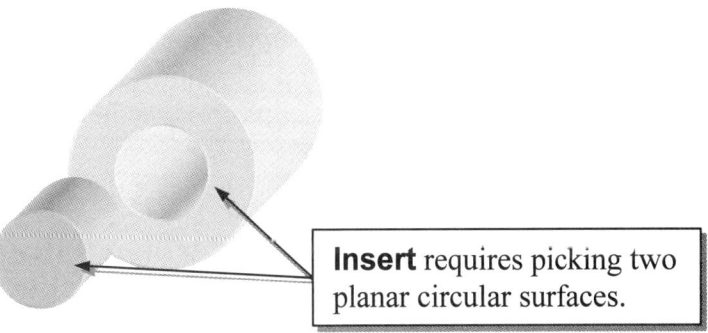

Insert requires picking two planar circular surfaces.

Apply the First Assembly Constraint

1. In the *Place Constraint* dialog box, confirm the constraint type is set to **Mate** constraint and select the **top horizontal surface** of the base part as the first part for the Mate alignment command.

2. On your own, dynamically rotate the displayed model to view the bottom of the *Bearing* part, as shown in the figure below.

3. Click on the bottom face of the *Bearing* part as the second part selection to apply the constraint. Note the direction normals shown in the figure; the **Mate** constraint requires the selection of opposite direction of surface normals.

4. Click on the **Apply** button to accept the selection and apply the **Mate** constraint.

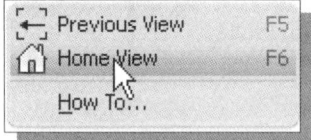

5. Move the cursor inside the graphics window, and then right-mouse-click to bring up the option menu.

6. Select the **Isometric View** to adjust the display of the assembly model.

❖ Notice the **DOF** symbol is adjusted automatically in the graphics window. The **Mate** constraint removes one degree of linear translation and two degrees of angular rotation between the selected planar surfaces. The *Bearing* part can still move along two axes and rotate about the third axis.

Apply a Second MATE Constraint

❖ The **Mate** constraint can also be used to align axes of cylindrical features.

1. In the *Place Constraint* dialog box, confirm the constraint type is set to **Mate** constraint and the *Offset* option is set to **0.00**.

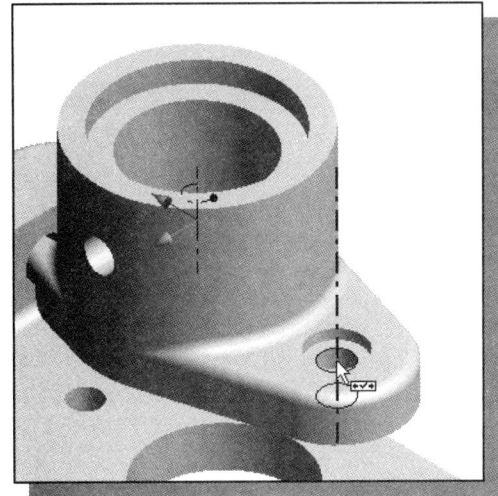

2. Move the cursor near the cylindrical surface of the right counter bore hole of the *Bearing* part. Select the axis when it is displayed as shown. (Hint: Use the *Dynamic Rotation* option to assist the selection.)

3. Move the cursor near the cylindrical surface of the small hole on the *Base-Plate* part. Select the axis when it is displayed as shown.

4. In the *Place Constraint* dialog box, click on the **Apply** button to accept the selection and apply the Mate constraint.

5. In the *Place Constraint* dialog box, click on the **Cancel** button to exit the Place Constraint command.

❖ The *Bearing* part appears to be placed in the correct position. But the DOF symbol indicates that this is not the case; the bearing part can still rotate about the displayed vertical axis.

Constrained Move

❖ To see how well a component is constrained, we can perform a constrained move. A constrained move is done by dragging the component in the graphics window with the left-mouse-button. A constrained move will honor previously applied assembly constraints. That is, the selected component and parts constrained to the component move together in their constrained positions. A grounded component remains grounded during the move.

1. Inside the graphics window, move the cursor on top of the top surface of the *Bearing* part as shown in the figure.

2. Press and hold down the left-mouse-button and drag the *Bearing* part downward.

❖ The *Bearing* part can freely rotate about the displayed axis.

3. On your own, use the dynamic rotation command to view the alignment of the *Bearing* part.

4. Rotate the *Bearing* part and adjust the display as shown in the figure.

5. Switch to the wireframe display mode before proceeding to the next section.

Apply a Flush Constraint

- Besides selecting the surfaces of solid models to apply constraints, we can also select the established work planes to apply the assembly constraints. This is an additional advantage of using the *BORN technique* in creating part models. For the *Bearing* part, we will apply a Mate constraint to two of the work planes and eliminate the last rotational DOF.

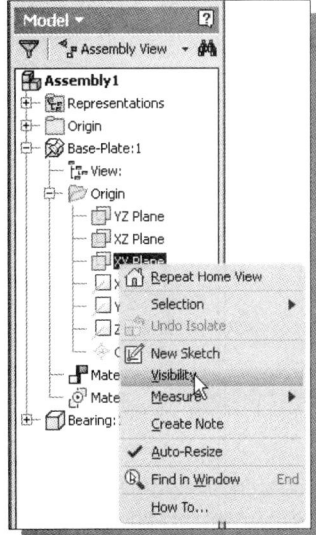

1. On your own, inside the *browser* window toggle ON the **Visibility** for the corresponding work planes that can be used for alignment of the *Base-Plate* and the *Bearing* parts.

2. In the *Assembly* panel, select the **Constrain** command by left-mouse-clicking once on the icon.

3. In the *Place Constraint* dialog box, confirm the constraint type is set to **Mate** constraint and the *Offset* option is set to **0.00**.

4. In the *Place Constraint* dialog box, switch the *Solution* option to **Flush** as shown.

5. Select the *work plane* of the *Base-Plate* part as the first part for the Flush alignment command.

6. Select the corresponding *work plane* of the *Bearing* part as the second part for the Flush alignment command.

❖ Note that the Flush constraint makes two planes coplanar with their faces aligned in the same direction.

7. In the *Place Constraint* dialog box, switch the *Solution* option to **Mate** and notice the *Bearing* part is rotated 180 degrees to satisfy the **Mate** constraint.

❖ Note that the *Show Preview* option allows us to preview the result before accepting the selection.

8. On your own, switch back to the **Flush** option and click on the **Apply** button to accept the settings.

9. In the *Place Constraint* dialog box, click on the **Cancel** button to exit the Place Constraint command.

❖ Note the DOF symbol disappears, which indicates the assembly is fully constrained.

Placing the Third Component

➢ We will retrieve the *Collar* part as the third component of the assembly model.

1. In the *Assembly* panel (the toolbar that is located to the left side of the graphics window) select the **Place Component** command by left-mouse-clicking the icon.

2. Select the *Collar* design (part file: *Collar.ipt*) in the list window. And click on the **Open** button to retrieve the model.

3. Place the *Collar* part toward the upper right corner of the graphics window, as shown in the figure.

4. Inside the graphics window, right-mouse-click once to bring up the option menu and select **Done** to end the placement of the *Collar* part.

❖ Notice the DOF symbol displayed on the screen. The *Collar* part can move linearly and rotate about the three axes (six degrees of freedom).

Applying an Insert Constraint

1. In the *Assembly* panel, select the **Constrain** command by left-mouse-clicking once on the icon.

2. In the *Place Constraint* dialog box, switch to the **Insert** constraint.

3. Select the inside corner of the *Collar* part as the first surface to apply the Insert constraint, as shown in the figure.

4. Select the inside circle on the top surface of the *Bearing* part as the second surface to apply the Insert constraint, as shown in the figure.

5. Click on the **Apply** button to accept the settings.

➢ Note that one rotational degree of freedom remains open; the *Collar* part can still freely rotate about the displayed DOF axis.

Assemble the Cap-Screws

❖ We will place two of the *Cap-Screw* parts to complete the assembly model.

1. In the *Assembly* panel (the toolbar that is located to the left side of the graphics window) select the **Place Component** command by left-mouse-clicking once on the icon.

2. Select the **Cap-Screw** design (part file: *Cap-Screw.ipt*) in the list window. And click on the **Open** button to retrieve the model.

3. Place two copies of the *Cap-Screw* part on both sides of the *Collar* by clicking twice on the screen as shown in the figure.

4. Inside the graphics window, right-mouse-click once to bring up the option menu and select **Done** to end the Place Component command.

❖ Notice the DOF symbols displayed on the screen. Each *Cap-Screw* has six degrees of freedom. Both parts are referencing the same external part file, but each can be constrained independently.

- Inside the *browser* window, the retrieved parts are listed in the order they are placed. The number behind the part name is used to identify the number of copies of the same part in the assembly model. Move the cursor to the last part name and notice the corresponding part is highlighted in the graphics window.

➢ On your own, use the Place Constraints command and assemble the *Cap-Screws* in place as shown in the figure below.

Exploded View of the Assembly

- Exploded assemblies are often used in design presentations, catalogs, sales literature, and in the shop to show all of the parts of an assembly and how they fit together. In *Autodesk Inventor*, an exploded assembly can be created by two methods: (1) using the Move Component and Rotate Component commands in the *Assembly Modeler*, which contains only limited options for the operation but can be done very quickly; (2) transferring the assembly model into the *Presentation Modeler*. For our example, we will create an exploded assembly by using the Move Component command that is available in the *Assembly Modeler*.

1. In the *Position* toolbar panel, select the **Move Component** command by left-mouse-clicking once on the icon.

2. Inside the graphics window, move the cursor on top of the top surface of the *Collar* part as shown in the figure.

3. Press and hold down the left-mouse-button and drag the *Collar* part toward the right side of the assembly as shown.

Assembly Modeling – Putting It All Together   10-23

4. On your own, repeat the above steps and create an exploded assembly by repositioning the components as shown in the figure below.

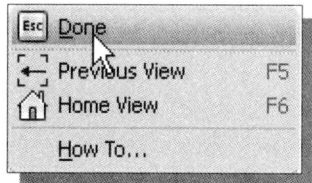

5. Inside the graphics window, right-mouse-click once to bring up the option menu and select **Done** to end the **Move Component** command.

❖ The **Move Component** and **Rotate Component** commands are used to temporarily reposition the components in the graphics window. The displayed image is temporary, but it can be printed with the **Print** command through the pull-down menu.

6. Click on the **Update** button in the *Standard* toolbar area.

❖ Note that the components are reset back to their assembled positions, based on the applied assembly constraints.

Editing the Components

- The *associative functionality* of *Autodesk Inventor* allows us to change the design at any level, and the system reflects the changes at all levels automatically.

1. Inside the *Desktop Browser*, move the cursor on top of the **Bearing** part. Right-mouse-click once to bring up the option menu and select **Edit** in the option list.

❖ Note that we are automatically switched back to *Part Editing Mode*.

2. On your own, adjust the diameter of the small *Drill Hole* to **0.25** as shown.

3. Click on the **Update** button in the *Standard* toolbar area to proceed with updating the model.

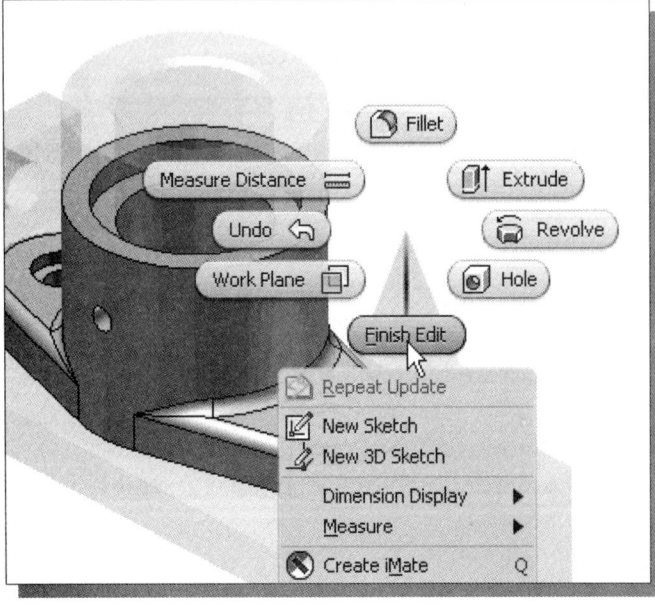

4. Inside the graphics window, click once with the right-mouse-button to display the option menu.

5. Select **Finish Edit** in the popup menu to exit *Part Editing Mode* and return to *Assembly Mode*.

➢ *Autodesk Inventor* has updated the part in all levels and in the current *Assembly Mode*. On your own, open the *Bearing* part file to confirm the modification is performed.

Adaptive Design Approach

- *Autodesk Inventor's **Adaptive Design** approach allows us to use the applied *assembly constraints* to control the sizes, shapes, and positions of ***underconstrained*** sketches, features, and parts. In this section, we will examine the procedure to apply the constraints directly on 3D parts; note that the adaptive design approach is also applicable to 2D sketches.

1. In the *Assembly* panel, select the **Create Component** command by left-mouse-clicking once on the icon.

2. In the *Create In-Place Component* dialog box, enter **A-Block** as the new file name.

3. Set the *File Location* to **Chapter13** as shown.

4. Click on the **OK** button to accept the settings.

5. Click on the **XY Plane** of the *Base-Plate* part, inside the *browser* window, to apply a Flush constraint.

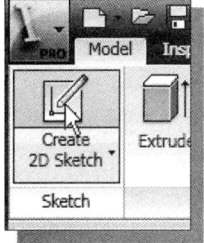

6. Activate the *Model* toolbar and select the **Sketch** command by left-clicking once on the icon.

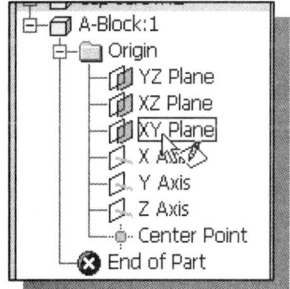

7. Select the **XY Plane**, in the *browser* window, of the *A-Block* part to align the sketch plane.

8. Select the **Two point rectangle** command by clicking once with the left-mouse-button on the icon in the *2D Sketch* panel.

9. On your own, create a rectangle of arbitrary size below the assembly model as shown in the figure.

10. Inside the graphics window, click once with the right-mouse-button to display the option menu and select **Done** to end the Rectangle command.

11. In the *Ribbon* toolbar panel, click on the **Model** tab then **Create → Extrude** as shown in the figure below.

Assembly Modeling – Putting It All Together   10-27

12. Inside the *Extrude* dialog box, select the **Both Sides** option and set the *Extents Distance* to **3 in** as shown.

13. In the *Extrude* dialog box, click on the **OK** button to proceed with creating the feature.

14. Right-mouse-click on the **Extrusion1** feature of the *A-Block* part, inside the *browser* window, and select **Adaptive** to allow the use of the adaptive design approach.

15. Click inside the graphics window to deselect any part or assembly.

16. Inside the graphics window, click once with the **right-mouse-button** to display the option menu.

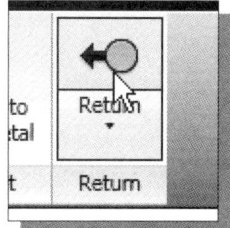

17. Select **Return** in the popup menu to exit *Part Editing Mode* and return to *Assembly Modeling Mode*.

- Note that the rectangular block is created with only one dimension, the extrude distance. The 2D sketch of the part is intentionally under-constrained.

18. Right-mouse-click on the **A-Block** part, inside the *browser* window, and confirm the **Adaptive** option is turned *ON*. This option allows the use of the *Adaptive Design* approach in the current assembly model.

- Note the **Adaptive** icon, the two-arrow symbol, appears in front of the part name in the *browser* window.

19. In the *Assembly* panel, select the **Constrain** command by left-mouse-clicking once on the icon.

20. On your own, use the **Flush** constraint to align the *A-block* to the left-edge of the *Base-Plate* as shown.

21. Create a **Mate** constraint to align the top of the *A-block* to the bottom of the *Base-Plate* part as shown.

22. Use the **Mate** constraint and align the right surface of the *A-block* to the bottom left surface of the *Base-Plate* part as shown.

- Note that the length of the *A-block* part is automatically adjusted to fit the defined constraint.

23. In the *Place Constraint* dialog box, click on the **Cancel** button to end the Place Constraint command.

Delete and Re-apply Assembly Constraints

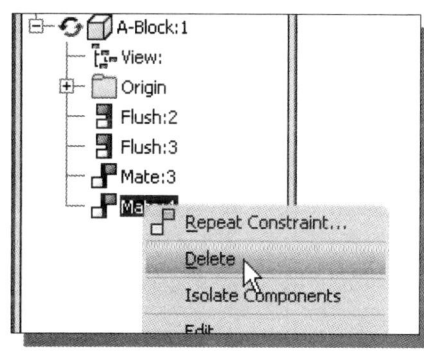

1. Inside the *browser* window, right-mouse-click on the last **Mate** constraint of the *A-Block* part to bring up the option menu.

2. Select **Delete** to remove the applied constraint.

3. On your own, switch *ON* the **Visibility** of the vertical work plane of the *Cap-Screw* part, the plane that is perpendicular to the length of the *Base-Plate* part, as shown.

4. In the *Assembly* position panel, select the **Constrain** command by left-mouse-clicking once on the icon.

5. On your own, align the right vertical surface of the *A-block* part to the vertical work plane as shown in the figure.

6. On your own, experiment with aligning the right vertical surface of the *A-block* part to other vertical surfaces of the assembly model.

• As can be seen, the length of the *A-block* is adjusted to the newly applied constraint. The ***Adaptive Design*** approach allows us to have greater flexibility and simplifies the design process.

7. On your own, save the assembly model as **Shaft-Support.iam** under the **Chapter13** folder.

Setup a Drawing of the Assembly Model

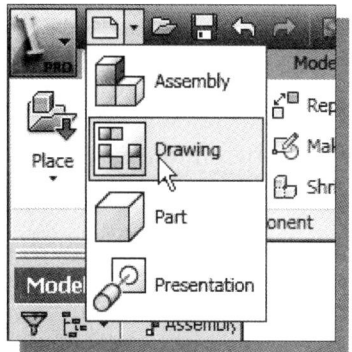

1. Click on the **drop-down arrow** next to the **New File** icon in the *Quick Access* toolbar area to display the available New File options.

2. Select **Drawing** from the option list.

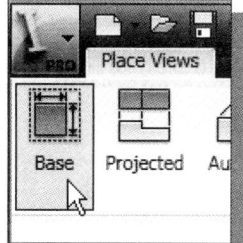

3. Click on the **Base View** in the *Drawing Views* panel to create a base view.

4. In the *Drawing View* dialog box, set *Orientation* to **Iso Top Right View** and **Hidden Line** as shown in the figure. (**DO NOT** click on the **OK** button at this point.)

5. Move the cursor inside the graphics window and place the *base* view near the lower left side of the *Border* as shown.

❖ Note that the default sheet size is much bigger than the created view. *Inventor* allows us to adjust the sheet size even when views have been created.

6. Inside the *Drawing Browser* window, right-mouse-click on **Sheet:1** to display the option menu.

7. Select **Edit Sheet** in the option menu to display the settings for the drawing.

8. Set the sheet size to **B-size** as shown.

9. Click on the **OK** button to accept the settings and exit the Edit Sheet command.

❖ Note that the *Border* and *Title Block* are automatically replaced as the sheet size is adjusted.

Assembly Modeling – Putting It All Together   10-33

Creating a Parts List

1. Left-mouse-click in the *title* area of the *Drawing Views* panel.

2. Select **Drawing Annotation Panel** by left-clicking once in the drop-down list.

3. In the *Drawing Annotation* window, click on the **Parts List** button.

4. In the prompt area, the message "*Select a view*" is displayed. Items in the selected view will be listed in the *Parts List*. Select the **base view**.

❖ The *Parts List* dialog box appears on the screen; options are available to make adjustments to the numbering system and table wrap settings.

➢ The *Parts List* – BOM options are as follows:

Structured: Creates a parts list in which subassemblies are assigned using a nested numbering system (for example, 1, 1.1, 1.1.1). The nested number extends as many levels as needed for the assembly levels in the model.

Only Parts: Creates a parts list that sequentially numbers all parts in the assembly, including parts that are contained in subassemblies.

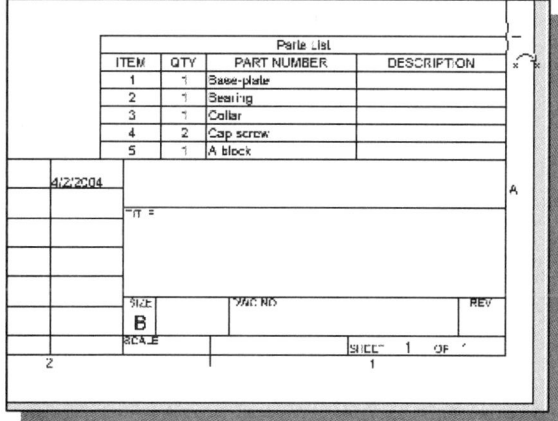

❖ Note that no subassemblies are currently used in the assembly; we will accept the default settings.

5. Click **OK** to accept the default settings.

6. Click **OK** again to enable the BOM view.

7. Place the *Parts List* above the *Title Block* as shown.

Editing the Parts List

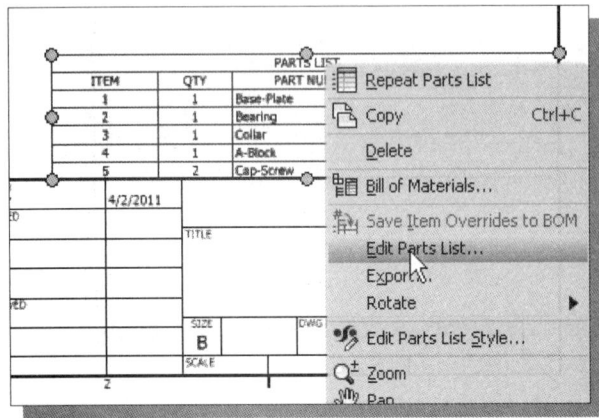

1. Move the cursor on top of the *Parts List* and right-mouse-click once to display the option menu.

2. Choose **Edit Parts List** in the option menu as shown.

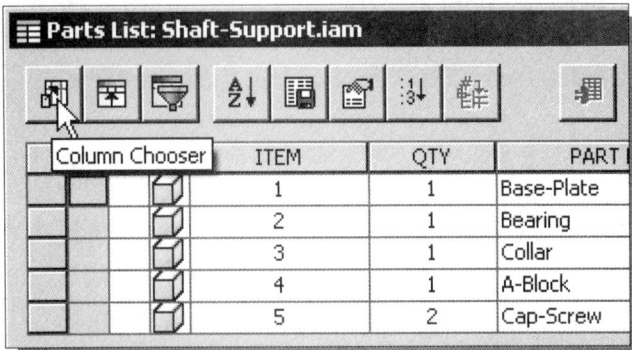

3. Click on the **Column Chooser** button as shown.

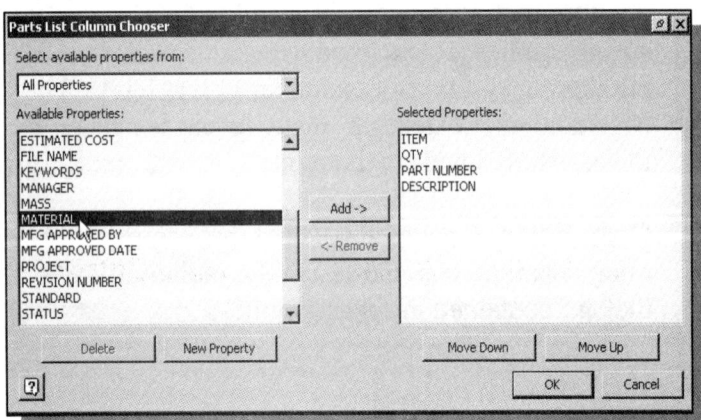

4. Select **MATERIAL** in the *Available Properties* list as shown.

5. Click **Add** to add the selected item to the *Selected Properties* list.

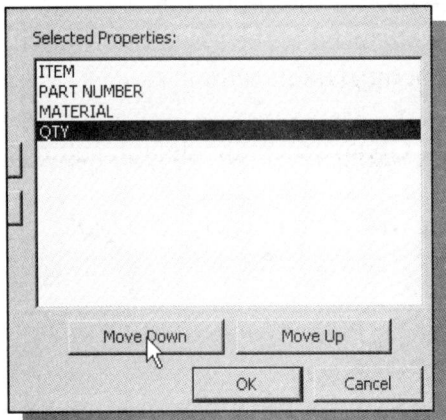

6. On your own, adjust the *Selected Properties* list as shown. (Hint: Use the **Move Up** and **Move Down** buttons to arrange the order of the list.)

7. Click **OK** to accept the settings.

❖ The *Parts List* is adjusted using the new settings. Note that, currently, all of the parts are using the **Default** material type.

8. Click on the **Table Layout** button as shown.

9. Set the *Table Direction* to **Add new parts to top** as shown.

10. Set the *Heading Placement* to **Bottom** as shown.

11. Turn **OFF** the *Parts List Title*.

12. Click **OK** to accept the settings.

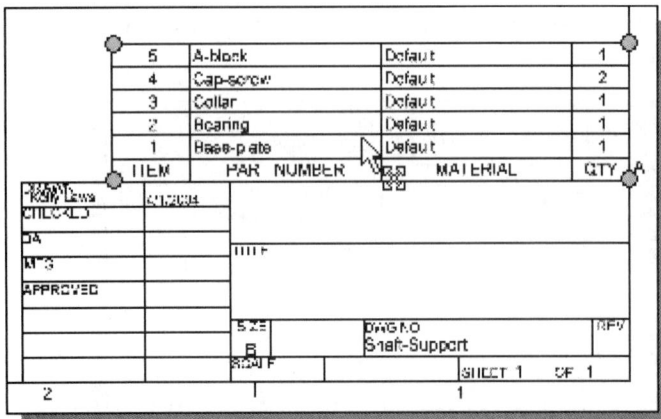

13. On your own, adjust the position of the *Parts List* so that it is aligned to the top edge of the *Title Block* as shown. (Hint: Look for the MOVE symbol next to the cursor.)

Changing the Material Type

❖ We will switch back to the assembly model to change the assignments of the material type.

1. Click on the *Shaft-Support.iam* window to switch back to the assembly model.

2. Inside the *Model Browser* window, right-mouse-click on **Base-Plate:1** to display the option menu.

3. Select **Edit** in the option menu to enter the *Edit Mode* for the selected part.

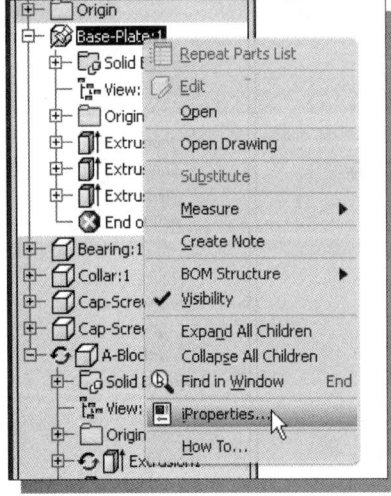

4. Inside the *Model Browser* window, select the **Base-plate** part by clicking once with the left-mouse-button.

5. Right-mouse-click on **Base-plate:1** to display the option menu and choose **iProperties** in the options list.

Assembly Modeling – Putting It All Together 10-37

6. Click on the **Physical** tab in the *Base-plate.ipt Properties* window.

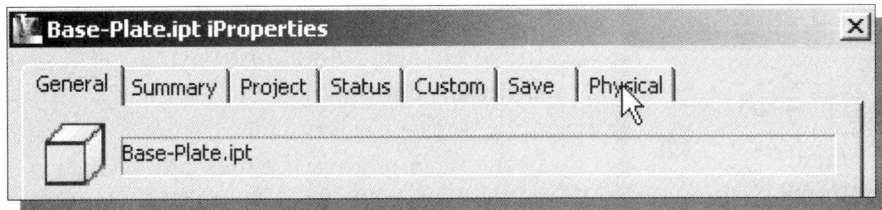

7. Choose the **Steel, Mild** in the *Material* list. Note the properties of the selected material are also displayed in the *Properties* list as shown in the figure.

❖ *Autodesk Inventor* comes with many materials that have pre-entered information; additional material types/properties can also be added/changed as well.

8. Click **OK** to accept the setting and exit the *Materials* dialog box.

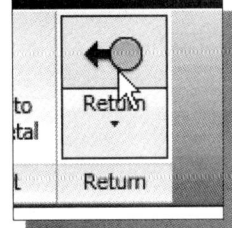

9. Select **Return** in the Standard toolbar to exit the *Part Editing Mode*.

10. On your own, switch back to the *Shaft-Support.idw* window and notice the *Material* information for the **Base-plate** part is now updated

11. On your own, repeat the above steps to change the material information for the other parts as shown in the figure below.

	5	A-block	Aluminum-6061	1
	4	Cap-screw	Steel, Mild	2
	3	Collar	Bronze, Soft Tin	1
	2	Bearing	Cast Iron	1
	1	Base-plate	Steel, Mild	1
	ITEM	PART NUMBER	MATERIAL	QTY
DRAWN Randy	5/3/2005			A
CHECKED				

Completing the Assembly Drawing

1. In the *Drawing Annotation* window, click on the **Balloon** button.

2. In the prompt area, the message "*Select a location*" is displayed. Click on the **Collar part** to attach an arrowhead to the part.

3. Pick another location to **place the balloon** as shown in the figure below.

4. Inside the graphics window, click once with the right-mouse-button to display the option menu.

5. Select **Continue** in the popup menu to proceed with the creation of the balloon.

6. On your own, repeat the above steps and complete the drawing as shown.

Bill of Materials

❖ A bill of materials (BOM) is a table that contains information about the parts within an assembly. The BOM can include information such as part names, quantities, costs, vendors, and all of the other information related to building the part. The **parts list**, which is used in an assembly drawing, is usually a partial list of the associated BOM.

In *Autodesk Inventor*, both the *bill of materials* and *parts list* can be derived directly from data generated by the assembly and the part properties. We can select which properties to be included in the *bill of materials* or *parts list*, in what order the information is presented, and in what format to export the information. The exported file can be used in an application such as a spreadsheet or text editor.

(a) BOM from Parts List

1. Move the cursor on top of the **Parts List** and right-mouse-click once to display the option menu.

2. Choose **Export...** in the option menu as shown.

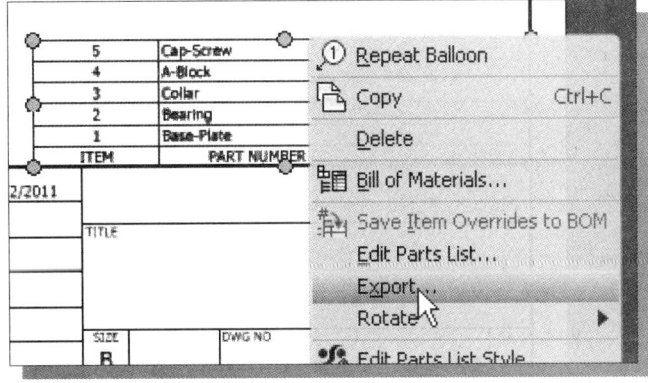

3. Confirm the *Save as type* list is set to **Microsoft Excel**.

4. Enter **Shaft-support.xls** as the filename and click **Save** to export the BOM.

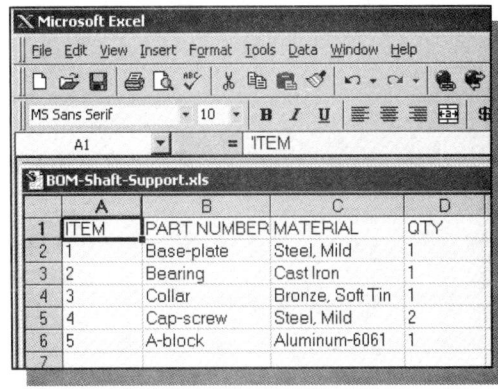

❖ On your own, examine the exported BOM by opening up the file in *Excel*.

(b) BOM from Assembly Model

1. Click on the ***Shaft-Support.iam*** tab to switch back to the assembly model.

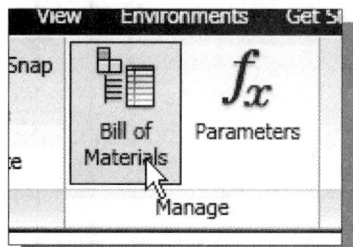

2. Select **Bill of Materials** in the *Assemble* tab of the *Ribbon* toolbar panel.

❖ Note that many of the controls and options are similar to those of the **Parts List** command in the *Drawing Mode*.

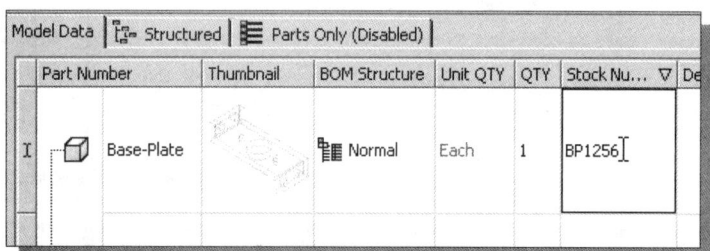

3. Click inside the ***Stock Number*** box to enter the *Edit Mode*.

4. Enter **BP1256** as the new *Stock Number*.

5. Click the **Export Bill of Materials** button.

6. On your own, export using the Microsoft Excel format and examine the *BOM* in Microsoft Excel.

Questions: (Time: 35 minutes)

1. What is the purpose of using *assembly constraints*?

2. List three of the commonly used *assembly constraints*.

3. Describe the difference between the **Mate** constraint and the **Flush** constraint.

4. In an assembly, can we place more than one copy of a part? How is it done?

5. How should we determine the assembly order of different parts in an assembly model?

6. How do we adjust the information listed in the **parts list** of an assembly drawing?

7. In *Autodesk Inventor*, describe the procedure to create a **bill of materials** (BOM)?

8. Create sketches showing the steps you plan to use to create the four parts required for the assembly shown on the next page:

Ex.1)

Ex.2)

Ex.3)

Ex.4)

Exercises: (Time: 60 minutes)

1. **Wheel Assembly** (Create a set of detail and assembly drawings. All dimensions are in mm.)

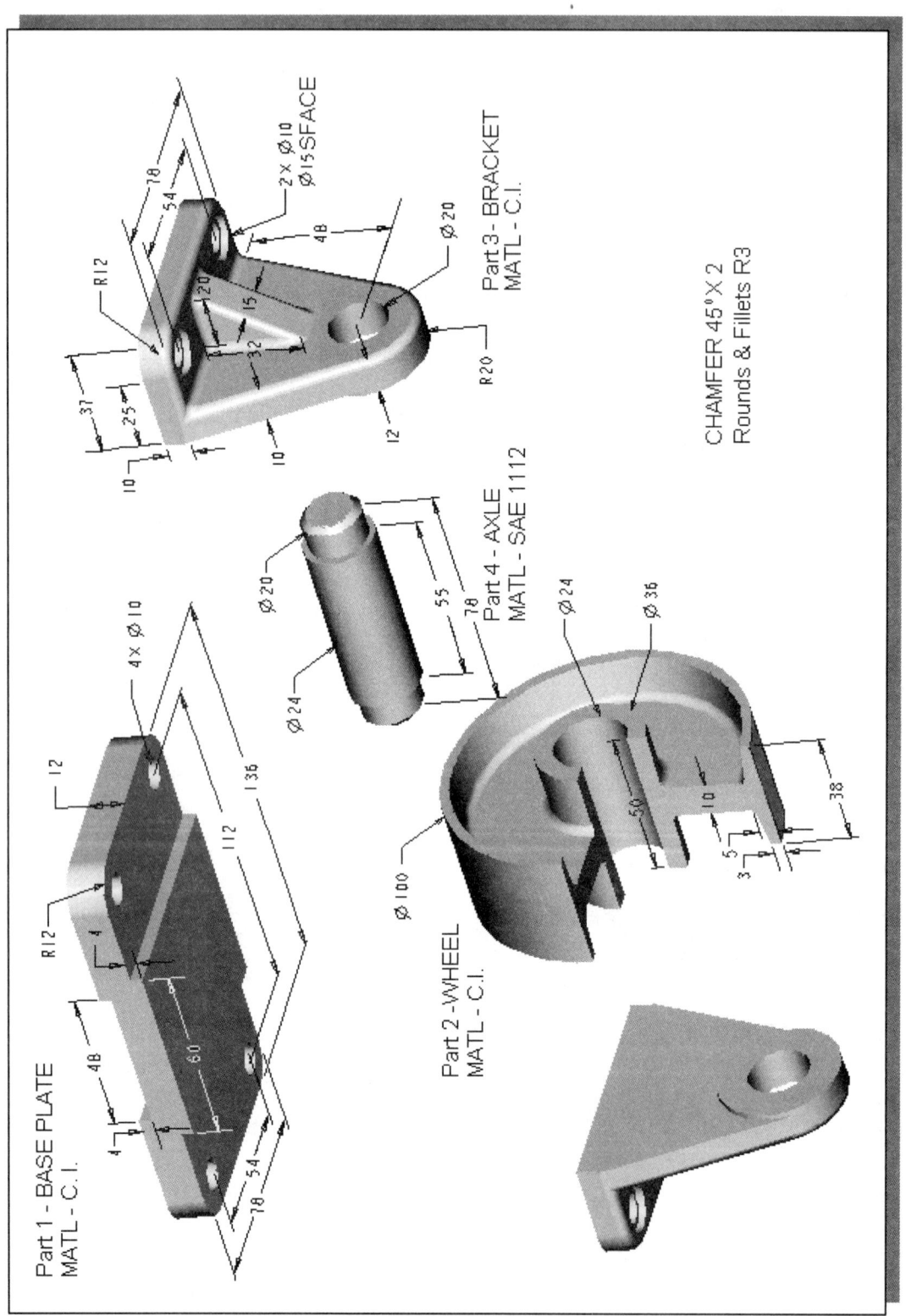

2. **Vise Assembly** (Create a set of detail and assembly drawings. All dimensions are in inches.)

(a) **Base:** The 1.5 inch wide and 1.25 inch wide slots are cut through the entire base. Material: **Gray Cast Iron**.

(b) **Jaw:** The shoulder of the jaw rests on the flat surface of the base and the jaw opening is set to 1.5 inches. Material: **Gray Cast Iron**.

(c) **Key: 0.1875 inch H x 0.375 inch W x 1.75 inch L**. The keys fit into the slots on the jaw with the edge faces flush as shown in the sub-assembly to the right. Material: **Alloy Steel**.

(d) **Screw:** There is one chamfered edge (0.0625 inch x 45°). The flat ⌀ 0.75" edge of the screw is flush with the corresponding recessed ⌀ 0.75 face on the jaw. Material: **Alloy Steel**.

(e) **Handle Rod:** **⌀ 0.375" x 5.0" L**. The handle rod passes through the hole in the screw and is rotated to an angle of 30° with the horizontal as shown in the assembly view. The flat ⌀ 0.375" edges of the handle rod are flush with the corresponding recessed ⌀ 0.735 faces on the handle knobs. Material: **Alloy Steel**.

(f) **Handle Knob:** There are two chamfered edges (0.0625 inch x 45°). The handle knobs are attached to each end of the handle rod. The resulting overall length of the handle with knobs is 5.50". The handle is aligned with the screw so that the outer edge of the upper knob is 2.0" from the central axis of the screw. Material: **Alloy Steel**.

Notes:

Chapter 11
Introduction to Stress Analysis

Learning Objectives

- **Create Simulation Study**
- **Apply Fixtures and Loads**
- **Perform Basic Stress Analysis**
- **View Results**
- **Assess Accuracy of Results**
- **Output the Associated Simulation Video File**

Introduction

In this chapter we will explore basic design analysis using the *Inventor Stress Analysis Module*. The *Stress Analysis Module* is a special module available for part, sheet metal, and assembly documents. The *Stress Analysis Module* has commands unique to its purpose. With Autodesk Inventor 2013, *contact analysis*, *frame analysis* and *dynamic analysis* can also be performed.

Inventor Stress Analysis Module provides a tool for basic stress analysis, allowing the user to examine the effects of applied forces on a design. Displacements, strains and stresses in a part are calculated based on material properties, fixtures, and applied loads. Stress results can be compared to material properties, such as yield strength, to perform failure analysis. The results can also be used to identify critical areas, calculate safety factors at various regions, and simulate deformation. *Inventor Stress Analysis Module* provides an easy-to-use method within the Autodesk Inventor's *Stress Analysis Module* to perform an initial stress analysis. The results can be used to improve the design.

In *Inventor Stress Analysis Module*, stresses are calculated using **linear static analysis** based on the **finite element method**. *Linear static analysis* is appropriate if deflections are small and vary only slowly. *Linear static analysis* omits time as a variable. It also excludes plastic action and deflections that change the way loads are applied. The *finite element method (FEM)* is a numerical method for finding approximate solutions to complex systems. The technique is widely used for the solution of complex problems in engineering mechanics. Analysis using the method is called *finite element analysis (FEA)*.

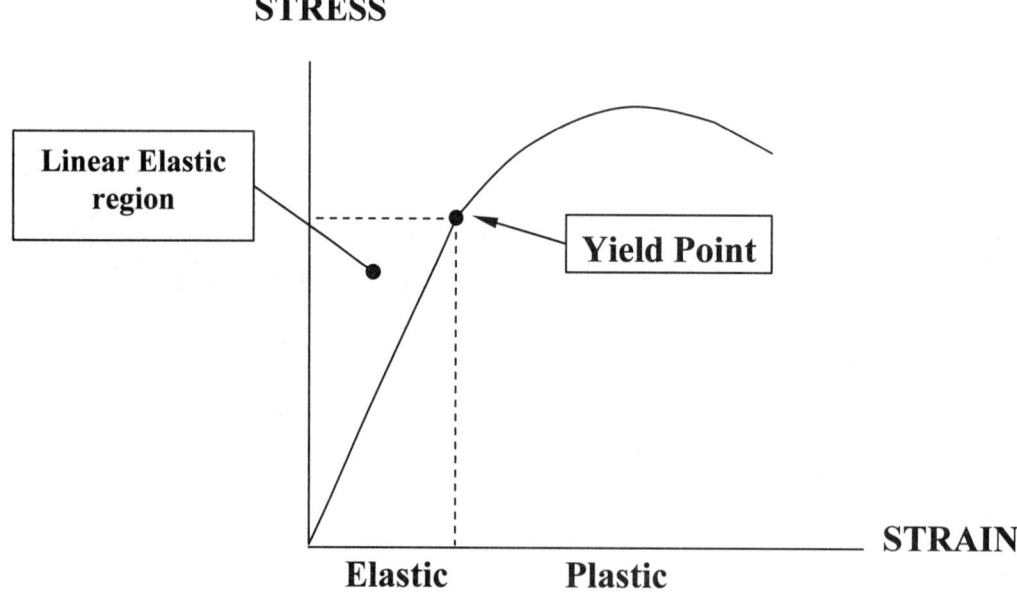

Stress-Strain diagram of typical ductile material

In the finite element method, a complex system is modeled as an equivalent system of smaller bodies of simple shapes, or *elements*, which are interconnected at common points called *nodes*. This process is called *discretization*; an example is shown in the figures below. The mathematical equations for the system are formulated first for each finite element, and the resulting system of equations is solved simultaneously to obtain an approximate solution for the entire system. In general, a better approximation is obtained by increasing the number of elements, which will require more computing time and resources.

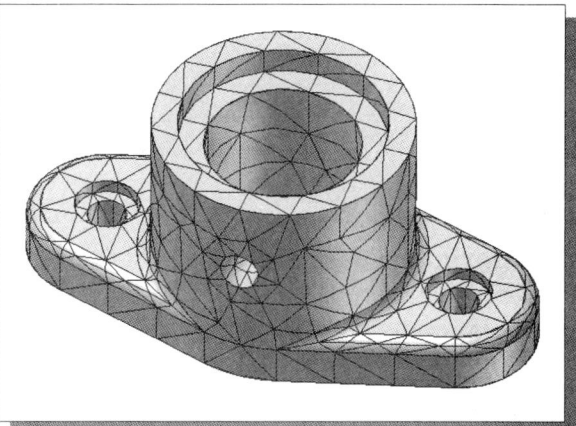

Inventor Stress Analysis Module utilizes tetrahedral elements for which the edges and faces can be curvilinear and which allow the modeling of curved surfaces, as seen in the figure above. The behavior of these elements is analyzed using linear static analysis and the appropriate material properties to relate local coordinate nodal displacements to local forces. The motion of each node is described by displacements in the X, Y, and Z directions, called *degrees of freedom* (DOFs). The equations describing the behavior of each element are assembled into a global system of equations, incorporating compatibility requirements based on connectivity among elements. Using the known material properties, supports, and loads, *Inventor Stress Analysis Module* solves the system of equations for the unknown displacements at each node. These displacements are used in the results stage to calculate strains and stresses.

While *Inventor Stress Analysis Module* is a powerful and easy-to-use tool, it is important to appreciate that it is the designer's responsibility to properly assess the accuracy of the results. A better FEA approximation is generally obtained by increasing the number of elements. An assessment must be made regarding the mesh used to discretize the model to ensure it is adequate. There are other important factors affecting the accuracy of the results. The material properties used in the analysis must accurately characterize the behavior of the material. The supports and loads must be applied in a manner which accurately reflects the actual conditions. Proper meshing and application of boundary conditions often require significant experience in FEA and may require tools and capabilities not available in *Inventor Stress Analysis Module*. *Inventor Stress Analysis Module* is an easy-to-use tool for a quick stress analysis.

Problem Statement

Determine the maximum normal stress that loading produces in the aluminum plate.

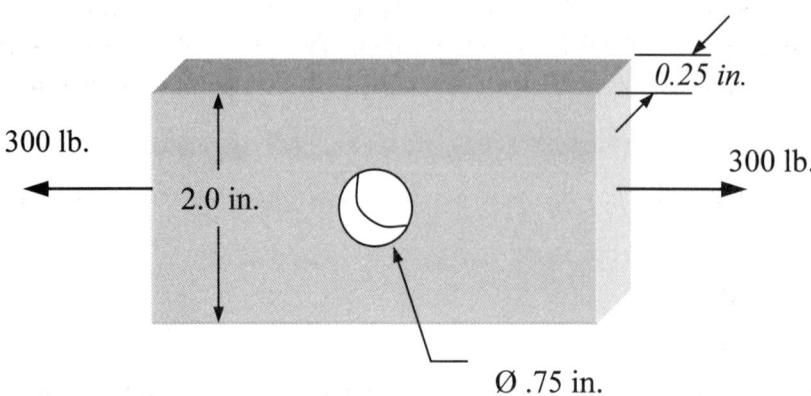

Preliminary Analysis

- **Maximum Normal Stress**

The nominal normal stress developed at the smallest cross section (through the center of the hole) in the plate is

$$\sigma_{nominal} = \frac{P}{A} = \frac{300}{(2 - 0.75) \times .25} = 960 \text{ psi.}$$

Stress Concentration factor K vs. Geometric factor (Hole Diameter / Plate width)

Geometric factor = .75/2 = 0.375

Stress concentration factor K is obtained from the graph, **K = 2.27**

$$\sigma_{MAX} = K\, \sigma_{nominal} = 2.27 \times 960 = 2180 \text{ psi.}$$

- **Maximum Displacement**

    We will also estimate the displacement under the loading condition. For a statically determinant system, the stress results depend mainly on the geometry. The material properties can be in error and still the FEA analysis comes up with the same stresses. However, the displacements always depend on the material properties. Thus, it is necessary to always estimate both the stress and displacement prior to a computer FEA analysis.

    The classic one-dimensional displacement can be used to estimate the displacement of the problem:

    $$\delta = \frac{PL}{EA}$$

    Where P=force, L=length, A=area, E= elastic modulus, and δ = deflection.

    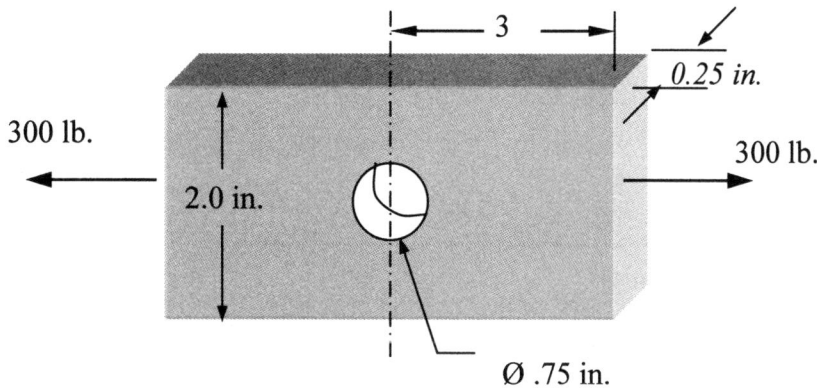

    A lower bound of the displacement of the right edge, measured from the center of the plate, is obtained by using the full area:

    $$\delta_{lower} = \frac{PL}{EA} = \frac{300 \times 3}{10E6 \times (2 \times 0.25)} = 1.8E\text{-}4 \text{ in.}$$

    and an upper bound of the displacement would come from the reduced section:

    $$\delta_{upper} = \frac{PL}{EA} = \frac{300 \times 3}{10E6 \times (1.25 \times 0.25)} = 2.88E\text{-}4 \text{ in.}$$

    but the best estimate is a sum from the two regions:

    $$\delta_{average} = \frac{PL}{EA} = \frac{300 \times 0.375}{10E6 \times (1.25 \times 0.25)} + \frac{300 \times 2.625}{10E6 \times (2.0 \times 0.25)}$$

    $$= 3.6E\text{-}5 + 1.58E\text{-}4 = 1.94E\text{-}4 \text{ in.}$$

Finite Element Analysis Procedure

In the previous section, an approximate preliminary analysis was performed prior to carrying out the finite element analysis; this will help us to gain some insights into the problem and also serves as a means of checking the finite element analysis results.

For a typical linear static analysis problem, the finite element analysis requires the following steps:

1. Preliminary Analysis.

2. Preparation of the finite element model:
   a. Model the problem into finite elements.
   b. Prescribe the geometric and material information of the system.
   c. Prescribe how the system is supported.
   d. Prescribe how the loads are applied to the system.

3. Perform calculations:
   a. Generate a stiffness matrix of each element.
   b. Assemble the individual stiffness matrices to obtain the overall, or global, stiffness matrix.
   c. Solve the global equations and compute displacements, strains, and stresses.

4. Post-processing of the results:
   a. Viewing the stress contours and the displaced shape.
   b. Checking any discrepancy between the preliminary analysis results and the FEA results.

Create the *Autodesk Inventor* Part

1. Select the **Autodesk Inventor** option on the *Start* menu or select the **Autodesk Inventor** icon on the desktop to start *Autodesk Inventor*. The *Autodesk Inventor* main window will appear on the screen.

2. Select the **New File** icon with a single click of the left-mouse-button in the *Launch* toolbar.

3. Select the **English** tab and in the *New File* area, select **Standard(in).ipt**.

4. Pick **OK** in the *New File* dialog box to accept the selected settings.

Create the 2D Sketch for the Plate

1. In the *Sketch* toolbar select the **Create 2D Sketch** command by left-clicking once on the icon.

2. In the *Status Bar* area, the message: "*Select face, workplane, sketch or sketch geometry.*" is displayed. Select the **XY Plane** by clicking the associated item in the graphics area or inside the *Model* history tree window.

3. Select the **Two point rectangle** command by clicking once with the left-mouse-button on the icon in the *Sketch* toolbar.

4. Create a rectangle of arbitrary size positioned near the center of the screen.

5. Select the **Center point circle** command by clicking once with the left-mouse-button on the icon in the *Sketch* toolbar.

6. Create a **circle** of arbitrary size and aligned to the *center point* as shown.

7. Select the **General Dimension** command in the *Constrain* panel.

8. On your own, create and adjust the dimensions of the rectangle and circle as shown. (Hint: Use parametric equations to position the geometry.)

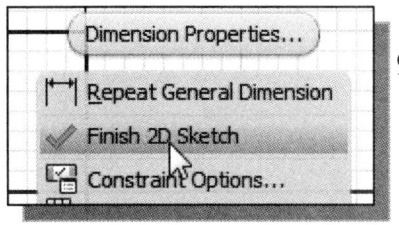

9. Inside the graphics window, click once with the right-mouse-button to display the option menu. Select **Finish 2D Sketch** in the popup menu to end the Sketch option.

10. In the *Part Features* toolbar, select the **Extrude** command by releasing the left-mouse-button on the icon.

11. On your own, create an **Extruded** feature with a thickness of **0.25 in** as shown.

Assigning the Material Properties

1. In the *browser*, **right-mouse-click** once on the *part name* to bring up the option menu, and then pick **iProperties** in the *pop-up* menu.

2. On your own, look at the different information listed in the *iProperties* dialog box.

3. Click on the **Physical** tab; this is the page that contains the physical properties of the selected model.

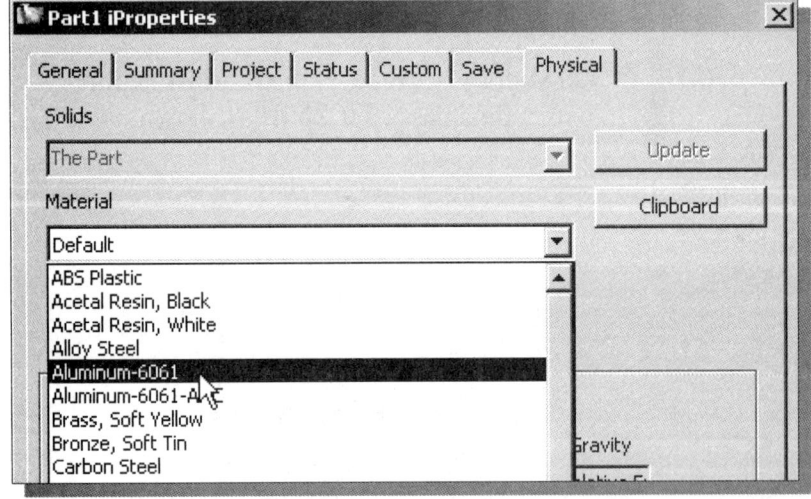

4. Click the down-arrow in the *Material* option to display the material list, and select **Aluminum-6061** as shown.

5. Click **OK** to accept the settings.

6. On your own, save the part with the filename **FEA_Al_Plate.ipt**.

Switch to the *Stress Analysis Module*

1. In the *Ribbon* toolbar, select the **Environments** tab as shown.

2. Click **Stress Analysis** to enter the *Inventor Stress Analysis Module*.

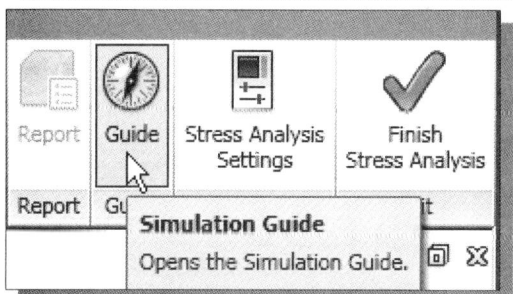

3. Select the **Simulation Guide** in the *Ribbon* toolbar as shown.

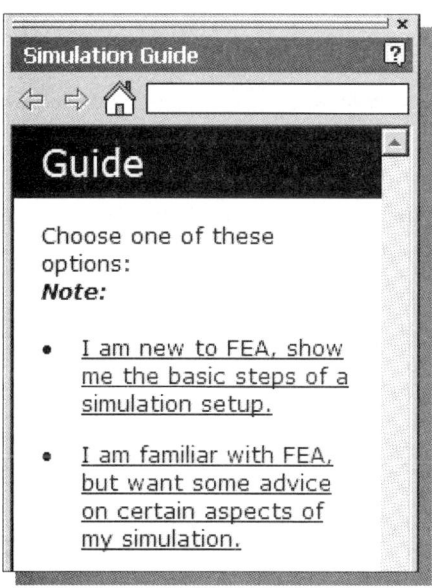

➢ Note the *Simulation Guide* provides an overall view of the *Inventor* FEA procedure. You are encouraged to read through the *Simulation Guide* to get familiar with the general procedure in performing the *Inventor* FEA simulation.

Create an FEA Simulation

1. Click **Create New Simulation** to start a new simulation.

2. Note the default settings include (1) *Simulation Type* set to perform **Static Analysis**, and (2) *Design Objective* set to **Single Point**. These settings are used for basic *linear static analysis*.

3. Click **OK** to accept the default settings.

➢ Notice the *Ribbon* toolbar and the *browser* window, to the left side of the graphics area, now display items associated with the S*tress Analysis Simulation Module*. The list in the *browser* window shows the elements necessary to perform the *Finite Element Stress Analysis*.

Introduction to Stress Analysis 11-13

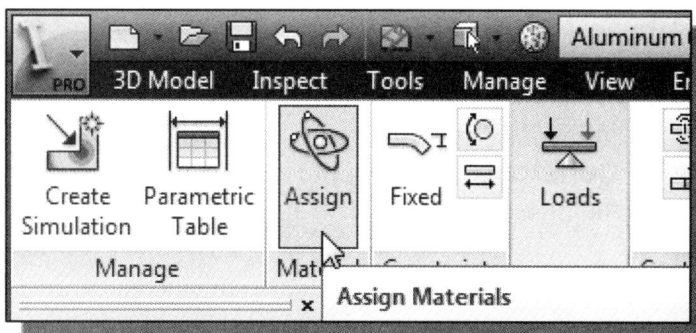

4. In the *Ribbon* toolbar area, select **Assign Materials** to examine the material assignment for the part.

- Note that the assigned material, **Aluminum-6061**, is shown under the *Original Material*; the *Override Material* option is available for us to examine the effects of using different materials.

5. Click **OK** to accept the settings.

- Note that the same command can also be accessed through the *browser* window.

Apply Constraints and Loads

1. In the *Ribbon* toolbar area, select **Fixed Constraint** to assign the support condition of the plate.

2. Click on the **top left corner** of the *ViewCube* to rotate the display; all DOFs to the left end of the plate will be removed, which simulates the end of the plate is clamped.

3. Select the small **vertical surface** of the left-end of the plane as shown.

4. Note the selection of the surface is recognized as the selection label is changed to **Faces**. Click **OK** to accept the selection.

Introduction to Stress Analysis   11-15

5. In the *Ribbon* toolbar area, select the **Force** command as shown.

6. Click on the **Home** icon above the *ViewCube* to reset the display back to the isometric view.

7. Click on the small vertical surface to the right end of the plate. In the *Force* dialog box, enter **300 lbf** as the force value and check the **Reverse Direction** option box. Notice the direction of the force load is now outward.

8. Click **OK** to accept the selection and exit the Force command.

➢ Notice the Fixed constraint and Force load appear in the *browser* window to the left of the graphics area with the default names Constraint:1 and Force:1.

Create a Mesh and Run the Solver

1. In the *Ribbon* toolbar area, select the **Mesh View** command as shown.

- Note that with the default settings, *Inventor Simulation* generated 663 nodes and 293 elements, which is a relatively coarse mesh.

- As a rule in creating the first FEA mesh, start with a relatively small number of elements and progressively move to more refined models. The main objective of the first coarse mesh analysis is to obtain a rough idea of the overall stress distribution. In most cases, use of a complex and/or a very refined FEA model is not justifiable since it most likely provides computational accuracy at the expense of unnecessarily increased processing time.

2. In the *Ribbon* toolbar area, select the **Simulate** command as shown.

Introduction to Stress Analysis   11-17

3. Click the **Run simulation** button to proceed with the FEA simulation.

4. On your own, set the *Visual Style* to **Realistic** for a better viewing of the stress result.

➢ A plot of equivalent stress (Von Mises stress) is generated and displayed in the graphics area. A color-coded scale is used with the associated scale bar displayed at the right. Red represents the regions of highest stress. The maximum stress is 2053 psi, which is well below the yield strength of the material (3999.3 psi), and is located at the stress concentration points at the upper and lower quadrants of the hole.

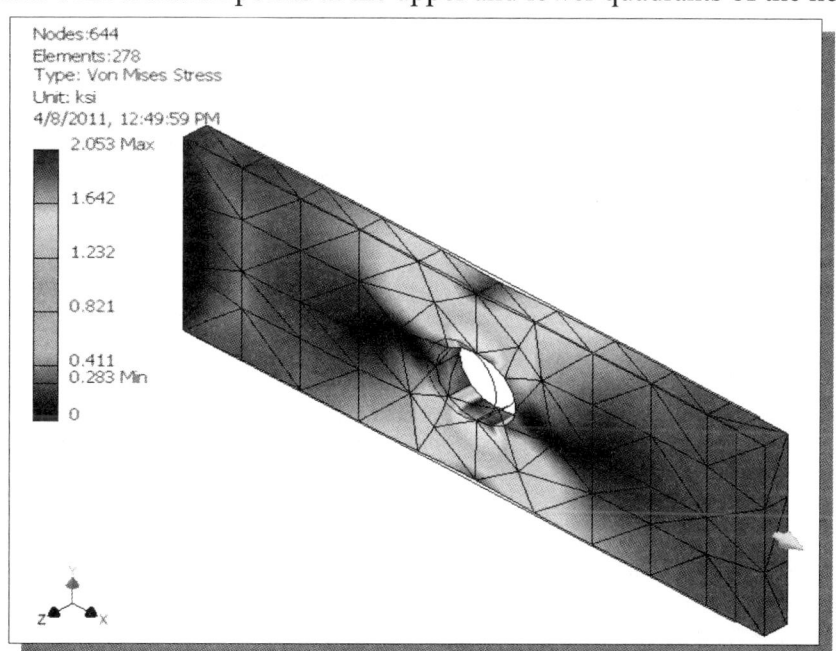

Refinement of the FEA Mesh – Global Element Size

- In order to gain accuracy for complex geometries or to represent a highly varying stress distribution, finer elements must be used. The increase in the number of elements will also increase the solution time and computer disk space. This is why the refinement of mesh around the high stress areas is required. The process of mesh refinement is called convergence analysis. As our first analysis confirmed the stress concentration points at the upper and lower quadrants of the hole, we will next refine the mesh to obtain a more accurate FEA result. One way of refinement is simply to adjust the element size to a smaller value. This can be done through adjusting the **Mesh Settings**.

1. In the *Ribbon* toolbar area, select the **Mesh Settings** command as shown.

2. In the *Mesh Settings* dialog box, adjust the *Average Element Size* to **0.05**, which will create twice as many elements. Note the number is a fraction of the length dimension of the plate.

3. Click **OK** to accept the new settings and exit the **Mesh Settings** command.

Introduction to Stress Analysis   11-19

4. It is necessary to update the mesh with the new settings through the *browser* window. Right-mouse-click on the **Mesh** item to bring up the **option list**.

5. Select **Update Mesh** in the option list to activate the mesh update.

• Note that with the new settings, *Inventor Simulation* generated 1946 nodes and 904 elements, which is almost three times more than the original coarse mesh.

6. On your own, perform the FEA analysis.

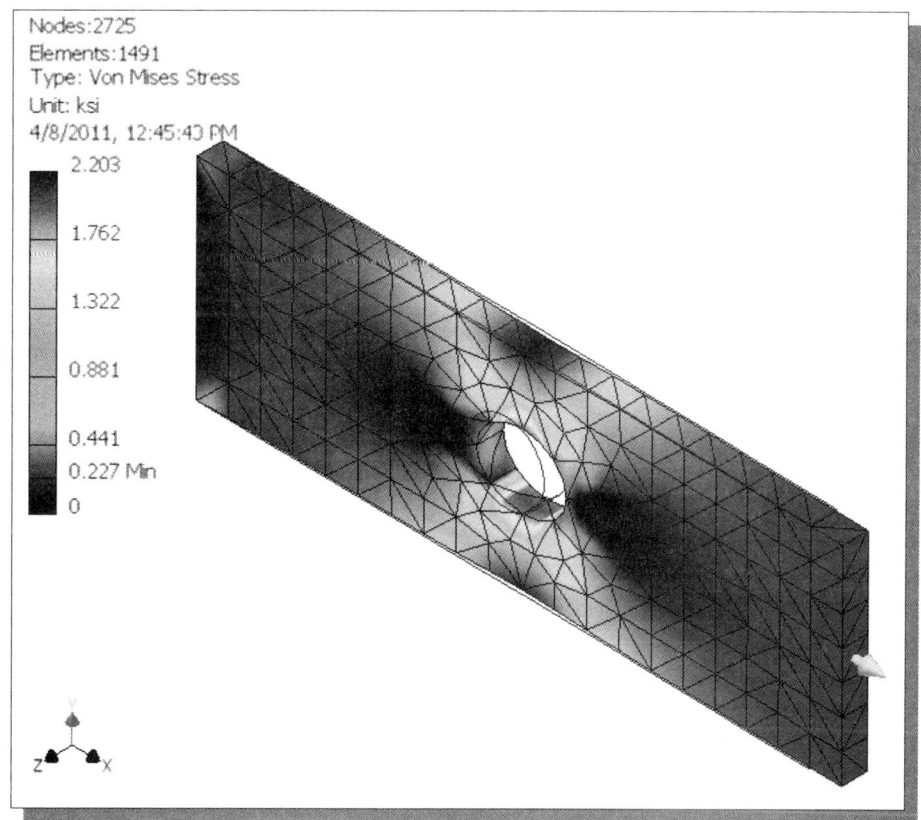

➢ The maximum stress with the refinement is now 2203 psi, which is higher than the first analysis, and much closer to the preliminary analysis. Next, we will further refine the mesh in the high stress area.

Refinement of the FEA Mesh – Local Element Size

1. In the *Ribbon* toolbar area, click the **Mesh View** icon to toggle *OFF* the mesh display as shown.

2. In the *Ribbon* toolbar area, select the **Local Mesh Control** command as shown.

3. Select the **inside cylindrical surface** of the hole as shown.

4. Set the local *Element Size* to **0.1** as shown.

5. Click **OK** to accept the new setting and exit the Local Mesh Control command.

6. On your own, activate the **Update Mesh** command as shown.

Introduction to Stress Analysis 11-21

- Note that with the new settings, *Inventor Simulation* generated 4370 nodes and 2402 elements, which is about seven times the original coarse mesh.

7. On your own, perform the FEA analysis.

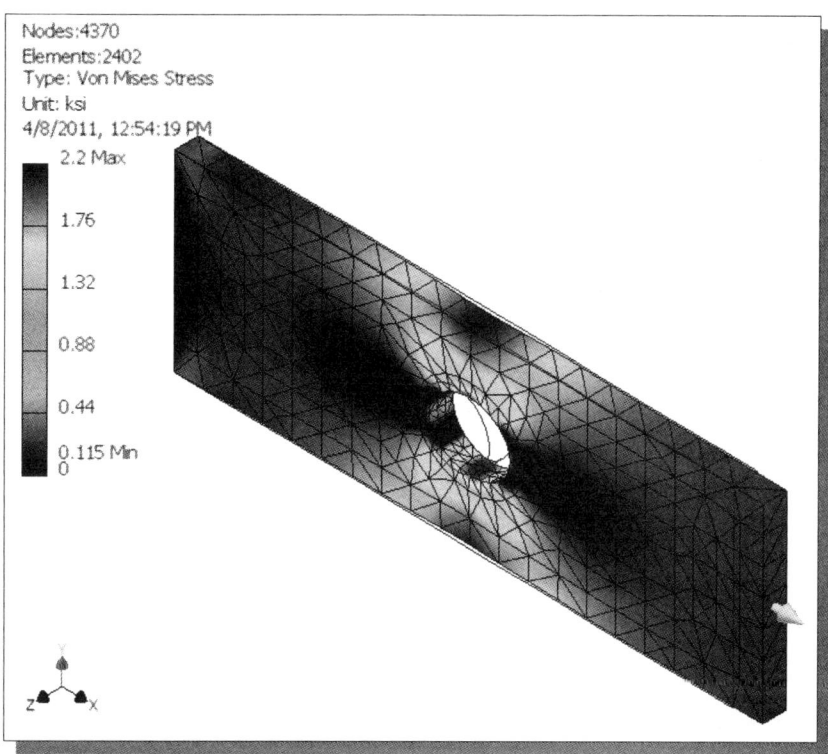

- The maximum stress with the refinement is now 2200 psi, which is just a bit higher than the second analysis. The refinement caused only a small difference compared to the previous mesh.

8. On your own, adjust the element size to **0.05** of the **Local Mesh Control** value as shown.

9. On your own, perform another FEA with the current settings.

10. Double-click on the **Displacement** item in the *browser* window to display the displacement of the plate.

- The FEA result showed the total displacement of 4.058e-4 inch, which matches quite well with the 3.88e-4 inch preliminary analysis calculation.

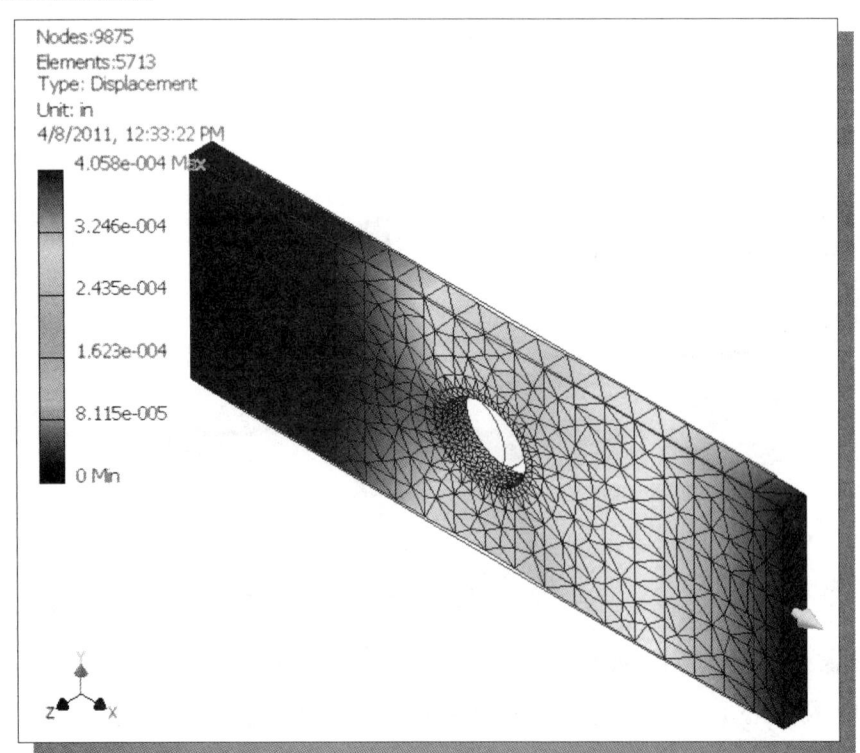

Comparison of Results

The accuracy of the *Inventor Simulation* results for this problem can be checked by comparing them to the analytical results presented earlier. In the **Preliminary Analysis** section, the maximum stress was calculated using a stress concentration factor and the value obtained was **2180 psi**. One should realize the analytical result is obtained through the use of charts from empirical data and therefore involves some degrees of error. The maximum stress obtained by finite element analysis using *Inventor Simulation* ranges from **2053** to **2203 psi**. In the Preliminary Analysis section, the maximum displacement was also estimated to be around **1.94E-4 inches**, measured from the center of the hole to one end of the plate. The maximum displacement obtained by finite element analysis using *Inventor Simulation* was around **2.0295E-4 inches**. The agreement between the analytical results and those from *Inventor Simulation* demonstrate the potential of *Inventor Simulation* as a very powerful design tool.

In FEA, the process of mesh refinement is called convergence analysis. For our analysis, the refinement of the mesh does show the FEA results converging near the analytical results. The refinement to the third mesh is quite adequate for our analysis. Any further refinement does not provide any additional insight and is therefore not necessary.

Number of Elements	σ_{max} (psi)	D_{max} (in)
278	2053	2.0215e-4
1491	2203	2.0275e-4
2402	2200	2.0280e-4
5713	2199	2.0295e-4

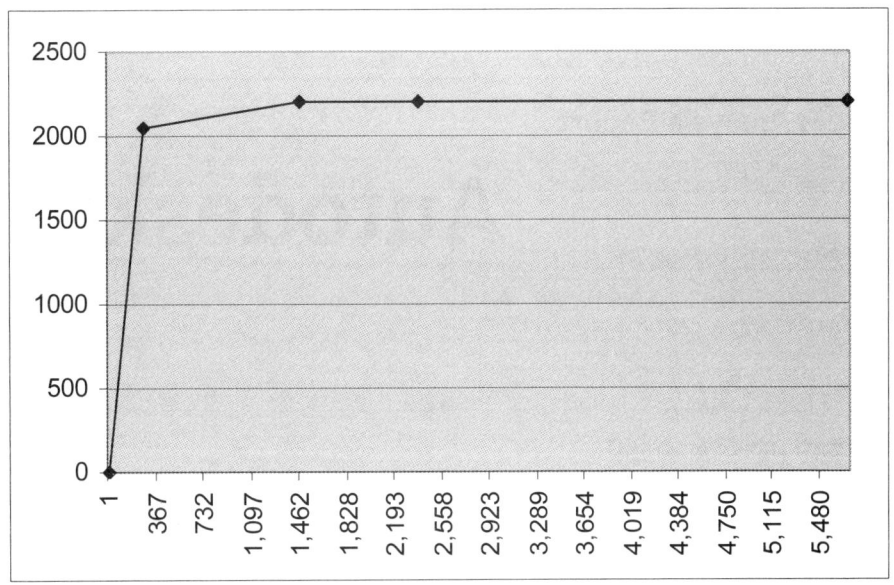

Create an HTML Report

- *Inventor Stress Analysis Simulation* module also includes options to create a report in HTML format which contains data related to the simulation.

1. Select the **Report** option as shown.

2. On your own, examine the different options available for the report. Click **OK** to generate a report.

➢ *Inventor Stress Analysis Environment* will create an HTML file and automatically open it in your default Web browser. The HTML file is saved in the location shown in the *File Information* section at the beginning of the report.

3. On your own, read through the report. Notice that all the relevant data are recorded.

Geometric Considerations of Finite Elements

In the previous sections, the entire plate was created and analyzed, but a closer examination of the associated geometry suggests a more effective approach can be used to analyze the plate.

For *linear statics analysis*, designs with symmetrical features can often be reduced to expedite the analysis.

For our plate problem, there are two planes of symmetry. Thus, we only need to create an FE model that is one-fourth of the actual system. By taking advantage of symmetry, we can use a finer subdivision of elements that will provide more accurate and faster results.

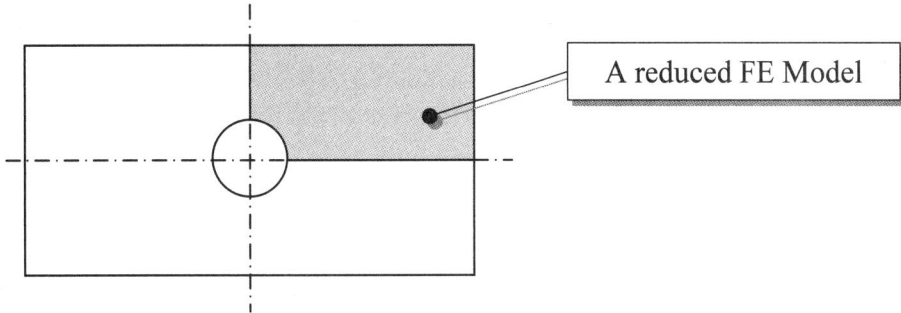

A reduced FE Model

In performing a stress analysis, it is necessary to consider the constraints in all directions. For our plate model, deformations will occur along the axes of symmetry; we will therefore place roller constraints along the two center lines as shown in the figure below. You are encouraged to perform the FEA on this more simplified model and compare the results obtained in the previous sections.

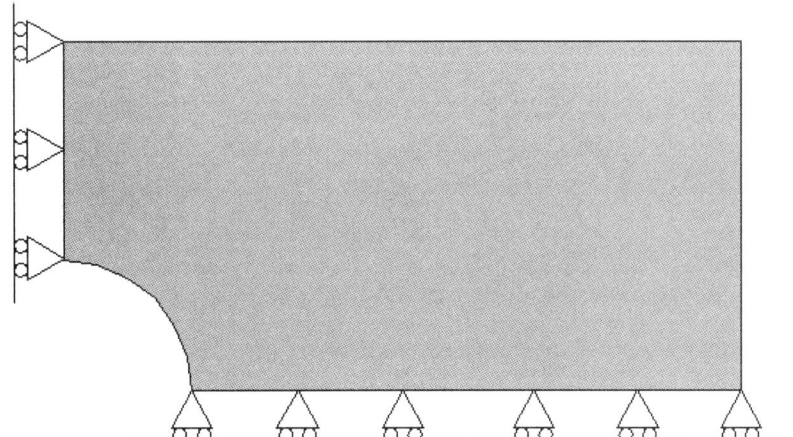

❖ One should also be cautious of using symmetrical characteristics in FEA. The symmetry characteristics of boundary conditions and loads should be considered. Also, note the symmetry characteristic that is used in *linear statics analysis* does not imply similar symmetrical results in vibration or buckling modes.

Conclusion

Design includes all activities involved from the original conception to the finished product. Design is the process by which products are created and modified. For many years designers sought ways to describe and analyze three-dimensional designs without building physical models. With advancements in computer technology, the creation of parametric models on computers offers a wide range of benefits. Parametric models are easier to interpret and can be easily altered. Parametric models can be analyzed using finite element analysis software, and simulation of real-life loads can be applied to the models and the results graphically displayed.

Throughout this text, various modeling techniques have been presented. Mastering these techniques will enable you to create intelligent and flexible solid models. The goal is to make use of the tools provided by *Autodesk Inventor* and to successfully capture the **DESIGN INTENT** of the product. In many instances, only one approach to the modeling tasks was presented; you are encouraged to repeat all of the lessons and develop different ways of accomplishing the same tasks. We have only scratched the surface of *Autodesk Inventor*'s functionality. The more time you spend using the system, the easier it will be to perform parametric modeling with *Autodesk Inventor*.

Summary of Modeling Considerations

- **Design Intent** – determine the functionality of the design; select features that are central to the design.

- **Order of Features** – consider the parent/child relationships necessary for all features.

- **Dimensional and Geometric Constraints** – the way in which the constraints are applied determines how the components are updated.

- **Relations** – consider the orientation and parametric relationships required between features and in an assembly.

Questions:

1. Describe the required steps in performing a stress analysis using *Inventor Stress Analysis Environment*.

2. Describe two ways the material properties can be defined or edited.

3. What is meant by the term *Constraints* in *Inventor Stress Analysis Module*?

4. How do we control whether a load applied to a face is in the *outward* or *inward* direction?

5. Define *degrees of freedom* (DOF).

6. How do we end the *Inventor Stress Analysis Module* and return to the model in *Autodesk Inventor*?

Exercises:

1. The shaft shown below is fixed at the large end and a 50 kN force is applied to the small end. Find the maximum stress and maximum deflection in the shaft. The material is AISI 1020. (Dimensions in mm).

2. For the hanging bracket, the top face is fixed and a 100 psi pressure load is applied to the horizontal surface as shown. Find the maximum stress and maximum deflection in the bracket. The material is Alloy Steel. (Dimensions in inches).

AutoCAD 2013
Tutorial

2D Fundamentals

Chapter 12
Getting Started

Learning Objectives

- **Development of Computer Aided Design**
- **Why use AutoCAD 2013?**
- **Getting started with AutoCAD 2013**
- **The AutoCAD Startup dialog box and Units setup**
- **AutoCAD 2013 screen layout**
- **Mouse buttons**

Introduction

Computer Aided Design (CAD) is the process of doing designs with the aid of computers. This includes the generation of computer models, analysis of design data, and the creation of the necessary drawings. **AutoCAD® 2013** is a computer aided design software developed by *Autodesk Inc*. The **AutoCAD® 2013** software is a tool that can be used for design and drafting activities. The two-dimensional and three-dimensional models created in **AutoCAD® 2013** can be transferred to other computer programs for further analysis and testing. The computer models can also be used in manufacturing equipment such as machining centers, lathes, mills, or rapid prototyping machines to manufacture the product.

The rapid changes in the field of **computer aided engineering** (CAE) have brought exciting advances in industry. Recent advances have made the long-sought goal of reducing design time, producing prototypes faster, and achieving higher product quality closer to a reality.

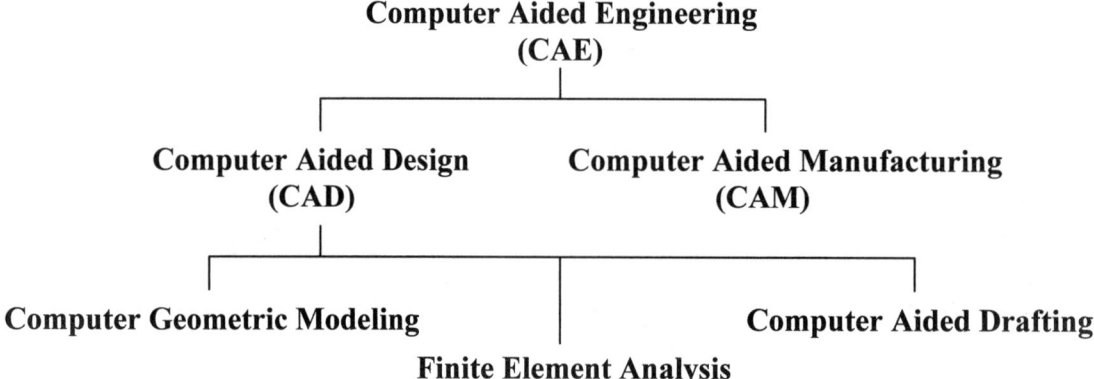

Development of Computer Geometric Modeling

Computer Aided Design is a relatively new technology and its rapid expansion in the last fifty years is truly amazing. Computer modeling technology advanced along with the development of computer hardware. The first generation CAD programs, developed in the 1950s, were mostly non-interactive; CAD users were required to create program codes to generate the desired two-dimensional (2D) geometric shapes. Initially, the development of CAD technology occurred mostly in academic research facilities. The Massachusetts Institute of Technology, Carnegie-Mellon University, and Cambridge University were the lead pioneers at that time. The interest in CAD technology spread quickly and several major industry companies, such as General Motors, Lockheed, McDonnell, IBM, and Ford Motor Co., participated in the development of interactive CAD programs in the 1960s. Usage of CAD systems was primarily in the automotive industry, aerospace industry, and government agencies that developed their own programs for their specific needs. The 1960s also marked the beginning of the development of finite element analysis methods for computer stress analysis and computer aided manufacturing for generating machine tool paths.

The 1970s are generally viewed as the years of the most significant progress in the development of computer hardware, namely the invention and development of **microprocessors**. With the improvement in computing power, new types of 3D CAD programs that were user-friendly and interactive became reality. CAD technology quickly expanded from very simple **computer aided drafting** to very complex **computer aided design**. The use of 2D and 3D wireframe modelers was accepted as the leading edge technology that could increase productivity in industry. The developments of surface modeling and solid modeling technology were taking shape by the late 1970s; but the high cost of computer hardware and programming slowed the development of such technology. During this time period, the available CAD systems all required extremely expensive room-sized mainframe computers.

In the 1980s, improvements in computer hardware brought the power of mainframes to the desktop at less cost and with more accessibility to the general public. By the mid-1980s, CAD technology had become the main focus of a variety of manufacturing industries and was very competitive with traditional design/drafting methods. It was during this period of time that 3D solid modeling technology had major advancements, which boosted the usage of CAE technology in industry.

In the 1990s, CAD programs evolved into powerful design/manufacturing/management tools. CAD technology has come a long way, and during these years of development, modeling schemes progressed from two-dimensional (2D) wireframe to three-dimensional (3D) wireframe, to surface modeling, to solid modeling and, finally, to feature-based parametric solid modeling.

The first generation CAD packages were simply 2D **Computer Aided Drafting** programs, basically the electronic equivalents of the drafting board. For typical models, the use of this type of program would require that several to many views of the objects be created individually as they would be on the drafting board. The 3D designs remained in the designer's mind, not in the computer database. The mental translation of 3D objects to 2D views is required throughout the use of the packages. Although such systems have some advantages over traditional board drafting, they are still tedious and labor intensive. The need for the development of 3D modelers came quite naturally, given the limitations of the 2D drafting packages.

The development of the 3D wireframe modeler was a major leap in the area of computer modeling. The computer database in the 3D wireframe modeler contains the locations of all the points in space coordinates and it is sufficient to create just one model rather than multiple models. This single 3D model can then be viewed from any direction as needed. The 3D wireframe modelers require the least computer power and achieve reasonably good representation of 3D models. But because surface definition is not part of a wireframe model, all wireframe images have the inherent problem of ambiguity.

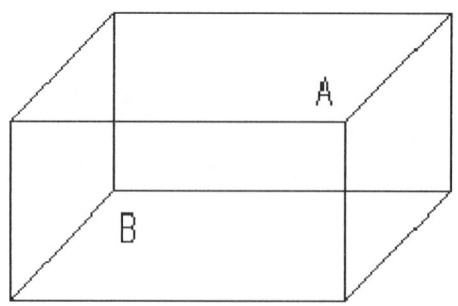

Wireframe Ambiguity: Which corner is in front, A or B?

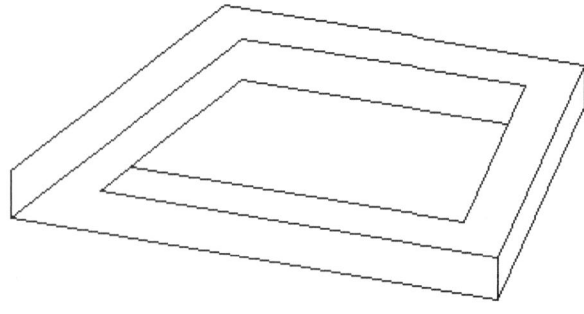

A non-realizable object: Wireframe models contain no surface definitions.

Surface modeling is the logical development in computer geometry modeling to follow the 3D wireframe modeling scheme by organizing and grouping edges that define polygonal surfaces. Surface modeling describes the part's surfaces but not its interiors. Designers are still required to interactively examine surface models to insure that the various surfaces on a model are contiguous throughout. Many of the concepts used in 3D wireframe and surface modelers are incorporated in the solid modeling scheme, but it is solid modeling that offers the most advantages as a design tool.

In the solid modeling presentation scheme, the solid definitions include nodes, edges, and surfaces, and it is a complete and unambiguous mathematical representation of a precisely enclosed and filled volume. Unlike the surface modeling method, solid modelers start with a solid or use topology rules to guarantee that all of the surfaces are stitched together properly. Two predominant methods for representing solid models are **constructive solid geometry** (CSG) representation and **boundary representation** (B-rep).

The CSG representation method can be defined as the combination of 3D solid primitives. What constitutes a "primitive" varies somewhat with the software but typically includes a rectangular prism, a cylinder, a cone, a wedge, and a sphere. Most solid modelers allow the user to define additional primitives, which can be very complex.

In the B-rep representation method, objects are represented in terms of their spatial boundaries. This method defines the points, edges, and surfaces of a volume, and/or issues commands that sweep or rotate a defined face into a third dimension to form a solid. The object is then made up of the unions of these surfaces that completely and precisely enclose a volume.

By the 1990s, a new paradigm called *concurrent engineering* had emerged. With concurrent engineering, designers, design engineers, analysts, manufacturing engineers, and management engineers all work closely right from the initial stages of the design. In this way, all aspects of the design can be evaluated and any potential problems can be identified right from the start and throughout the design process. Using the principles of concurrent engineering, a new type of computer modeling technique appeared. The technique is known as the *feature-based parametric modeling technique*. The key advantage of the *feature-based parametric modeling technique* is its capability to produce very flexible designs. Changes can be made easily and design alternatives can be evaluated with minimum effort. Various software packages offer different approaches to feature-based parametric modeling, yet the end result is a flexible design defined by its design variables and parametric features.

In this text, we will concentrate on creating designs using two-dimensional geometric construction techniques. The fundamental concepts and use of different **AutoCAD® 2013** commands are presented using step-by-step tutorials. We will begin with creating simple geometric entities and then move toward creating detailed working drawings and assembly drawings. The techniques presented in this text will also serve as the foundation for entering the world of three-dimensional solid modeling using packages such as **AutoCAD Mechanical Desktop, AutoCAD Architecture** and **Autodesk Inventor**.

Why use AutoCAD® 2013?

AutoCAD® was first introduced to the public in late 1982, and was one of the first CAD software products that were available for personal computers. Since 1984, **AutoCAD®** has established a reputation for being the most widely used PC-based CAD software around the world. By 2007, it was estimated that there were over 6 million **AutoCAD®** users in more than 150 countries worldwide. **AutoCAD® 2013** is the twenty-sixth release, with many added features and enhancements, of the original **AutoCAD®** software produced by *Autodesk Inc*.

CAD provides us with a wide range of benefits; in most cases, the result of using CAD is increased accuracy and productivity. First of all, the computer offers much higher accuracy than the traditional methods of drafting and design. Traditionally, drafting and detailing are the most expensive cost element in a project and the biggest bottleneck. With CAD systems, such as **AutoCAD® 2013**, the tedious drafting and detailing tasks are simplified through the use of many of the CAD geometric construction tools, such as *grids*, *snap*, *trim*, and *auto-dimensioning*. Dimensions and notes are always legible in CAD drawings, and in most cases, CAD systems can produce higher quality prints compared to traditional hand drawings.

CAD also offers much-needed flexibility in design and drafting. A CAD model generated on a computer consists of numeric data that describe the geometry of the object. This allows the designers and clients to see something tangible and to interpret the ramifications of the design. In many cases, it is also possible to simulate operating conditions on the computer and observe the results. Any kind of geometric shape stored in the database can be easily duplicated. For large and complex designs and drawings, particularly those involving similar shapes and repetitive operations, CAD approaches are very efficient and effective. Because computer designs and models can be altered easily, a multitude of design options can be examined and presented to a client before any construction or manufacturing actually takes place. Making changes to a CAD model is generally much faster than making changes to a traditional hand drawing. Only the affected components of the design need to be modified and the drawings can be plotted again. In addition, the greatest benefit is that, once the CAD model is created, it can be used over and over again. The CAD models can also be transferred into manufacturing equipment such as machining centers, lathes, mills, or rapid prototyping machines to manufacture the product directly.

CAD, however, does not replace every design activity. CAD may help, but it does not replace the designer's experience with geometry and graphical conventions and standards for the specific field. CAD is a powerful tool, but the use of this tool does not guarantee correct results; the designer is still responsible for using good design practice and applying good judgment. CAD will supplement these skills to ensure that the best design is obtained.

CAD designs and drawings are stored in binary form, usually as CAD files, to magnetic devices such as diskettes and hard disks. The information stored in CAD files usually requires much less physical space in comparison to traditional hand drawings. However, the information stored inside the computer is not indestructible. On the contrary, the electronic format of information is very fragile and sensitive to the environment. Heat or cold can damage the information stored on magnetic storage devices. A power failure while you are creating a design could wipe out the many hours you spent working in front of the computer monitor. It is a good habit to save your work periodically, just in case something might go wrong while you are working on your design. In general, one should save one's work onto a storage device at an interval of every 15 to 20 minutes. You should also save your work before you make any major modifications to the design. It is also a good habit to periodically make backup copies of your work and put them in a safe place.

Getting started with AutoCAD® 2013

How to start **AutoCAD® 2013** depends on the type of workstation and the particular software configuration you are using. With most *Windows* systems, you may select the **AutoCAD 2013** option on the *Start* menu or select the **AutoCAD 2013** icon on the *Desktop*. Consult with your instructor or technical support personnel if you have difficulty starting the software.

The program takes a while to load, so be patient. Eventually the **AutoCAD® 2013** main *drawing screen* will appear on the screen. The tutorials in this text are based on the assumption that you are using **AutoCAD® 2013**'s default settings. If your system has been customized for other uses, some of the settings may not work with the step-by-step instructions in the tutorials. Contact your instructor and/or technical support personnel to restore the default software configuration.

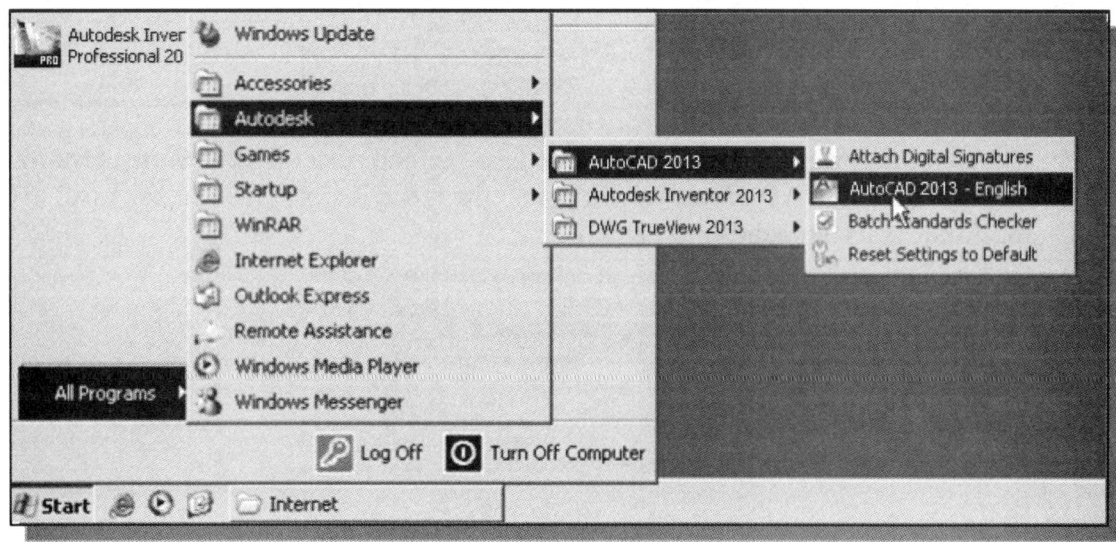

AutoCAD® 2013 Screen Layout

The default **AutoCAD® 2013** *drawing screen* contains the *pull-down* menus, the *Standard* toolbar, the *InfoCenter Help system,* the *scrollbars,* the *command prompt area*, the *Status Bar*, and the *Ribbon Tabs* and *Panels* that contains several *control panels* such as the *Draw and Modify* panel and the *Annotation* panel. You may resize the **AutoCAD® 2013** drawing window by click and drag at the edges of the window, or relocate the window by click and drag at the window title area.

[Screen layout diagram with labels: Application Menu, Quick Access Toolbar, InfoCenter, Ribbon Tabs and Panels, Graphics Window, Graphics Cursor, ViewCube and Navigation Toolbar, Command Line area, Cursor Coordinates Display, Status Bar, Assorted Quick Access Toolbars]

❖ Click on the down-arrow in the *Quick Access* bar and select **Show Menu Bar** to display the **AutoCAD** *Menu* bar. Note that the menu bar provides access to all of the AutoCAD commands.

- **Application Menu**

The *Application Menu* at the top of the main window contains commonly used file operations.

- **Workspace Switching**

The Workspace Switching icon allows us to switch between different system settings.

- **Quick Access Toolbar**

The *Quick Access* toolbar at the top of the *AutoCAD* window allows us quick access to frequently used commands, such as **Qnew, Open, Save** and also the **Undo** command. Note that we can customize the quick access toolbar by adding and removing sets of options or individual commands.

- **AutoCAD Menu Bar**

The *Menu* bar is the pull-down menu where all operations of AutoCAD can be accessed.

- **Graphics Window**
  The *graphics window* is the area where models and drawings are displayed.

- **Graphics Cursor or Crosshairs**

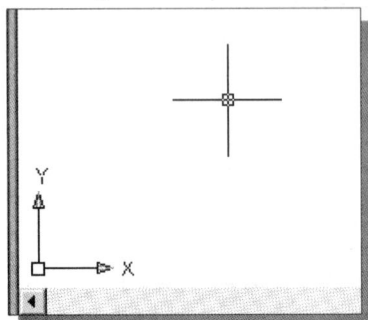

  The *graphics cursor*, or *crosshairs*, shows the location of the pointing device in the graphics window. The coordinates of the cursor are displayed at the bottom of the screen layout. The cursor's appearance depends on the selected command or option.

- **Command Prompt Area**

  The bottom section of the screen layout provides status information for an operation and it is also the area for data input.

- **Cursor Coordinates**

  The bottom left section of the screen layout displays the coordinate information of the cursor.

- **Status Toolbar**

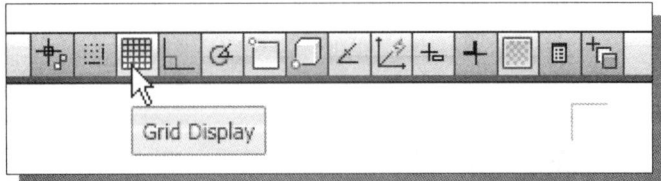

  Next to the cursor coordinate display is the *Status* toolbar, showing the status of several commonly used display and construction options.

- **Ribbon Tabs and Panels**
  The top section of the screen layout contains customizable icon panels, which contain groups of buttons that allow us to pick commands quickly, without searching through a menu structure. These panels allow us to quickly access the commonly used commands available in AutoCAD.

Getting Started 12-11

- **Draw and Modify Toolbar Panels**
  The *Draw* and *Modify* toolbar panels contain icons for basic draw and modify commands.

- **Layers Control Toolbar Panel**

The *Layers Control* toolbar panel contains tools to help manipulate the properties of graphical objects.

- **Annotation Toolbar Panel**

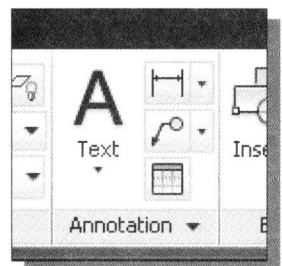

The *Annotation* toolbar panel contains tools for creating and editing dimensions.

- **Layout/Model Toolbar**

The *Layout/Model* toolbar contains tools for creating and editing layouts.

- **Viewport/View/Display Controls**

The *Viewport/View/Display controls panel* is located at the upper left corner of the graphics area and it can be used to quickly access viewing related commands, such as **Viewport** and **Display style**.

Mouse Buttons

AutoCAD® 2013 utilizes the mouse buttons extensively. In learning **AutoCAD® 2013**'s interactive environment, it is important to understand the basic functions of the mouse buttons. It is highly recommended that you use a mouse or a tablet with **AutoCAD® 2013** since the package uses the buttons for various functions.

- **Left mouse button**
  The **left-mouse-button** is used for most operations, such as selecting menus and icons, or picking graphic entities. One click of the button is used to select icons, menus and form entries, and to pick graphic items.

- **Right mouse button**
  The **right-mouse-button** is used to bring up additional available options. The software also utilizes the **right-mouse-button** as the same as the **ENTER** key, and is often used to accept the default setting to a prompt or to end a process.

- **Middle mouse button/wheel**
  The middle mouse button/wheel can be used to Pan (hold down the wheel button and drag the mouse) or Zoom (rotate the wheel) realtime.

[Esc] – Canceling commands

The [**Esc**] key is used to cancel a command in **AutoCAD® 2013**. The [**Esc**] key is located near the top-left corner of the keyboard. Sometimes, it may be necessary to press the [**Esc**] key twice to cancel a command; it depends on where we are in the command sequence. For some commands, the [**Esc**] key is used to exit the command.

On-Line Help

❖ Several types of on-line help are available at any time during an **AutoCAD® 2013** session. The **AutoCAD® 2013** software provides many on-line help options:

- **Autodesk Exchange**:
  Autodesk Exchange is a central portal in AutoCAD 2013; AutoCAD Exchange provides a user interface for Help, learning aids, tips and tricks, videos, and downloadable apps. By default, *Autodesk Exchange* is displayed at **startup**. This allows access to a dynamic selection of tools from the *Autodesk community*, note that internet connection is required to use this option.

- To use *Autodesk Exchange*, simply type in a question in the *input box* to search through the Autodesk's *Help* system as shown in the above figure.

- A list of the search options appears in the *Autodesk Exchange* window; and we can determine the level and type of searches of the associated information.

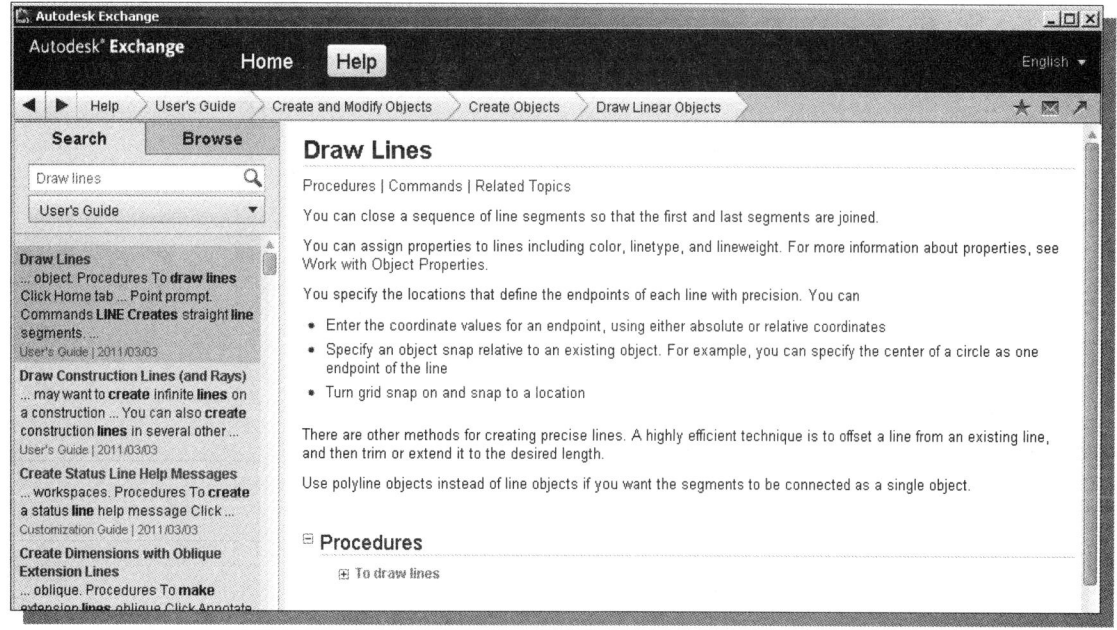

Leaving AutoCAD® 2013

➢ To leave **AutoCAD® 2013**, use the left-mouse-button and click the **Application Menu** button at the top left corner of the **AutoCAD® 2013** screen window, then choose **Exit AutoCAD** from the pull-down menu or type **QUIT** in the command prompt area.

Creating a CAD file folder

❖ It is a good practice to create a separate folder to store your CAD files. You should not save your CAD files in the same folder where the **AutoCAD® 2013** application is located. It is much easier to organize and backup your project files if they are in a separate folder. Making folders within this folder for different types of projects will help you organize your CAD files even further. When creating CAD files in **AutoCAD® 2013**, it is strongly recommended that you *save* your CAD files on the hard drive.

➢ To create a new folder in the *Microsoft Windows* environment:

1. In *My Computer*, or start the **Windows Explorer** under the *Start* menu, open the folder in which you want to create a new folder.

2. On the **File** menu, point to **New**, and then click **Folder**. The new folder appears with a temporary name.

3. Type a name for the new folder, and then press **ENTER**.

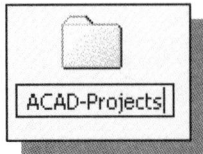

Chapter 13
AutoCAD Fundamentals

Learning Objectives

- Create and Save AutoCAD drawing files
- Use the AutoCAD visual reference commands
- Draw, using the LINE and CIRCLE commands
- Use the ERASE command
- Define Positions using the Basic Entry methods
- Use the AutoCAD Pan Realtime option

Introduction

Learning to use a CAD system is similar to learning a new language. It is necessary to begin with the basic alphabet and learn how to use it correctly and effectively through practice. This will require learning some new concepts and skills as well as learning a different vocabulary. Today, the majority of the Mechanical CAD systems are capable of creating three-dimensional solid models. Nonetheless, all CAD systems create designs using basic geometric entities and many of the constructions used in technical designs are based upon two-dimensional planar geometry. The method and number of operations that are required to accomplish the basic planar constructions are different from one system to another.

In order to become effective and efficient in using a CAD system, we must learn to create geometric entities quickly and accurately. In learning to use a CAD system, **lines** and **circles** are the first two, and perhaps the most important two, geometric entities that one should master the skills of creating and modifying. Straight lines and circles are used in almost all technical designs. In examining the different types of planar geometric entities, the importance of lines and circles becomes obvious. Triangles and polygons are planar figures bounded by straight lines. Ellipses and splines can be constructed by connecting arcs with different radii. As one gains some experience in creating lines and circles, similar procedures can be applied to create other geometric entities. In this chapter, the different ways of creating lines and circles in **AutoCAD® 2013** are examined.

Starting Up AutoCAD® 2013

1. Select the **AutoCAD 2013** option on the *Program* menu or select the **AutoCAD 2013** icon on the *Desktop*.

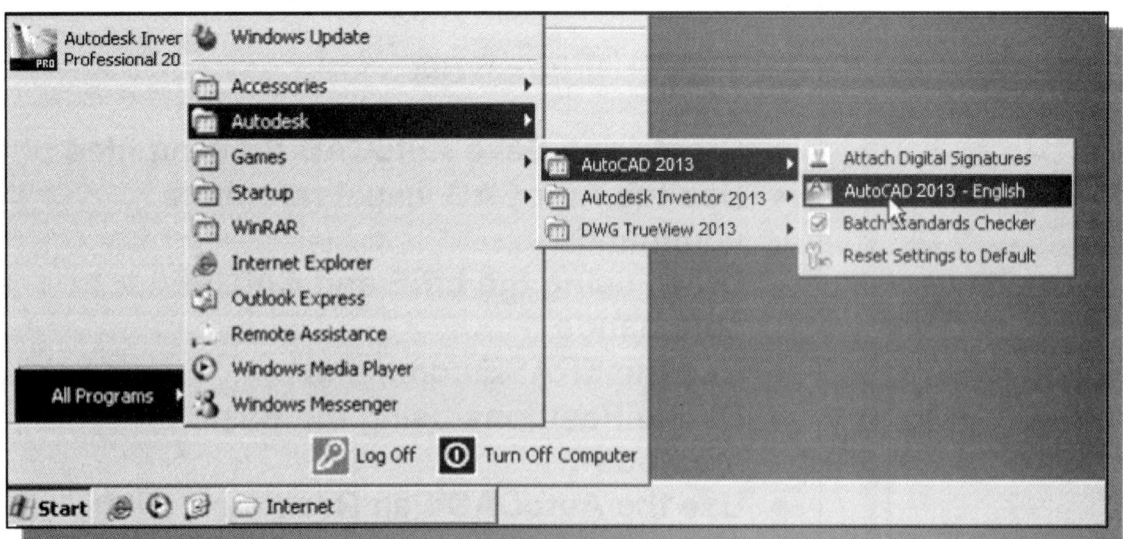

❖ Once the program is loaded into memory, the **AutoCAD® 2013** drawing screen will appear on the screen.

AutoCAD Fundamentals **13-3**

> Note that AutoCAD automatically assigns generic name, *Drawing X*, as new drawings are created. In our example, AutoCAD opened the graphics window using the default system units and assigned the drawing name *Drawing1*.

2. If necessary, click on the down-arrow in the *Quick Access* bar and select **Show Menu** to display the **AutoCAD** *Menu Bar*. The *Menu Bar* provides access to all AutoCAD commands.

Drawing Units Setup

> Every object we construct in a CAD system is measured in **units**. We should determine the system of units within the CAD system before creating the first geometric entities.

1. In the *Menu Bar* select:
   [Format] → **[Units]**

- The AutoCAD *Menu Bar* contains multiple pull-down menus, where all of the AutoCAD commands can be accessed. Note that many of the menu items listed in the pull-down menus can also be accessed through the *Quick Access* toolbar and/or *Ribbon* panels.

2. Click on the *Length Type* option to display the different types of length units available. Confirm the *Length Type* is set to **Decimal**.

3. On your own, examine the other settings that are available.

4. In the *Drawing Units* dialog box, set the *Length Type* to **Decimal**. This will set the measurement to the default *English* units, inches.

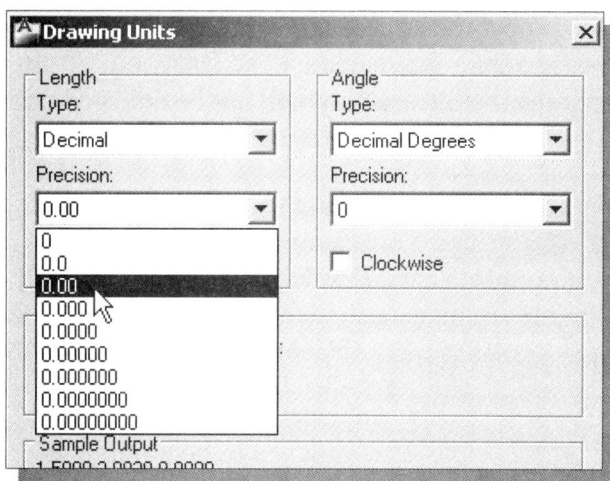

5. Set the *Precision* to **two digits** after the decimal point as shown in the above figure.

6. Pick **OK** to exit the *Drawing Units* dialog box.

Drawing Area Setup

❖ Next, we will set up the **Drawing Limits** by entering a command in the command prompt area. Setting the Drawing Limits controls the extents of the display of the *grid*. It also serves as a visual reference that marks the working area. It can also be used to prevent construction outside the grid limits and as a plot option that defines an area to be plotted/printed. Note that this setting does not limit the region for geometry construction.

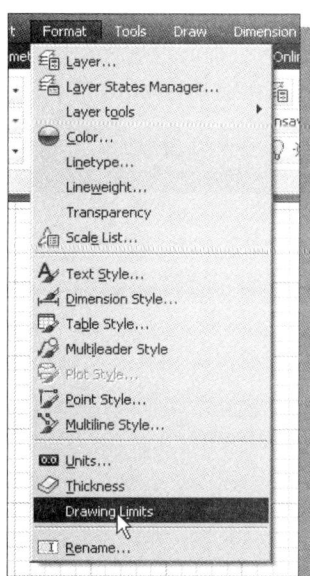

1. In the *Menu Bar* select:
   [Format] → **[Drawing Limits]**

2. In the command prompt area, the message "*Reset Model Space Limits: Specify lower left corner or [On/Off] <0.00,0.00>:*" is displayed. Press the **ENTER** key once to accept the default coordinates <**0.00,0.00**>.

3. In the command prompt area, the message "*Specify upper right corner <12.00,9.00>:*" is displayed. Press the **ENTER** key again to accept the default coordinates <**12.00,9.00**>.

4. On your own, move the graphic cursor near the upper-right corner inside the drawing area and note that the drawing area is unchanged. (The **Drawing Limits** command is used to set the drawing area, but the display will not be adjusted until a display command is used.)

5. Inside the *Menu Bar* area select:
   [View] → [Zoom] → [All]

❖ The **Zoom All** command will adjust the display so that all objects in the drawing are displayed to be as large as possible. If no objects are constructed, the **Drawing Limits** are used to adjust the current viewport.

6. Move the graphic cursor near the upper-right corner inside the drawing area and note that the display area is updated.

7. Hit the function key **[F7]** once to turn **off** the display of the *Grid* lines.

- Note that function key [F7] is a quick key which can be used to quickly toggle on/off the grid display.

Drawing lines with the *LINE* command

1. Move the graphics cursor to the first icon in the *Draw* panel. This icon is the **Line** icon. Note that a brief description of the Line command appears next to the cursor.

2. Select the icon by clicking once with the **left-mouse-button**, which will activate the Line command.

3. In the command prompt area, near the bottom of the AutoCAD drawing screen, the message "*_line Specify first point:*" is displayed. AutoCAD expects us to identify the starting location of a straight line. Move the graphics cursor inside the graphics window and watch the display of the coordinates of the graphics cursor at the bottom of the AutoCAD drawing screen. The three numbers represent the location of the cursor in the X, Y, and Z directions. We can treat the graphics window as if it was a piece of paper and we are using the graphics cursor as if it were a pencil with which to draw.

Coordinates of the graphics cursor.

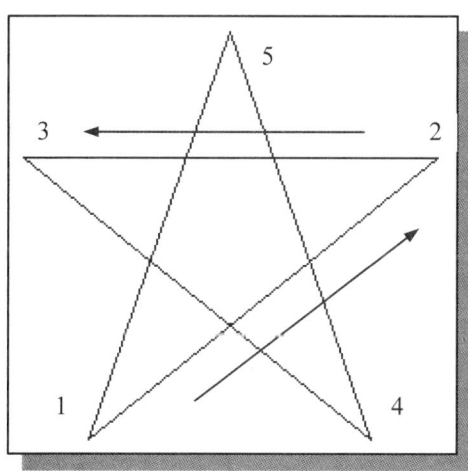

❖ We will create a freehand sketch of a five-point star using the Line command. Do not be overly concerned with the actual size or the accuracy of your freehand sketch. This exercise is to give you a feel for the **AutoCAD® 2013** user interface.

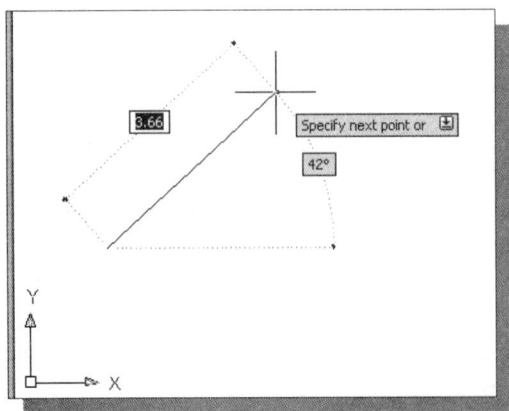

4. We will start at a location about one-third from the bottom of the graphics window. Left-click once to position the starting point of our first line. This will be *point 1* of our sketch. Next move the cursor upward and toward the right side of *point 1*. Notice the rubber-band line that follows the graphics cursor in the graphics window. Left-click again (*point 2*) and we have created the first line of our sketch.

5. Move the cursor to the left of *point 2* and create a horizontal line about the same length as the first line on the screen.

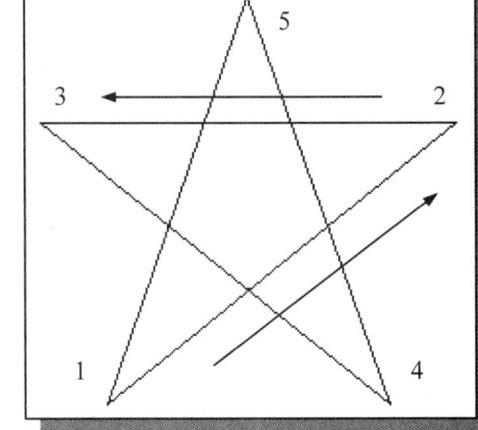

6. Repeat the above steps and complete the freehand sketch by adding three more lines (from *point 3* to *point 4*, *point 4* to *point 5*, and then connect to *point 5* back to *point 1*).

7. Notice that the Line command remains activated even after we connected the last segment of the line to the starting point *(point 1)* of our sketch. Inside the graphics window, **click once** with the **right-mouse-button** and a popup menu appears on the screen.

8. Select **Enter** with the left-mouse-button to end the Line command. (This is equivalent to hitting the [**ENTER**] key on the keyboard.)

9. Move the cursor near *point 2* and *point 3*, and estimate the length of the horizontal line by watching the displayed coordinates for each point.

Visual reference

The method we just used to create the freehand sketch is known as the **interactive method**, where we use the cursor to specify locations on the screen. This method is perhaps the fastest way to specify locations on the screen. However, it is rather difficult to try to create a line of a specific length by watching the displayed coordinates. It would be helpful to know what one inch or one meter looks like on the screen while we are creating entities. **AutoCAD® 2013** provides us with many tools to aid the construction of our designs. For example, the **GRID** and **SNAP MODE** options can be used to get a visual reference as to the size of objects and learn to restrict the movement of the cursor to a set increment on the screen.

The **GRID** and **SNAP MODE** options can be turned *ON* or *OFF* through the *Status Bar*. The *Status Bar* area is located at the bottom left of the AutoCAD drawing screen, next to the cursor coordinates.

The second button in the *Status Bar* is the *SNAP MODE* option and the third button is the *GRID DISPLAY* option. Note that the buttons in the *Status Bar* area serve two functions: (1) the status of the specific option, and (2) as toggle switches that can be used to turn these special options *ON* and *OFF*. When the corresponding button is *highlighted*, the specific option is turned *ON*. Using the buttons is a quick and easy way to make changes to these *drawing aid* options. Another aspect of the buttons in the *Status Bar* is these options can be switched on and off in the middle of another command.

GRID ON

1. Left-click the **GRID** button in the *Status Bar* to turn **ON** the *GRID DISPLAY* option. (Notice in the command prompt area, the message *"<Grid on>"* is also displayed.)

2. Move the cursor inside the graphics window, and estimate the distance in between the grid lines by watching the coordinates display at the bottom of the screen.

➢ The *GRID* option creates a pattern of lines that extends over an area on the screen. Using the grid is similar to placing a sheet of grid paper under a drawing. The grid helps you align objects and visualize the distance between them. The grid is not displayed in the plotted drawing. The default grid spacing, which means the distance in between two lines on the screen, is 0.5 inches. We can see that the sketched horizontal line in the sketch is about 4.5 inches long.

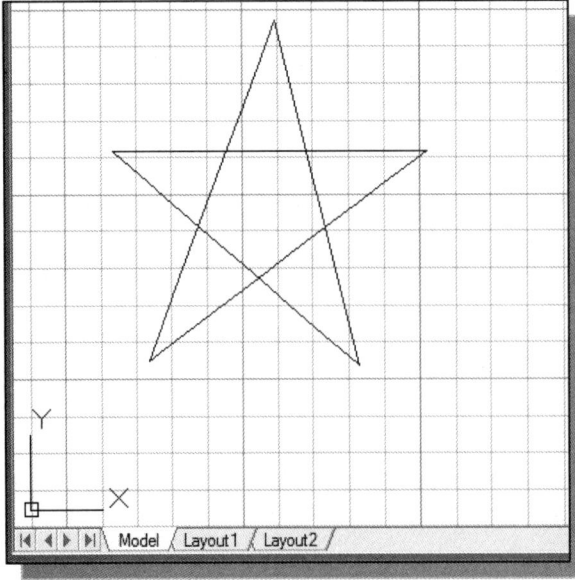

SNAP MODE ON

1. Left-click the **SNAP MODE** button in the *Status Bar* to turn **ON** the *SNAP* option.

2. Move the cursor inside the graphics window, and move the cursor diagonally on the screen. Observe the movement of the cursor and watch the *coordinates display* at the bottom of the screen.

> The *SNAP* option controls an invisible rectangular grid that restricts cursor movement to specified intervals. When *SNAP* mode is on, the screen cursor and all input coordinates are snapped to the nearest point on the grid. The default snap interval is 0.5 inches, and aligned to the grid points on the screen.

3. Click on the **Line** icon in the *Draw* toolbar. In the command prompt area, the message "*_line Specify first point:*" is displayed.

4. On your own, create another sketch of the five-point star with the *GRID* and *SNAP* options switched *ON*.

5. Use the **right-mouse-button** and select **Enter** in the popup menu to end the **Line** command if you have not done so.

Using the ERASE command

❖ One of the advantages of using a CAD system is the ability to remove entities without leaving any marks. We will erase two of the lines using the Erase command.

1. Pick **Erase** in the *Modify* toolbar. (The icon is a picture of an eraser at the end of a pencil.) The message "*Select objects*" is displayed in the command prompt area and AutoCAD awaits us to select the objects to erase.

2. Left-click the **SNAP MODE** button on the *Status Bar* to turn **OFF** the *SNAP MODE* option so that we can more easily move the cursor on top of objects. We can toggle the *Status Bar* options *ON* or *OFF* in the middle of another command.

3. Select any two lines on the screen; the selected lines are displayed as dashed lines as shown in the figure below.

➢ To **deselect** an object from the selection set, hold down the [**SHIFT**] key and select the object again.

4. **Right-mouse-click** once to accept the selections. The selected two lines are erased.

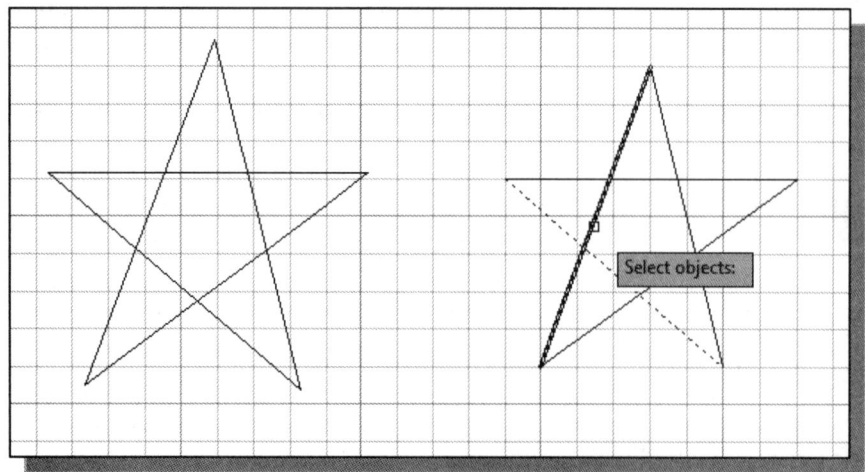

Repeat the last command

1. Inside the graphics window, click once with the right-mouse-button to bring up the popup option menu.

2. Pick **Repeat Erase**, with the left-mouse-button, in the popup menu to repeat the last command. Notice the other options available in the popup menu.

➢ **AutoCAD® 2013** offers many options to accomplish the same task. Throughout this text, we will emphasize the use of the **AutoCAD Heads-up Design**™ interface, which means we focus on the screen, not on the keyboard.

3. Move the cursor to a location that is above and toward the left side of the entities on the screen. Left-mouse-click once to start a corner of a rubber-band window.

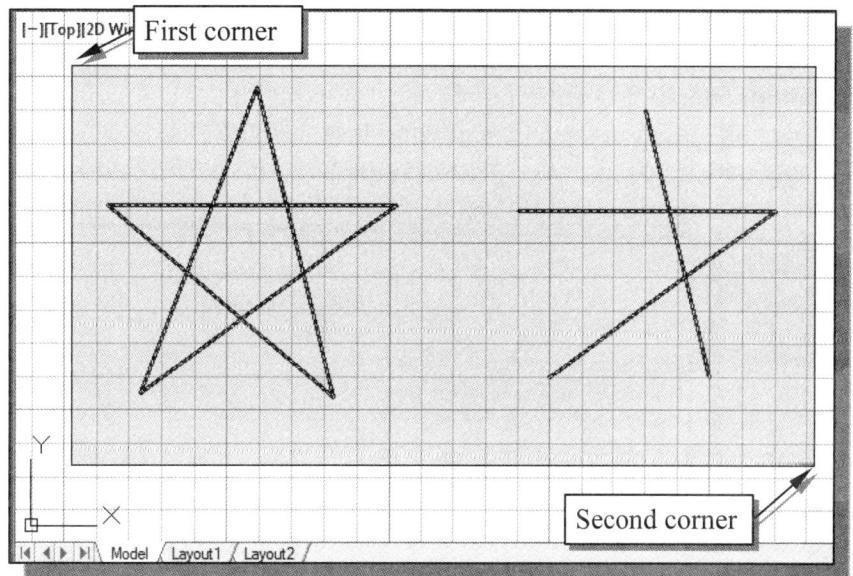

4. Move the cursor toward the right and below the entities, and then left-mouse-click to enclose all the entities inside the **selection window**. Notice all entities that are inside the window are selected.

5. Inside the graphics window, right-mouse-click once to proceed with erasing the selected entities.

➢ On your own, create a free-hand sketch of your choice using the **Line** command. Experiment with using the different commands we have discussed so far. Reset the status buttons so that only the *GRID DISPLAY* option is turned *ON* as shown.

The CAD Database and the User Coordinate System

- Designs and drawings created in a CAD system are usually defined and stored using sets of points in what is called **world space**. In most CAD systems, the world space is defined using a three-dimensional *Cartesian coordinate system*. Three mutually perpendicular axes, usually referred to as the X-, Y-, and Z-axes, define this system. The intersection of the three coordinate axes forms a point called the **origin**. Any point in world space can then be defined as the distance from the origin in the X-, Y- and Z-directions. In most CAD systems, the directions of the arrows shown on the axes identify the positive sides of the coordinates.

A CAD file, which is the electronic version of the design, contains data that describes the entities created in the CAD system. Information such as the coordinate values in world space for all endpoints, center points, etc., along with the descriptions of the types of entities are all stored in the file. Knowing that AutoCAD stores designs by keeping coordinate data helps us understand the inputs required to create entities.

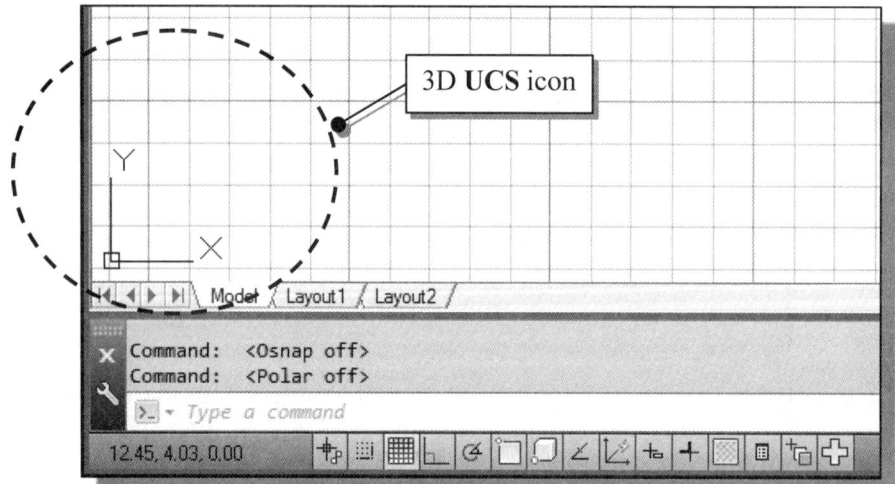

The icon near the bottom left corner of the default AutoCAD graphics window shows the positive X-direction and positive Y-direction of the coordinate system that is active. In AutoCAD, the coordinate system that is used to create entities is called the **user coordinate system** (UCS). By default, the **user coordinate system** is aligned to the **world coordinate system** (WCS). The **world coordinate system** is a coordinate system used by AutoCAD as the basis for defining all objects and other coordinate systems defined by the users. We can think of the **origin** of the **world coordinate system** as a fixed point being used as a reference for all measurements. The default orientation of the Z-axis can be considered as positive values in front of the monitor and negative values inside the monitor.

AutoCAD Fundamentals   13-15

Changing to the 2D UCS Icon Display

❖ In **AutoCAD® 2013**, the **UCS** icon is displayed in various ways to help us visualize the orientation of the drawing plane.

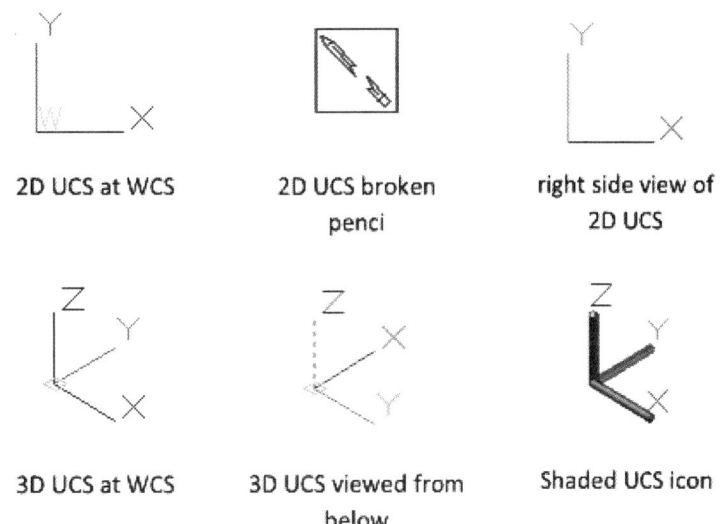

2D UCS at WCS   2D UCS broken   right side view of
                   penci   2D UCS

3D UCS at WCS   3D UCS viewed from   Shaded UCS icon
                   below

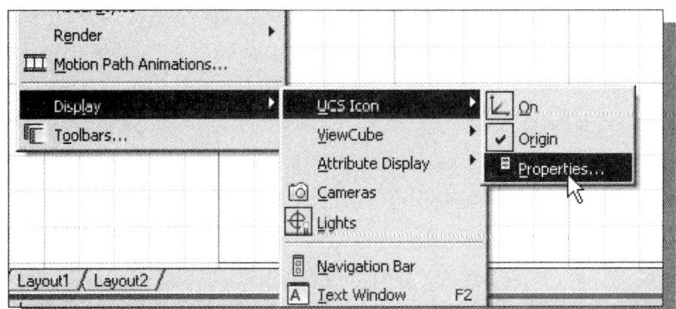

1. Click on the **View** pull-down menu and select

   [Display] → [UCS Icon] → [Properties...]

2. In the *UCS icon style* section, switch to the **2D** option as shown.

3. Click **OK** to accept the settings.

❖ Note the W symbol in the UCS icon indicates the UCS is aligned to the world coordinate system.

Cartesian and Polar Coordinate Systems

In a two-dimensional space, a point can be represented using different coordinate systems. The point can be located, using a *Cartesian coordinate system*, as X and Y units away from the origin. The same point can also be located using the *polar coordinate system*, as r and θ units away from the origin.

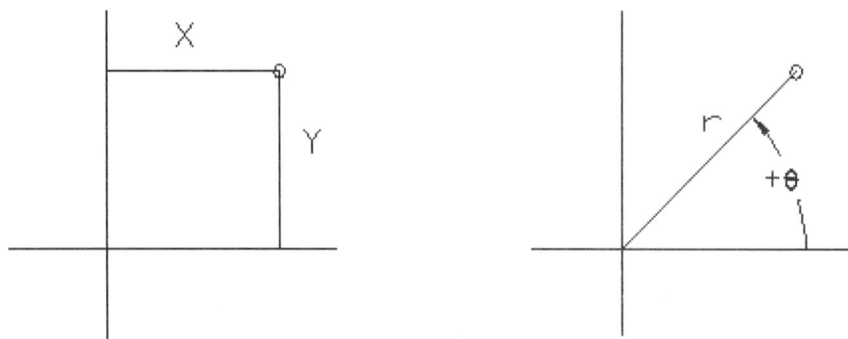

For planar geometry, the polar coordinate system is very useful for certain applications. In the polar coordinate system, points are defined in terms of a radial distance, r, from the origin and an angle θ between the direction of r and the positive X axis. The default system for measuring angles in **AutoCAD® 2013** defines positive angular values as counter-clockwise from the positive X-axis.

Absolute and Relative Coordinates

- **AutoCAD® 2013** also allows us to use *absolute* and *relative coordinates* to quickly construct objects. **Absolute coordinate values** are measured from the current coordinate system's origin point. **Relative coordinate values** are specified in relation to previous coordinates.

➢ Note that the *coordinate display area* can also be used as a toggle switch; each left-mouse-click will toggle the coordinate display *on* or *off*.

In **AutoCAD® 2013**, the *absolute* coordinates and the *relative* coordinates can be used in conjunction with the *Cartesian* and *polar* coordinate systems. By default, AutoCAD expects us to enter values in *absolute Cartesian coordinates*, distances measured from the current coordinate system's origin point. We can switch to using the *relative coordinates* by using the @ symbol. The @ symbol is used as the *relative coordinates specifier*, which means that we can specify the position of a point in relation to the previous point.

Defining Positions

In AutoCAD, there are five methods for specifying the locations of points when we create planar geometric entities.

> **Interactive method**: Use the cursor to select on the screen.

> **Absolute coordinates (Format: X,Y)**: Type the X and Y coordinates to locate the point on the current coordinate system relative to the origin.

> **Relative rectangular coordinates (Format: @X,Y)**: Type the X and Y coordinates relative to the last point.

> **Relative polar coordinates (Format: @Distance<angle)**: Type a distance and angle relative to the last point.

> **Direct Distance entry technique**: Specify a second point by first moving the cursor to indicate direction and then entering a distance.

GRID Style Setup

1. In the *Status Bar* area, **right-mouse-click** on *SnapMode* and choose **[Settings]**

2. In the *Drafting Settings* dialog box, select the **Snap and Grid** tab if it is not the page on top.

3. Change *Grid Style* to **Display dotted grid in 2D model Space** as shown in the below figure.

4. Pick **OK** to exit the *Drafting Settings* dialog box.

The *GuidePlate*

We will next create a mechanical design using the different coordinate entry methods.

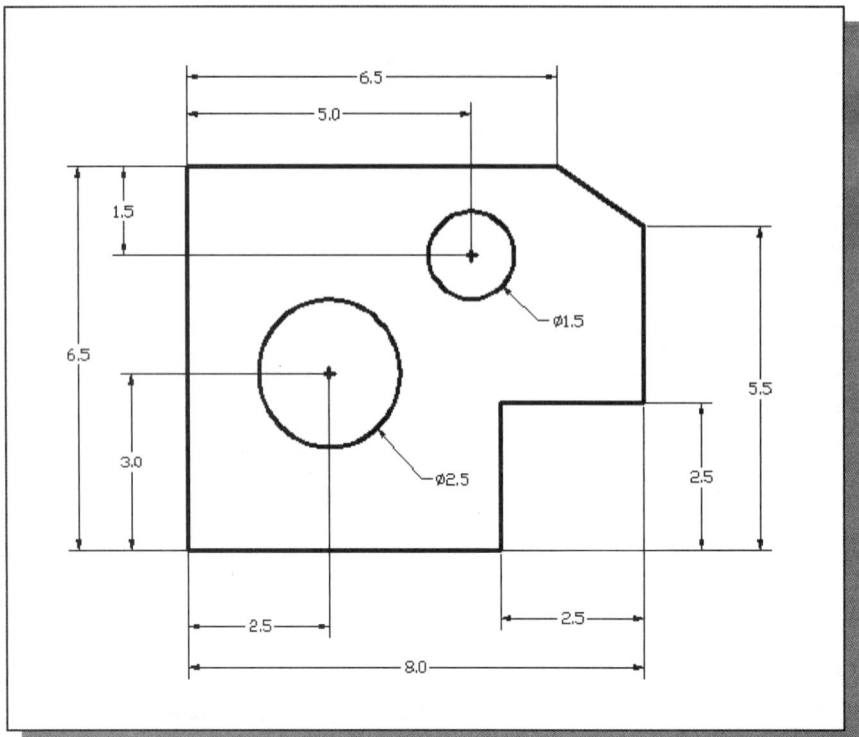

❖ The rule for creating CAD designs and drawings is that they should be created at **full size** using real-world units. The CAD database contains all the definitions of the geometric entities and the design is considered as a virtual, full-sized object. Only when a printer or plotter transfers the CAD design to paper is the design scaled to fit on a sheet. The tedious task of determining a scale factor so that the design will fit on a sheet of paper is taken care of by the CAD system. This allows the designers and CAD operators to concentrate their attention on the more important issues – the design.

1. Select the **Line** command icon in the *Draw* toolbar. In the command prompt area, near the bottom of the AutoCAD graphics window, the message "*_line Specify first point:*" is displayed. AutoCAD expects us to identify the starting location of a straight line.

2. We will locate the starting point of our design at the origin of the *world coordinate system*.

   Command: _line Specify first point: **0,0**
   (Type **0,0** and press the [**ENTER**] key once.)

3. We will create a horizontal line by entering the absolute coordinates of the second point.
   Specify next point or [Undo]: **5.5,0** [ENTER]

- Note that the line we created is aligned to the bottom edge of the drawing window. Let us adjust the view of the line by using the Pan Realtime command.

4. In the *Menu Bar* area select: **[View] → [Pan] → [Realtime]**

❖ The available Pan commands enable us to move the view to a different position. The *Pan-Realtime* function acts as if you are using a video camera.

5. Move the cursor, which appears as a hand inside the graphics window, near the center of the drawing window, then push down the left-mouse-button and drag the display toward the right and top side until we can see the sketched line. (Notice the scroll bars can also be used to adjust viewing of the display.)

6. Press the [Esc] key to exit the Pan-Realtime command. Notice that AutoCAD goes back to the Line command.

7. We will create a vertical line by using the *relative rectangular coordinates entry method*, relative to the last point we specified:
   Specify next point or [Close/Undo]: **@0,2.5** **[ENTER]**

8. We can mix any of the entry methods in positioning the locations of the endpoints. Move the cursor to the *Status Bar* area, and turn **ON** the *SNAP MODE* option.

❖ Note that the Line command is resumed as the settings are adjusted.

9. Left-click once on the coordinates display area to switch to a different coordinate display option.

10. Note the coordinates display area has changed to show the length of the new line and its angle. Left-click once on the coordinates display area to switch back to using the world coordinate system.

11. Create the next line by picking the location, world coordinates (**8,2.5**), on the screen.

12. We will next use the *relative polar coordinates entry method*, relative to the last point we specified:
    Specify next point or [Close/Undo]: **@3<90** [ENTER]
    (Distance is **3** inches with an angle of **90** degrees.)

13. Using the *relative rectangular coordinates entry method* to create the next line, we can imagine a *reference coordinate system* aligned at the previous point. Coordinates are measured along the two reference axes.

    Specify next point or [Close/Undo]: **@-1.5,1** [ENTER]

    (**-1.5** and **1** inches are measured relative to the reference point.)

14. Move the cursor directly to the left of the last point and use the *direct distance entry technique* by entering **6.5** [ENTER].

15. For the last segment of the sketch, we can use the **Close** option to connect back to the starting point. Inside the graphics window, **right-mouse-click** and a *popup menu* appears on the screen.

16. Select **Close** with the left-mouse-button to connect back to the starting point and end the Line command.

Creating *Circles*

- The menus and toolbars in **AutoCAD® 2013** are designed to allow the CAD operators to quickly activate the desired commands.

1. In the *Draw* toolbar, click on the little triangle below the circle icon. Note that the little triangle indicates additional options are available.

2. In the option list, select: **[Center, Diameter]**

Notice the different options available under the circle submenu:

- **Center, Radius**: Draws a circle based on a center point and a radius.

- **Center, Diameter**: Draws a circle based on a center point and a diameter.

- **2 Points**: Draws a circle based on two endpoints of the diameter.

- **3 Points**: Draws a circle based on three points on the circumference.

- **TTR–Tangent, Tangent**, **Radius**: Draws a circle with a specified radius tangent to two objects.

- **TTT–Tangent, Tangent, Tangent**: Draws a circle tangent to three objects.

3. In the command prompt area, the message *"Specify center point for circle or [3P/2P/Ttr (tan tan radius)]:"* is displayed. AutoCAD expects us to identify the location of a point or enter an option. We can use any of the four coordinate entry methods to identify the desired location. We will enter the **world coordinates** (**2.5,3**) as the center point for the first circle.

Specify center point for circle or [3P/2P/Ttr (tan tan radius)]: **2.5,3** [ENTER]

4. In the command prompt area, the message *"Specify diameter of circle:"* is displayed.
Specify diameter of circle: **2.5** [ENTER]

5. Inside the graphics window, right-mouse-click to bring up the popup option menu.

6. Pick **Repeat CIRCLE** with the left-mouse-button in the popup menu to repeat the last command.

7. Using the *relative rectangular coordinates entry method*, relative to the center-point coordinates of the first circle, we specify the location as (**2.5,2**).

Specify center point for circle or [3P/2P/Ttr (tan tan radius)]: **@2.5,2** [ENTER]

8. In the command prompt area, the message "*Specify Radius of circle: <2.50>*" is displayed. The default option for the Circle command in AutoCAD is to specify the *radius* and the last radius used is also displayed in brackets.

9. Inside the graphics window, **right-mouse-click** to bring up the popup option menu and select **Diameter** as shown.

10. In the command prompt area, enter **1.5** as the diameter.

   Specify Diameter of circle<2.50>: **1.5 [ENTER]**

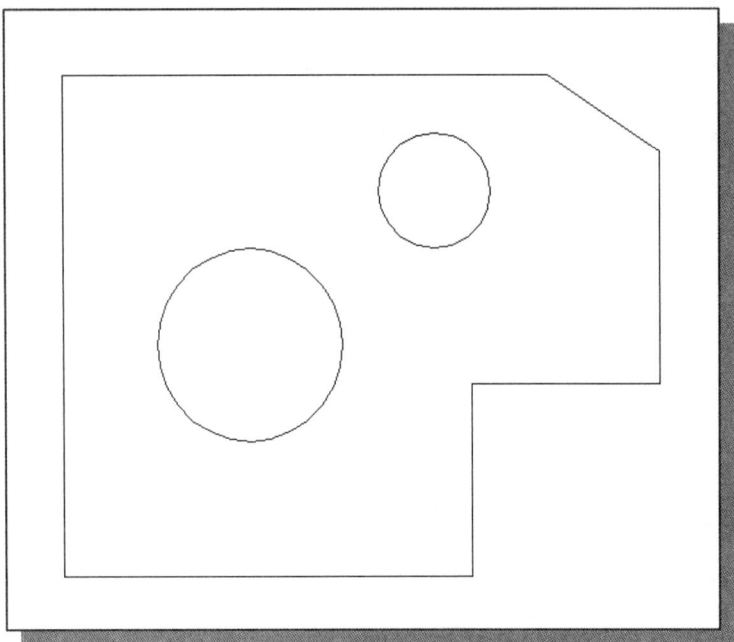

Saving the CAD Design

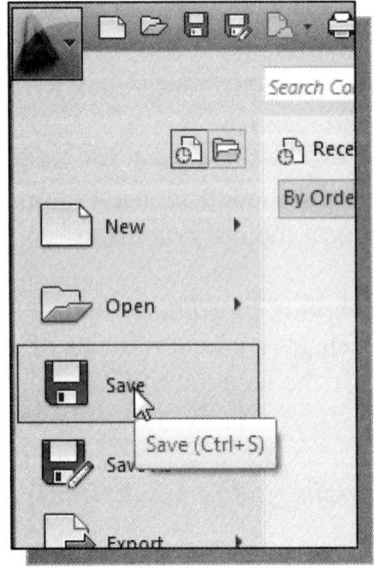

1. In the *Application Menu*, select:

   [Application] → [Save]

   ❖ Note the command can also be activated with quick-key combination of **[Ctrl]+[S]**.

2. In the *Save Drawing As* dialog box, select the folder in which you want to store the CAD file and enter **GuidePlate** in the *File name* box.

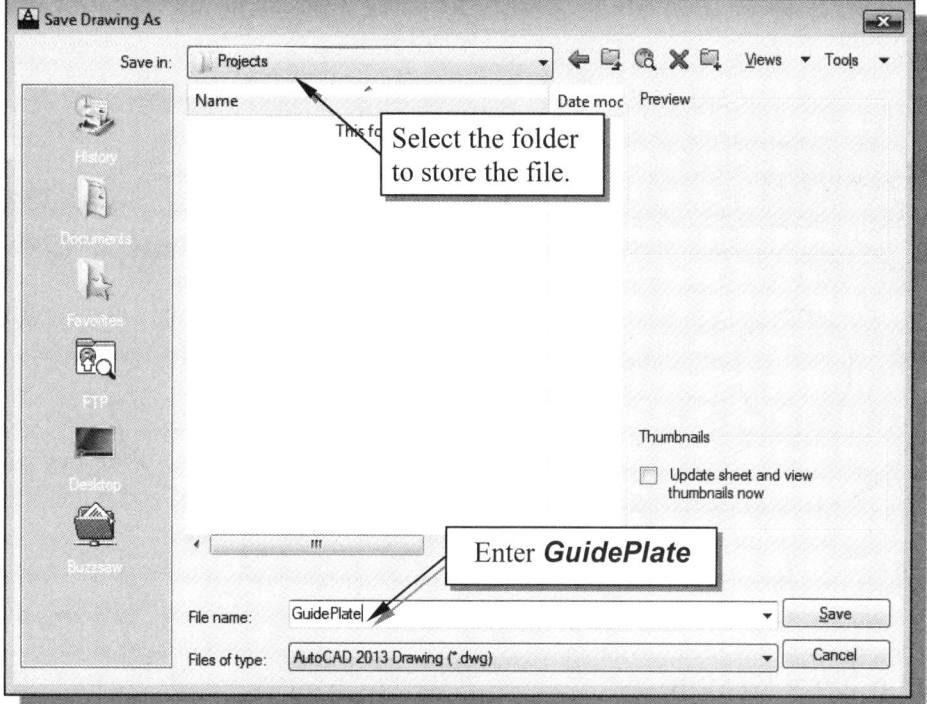

3. Click **Save** in the *Save Drawing As* dialog box to accept the selections and save the file. Note the default file type is DWG, which is the standard AutoCAD drawing format.

Close the Current Drawing

❖ Several options are available to close the current drawing:

➢ Select **[Close]** → **[Current Drawing]** in the *Application Menu Bar* as shown.

➢ Enter **Close** at the command prompt.

➢ The third option is to click on the **[Close]** icon, located at the upper-right-hand corner of the drawing window.

The *Spacer* design

❖ We will next create the spacer design using more of the AutoCAD's drawing tools.

Start a New Drawing

1. In the *Application Menu,* select **[New]** to start a new drawing.

2. The **Select Template** dialog box appears on the screen. Accept the **default acad.dwt** as the template to open.

➢ The dwt file type is the AutoCAD template file format. An AutoCAD template file contains pre-defined settings to reduce the amount of tedious repetitions.

Drawing Units Setup

➢ Every object we construct in a CAD system is measured in **units**. We should determine the system of units within the CAD system before creating the first geometric entities.

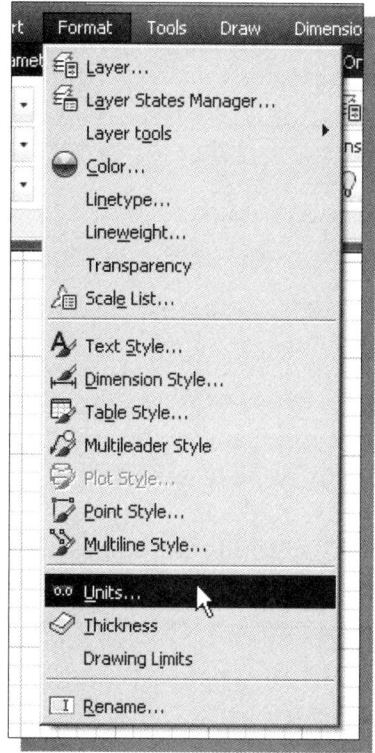

1. In the *Menu Bar* select:
   [Format] → [Units]

- The AutoCAD *Menu Bar* contains multiple pull-down menus, where all of the AutoCAD commands can be accessed. Note that many of the menu items listed in the pull-down menus can also be accessed through the *Quick Access* toolbar and/or *Ribbon* panels.

2. Click on the *Length Type* option to display the different types of length units available. Confirm the *Length Type* is set to **Decimal**.

3. On your own, examine the other settings that are available.

4. In the *Drawing Units* dialog box, set the *Length Type* to **Decimal**. This will set the measurement to the default *English* units, inches.

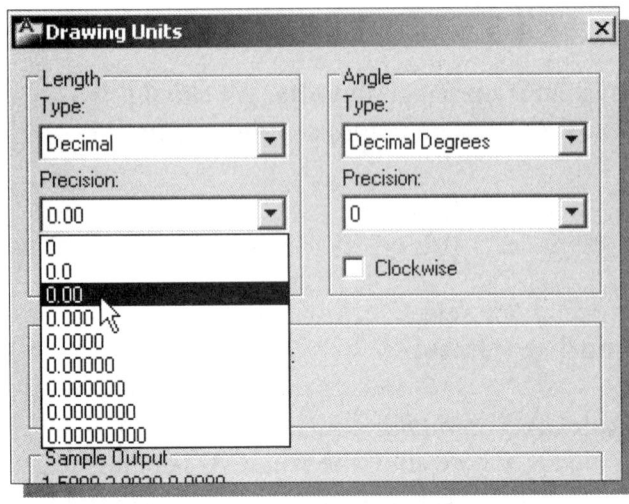

5. Set the *Precision* to **two digits** after the decimal point as shown in the above figure.

6. Pick **OK** to exit the *Drawing Units* dialog box.

Drawing Area Setup

❖ Next, we will set up the **Drawing Limits** by entering a command in the command prompt area. Setting the Drawing Limits controls the extents of the display of the *grid*. It also serves as a visual reference that marks the working area. It can also be used to prevent construction outside the grid limits and as a plot option that defines an area to be plotted/printed. Note that this setting does not limit the region for geometry construction.

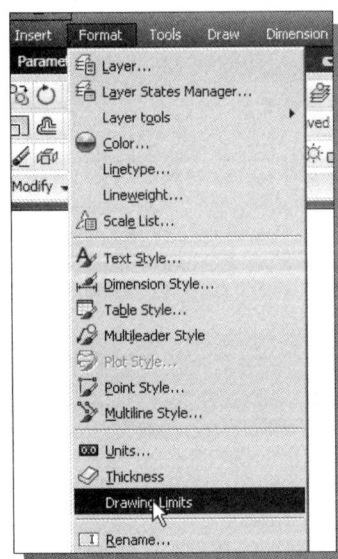

1. In the *Menu Bar* select:
   [Format] → [Drawing Limits]

2. In the command prompt area, the message "*Reset Model Space Limits: Specify lower left corner or [On/Off] <0.00,0.00>:*" is displayed. Press the **ENTER** key once to accept the default coordinates **<0.00,0.00>**.

3. In the command prompt area, the message "*Specify upper right corner <12.00,9.00>:*" is displayed. Press the **ENTER** key again to accept the default coordinates **<12.00,9.00>**.

AutoCAD Fundamentals   13-29

4. On your own, move the graphic cursor near the upper-right corner inside the drawing area and note that the drawing area is unchanged. (The Drawing Limits command is used to set the drawing area, but the display will not be adjusted until a display command is used.)

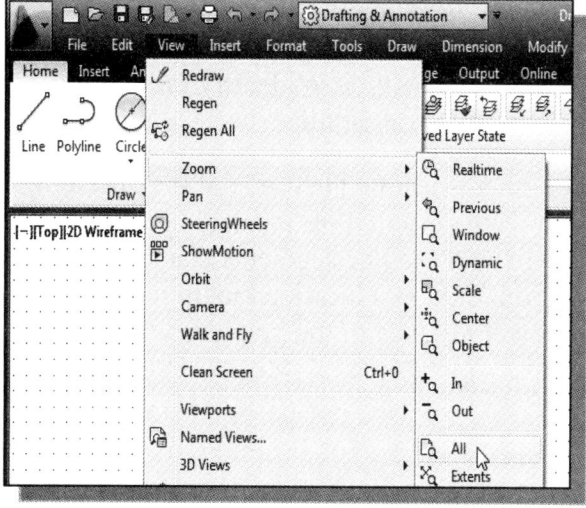

5. Inside the *Menu Bar* area select: **[View] → [Zoom] → [All]**

❖ The **Zoom All** command will adjust the display so that all objects in the drawing are displayed to be as large as possible. If no objects are constructed, the Drawing Limits are used to adjust the current viewport.

6. Move the graphic cursor near the upper-right corner inside the drawing area and note that the display area is updated.

7. In the *Status Bar* area, **right-mouse-click** on *SnapMode* and choose **[Settings]**.

8. In the *Drafting Settings dialog box*, switch **on** the **Snap** and **Grid** options as shown.

➢ On your own, exit the *Drafting Settings dialog box* and reset the status buttons so that only **GRID DISPLAY** and **SNAP MODE** are turned **ON** as shown.

Using the Line Command

1. Select the **Line** command icon in the *Draw* toolbar. In the command prompt area, near the bottom of the AutoCAD graphics window, the message "*_line Specify first point:*" is displayed. AutoCAD expects us to identify the starting location of a straight line.

2. To further illustrate the usage of the different input methods and tools available in AutoCAD, we will start the line segments at an arbitrary location. Start at a location that is somewhere in the lower left side of the graphics window.

3. We will create a horizontal line by using the *relative rectangular coordinates entry method*, relative to the last point we specified: **@6,0 [ENTER]**

4. Next, create a vertical line by using the *relative polar coordinates entry method*, relative to the last point we specified: **@3<90 [ENTER]**

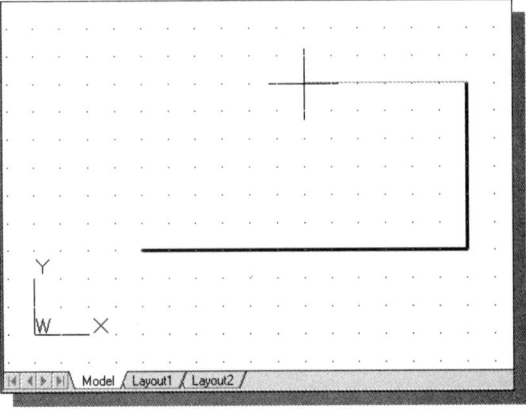

5. Next, we will use the direct input method; first, move the cursor directly to the left of the last endpoint of the line segments.

AutoCAD Fundamentals   13-31

6. Use the *direct distance entry technique* by entering **2 [ENTER]**.

7. On your own, repeat the above steps and create the four additional line segments, using the dimensions as shown.

8. To end the line command, we can either hit the [Enter] key on the key board or use the **Enter** option, **right-mouse-click** and a *popup menu* appears on the screen.

9. Select **Enter** with the left-mouse-button to end the Line command.

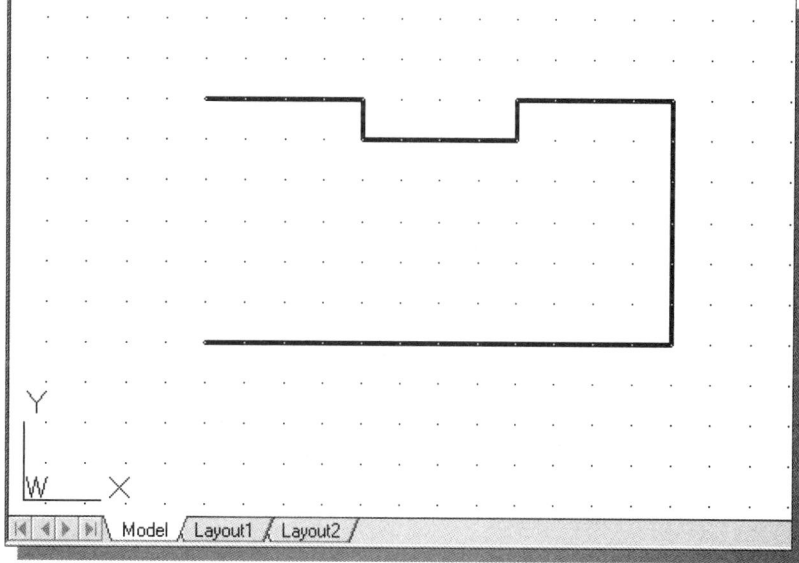

Using the *ERASE* command

❖ The vertical line on the right was created as a construction line, to aide the construction of the rest of the lines for the design. We will use the Erase command to remove it.

1. Pick **Erase** in the *Modify* toolbar. The message "*Select objects*" is displayed in the command prompt area and AutoCAD awaits us to select the objects to erase.

2. Select the vertical line as shown.

3. Click once with the **right-mouse-button** to accept the selection and delete the line.

Using the Arc Command

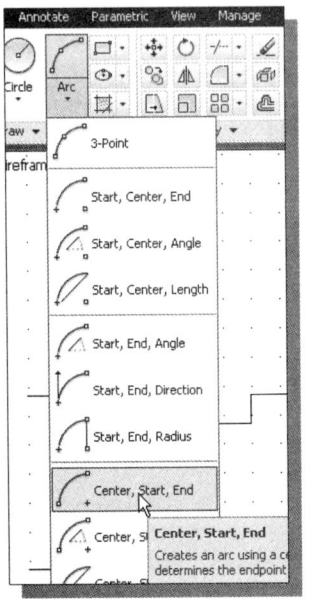

1. Click the down-arrow icon of the **Arc** command in the *Draw* toolbar to display the different Arc construction options.

➢ AutoCAD provides eleven different ways to create arcs. Note that the different options are used based on the geometry conditions of the design. The more commonly used options are the **3-Points** option and the **Center-Start-End** option.

2. Select the **Center-Start-End** option as shown. This option requires the selection of the center point, start point and end point location, in that order, of the arc.

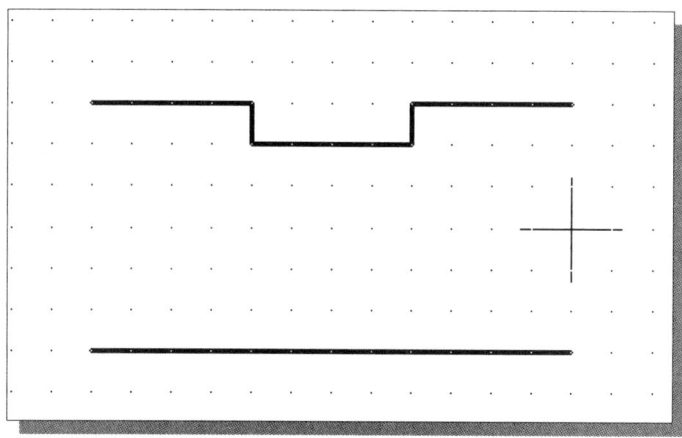

3. Move the cursor to the middle of the two horizontal lines and align the cursor to the two endpoints as shown. Click once with the **right-mouse-button** to select the location as the center point of the new arc.

4. Move the cursor downward and select the right endpoint of the bottom horizontal line as the start point of the arc.

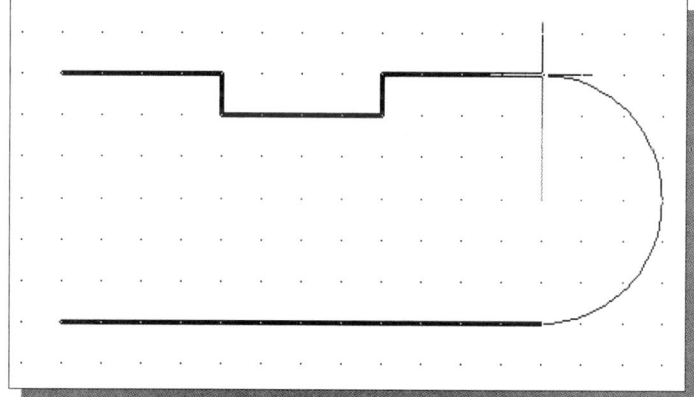

5. Move the cursor to the right endpoint of the top horizontal line as shown. Pick this point as the endpoint of the new arc.

6. On your own, repeat the above steps and create the other arc as shown. Note that in most CAD packages, positive angles are defined as going counterclockwise; therefore the starting point of the second arc is the endpoint on top.

Using the Circle command

1. Select the **[Circle]** → **[Center, Diameter]** option as shown.

2. Select the same location for the arc center as the center point for the new circle.

3. In the command prompt area, the message "*Specify diameter of circle:*" is displayed. *Specify diameter of circle:* **1.25 [ENTER]**

4. On your own, create the other circle and complete the drawing as shown.

Saving the CAD Design

1. In the *Quick Access Toolbar*, select: **[Save]**

- Note the command can also be activated with quick-key combination of **[Ctrl]+[S]**.

2. In the *Save Drawing As* dialog box, select the folder in which you want to store the CAD file and enter **Spacer** in the *File name* box.

3. Click **Save** in the *Save Drawing As* dialog box to accept the selections and save the file. Note the default file type is DWG, which is the standard AutoCAD drawing format.

Exit AutoCAD 2013

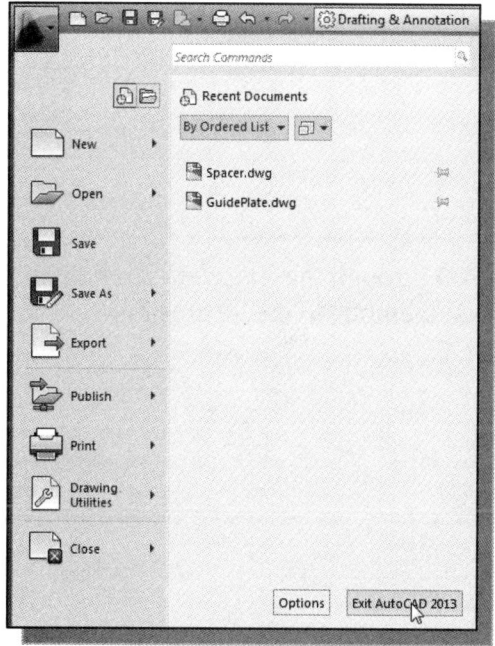

- To exit **AutoCAD® 2013**, select **Exit AutoCAD** in the *Menu Bar* or type **QUIT** at the command prompt. Note the command can also be activated with quick-key combination of **[Ctrl]+[Q]**.

Review Questions: (Time: 20 minutes)

1. What are the advantages and disadvantages of using CAD systems to create engineering drawings?

2. What is the default AutoCAD filename extension?

3. How do the **GRID** and **SNAP** options assist us in sketching?

4. List and describe the different **coordinate entry methods** available in AutoCAD?

5. When using the Line command, which option allows us to quickly create a line-segment connecting back to the starting point?

6. List and describe the two types of coordinate systems commonly used for planar geometry.

7. Which key do you use to quickly cancel a command?

8. When you use the Pan command, do the coordinates of objects get changed?

9. Find information on how to draw ellipses in AutoCAD through the *Autodesk Exchange* and create the following arc. If it is desired to position the center of the ellipse to a specific location, which ellipse command is more suitable?

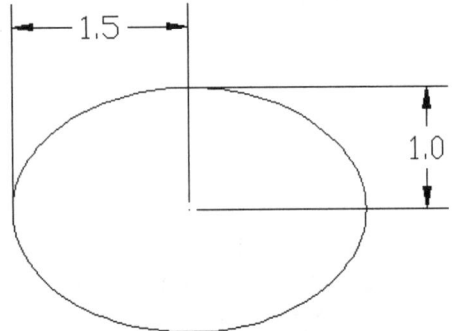

10. Find information on how to draw arcs in AutoCAD through the *Autodesk Exchange* and create the following arc. List and describe two methods to create arcs in AutoCAD.

Exercises: (All dimensions are in inches.) (Time: 60 minutes)

1. **Angle Spacer**

2. **Base Plate**

3. T-Clip

4. Channel Plate

Chapter 14
Basic Object Construction and Dynamic Input

Learning Objectives

- **Referencing the WCS**
- **Use the Startup dialog box**
- **Set up GRID & SNAP intervals**
- **Display AutoCAD's toolbars**
- **Set up and use OBJECT SNAPS**
- **Edit, using the TRIM command**
- **Use the POLYGON command**
- **Create TTR circles**
- **Create Tangent lines**

Introduction

The main characteristic of any CAD system is its ability to create and modify 2D/3D geometric entities quickly and accurately. Most CAD systems provide a variety of object construction and editing tools to relieve the designer of the tedious drudgery of this task, so that the designer can concentrate more on design content. It is important to note that CAD systems can be used to replace traditional drafting with pencil and paper, but the CAD user must have a good understanding of the basic geometric construction techniques to fully utilize the capability of the CAD systems.

One of the major enhancements of AutoCAD® 2006 was the introduction of the *Dynamic Input* feature. This addition, which is also available in AutoCAD® 2013, greatly enhanced the **AutoCAD Heads-up Design™** interface.

The use of the **User Coordinate System (UCS)** and the **World Coordinate System (WCS)** is further discussed in this chapter. In working CAD, one simple approach to creating designs in CAD systems is to create geometry by referencing the **World Coordinate System**. The general procedure of this approach is illustrated in this chapter.

In this chapter, we will examine the *Dynamic Input* options, the basic geometric construction and editing tools provided by **AutoCAD® 2013**. We will first look at the *Dynamic Input* options, also tools such as *UNITS, GRID, SNAP MODE* intervals setup and the *OSNAP* option, followed by construction tools such as circles and polygons; we will also look at the basic Trim command.

Starting Up AutoCAD® 2013

1. Start **AutoCAD® 2013** by selecting the *Autodesk* folder in the **Start** menu as shown. Once the program is loaded into the memory, the **AutoCAD® 2013** drawing screen will appear on the screen.

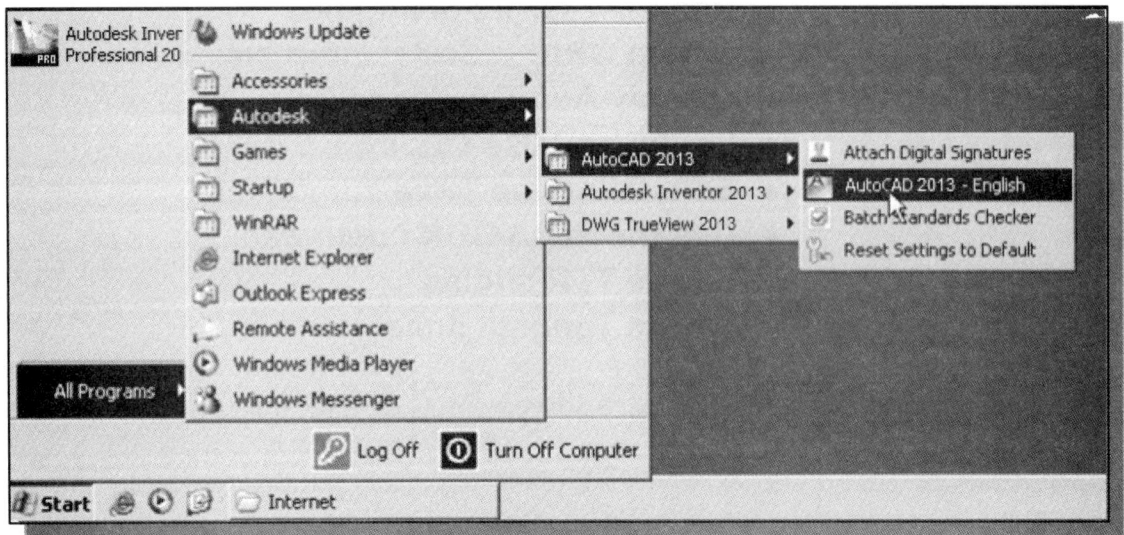

Basic Object Construction Tools   14-3

Dynamic Input

In AutoCAD® 2013, the **Dynamic Input** feature provides the user with **visual tooltips** and **entry options** right on the screen.

Dynamic Input provides a convenient command interface near the cursor to help the user focus in the graphics area. When *Dynamic Input* is *ON*, tooltips display information near the cursor that is dynamically updated as the cursor moves.

The tooltips also provide a place for user entry when a command is activated. The actions required to complete a command remain the same as those for the command line. Note that **Dynamic Input** is **not** designed to replace the *command line*. The main advantage of using the *Dynamic Input* options is to keep our attention near the cursor.

The *Dynamic Input* features simply enhance the five methods for specifying the locations of points as described in Chapter 1, page 1-18.

1. Switch **ON** only the *Dynamic Input* option by clicking on the button in the *Status Bar* area as shown.

2. Click on the **Line** icon in the *Draw* toolbar. In the command prompt area, the message "*_line Specify first point:*" is displayed.

3. Move the cursor inside the graphics window and notice the displayed tooltip, which shows the coordinates of the cursor position.

4. Type **3** and notice the input is entered in the first entry box.

5. Hit the **TAB** key once to move the input focus to the second entry box.

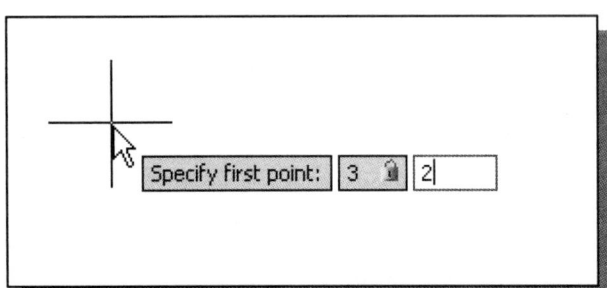

6. Type **2** and notice the input is displayed in the second entry box.

7. Hit the **ENTER** key once to accept the inputs.

❖ We have placed the first endpoint at the world coordinate of 3,2.

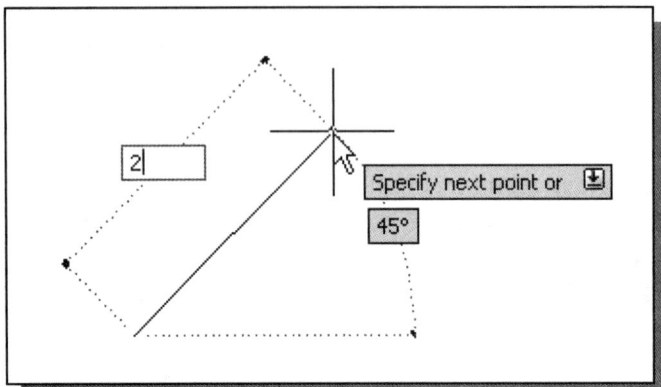

8. Move the cursor upward and toward the right side of the screen. Notice the tooltip is set to use polar coordinates by default.

9. Type **2** and notice the input is displayed in the entry box as shown.

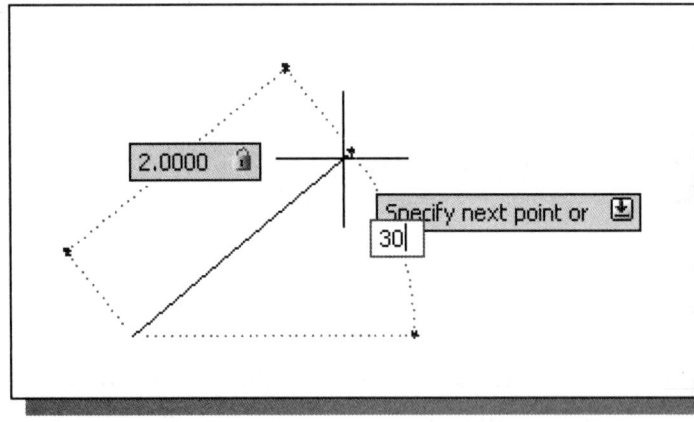

10. Hit the **TAB** key once to move the input focus to the second entry box.

11. Type **30** and notice the input is displayed in the angle entry box.

12. Hit the **ENTER** key once to accept the inputs and create the line that is 2 units long and at an angle of 30 degrees.

Basic Object Construction Tools   14-5

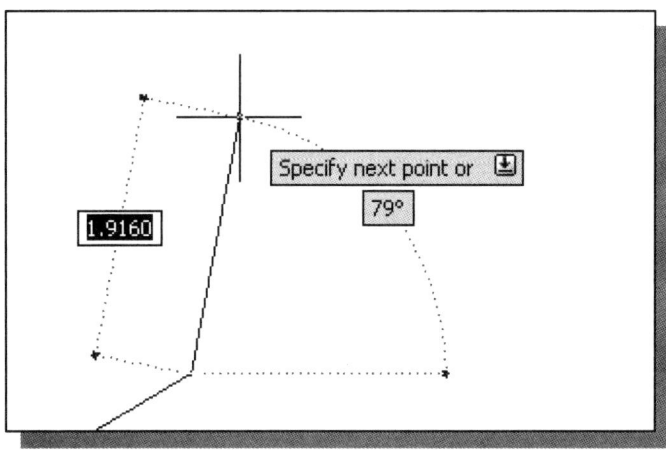

13. Move the cursor upward and toward the right side of the screen. Notice the tooltip is still set to using polar coordinates.

> To switch to using the relative Cartesian coordinates input method, use a **comma** as the **specifier** after entering the first number.

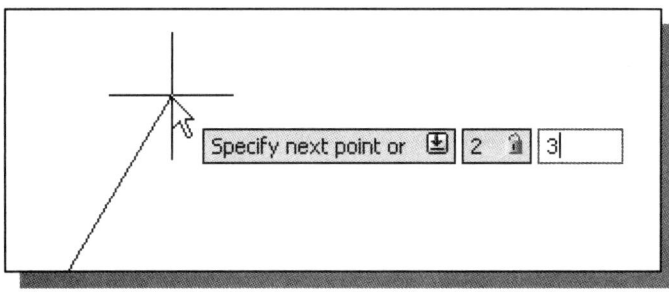

14. Type **2,3** and notice the input option is now set to using relative Cartesian coordinates as shown.

15. Hit the **ENTER** key once to accept the inputs.

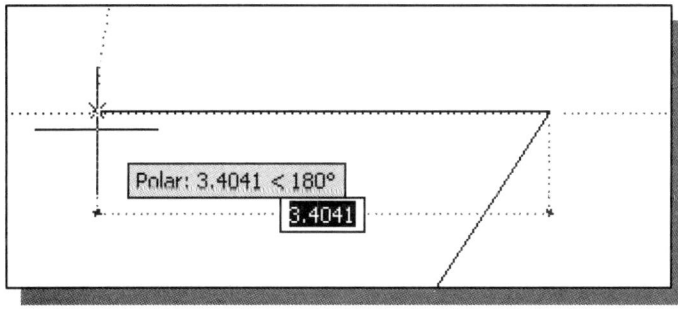

16. Move the cursor toward the right side of the last position until the angle is near 180 degrees as shown.

17. Type **4** and notice the input is displayed on the screen.

18. Hit the **ENTER** key once to accept the input and note a horizontal line is created.

> In effect, we just created a line using the *Direct Distance* option.

19. In the *Status Bar* area, **right-mouse-click** on *Dynamic Input* and choose **Settings**.

❖ The *Settings* dialog allows us to control what is displayed when *Dynamic Input* is on.

➢ Note that the *Dynamic Input* feature has three components: ***Pointer Input***, ***Dimensional Input***, and ***Dynamic Prompts***.

20. On your own, toggle *ON/OFF* the three options and create additional line-segments to see the different effects of the settings.

The *RockerArm* design:

❖ Before continuing to the next page, on your own, make a rough freehand sketch showing the steps that can be used to create the design. Be aware that there are many different approaches to accomplishing the same task.

Basic Object Construction Tools 14-7

Activate the Startup option

❖ In **AutoCAD® 2013**, we can use the *Startup* dialog box to establish different types of drawing settings. The startup dialog box can be activated through the use of the **STARTUP** system variable.

The STARTUP system variable can be set to either 0 or 1:
- 1: displays the *Create New Drawing* dialog box.
- 0: displays the *Select Template* dialog box (default).

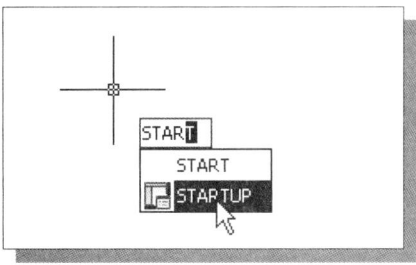

1. In the command prompt area, choose the Startup option from the list or enter the system variable name:
   STARTUP [ENTER]

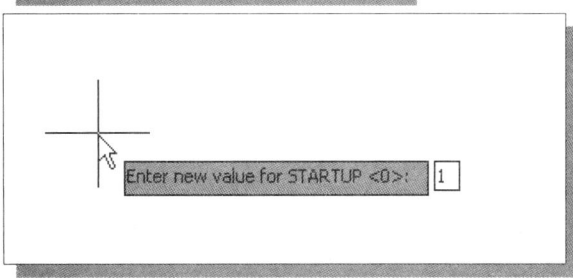

2. Enter **1** as the new value for the *Startup* system variable.

3. To show the effect of the *Startup* option, **exit** AutoCAD by clicking on the **Close** icon as shown.

4. Restart AutoCAD by selecting the **AutoCAD 2013** option through the *Start* menu.

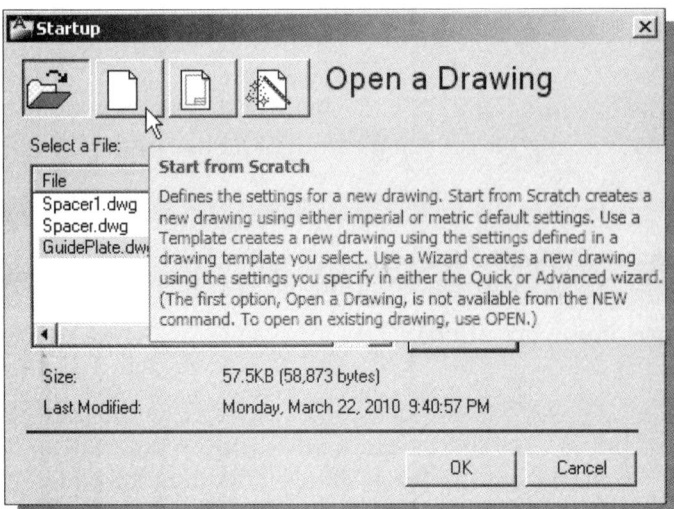

5. The *Startup* dialog box appears on the screen with different options to assist the creation of drawings. Move the cursor on top of the four icons and notice the four options available:
   (1) **Open a drawing**
   (2) **Start from Scratch**
   (3) **Use a Template**
   (4) **Use a Setup Wizard**

6. In the *Startup* dialog box, select the **Start from Scratch** option as shown in the figure.

7. Choose **Metric** to use the metric settings.

8. Click **OK** to accept the setting.

Drawing Units Display Setup

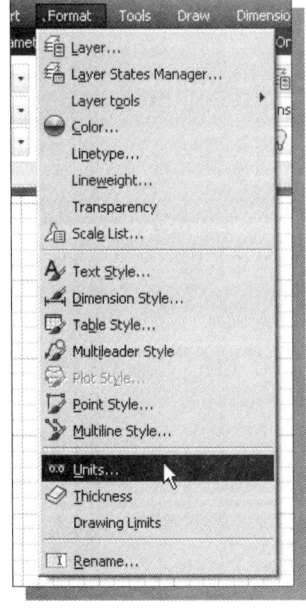

1. On your own, activate the display of the AutoCAD *Menu Bar*. (Refer to page 1-4 for the procedure.)

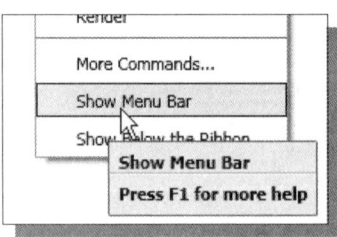

2. Click the *Menu Bar* area, select:
   [Format] → [Units]

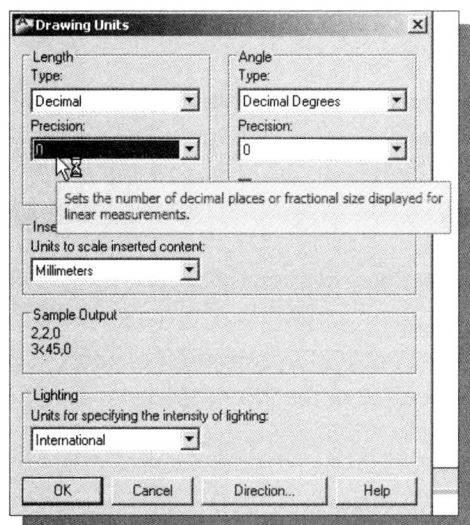

3. Set the *Precision* to **no digits** after the decimal point.

4. Click **OK** to exit the *Drawing Units* dialog box.

5. On your own, adjust the option settings so that only the **Dynamic Input** option is turned *ON* in the *Status Bar* area.

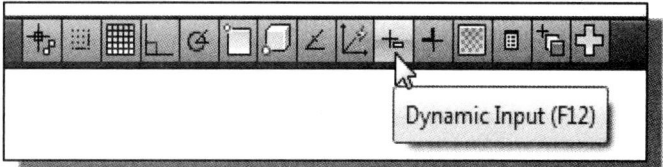

GRID and *SNAP* Intervals Setup

1. In the *Status Bar* area, **right-mouse-click** on *Grid Mode* and choose **[Settings]**

2. In the *Drafting Settings* dialog box, select the **Snap and Grid** tab if it is not the page on top.

3. Change *Grid Spacing* and *Snap Spacing* to **10** for both X and Y directions.

4. Switch *ON* the *Display dotted grid in 2D model Space* option as shown

5. Switch *ON* the *Grid On* and *Snap On* options as shown.

6. Click **OK** to exit the *Drawing Units* dialog box.

Drawing Area Setup

❖ Next, we will set up the **Drawing Limits**; setting the Drawing Limits controls the extents of the display of the *grid*. It also serves as a visual reference that marks the working area. Note that this setting can also be adjusted through the use of the command prompt area.

1. Click inside the *command prompt* area.

2. Inside the command prompt area, enter **Limits** and press the **[Enter]** key.

3. In the command prompt area, near the bottom of the AutoCAD drawing screen, the message "*Reset Model Space Limits: Specify lower left corner or [On/Off] <0,0>:*" is displayed. Enter **-200,-150** through the *Dynamic Input* entry boxes.

4. In the command prompt area, the message "*Specify upper right corner <420,297>:*" is displayed. Enter **200,150** as the new upper right coordinates as shown.

5. On your own, use the *Menu Bar* and confirm the **[View]** → **[Display]** → **[UCS Icon]** → **[Origin]** option is switched *ON* as shown. (The little checked icon next to the option indicates it is switched *ON*.)

6. On your own, use the **Zoom Extents** command, under the **View** tab, to reset the display.

❖ Notice the *UCS Icon*, which is aligned to the origin, is displayed at the center of the graphics window.

Referencing the World Coordinate System

Design modeling software is becoming more powerful and user friendly, yet the system still does only what the user tells it to do. When using a geometric modeler, we therefore need to have a good understanding of what the inherent limitations are. We should also have a good understanding of what we want to do and what to expect, as the results are based on what is available.

In most geometric modelers, objects are located and defined in what is usually called **world space** or **global space**. Although a number of different coordinate systems can be used to create and manipulate objects in a 3D modeling system, the objects are typically defined and stored using the *world space*. The *world space* is usually a **3D Cartesian coordinate system** that the user cannot change or manipulate.

In most engineering designs, models can be very complex, and it would be tedious and confusing if only one coordinate system were available in CAD systems. Practical CAD systems provide the user with definable **Local Coordinate Systems (LCS)** or **User Coordinate Systems (UCS)**, which are measured relative to the world coordinate system. Once a local coordinate system is defined, we can then create geometry in terms of this more convenient system. For most CAD systems, the default construction coordinate system is initially aligned to the world coordinate system.

In AutoCAD, the default **User Coordinate System (UCS)** is initially aligned to the XY plane of the **World Coordinate System (WCS)**. One simple approach to creating designs in CAD systems is to create geometry by referencing the **World Coordinate System**. The general procedure of this approach is illustrated in the following sections.

Creating *Circles*

1. Click on and switch back to the **Home** tab in the *Ribbon* tabs and panels area.

2. Select the **Circle – Center, Radius** command icon in the *Draw* toolbar. In the command prompt area, the message "*_circle Specify center point for the circle or [3P/2P/Ttr (tan tan radius)]:*" is displayed.

3. Select the **origin** of the world coordinate system as the center point location.

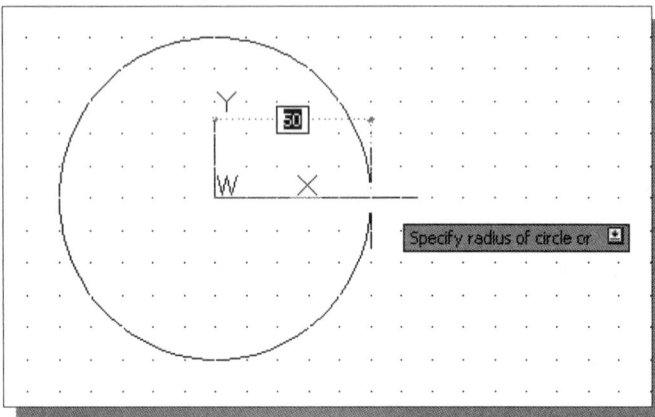

4. In the command prompt area, the message "*Specify radius of circle or [Diameter]:*" is displayed. AutoCAD expects us to identify the radius of the circle. Set the radius to **50** by observing the tooltips as shown.

5. Hit the [**SPACE BAR**] once to repeat the circle command.

6. On your own, select **70,40** as the absolute coordinate values of the center point coordinates of the second circle.

7. Set the value of the radius to **25**.

8. On your own, repeat the above procedure and create another circle (radius **25**) at absolute coordinates of **-50,-60** as shown in the figure.

Object Snap Toolbar

1. Move the cursor to the *Menu Bar* area and choose **[Tools]** → **[Toolbars]** → **[AutoCAD]**.

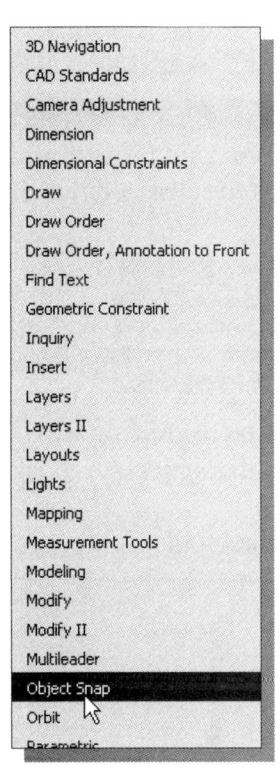

   ❖ AutoCAD provides 44 predefined toolbars for access to frequently used commands, settings, and modes. A *checkmark* (next to the item) in the list identifies the toolbars that are currently displayed on the screen.

2. Select **Object Snap**, with the left-mouse-button, to display the *Object Snap* toolbar on the screen.

   ❖ **Object Snap** is an extremely powerful construction tool available on most CAD systems. During an entity's creation operations, we can snap the cursor to points on objects such as endpoints, midpoints, centers, and intersections. For example, we can turn on **Object Snap** and quickly draw a line to the center of a circle, the midpoint of a line segment, or the intersection of two lines.

3. Move the cursor over the icons in the *Object Snap* toolbar and read the description of each icon.

4. We will next turn **OFF** the *GRID SNAP* option by toggling off the **SNAP Mode** button in the *Status Bar* area.

5. On your own, reset the option buttons in the *Status Bar* area, so that only the *GRID DISPLAY* option is switched **ON**.

Using the *LINE* command

1. Select the **Line** command icon in the *Draw* toolbar. In the command prompt area, near the bottom of the AutoCAD drawing screen, the message "*_line Specify first point:*" is displayed.

2. Pick **Snap to Tangent** in the *Object Snap* toolbar. In the command prompt area, the message "*_tan to*" is displayed. AutoCAD now expects us to select a circle or an arc on the screen.

❖ The **Snap to Tangent** option allows us to snap to the point on a circle or arc that, when connected to the last point, forms a line tangent to that object.

3. Pick a location that is near the top left side of the smaller circle on the right; note the tangent symbol is displayed as shown.

❖ Note that the note "Deferred Tangent" indicates that AutoCAD will calculate the tangent location when the other endpoint of the line is defined.

4. Pick **Snap to Tangent** in the *Object Snap* toolbar. In the command prompt area, the message "*_tan to*" is displayed. AutoCAD now expects us to select a circle or an arc on the screen.

Basic Object Construction Tools   14-15

5. Pick a location that is near the top left side of the center circle; note the tangent symbol is displayed as shown.

6. Inside the graphics window, **right-mouse-click** to activate the option menu and select **Enter** with the left-mouse-button to end the Line command.

❖ A line tangent to both circles is constructed as shown in the figure.

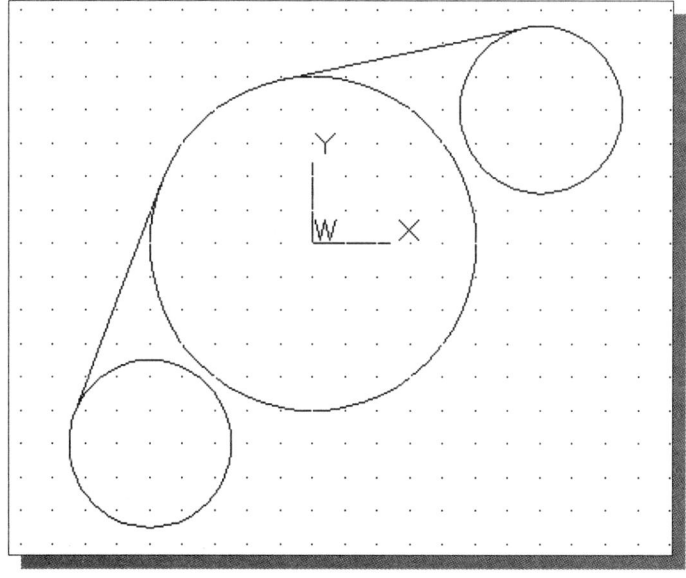

7. On your own, repeat the above steps and create the other tangent line between the center circle and the circle on the left. Your drawing should appear as the figure.

Creating *TTR Circles*

1. Select the **Circle** command icon in the *Draw* toolbar. In the command prompt area, the message "*Specify center point for circle or [3P/2P/Ttr (tan tan radius)]:*" is displayed.

2. Inside the graphics window, right-mouse-click to activate the option menu and select the **Ttr (tan tan radius)** option. This option allows us to create a circle that is tangent to two objects.

3. Pick a location near the **bottom of the smaller circle** on the right. We will create a circle that is tangent to this circle and the center circle.

4. Pick the **center circle** by selecting a location that is near the right side of the circle. AutoCAD interprets the locations we selected as being near the tangency.

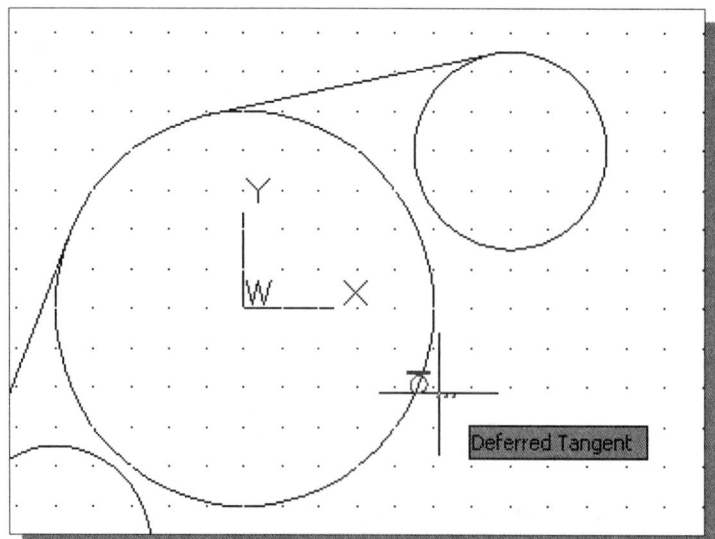

5. In the command prompt area, the message "*Specify radius of circle*" is displayed. Enter **50** as the radius of the circle.

Specify radius of circle: **50 [ENTER]**

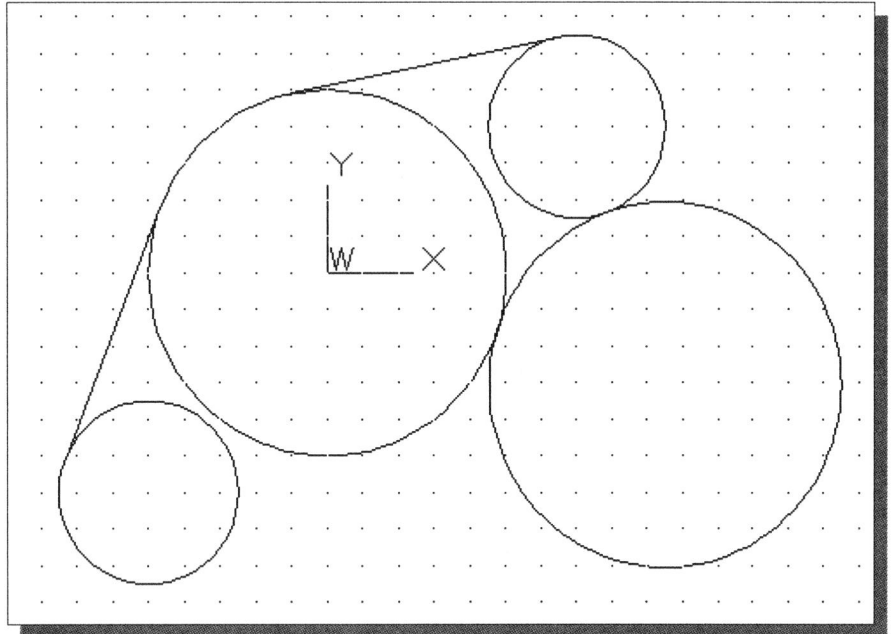

6. On your own, repeat the above steps and create the other TTR circle (radius **40**). Your drawing should appear as the figure below.

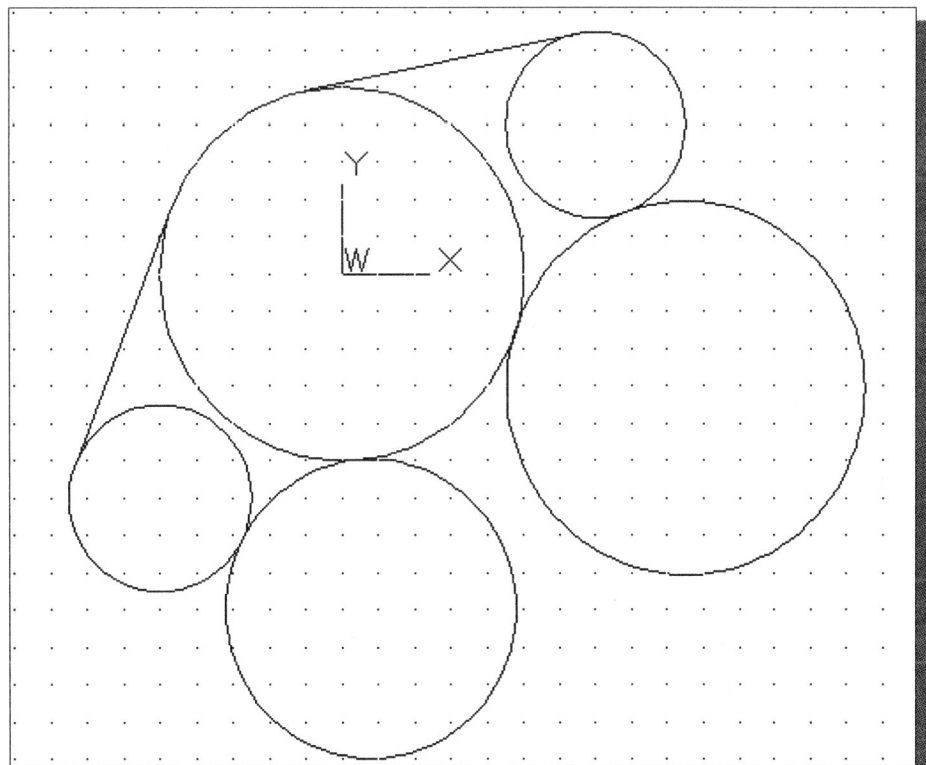

Using the *TRIM* Command

- The **Trim** command shortens an object so that it ends precisely at a selected boundary.

1. Select the **Trim** command icon in the *Modify* toolbar, click on the down-triangle to display additional icons as shown. In the command prompt area, the message "*Select boundary edges... Select objects:*" is displayed.

- First, we will select the objects that define the boundary edges to which we want to trim the object.

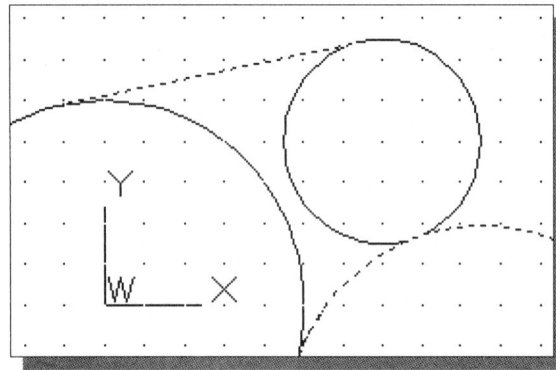

2. Pick the tangent line connecting the center circle and the top right circle.

3. Pick the lower right circle. The two selected entities are highlighted as shown in the figure.

4. Inside the graphics window, **right-mouse-click** once to proceed with the Trim command.

5. The message "*Select object to trim or shift-select object to extend or [Project/Edge/Undo]:*" is displayed in the command prompt area. Pick the **left** section of the upper right circle and note the selected portion is trimmed as shown.

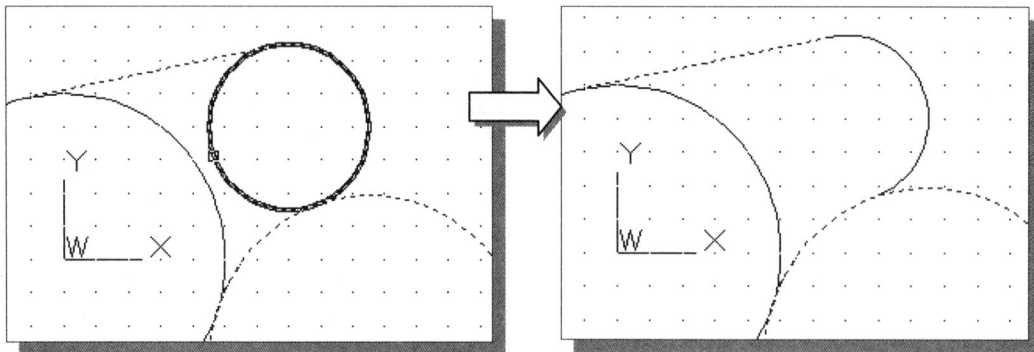

❖ In AutoCAD, the Trim command requires first selection of objects that define the cutting edges at which an object is to stop. Valid cutting edge objects include most 2D geometry such as lines, arcs, circles, ellipses, polylines, splines, and text. For 3D objects, a 2D projection method is used where objects are projected onto the XY plane of the current user coordinate system (UCS).

6. Select the upper right side of the center circle to remove the selected portion.

7. Inside the graphics window, **right-mouse-click** to activate the option menu and select **Enter** to end the Trim command.

8. Hit the [**SPACE BAR**] once to repeat the **Trim** command.

9. Select the two arcs that were trimmed as the two cutting edges and trim the lower section of the TTR circle as shown.

10. On your own, trim the other geometry so that the drawing appears as shown.

11. Inside the graphics window, **right-mouse-click** to activate the option menu and select **Enter** with the left-mouse-button to end the Trim command.

Using the POLYGON command

1. Select the **Polygon** command icon in the *Draw* toolbar. Click on the triangle icon next to the rectangle icon to display the additional icon list.

2. Enter **6** to create a six-sided hexagon.
   polygon Enter number of sides <4>:
   6 [ENTER]

3. The message "*Specify center of polygon or [Edge]:*" is displayed. Since the center of the large circle is aligned to the origin of the WCS, the center of the polygon can be positioned using several methods. Set the center point to the origin by entering the absolute coordinates. *Specify center of polygon or [Edge]:* **0,0 [ENTER]**

4. In the command prompt area, the message "*Enter an option [Inscribed in circle/Circumscribed about circle] <I>:*" is displayed. Click **Circumscribed** to select the *Circumscribed about circle* option.

5. In the command prompt area, the message *Specify radius of circle:*" is displayed. Enter **30** as the radius.
   Specify radius of circle : **30 [ENTER]**

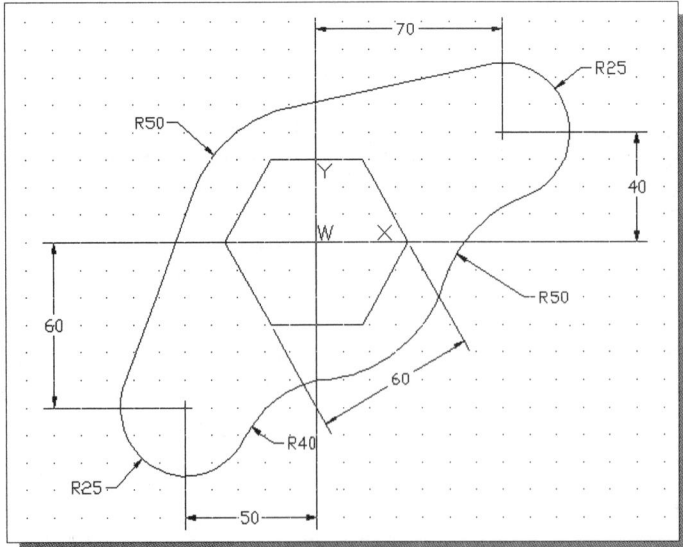

❖ Note that the polygon option [Inscribed in circle/Circumscribed about circle] allows us to create either **flat to flat** or **corner to corner** distance.

Basic Object Construction Tools   14-21

6. Inside the graphics window, **right-mouse-click** to activate the option menu and select **Repeat Polygon**. In the command prompt area, the message "*_polygon Enter number of sides <6>:*" is displayed.

7. Enter **4** to create a four-sided polygon.
   _polygon Enter number of sides <6>: **4 [ENTER]**

8. In the command prompt area, the message "*Specify center of polygon or [Edge]:*" is displayed. Let's use the *Object Snap* options to locate its center location. Pick **Snap to Center** in the *Object Snap* toolbar as shown.

9. Move the cursor on top of the arc on the right and notice the center point is automatically highlighted. Select the arc to accept the highlighted location.

10. Inside the graphics window, **right-mouse-click** to activate the option menu and select **Circumscribed about circle**.

11. Switch *ON* the *GRID SNAP* option in the *Status Bar* as shown.

12. Create a square by selecting one of the adjacent grid points next to the center point as shown. Note that the orientation of the polygon can also be adjusted as the cursor is moved to other locations.

Creating a Concentric *Circle*

1. Select the **Circle** command icon in the *Draw* toolbar. In the command prompt area, the message "*Specify center point for circle or [3P/2P/Ttr (tan tan radius)]:*" is displayed.

2. Let's use the *Object Snap* options to assure the center location is aligned properly. Pick **Snap to Center** in the *Object Snap* toolbar as shown.

3. Move the cursor on top of the lower arc on the left and notice the center point is automatically highlighted. Select the arc to accept the highlighted location.

4. In the command prompt area, the message "*Specify radius of circle <25>*" is displayed. Enter **10** to complete the Circle command.
   Specify radius of circle <25>: **10 [ENTER]**

Basic Object Construction Tools   14-23

Using the QuickCal calculator to Measure Distance and Angle

- AutoCAD also provides several tools that will allow us to measure distance, area, perimeter, and even mass properties. With the use of the *Object Snap* options, getting measurements of the completed design can be done very quickly.

1. Inside the *graphics window*, **right-mouse-click** once to bring up the option menu.

2. Select **QuickCalc** in the option menu as shown.

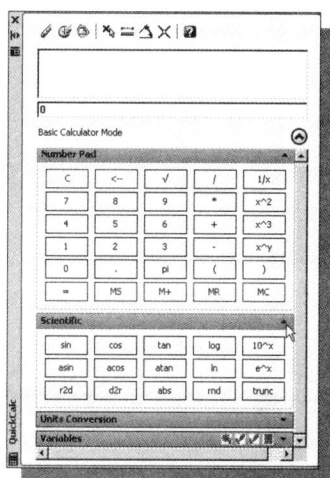

❖ Note that the QuickCalc option brings up the AutoCAD calculator, which can be used to perform a full range of mathematical, scientific, and geometric calculations. We can also use QuickCalc to create and use variables, as well as to convert units of measurement.

3. Click the **Measure Distance** icon, which is located on the top section of the *QuickCalc* calculator pad.

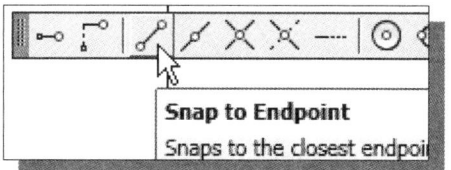

4. Pick **Snap to Endpoint** in the *Object Snap* toolbar.

5. Select the tangent line, near the lower endpoint, as shown.

6. Pick **Snap to Endpoint** in the *Object Snap* toolbar.

7. Select the tangent line, near the upper endpoint, as shown.

❖ The length of the line is displayed in the *Quickcalc* calculator as shown.

8. Click the **Clear** icon to remove the number displayed.

9. On your own, repeat the above steps and measure the center to center distance of the lower region of the design as shown. (Hint: use the **Snap to Center** option.)

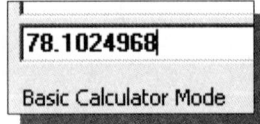

10. Click the **Measure Angle** icon, which is located on the top section of the *QuickCalc* calculator pad.

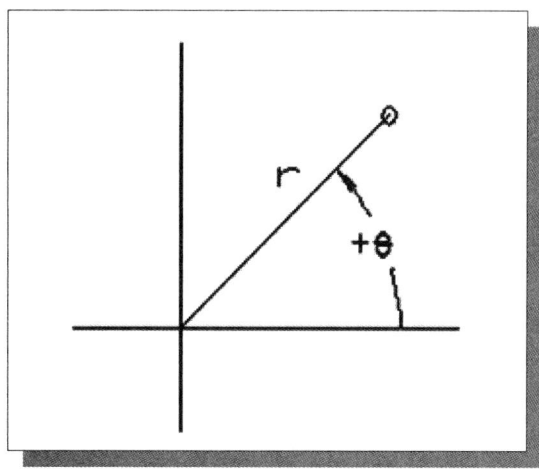

❖ Note that this option allows us to measure the angle between the horizontal axis and the line formed by the selected two points. A positive angle indicates a counterclockwise direction.

11. Pick **Snap to Endpoint** in the *Object Snap* toolbar.

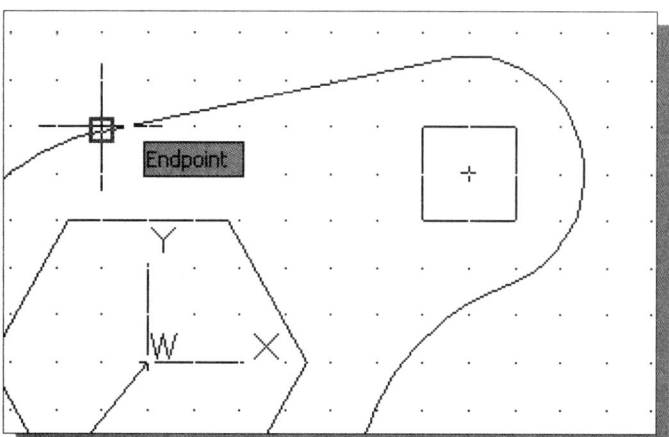

12. Select the tangent line, near the lower endpoint, as shown.

13. Pick **Snap to Endpoint** in the *Object Snap* toolbar.

14. Select the tangent line, near the upper endpoint, as shown.

> The measured angle is displayed in the calculator pad as shown.

15. On your own, experiment with the available **Get Coordinates** options.

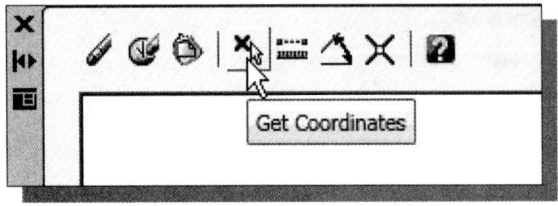

> Note also that the QuickCalc calculator can remain active while you are using the other AutoCAD commands.

Saving the CAD file

1. In the *Application Menu*, select:

   [Application] → [Save]

   ❖ Note the command can also be activated with quick-key combination of **[Ctrl]+[S]**.

2. In the *Save Drawing As* dialog box, select the folder in which you want to store the CAD file and enter **RockerArm** in the *File name* box.

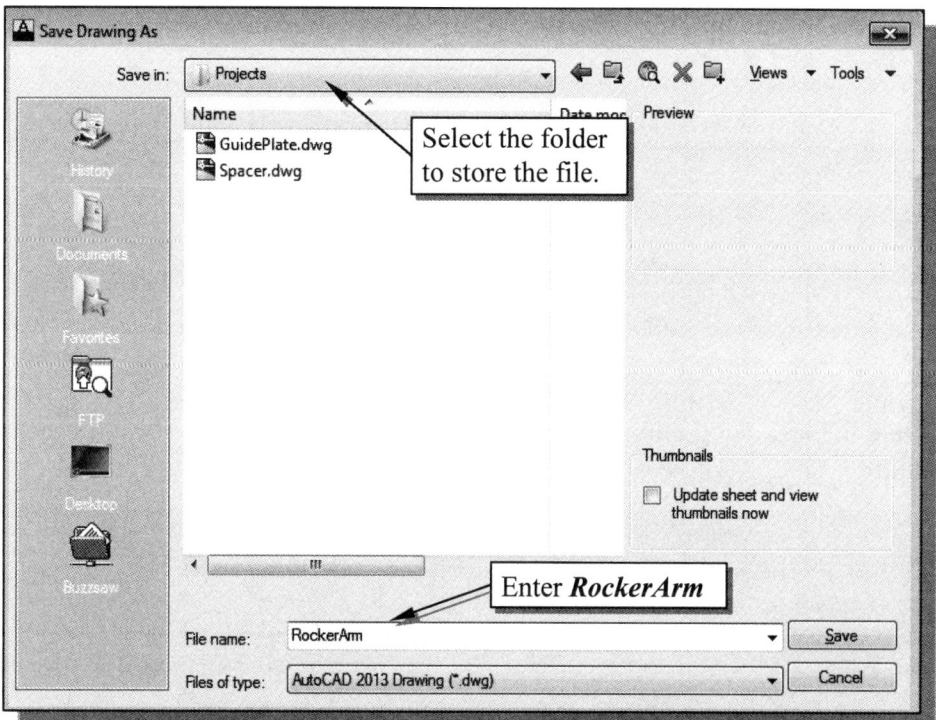

3. Pick **Save** in the *Save Drawing As* dialog box to accept the selections and save the file.

Exit AutoCAD

- To exit **AutoCAD® 2013**, select **Exit AutoCAD** from the *Application Menu* or type **QUIT** at the command prompt.

Review Questions: (Time: 20 minutes)

1. Describe the procedure to activate the AutoCAD **Startup** option.

2. List and describe three options in the AutoCAD *Object Snap* toolbar.

3. Which AutoCAD command can we use to remove a portion of an existing entity?

4. Describe the difference between the *circumscribed* and *inscribed* options when using the AutoCAD **Polygon** command.

5. Create the following triangle and fill in the blanks: Length = ____, Angle = ____. (Dimensions are in inches.)

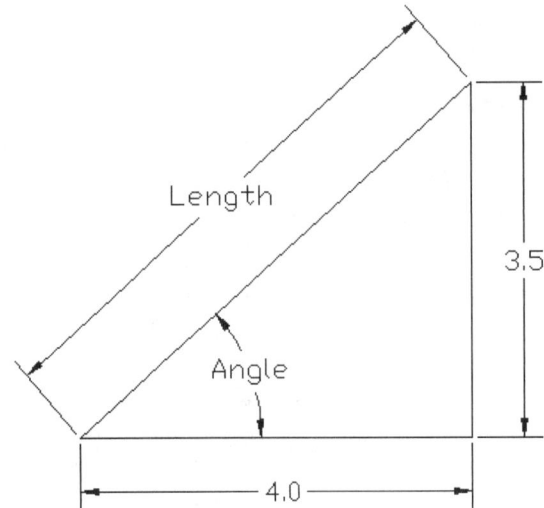

6. Create the following drawing; line *AB* is tangent to both circles. Fill in the blanks: Length = ____, Angle = ____. (Dimensions are in inches.)

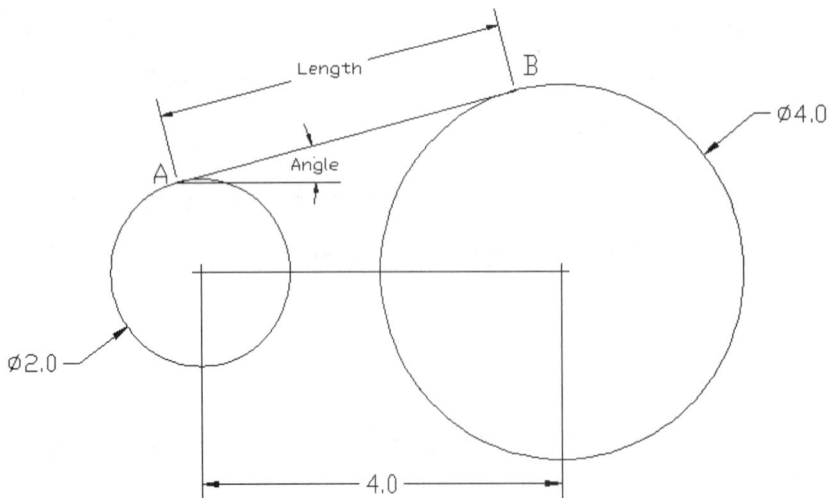

Exercises:

(Unless otherwise specified, dimensions are in inches. Time: 90 minutes.)

1. Adjustable Support

2. V-Slide Plate (The design has two sets of parallel lines with implied tangency.)

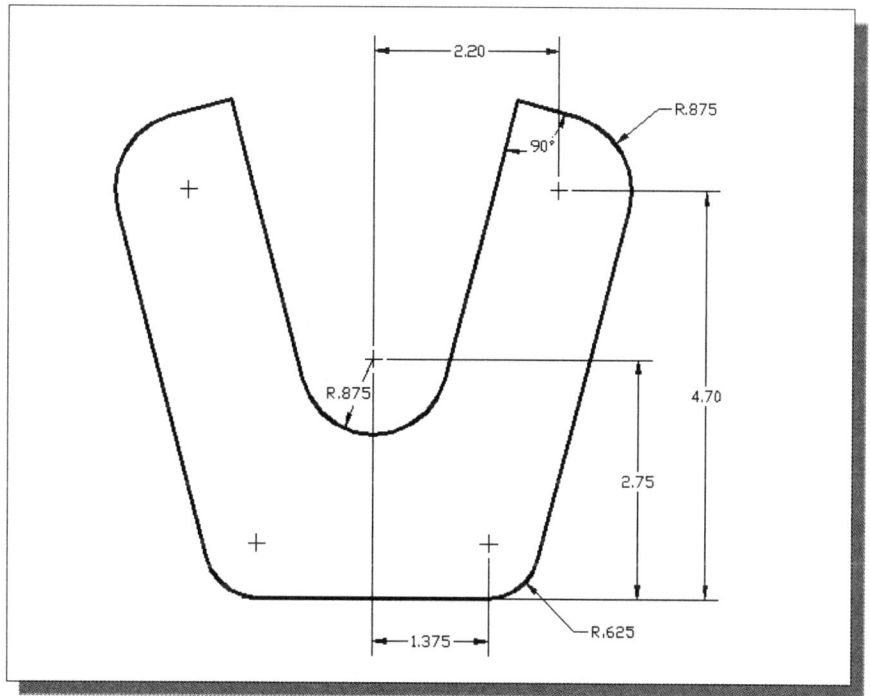

3. **Swivel Base** (Dimensions are in Millimeters.)

4. **Sensor Mount**

5. Flat Hook (Dimensions are in Millimeters. Thickness: 25 mm.)

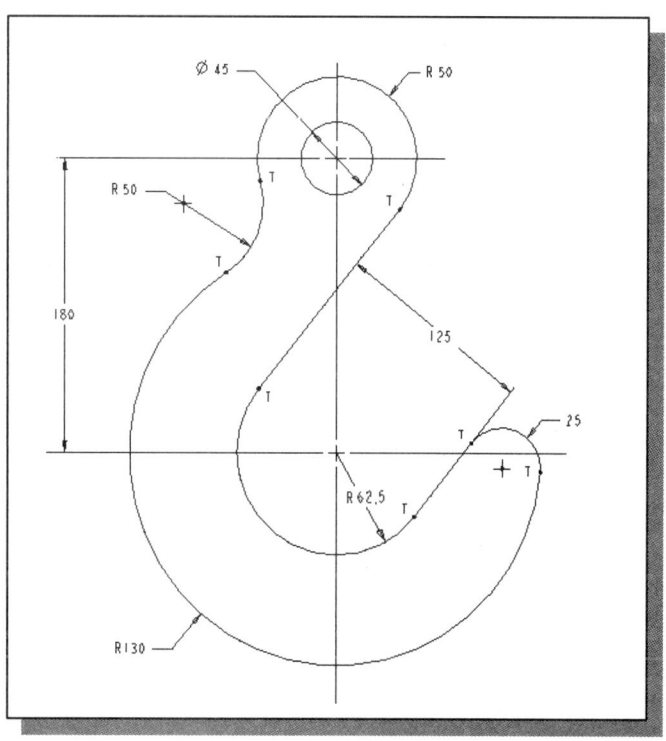

Notes:

Chapter 15
Geometric Construction and Editing Tools

Learning Objectives

- **Set up the display of Drawing Units**
- **Display AutoCAD's toolbars**
- **Set up and use OBJECT SNAPS**
- **Edit, using EXTEND and TRIM**
- **Use the FILLET command**
- **Create parallel geometric entities**
- **Using the PEDIT command**
- **Use the EXPLODE command**

Geometric Constructions

The creation of designs usually involves the manipulations of geometric shapes. Traditionally, manual graphical construction uses simple hand tools like a T-square, straightedge, scales, triangles, compass, dividers, pencils, and paper. The manual drafting tools are designed specifically to assist the construction of geometric shapes. For example, the T-square and drafting machine can be used to construct parallel and perpendicular lines very easily and quickly. Today, modern CAD systems provide designers much better control and accuracy in the construction of geometric shapes.

In technical drawings, many of the geometric shapes are constructed with specific geometric properties, such as perpendicularity, parallelism and tangency. For example, in the drawing below, quite a few implied geometric properties are present.

Geometric Construction and Editing Tools   15-3

Starting Up AutoCAD® 2013

1. Select the AutoCAD 2013 option on the *Program* menu or select the AutoCAD 2013 icon on the *Desktop*. Once the program is loaded into the memory, the **AutoCAD® 2013** drawing screen will appear on the screen.

2. In the *Startup* window, select **Start from Scratch**, as shown in the figure below.

3. In the *Default Settings* section, pick **Imperial (feet and inches)** as the drawing units.

4. Pick **OK** in the *Startup* dialog box to accept the selected settings.

Geometric Construction – CAD Method

The main characteristic of any CAD system is its ability to create and modify 2D/3D geometric entities quickly and accurately. Most CAD systems provide a variety of object construction and editing tools to relieve the designer of the tedious drudgery of this task, so that the designer can concentrate more on design content. A good understanding of the computer geometric construction techniques will enable the CAD users to fully utilize the capability of the CAD systems.

➢ Note that with CAD systems, besides following the classic geometric construction methods; quite a few options are also feasible.

- **Bisection of a Line or Arc**

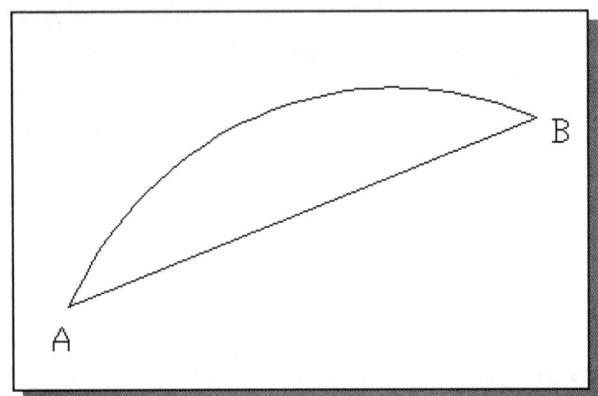

1. Create an arbitrary arc **AB** at any angle, and create line **AB** by connecting the two endpoints of the arc.

2. Switch *ON* only the *Dynamic Input* option by clicking on the buttons in the *Status Bar* area as shown.

3. Select the **Line** command icon in the *Draw* toolbar. In the command prompt area, near the bottom of the AutoCAD drawing screen, the message "*_line Specify first point:*" is displayed. AutoCAD expects us to identify the starting location of a straight line.

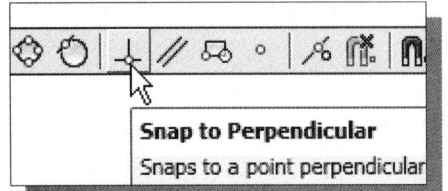

4. Pick **Snap to Perpendicular** in the *Object Snap* toolbar. In the command prompt area, the message "*_per to*" is displayed.

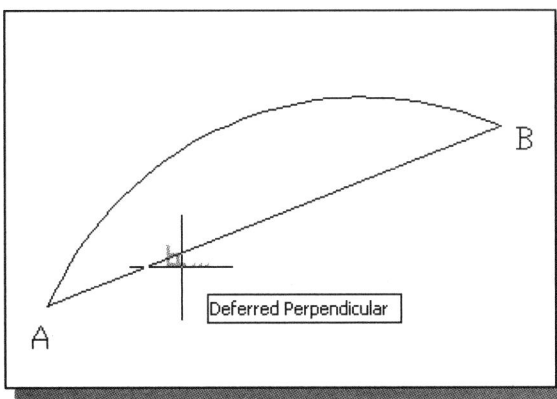

5. Select line **AB** at any position.

❖ Note the tooltip *Deferred Perpendicular* is displayed indicating the construction is deferred until all inputs are completed.

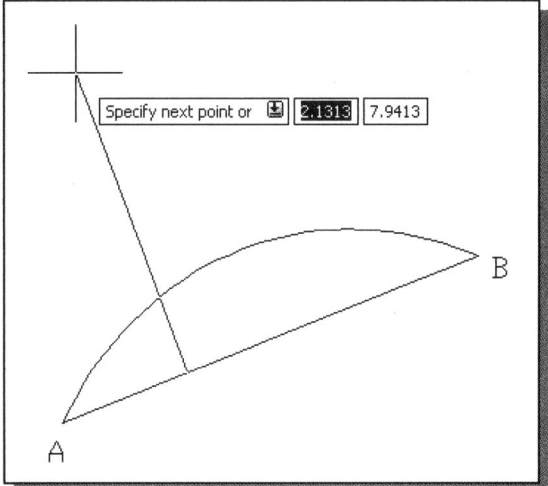

6. Select an arbitrary point above the line as shown.

7. Inside the graphics window, **right-mouse-click** to activate the option menu and select **Enter** with the left-mouse-button to end the **Line** command.

8. Select **Move** in the *Modify* toolbar as shown.

9. Select the perpendicular line we just created.

❖ In the command prompt area, the message: "*Specify the base point or [Displacement]*" is displayed. AutoCAD expects us to select a reference point as the base point for moving the selected object.

10. Pick **Snap to Endpoint** in the *Object Snap* toolbar.

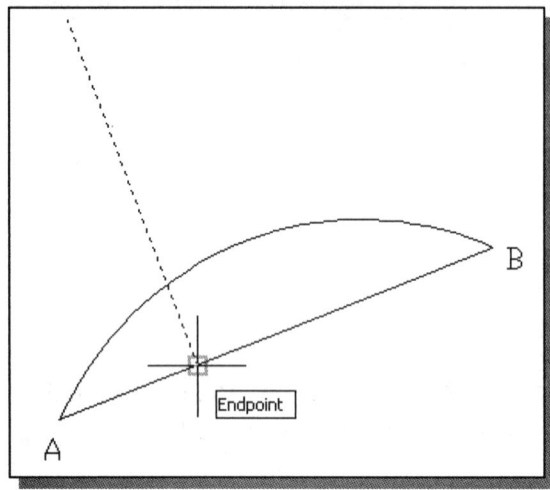

11. Select the lower **Endpoint** of the selected line as shown.

12. Move the cursor inside the graphics window, and notice the line is moved to the new cursor location on the screen,

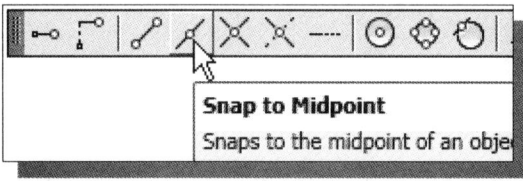

13. Pick **Snap to Midpoint** in the *Object Snap* toolbar.

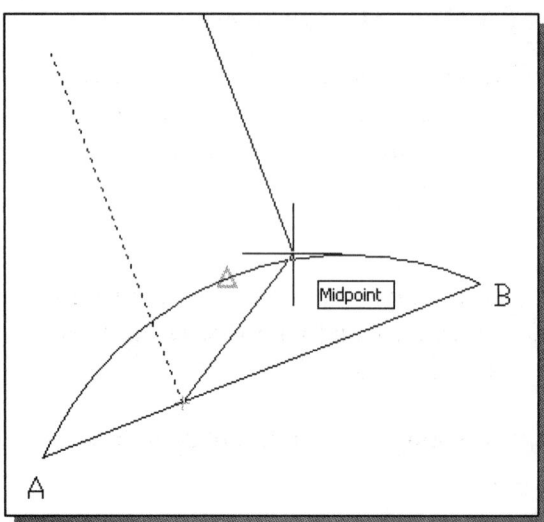

❖ In the command prompt area, the message "_mid to" is displayed. AutoCAD now expects us to select an existing arc or line on the screen.

14. Select the arc to move the line to the midpoint of the arc. Note that the midpoint of an arc or a line is displayed when the cursor is on top of the object.

15. On your own, repeat the above process and move the perpendicular line to the midpoint of line **AB**.

➢ The constructed bisecting line is perpendicular to line **AB** and passes through the midpoint of the line or arc **AB**.

- **Bisection of an Angle**

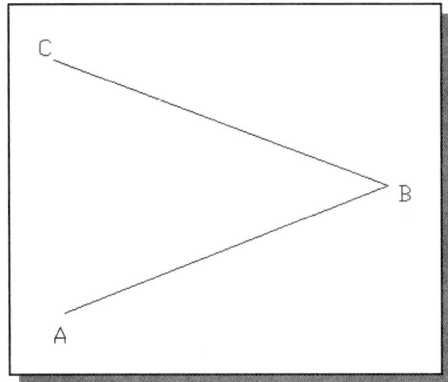

1. Create an arbitrary angle **ABC** as shown in the figure.

2. Click once with the left-mouse-button on the small triangle in the titlebar of the *Draw* toolbar as shown.

3. Select the **Construction Line** icon in the *Draw* toolbar. In the command prompt area, the message " *xline Specify a point or [Hor/Ver/Ang/Bisect/Offset]:*" is displayed.

 ➢ *Construction lines* are lines that extend to infinity. Construction lines are usually used as references for creating other objects.

4. Inside the graphics window, **right-mouse-click** once to bring up the option menu.

5. Select **Bisect** from the option list as shown. In the command prompt area, the message "*Specify angle vertex point:*" is displayed.

6. Pick **Snap to Endpoint** in the *Object Snap* toolbar.

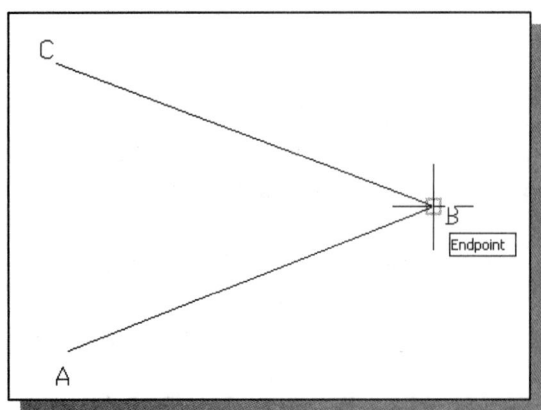

7. Select the vertex point of the angle as shown. In the command prompt area, the message "*Specify angle start point:*" is displayed.

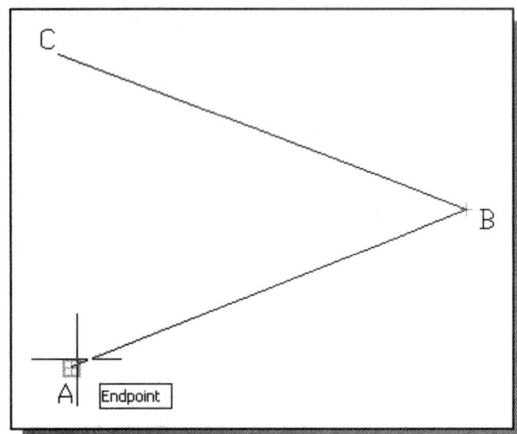

8. Pick **Snap to Endpoint** in the *Object Snap* toolbar.

9. Select one of the endpoints of the angle.

10. Pick **Snap to Endpoint** in the *Object Snap* toolbar.

11. Select the other endpoint of the angle.

➢ Note that the constructed bisection line divides the angle into two equal parts.

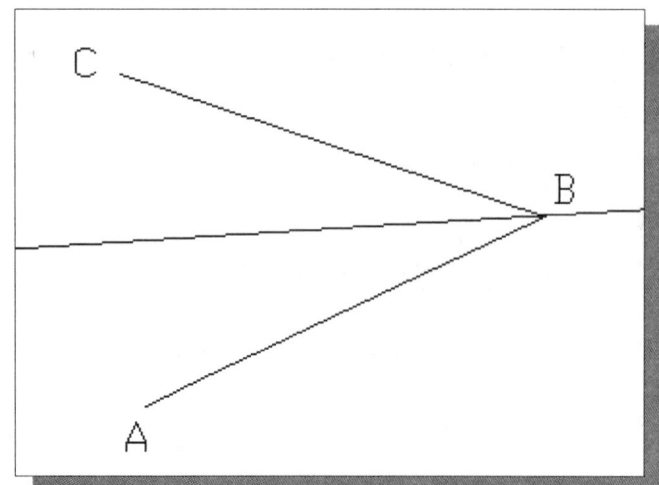

- **Transfer of an Angle**

1. Create an arbitrary angle ABC and a separate line **XY** as shown in the figure.

    ➤ Besides using the classical transfer method (see page 3-14), CAD systems provide several options to allow the user to accurately measure any constructed objects. In this section, we will use the QuickCalc option to transfer the angle.

2. Select **Copy** in the *Modify* toolbar as shown.

3. Select line XY as the object to be copied.

4. **Right-mouse-click** once to proceed with the Copy command.

5. Pick **Snap to Endpoint** in the *Object Snap* toolbar.

6. Select point **X** as the base point.

7. Use the **Snap to Endpoint** option and select point **X** again to place another line on top of line **XY**.

8. Hit the **ENTER** key once to end the Copy command.

9. Select **Rotate** in the *Draw* toolbar as shown.

10. Select one of the two lines at **XY**.

11. **Right-mouse-click** once to proceed with the Rotate command.

12. Pick **Snap to Endpoint** in the *Object Snap* toolbar.

13. Select point **X** as the base point for the rotation.

14. Inside the graphics window, **right-mouse-click** once to bring up the option menu.

15. Select **QuickCalc** in the option menu as shown.

16. Select **Angle of Line Defined by Two Points** as shown.

> Note the **Distance** option is also available in the toolbar region.

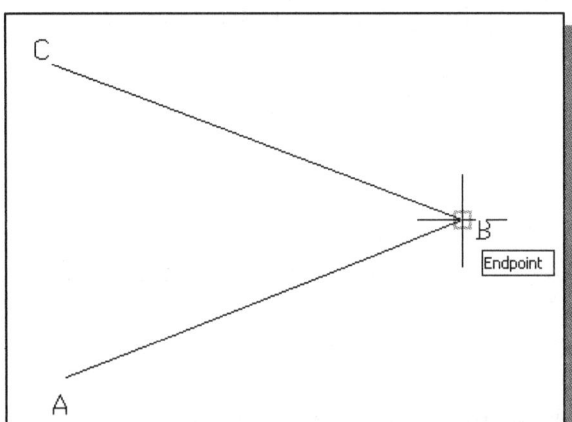

17. Pick **Snap to Endpoint** in the *Object Snap* toolbar.

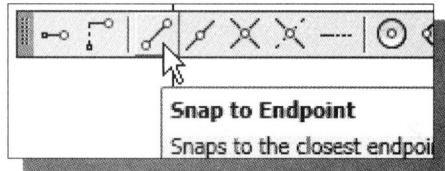

18. Select the vertex, point **B**, of the angle **ABC** as shown.

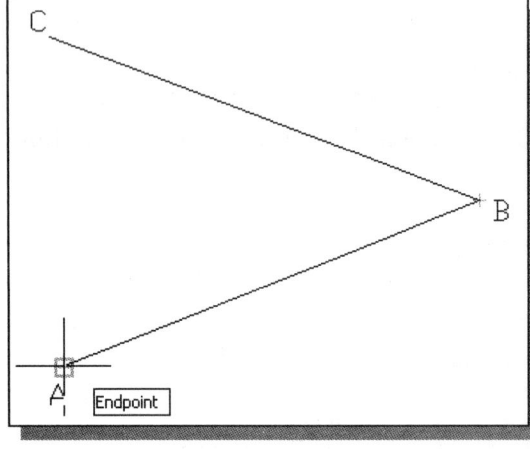

19. Pick **Snap to Endpoint** in the *Object Snap* toolbar.

20. Select point **A** as the second point to measure the angle as shown.

> The default system for measuring angles in **AutoCAD® 2013** defines positive angular values as counterclockwise from the positive X-axis.

Geometric Construction and Editing Tools 15-11

21. Enter a **minus sign** behind the displayed angle in the *QuickCalc* window.

➢ Note the display of **Active Command: Rotate** in the *QuickCalc* window.

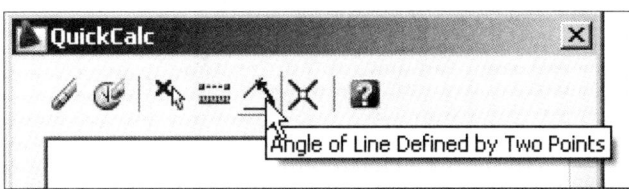

22. Select the **Angle of Line Defined by Two Points** option as shown.

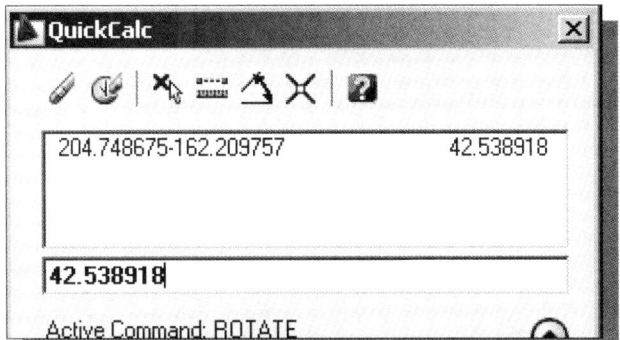

23. Repeat the above process and measure the angle formed by line **BC** and the positive X-axis.

24. Press the **ENTER** key once to calculate the difference between the two values, which is the angle formed by line **AB** and line **BC**.

25. Enter a **minus sign** in front of the calculated value in the *QuickCalc* window as shown.

➢ The minus sign is used to create the new line in the clock-wise direction. (We will rotate the line in a clockwise direction relative to the current **XY** line.)

26. Click **Apply** to transfer the calculated value to the command prompt area.

➢ The calculated value is now transferred in the command prompt area.

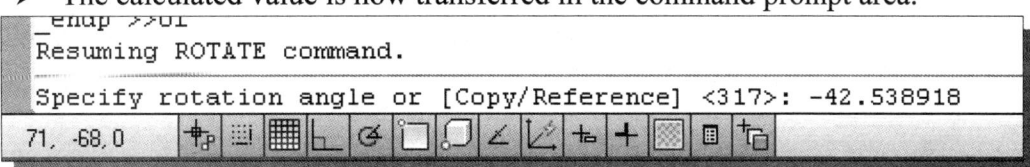

27. Press the **ENTER** key once to accept the displayed value and complete the **Rotate** command.

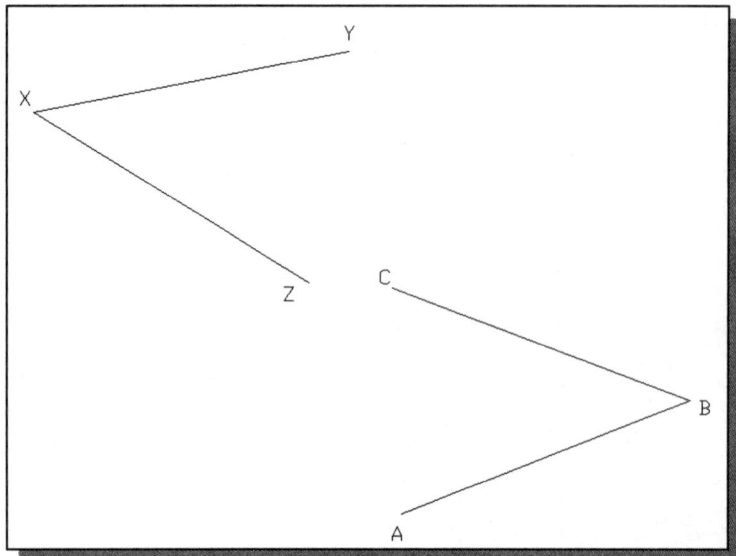

➢ You are also encouraged to perform this geometric construction using the classical method as described below. (Note that R is an arbitrary distance.)

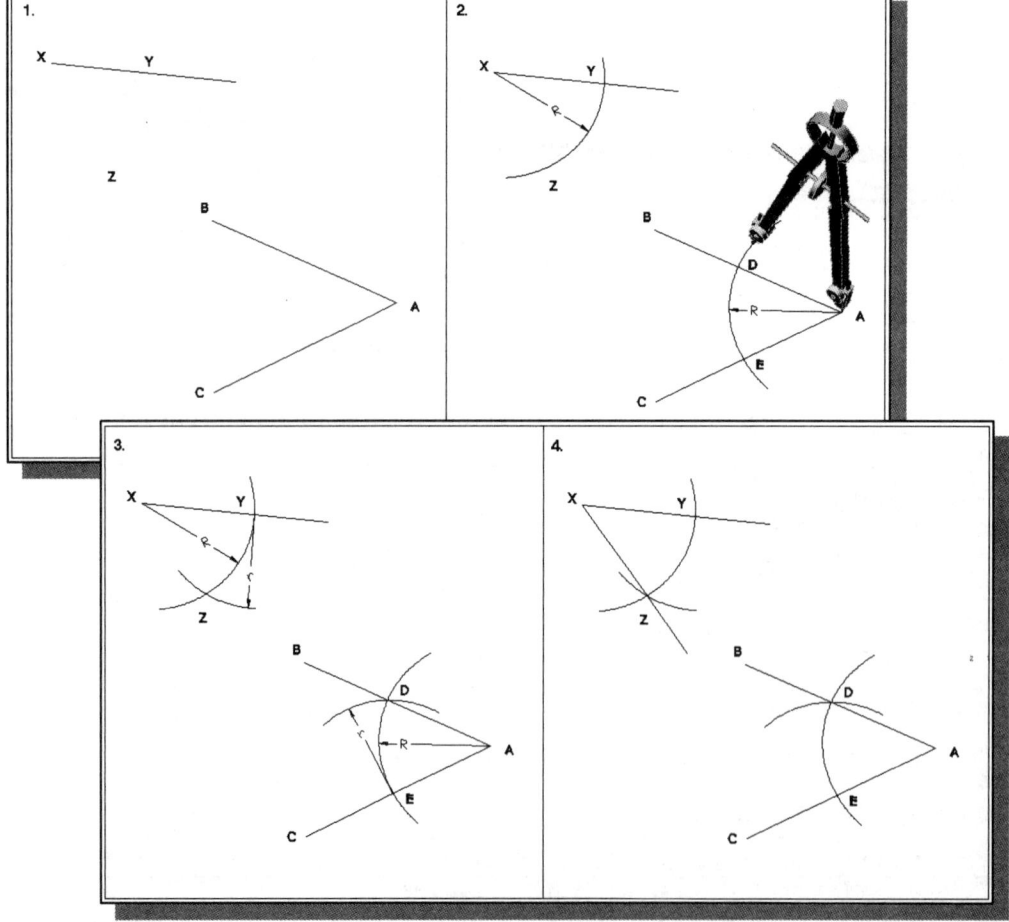

• Dividing a Given Line into a Number of Equal Parts

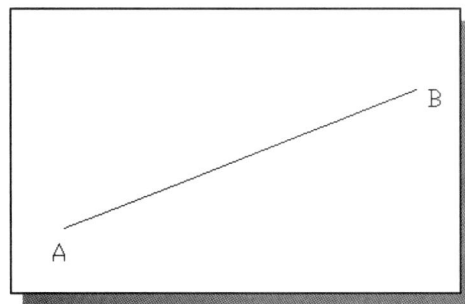

1. Create a line **AB** at an arbitrary angle; the line is to be divided into five equal parts.

2. From the *Draw* toolbar, select:

   [Divide]

3. Select line **AB**. In the message area, the message "*Enter the number of segments or [Block]:*" is displayed.

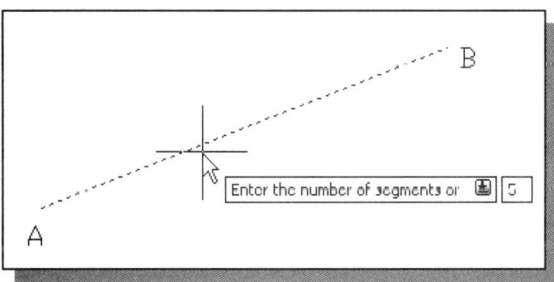

4. Enter **5** as the number of segments needed.

5. On your own, create an arbitrary short line segment at point **A**.

6. Select **Copy** in the *Modify* toolbar as shown.

7. Select the short line as the object to be copied.

8. **Right-mouse-click** once to proceed with the Copy command.

9. Pick **Snap to Endpoint** in the *Object Snap* toolbar.

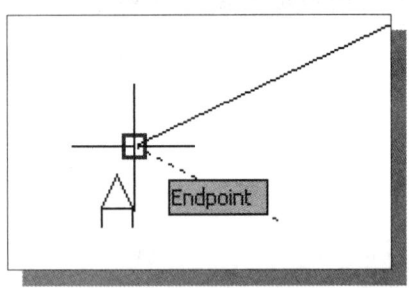

10. **Select** point **A** as the base reference point.

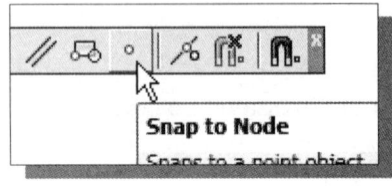

11. Pick **Snap to Node** in the *Object Snap* toolbar.

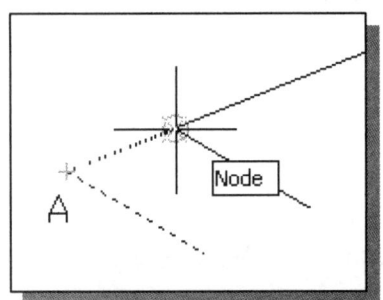

12. Move the cursor along line **AB**, and select the next node point as shown.

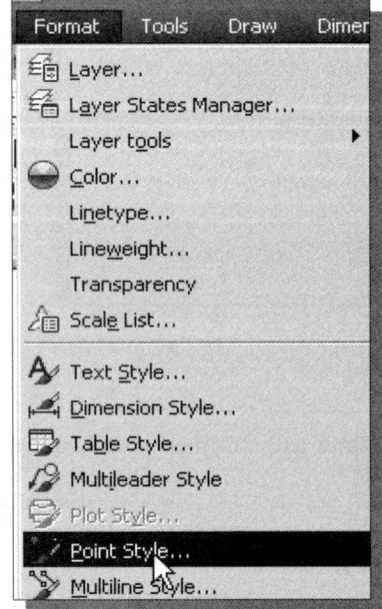

➢ We can also change the display of the created Points.

13. In the *Menu Bar*, select:

   [Format] → [Point Style]

14. In the *Point Style* window, choose the 4th icon in the second row, as shown.

15. Click **OK** to accept the selection and adjust the point style.

- **Circle through Three Points**

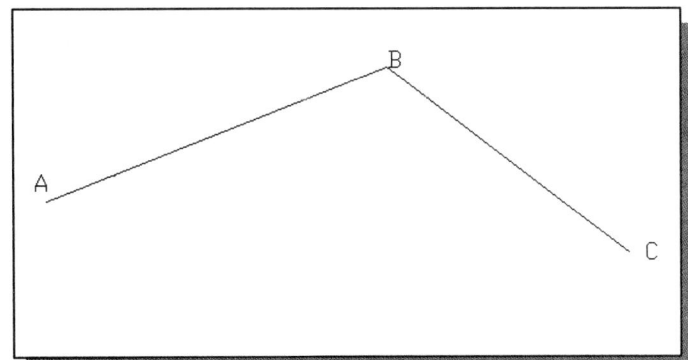

1. Create two arbitrary line segments, **AB** and **BC**, as shown.

2. Select the **3-Point Circle** command in the *Draw* toolbar as shown.

3. Pick **Snap to Endpoint** in the *Object Snap* toolbar.

4. Select the first point, point **A**.

5. Repeat the above steps and select points **B** and **C** to create the circle that passes through all three points.

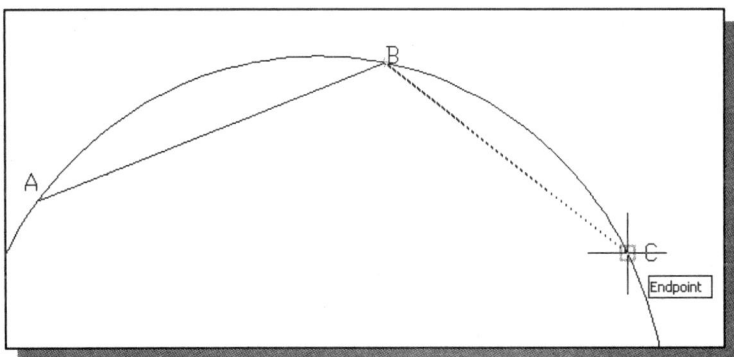

- **Line Tangent to a Circle from a Given Point**

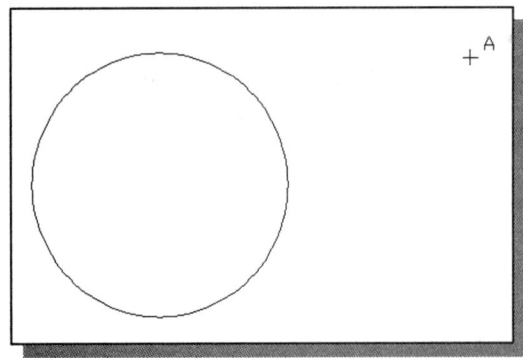

1. Create a circle and a point **A**. (Use the Point command to create point **A**.)

2. Select the **Line** command icon in the *Draw* toolbar. In the command prompt area, near the bottom of the AutoCAD drawing screen, the message "*_line Specify first point:*" is displayed. AutoCAD expects us to identify the starting location of a straight line.

3. Pick **Snap to Node** in the *Object Snap* toolbar.

4. Select point **A** as the starting point of the new line.

5. Pick **Snap to Tangent** in the *Object Snap* toolbar.

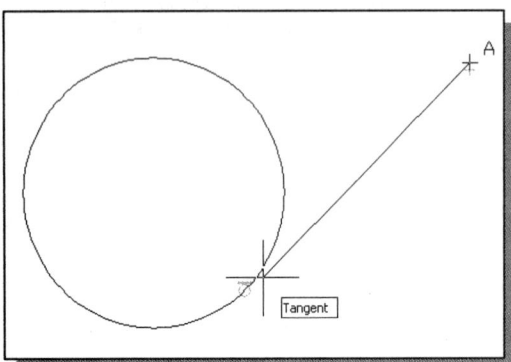

6. Move the cursor on top of the circle and notice the Tangent symbol is displayed.

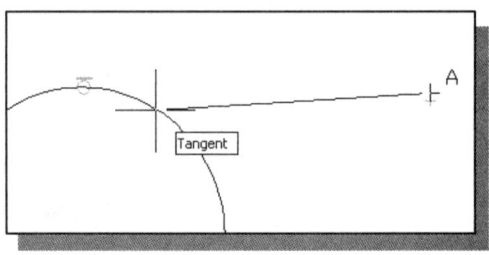

➢ Note that we can create two tangent lines, one to the top and one to the bottom of the circle, from point **A**.

- **Circle of a Given Radius Tangent to two Given Lines**

    Option I: TTR circle

    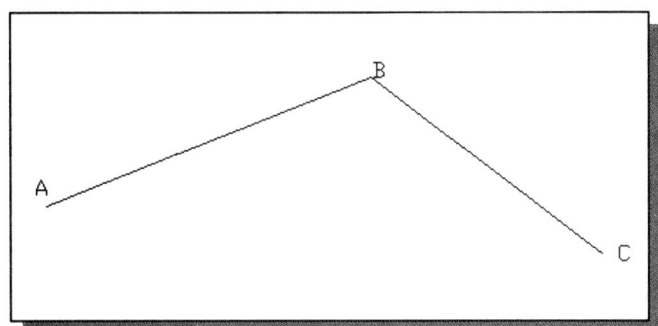

    1. Create two arbitrary line segments as shown.

    2. Select **TTR Circle** in the *Draw* toolbar as shown.

    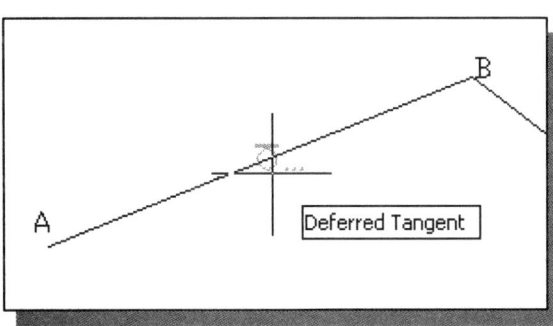

    3. Select one of the line segments; note the tangency is deferred until all inputs are completed.

    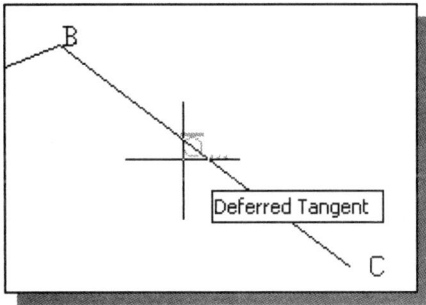

    4. Select the other line segment; note the tangency is also deferred until all inputs are completed.

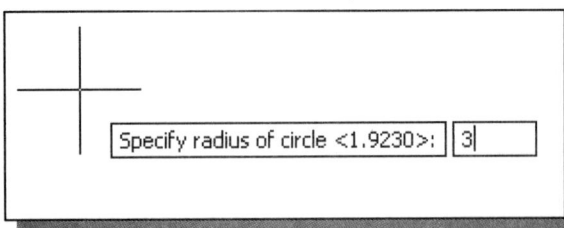

5. Enter **3** as the radius of the circle.

   ➢ The circle is constructed exactly tangent to both lines.

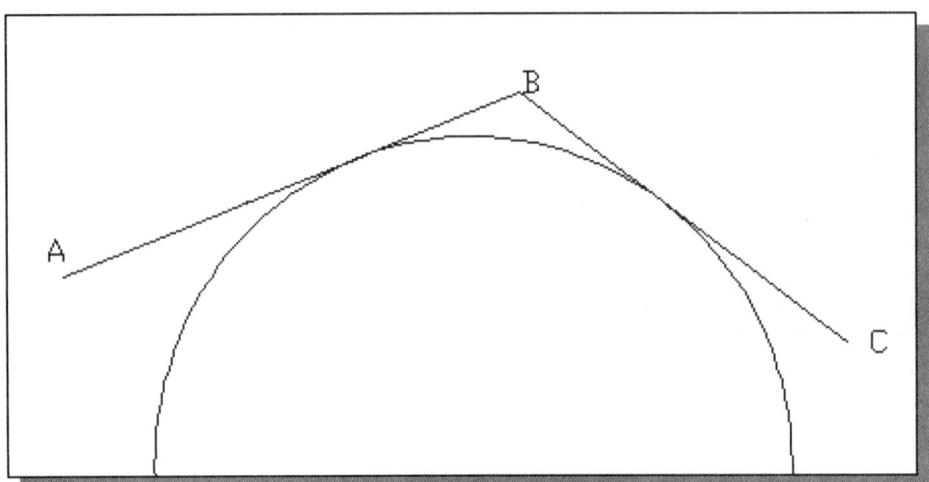

Option II: Fillet command

1. Select the **Undo** icon in the *Standard* toolbar as shown. This will undo the last step, the circle.

2. Select **Fillet** in the *Modify* toolbar as shown.

3. In the command prompt area, the message "*Select first object or [Undo/Polyline/Radius/Trim/Multiple]*" is displayed. By default *Mode* is set to **Trim** and the current arc *Radius* is set to **0**.

Geometric Construction and Editing Tools   15-19

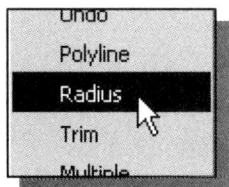

4. Inside the graphics window, **right-mouse-click** once to bring up the option menu.

5. Select **Radius** to adjust the radius of the fillet.

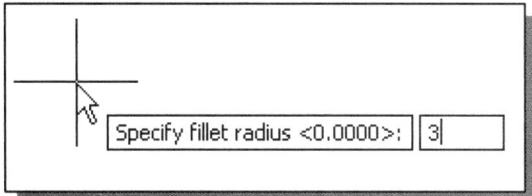

6. Enter **3** as the new radius of the Fillet command.

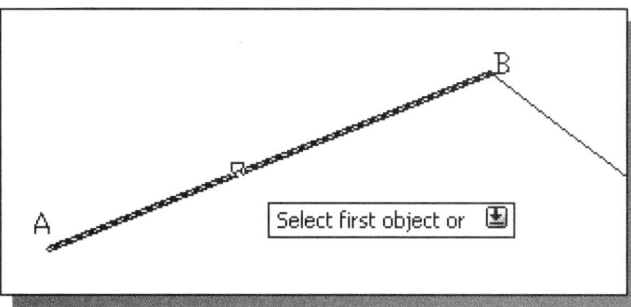

7. Select one of the lines as the first object.

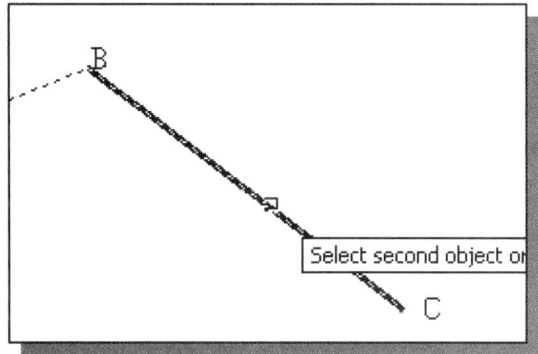

8. Select the other line as the second object.

➢ Note that the default setting of the Fillet command is to trim the edges as shown in the figure below.

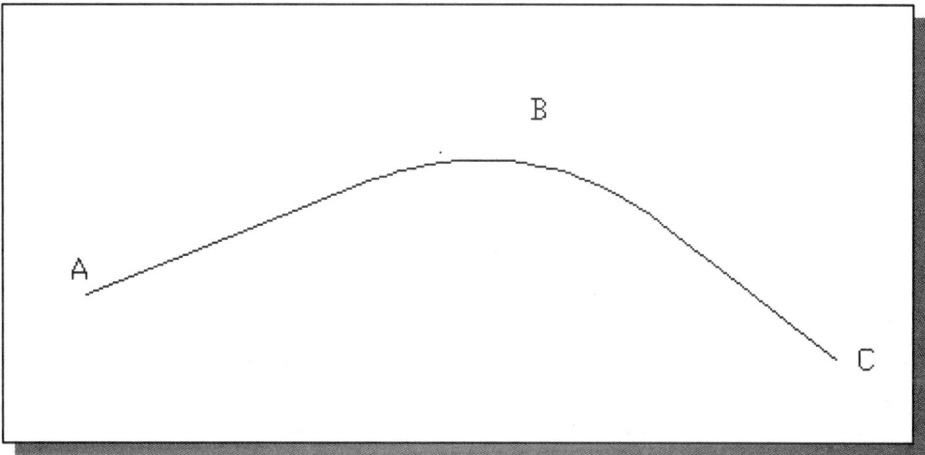

- Note that all of the classical methods for geometric construction, such as the one shown on page 3-14, can also be created in CAD systems.

The *Gasket* design

Exploring the possibilities of a CAD system can be very exciting. For persons who have board drafting experience, the transition from the drafting board to the computer does require some adjusting. But, the essential skills required to work in front of a computer are not that much different from those needed for board drafting. In fact, many of the basic skills acquired in board drafting can also be applied to a computer system. For example, the geometric construction techniques that are typically used in board drafting can be used in AutoCAD. The main difference between using a CAD system over the traditional board drafting is the ability to create and modify geometric entities very quickly and accurately. As it was illustrated in the previous sections, a variety of object construction and editing tools, which are available in AutoCAD, are fairly easy to use. It is important to emphasize that a good understanding of the geometric construction fundamentals remains the most important part of using a CAD system. The application of the basic geometric construction techniques in a CAD system is one of the main tasks in using a CAD system.

In the following sections, we will continue to examine more of the geometric construction and editing tools provided by **AutoCAD® 2013**. We will be looking at the geometric construction tools, such as Trim, Extend, Edit Polyline and Offset that are available in **AutoCAD® 2013**.

❖ Before continuing to the next page, on your own make a rough sketch showing the steps that can be used to create the design. Be aware that there are many different approaches to accomplishing the same task.

Drawing Units Display Setup

Before creating the first geometric entity, the value of the units within the CAD system should be determined. For example, in one drawing, a unit might equal one millimeter of the real-world object. In another drawing, a unit might equal an inch. The unit type and number of decimal places for object lengths and angles can be set through the **UNITS** command. These *drawing units settings* control how AutoCAD interprets the coordinate and angle entries and how it displays coordinates and units in the *Status Bar* and in the dialog boxes.

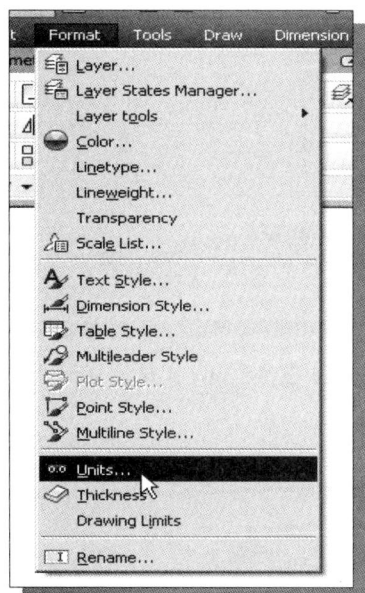

1. In the *Menu Bar* select:

   [Format] → [Units]

2. In the *Drawing Units* dialog box, confirm the *Length Type* to **Decimal**. This is the default measurement to English units, inches.

3. Set the *Precision* to **two digits** after the decimal point.

4. Pick **OK** to exit the *Drawing Units* dialog box.

GRID and SNAP Intervals Setup

1. In the *Menu Bar*, select:

   [Tools] → [Drafting Settings]

2. In the *Drafting Settings* dialog box, select the **Snap and Grid** tab if it is not the page on top.

3. Change *Grid Spacing* to **1.00** for both X and Y directions.

4. Switch **ON** the *Grid On* and *Snap On* options as shown.

5. Pick **OK** to exit the *Drawing Units* dialog box.

Geometric Construction and Editing Tools   15-23

6. On your own, use the **Zoom Extents** command, under the **View** tab, to reset the display.

❖ Notice in the *Status Bar* area, the *GRID* and *SNAP* options are pressed down indicating they are switched *ON*. Currently, the grid spacing is set to 1 inch and the snap interval is set to 0.5 inch.

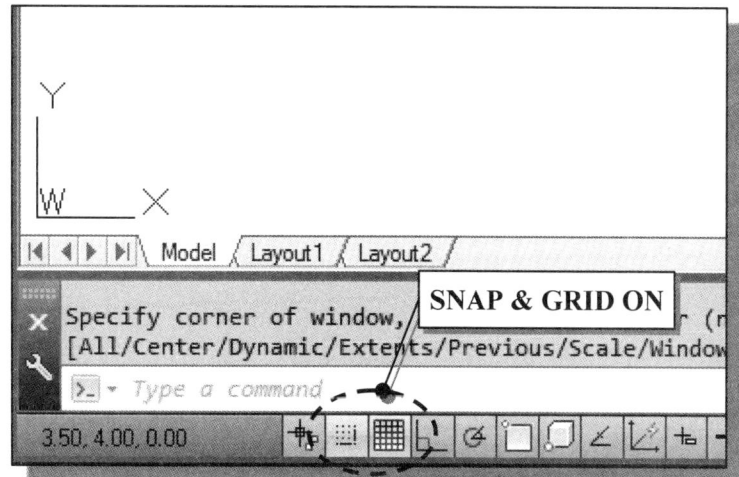

Using the *LINE* command

1. Select the **Line** command icon in the *Draw* toolbar. In the command prompt area, near the bottom of the AutoCAD drawing screen, the message "*_line Specify first point:*" is displayed. AutoCAD expects us to identify the starting location of a straight line.

2. In the graphics window, move the cursor to **world coordinates (4,6). Left-click** to position the starting point of the line at that location.

3. We will next turn *ON* the *ORTHO* option by toggling on the ***ORTHO*** button in the *Status Bar* area.

❖ The *ORTHO* option constrains cursor movement to the horizontal or vertical directions, relative to the current coordinate system. With the **Line** command, we are now restricted to creating only horizontal or vertical lines with the *ORTHO* option.

4. Move the graphics cursor below the last point we selected on the screen and create a vertical line that is two units long (*Y coordinate:* **4.00**).

5. Move the graphics cursor to the right of the last point and create a horizontal line that is one unit long (*X coordinate:* **5.00**).

6. Move the graphics cursor below the last point and create a vertical line that is 2.5 units long (*Y coordinate:* **1.50**).

7. Turn **OFF** the *SNAP* option in the *Status Bar* area.

8. Move the graphics cursor to the right of the last point and create a horizontal line that is about seven units long (near *X coordinate:* **12.00**). As is quite common during the initial design stage, we might not always know all of the dimensions at the beginning.

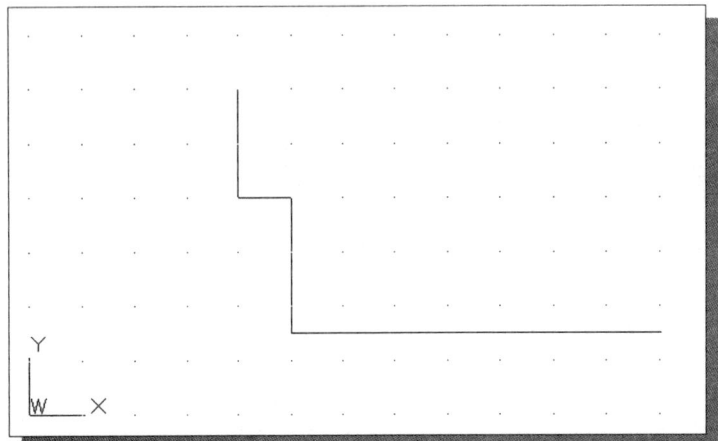

9. Inside the graphics window, **right-mouse-click** to activate the option menu and select **Enter** with the left-mouse-button to end the Line command.

10. In the *Status Bar* area, reset the option buttons so that only the *GRID DISPLAY*, and *ORTHO MODE* options are switched **ON**.

11. Activate the **Line** command by picking the icon in the *Draw* toolbar or **right-mouse-click** to activate the option menu and select **Repeat Line**.

Object Snap Toolbar

❖ **Object Snap** is an extremely powerful construction tool available on most CAD systems. During an entity's creation operations, we can snap the cursor to points on objects such as endpoints, midpoints, centers, and intersections. For example, we can quickly draw a line to the center of a circle, the midpoint of a line segment, or the intersection of two lines.

1. Bring up the *Object Snap* toolbar through the **[Tools]** → **[Toolbars]** menu.

2. In the *Object Snap* toolbar, pick **Snap to Endpoint**. In the command prompt area, the message "*_endp of*" is displayed. AutoCAD now expects us to select a geometric entity on the screen.

❖ The Snap to Endpoint option allows us to snap to the closest endpoint of objects such as lines or arcs. AutoCAD uses the midpoint of the entity to determine which end to snap to.

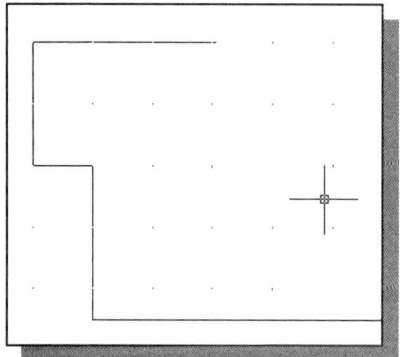

3. Pick the **top left vertical line** by selecting a location above the midpoint of the line. Notice AutoCAD automatically snaps to the top endpoint of the line.

4. Move the graphics cursor to the right of the last point and create a horizontal line that is about three units long (near *X coordinate: 7.00*).

5. Inside the graphics window, **right-mouse-click** to activate the option menu and select **Enter** with the left-mouse-button to end the Line command.

6. Select the **Circle-Radius** command icon in the *Draw* toolbar. In the command prompt area, the message "*Specify center point for circle or [3P/2P/Ttr (tan tan radius)]:*" is displayed.

7. In the *Status Bar* area, switch *ON* the *SNAP* option.

8. In the graphics window, move the cursor to world coordinates (**11.5,6**). **Left-click** to position the center point of the circle at this location.

9. Move the graphics cursor to world coordinates (**13,6**). **Left-click** at this location to create a circle (radius **1.5** inches).

10. Select the **Line** command icon in the *Draw* toolbar. In the command prompt area, the message "*_line Specify first point:*" is displayed.

11. In the graphics window, move the cursor to world coordinates (**11,1.5**). **Left-click** to position the first point of a line at this location.

12. Pick **Snap to Tangent** in the *Object Snap* toolbar. In the command prompt area, the message "*_tan to*" is displayed. AutoCAD now expects us to select a circle or an arc on the screen.

❖ The **Snap to Tangent** option allows us to snap to the point on a circle or arc that, when connected to the last point, forms a line tangent to that object.

13. Pick a location on the right side of the circle and create the line tangent to the circle. Note that the *Object Snap* options take precedence over the *ORTHO* option.

14. Inside the graphics window, **right-mouse-click** to activate the option menu and select **Enter** with the left-mouse-button to end the Line command.

15. In the *Status Bar* area, reset the option buttons so that none of the buttons are switched *ON*.

16. Close the *Object Snap* toolbar by **left-clicking** the upper right corner **X** icon.

Using the *EXTEND* command

- The **Extend** command lengthens an object so that it ends precisely at a selected boundary.

1. Select the **Extend** command icon in the *Modify* toolbar. In the command prompt area, the message "*Select boundary edges... Select objects:*" is displayed.

   ❖ First, we will select the objects that define the boundary edges to which we want to extend the object.

2. Pick the **circle** as the *boundary edge*.

3. Inside the graphics window, **right-mouse-click** to proceed with the Extend command.

4. The message "*Select object to extend or shift-select object to trim or [Project/Edge/Undo]:*" is displayed in the command prompt area. Extend the **horizontal line** that is to the left side of the circle by clicking near the right endpoint of the line.

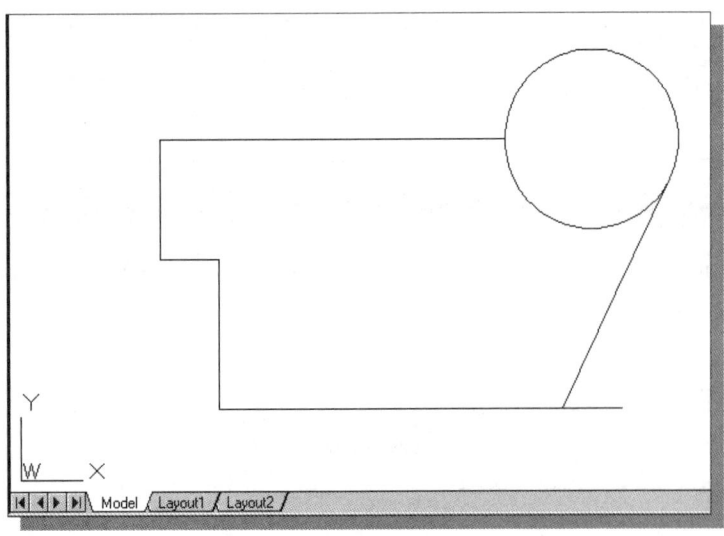

5. Inside the graphics window, **right-mouse-click** to activate the option menu and select **Enter** with the left-mouse-button to end the Extend command.

Geometric Construction and Editing Tools   15-29

Using the *TRIM* command

- The Trim command shortens an object so that it ends precisely at a selected boundary.

1. Select the **Trim** command icon in the *Modify* toolbar. In the command prompt area, the message "*Select boundary edges... Select objects:*" is displayed.

❖ First, we will select the objects that define the boundary edges to which we want to trim the object.

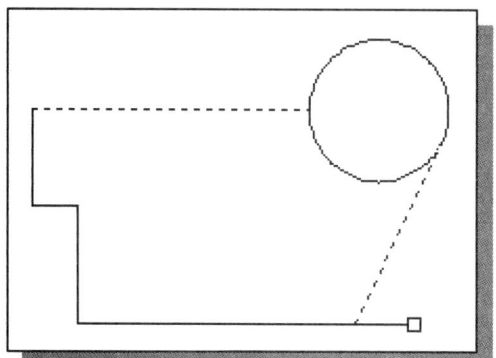

2. Pick the **inclined line** and the **top horizontal line** as the *boundary edges*.

3. Inside the graphics window, **right-mouse-click** to proceed with the Trim command.

4. The message "*Select object to trim or shift-select object to extend or [Fence/Crossing/Project/Edge/eRase/Undo]:*" is displayed in the command prompt area. Pick the **right endpoint** of the bottom horizontal line.

5. Pick the **bottom of the circle** by clicking on the lower portion of the circle.

6. Inside the graphics window, **right-mouse-click** to activate the option menu and select **Enter** with the left-mouse-button to end the Trim command.

- Note that in **AutoCAD® 2013**, we can use the Extend command or the Trim command for trimming or extending an object. For example, when using the **Extend** command, we can select an object to *extend* or hold down **SHIFT** and select an object to *trim*.

Creating a TTR CIRCLE

1. In the *Draw* toolbar, click the triangle next to the **Circle** icon to show the additional options.

2. In the displayed list, select the **Ttr (Tan Tan Radius)** option. This option allows us to create a circle that is tangent to two objects.

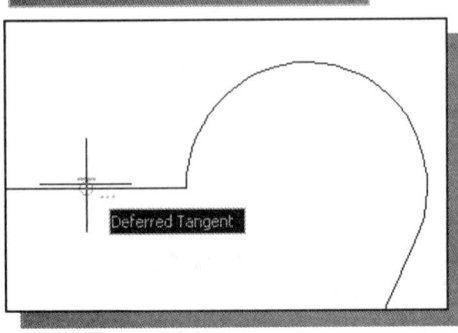

3. Pick the **top horizontal line** that is to the left side of the arc. We will create a circle that is tangent to this line and the circle.

4. Pick the **arc** by selecting a location that is above the right endpoint of the horizontal line. AutoCAD interprets the location we selected as being near the tangency.

5. In the command prompt area, the message "*Specify radius of circle <1.50>*" is displayed.
   Specify radius of circle <1.50>: **1.0** [ENTER]

➢ On your own, use the **Trim** command and trim the circle, the horizontal line, and the arc as shown.

Using the *FILLET* command

- Fillet rounds or fillets the edges of two arcs, circles, elliptical arcs, or lines with an arc of a specified radius.

1. Select the **Fillet** command icon in the *Modify* toolbar. In the command prompt area, the message "*Select first object or [Polyline/Radius/Trim]:*" is displayed.

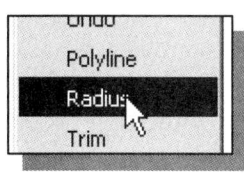

2. Inside the graphics window, right-mouse-click to activate the option menu and select the **Radius** option with the left-mouse-button to specify the radius of the fillet.

3. In the command prompt area, the message "*Specify fillet radius:*" is displayed.

   Specify fillet radius: **0.75** [ENTER]

4. Pick the **bottom horizontal line** and the **adjacent vertical line** to create a rounded corner as shown.

➢ On your own, use the Fillet command and create a radius **0.25** fillet at the corner as shown.

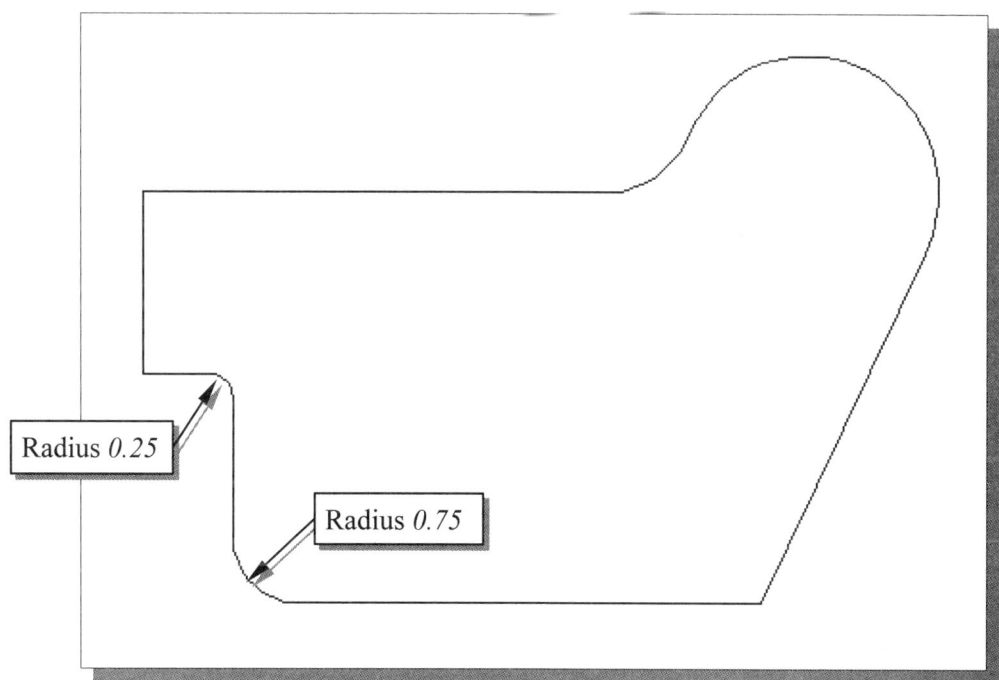

Converting objects into a *Polyline*

- The next task in our project is to use the **Offset** command and create a scaled copy of the constructed geometry. Prior to using the **Offset** command, we will simplify the procedure by converting all objects into a **compound object** – a *polyline*.

❖ A *polyline* in AutoCAD is a 2D line of adjustable width composed of line and arc segments. A polyline is treated as a single object with definable options.

1. In the Ribbon Toolbars, select:

   [Modify] → **[Edit Polyline]**

2. The message "*Select polyline:*" is displayed in the command prompt area. Select **any** of the objects on the screen.

3. The message "*Object selected is not a polyline, Do you want to turn it into one? <Y>*" is displayed in the command prompt area. **Right-mouse-click** to accept the *Yes* default.

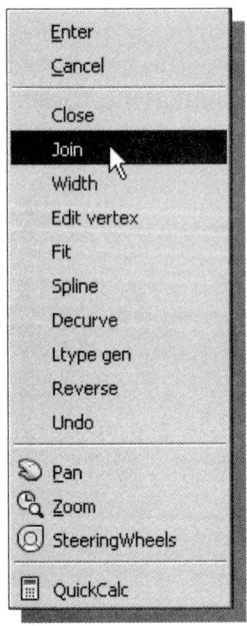

4. Inside the graphics window, **right-mouse-click** to activate the option menu and select the **Join** option with the left-mouse-button to add objects to the polyline.

5. **Pick all objects** by enclosing them inside a *selection window*.

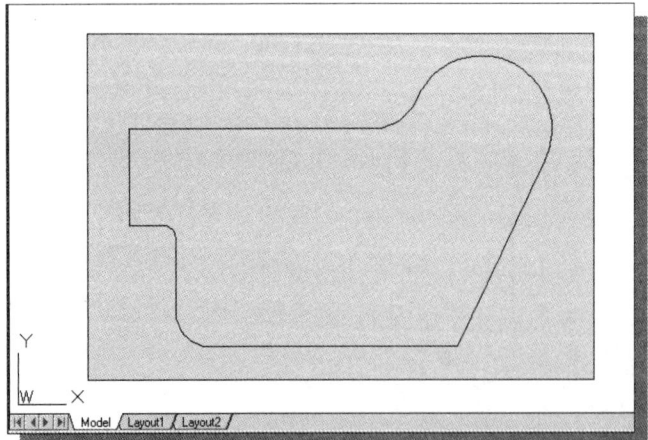

6. Inside the graphics window, **right-mouse-click** to accept the selected objects.

7. Inside the graphics window, right-mouse-click to activate the option menu and select **Enter** to end the Edit Polyline command.

Using the *OFFSET* command

- The Offset command creates a new object at a specified distance from an existing object or through a specified point.

1. Select the **Offset** command icon in the *Modify* toolbar. In the command prompt area, the message "*Specify offset distance or [Through]:*" is displayed.

   Specify offset distance or [Through]:
   0.5 [ENTER]

2. In the command prompt area, the message "*Select object to offset or <exit>:*" is displayed. Select **any segment** of the polyline on the screen.

> Since all the lines and arcs have been converted into a single object, all segments are now selected.

3. AutoCAD next asks us to identify the direction of the offset. Pick a location that is *inside* the polyline.

4. Inside the graphics window, **right-mouse-click** and select **Enter** to end the Offset command.

Using the Area Inquiry Tool to Measure Area and Perimeter

- AutoCAD also provides several tools that will allow us to measure distance, area, perimeter, and even mass properties. With the use of polylines, measurements of areas and perimeters can be done very quickly.

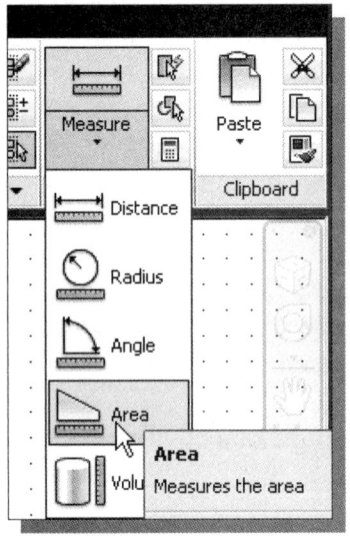

1. In the *Ribbon* tabs area, left-mouse-click once on the **Measure** title in the *Utilities* toolbar as shown.

2. In the *Inquiry* toolbar, click on the **Area** icon to activate the Calculates the area and perimeter of selected objects command.

- Note the different **Measure** options that are available in the list.

3. In the command prompt area, the message "*Specify first corner point or [Object/Add/Subtract]:*" is displayed. By default, AutoCAD expects us to select points that will form a polygon. The area and perimeter of the polygon will then be calculated.

4. AutoCAD can also calculate the area and perimeter of objects that define closed regions. For example, a circle or a rectangle can be selected as both of these objects define closed regions. We can also select a region defined by a *polyline*. To activate this option, **right-mouse-click** once inside the graphics window and select **Object** as shown.

5. In the command prompt area, the message "*Select objects:*" is displayed. Pick the **inside polyline** and the associated area and perimeter information are shown in the prompt area.

Geometric Construction and Editing Tools 15-35

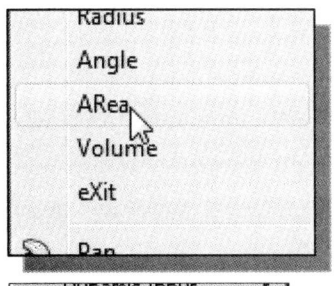

6. Inside the graphics window, right-mouse-click once to bring up the option menu and select **Repeat AREA** as shown.

7. We can also select a region defined by multiple *polylines*. To activate this option, **right-mouse-click** once inside the graphics window and select **Add area** as shown.

8. To also activate selection of regions *defined* by polylines, **right-mouse-click** once inside the graphics window and select **Object** as shown.

9. In the command prompt area, the message "*[Add Mode] Select objects:*" is displayed. Pick the outside polyline. The associated area and perimeter information are shown in the prompt area.

10. Next we will subtract the region defined by the inside polyline. In the command prompt area, select **Subtract area** as shown.

11. To also activate selection of regions defined by polylines, select **Object** in the command prompt area as shown.

12. In the command prompt area, the message "*Select objects:*" is displayed. Pick the inside polyline and the area between the two polylines is shown in the command prompt area.

Using the *EXPLODE* command

- The **Explode** command breaks a compound object into its component objects.

    1. Select the **Explode** command icon in the *Modify* toolbar. In the command prompt area, the message "*Select objects:*" is displayed.

    2. Pick the ***inside polyline*** that we created using the Offset command.

    3. Inside the graphics window, **right-mouse-click** to end the Explode command.

Create another *Fillet*

1. Select the **Fillet** command icon in the *Modify* toolbar. In the command prompt area, the message "*Select first object or [Polyline/Radius/Trim]:*" is displayed.

2. On your own, set the *Fillet Radius* to **0.5**.
   Specify fillet radius: **0.5** [ENTER]

3. Pick the **horizontal line** and the **adjacent inclined line** to create a rounded corner as shown.

Saving the CAD file

1. In the pull-down menus, select:

   [File] → [Save As]→ [AutoCAD Drawing]

2. In the *Save Drawing As* dialog box, select the folder in which you want to store the CAD file and enter **Gasket** in the *File name* box.

3. Pick **Save** in the *Save Drawing As* dialog box to accept the selections and save the file.

Exit AutoCAD

- To exit **AutoCAD® 2013**, select **Exit AutoCAD** from the *Application Menu* or type **QUIT** at the command prompt.

Review Questions: (Time: 20 minutes)

1. Describe when and why you would use the AutoCAD **ORTHO** option.

2. What is the difference between a *line* and a *polyline* in AutoCAD?

3. Which AutoCAD command can we use to break a compound object, such as a polyline, into its component objects?

4. Which AutoCAD command can we use to quickly calculate the area and perimeter of a closed region defined by a polyline?

5. Describe the procedure to calculate the area and perimeter of a closed region defined by a polyline?

6. What does the **Offset** command allow us to do?

7. Create the following triangle and measure the area and perimeter of the triangle.

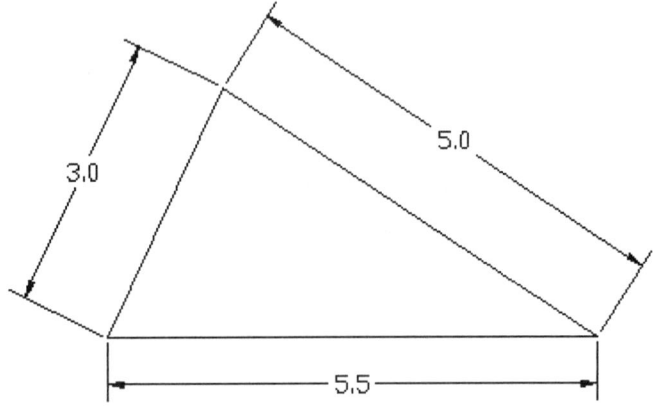

8. Create the following triangle and measure the area and perimeter of the triangle. Also find the angle Θ.

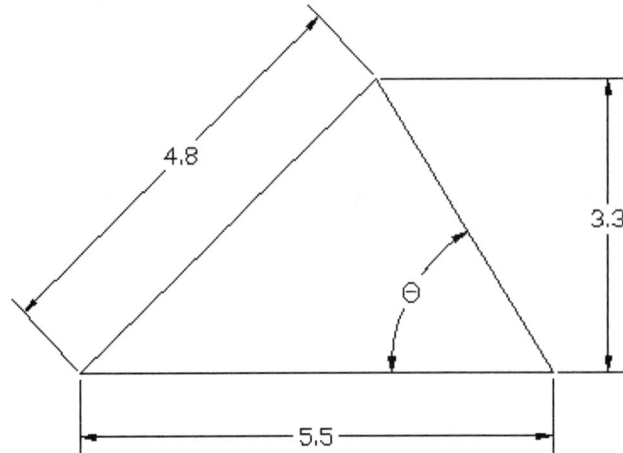

Exercises: (Time: 90 minutes)
(Unless otherwise specified, dimensions are in inches.)

1. Lines & Squares Pattern

2. Interlacement Design

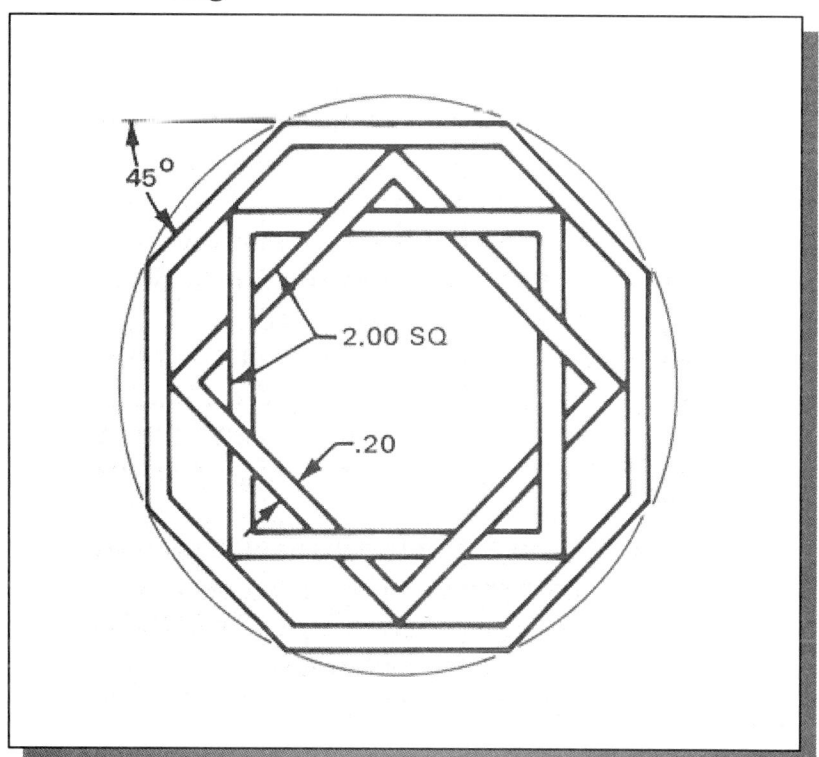

3. **Positioning Spacer** (Dimensions are in inches.)

4. **Indexing Base** (Dimensions are in inches.)

5. Guide Block (Create the front view of the design. Dimensions are in inches.)

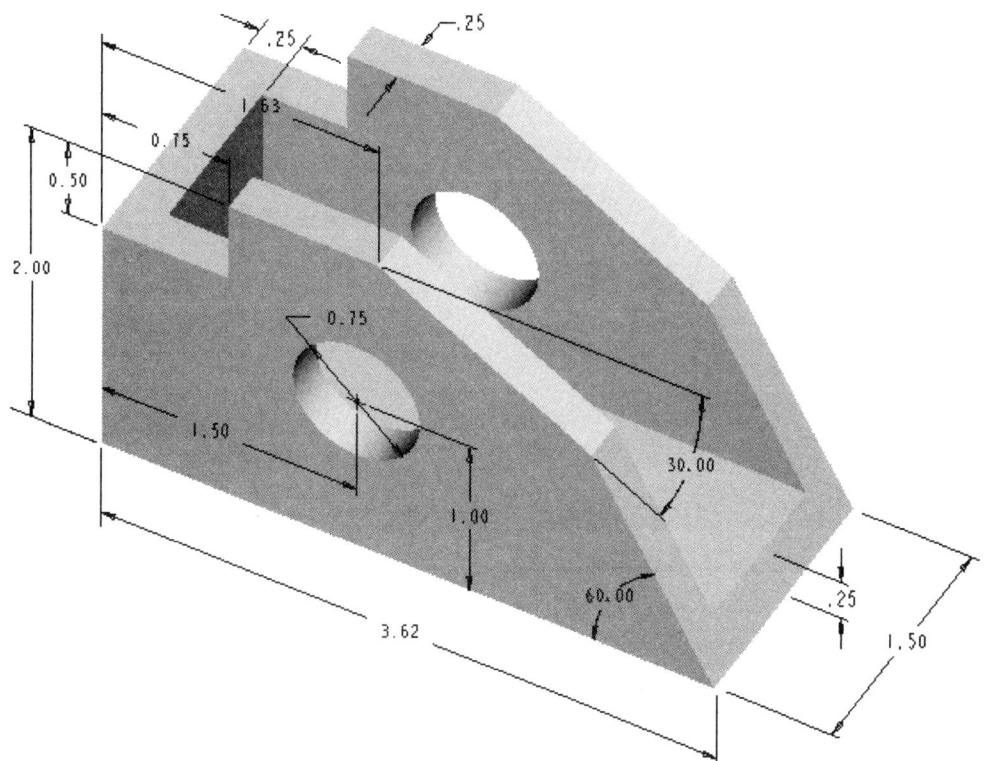

Notes:

Chapter 16
Orthographic Views in Multiview Drawings

Learning Objectives

- **Create 2D orthographic views using AutoCAD**
- **Using the CONSTRUCTION LINE command to draw**
- **Using Running Object Snaps**
- **Use AutoCAD's *AutoSnap* and *AutoTrack* features**
- **Create a Miter line to transfer dimensions**
- **Using Projection lines between orthographic views**
- **Use the POLAR Tracking option**

Introduction

Most drawings produced and used in industry are *multiview drawings*. Multiview drawings are used to provide accurate three-dimensional object information on two-dimensional media, a means of communicating all of the information necessary to transform an idea or concept into reality. The standards and conventions of multiview drawings have been developed over many years, which equip us with a universally understood method of communication. The age of computers has greatly altered the design process, and several CAD methods are now available to help generate multiview drawings using CAD systems.

Multiview drawings usually require several orthographic views to define the shape of a three-dimensional object. Each orthographic view is a two-dimensional drawing showing only two of the three dimensions of the three-dimensional object. Consequently, no individual view contains sufficient information to completely define the shape of the three-dimensional object. All orthographic views must be looked at together to comprehend the shape of the three-dimensional object. The arrangement and relationship between the views are therefore very important in multiview drawings. In this chapter, the common methods of creating two-dimensional orthographic views with AutoCAD are examined.

The *Locator* design

The *Locator* part

> Before going through the tutorial, make a rough sketch of a multiview drawing of the part. How many 2D views will be necessary to fully describe the part? Based on your knowledge of **AutoCAD® 2013** so far, how would you arrange and construct these 2D views? Take a few minutes to consider these questions and do preliminary planning by sketching on a piece of paper. You are also encouraged to construct the orthographic views on your own prior to following through the tutorial.

Starting Up AutoCAD® 2013

1. Select the **AutoCAD 2013** option on the *Program* menu or select the **AutoCAD 2013** icon on the *Desktop*.

2. In the *Startup* dialog box, select the **Start from Scratch** option with a single click of the left-mouse-button.

3. In the *Default Settings* section, pick **Imperial** as the drawing units.

4. On your own, open up the *Drafting Settings* dialog box, and select the **SNAP and GRID** tab.

5. Change *Grid Spacing* to **0.5** for both X and Y directions.

6. Also adjust the *Snap Spacing* to **0.5** for both X and Y directions.

Layers setup

1. Pick **Layer Properties Manager** in the *Layers* toolbar.

2. Click on the **New** icon to create new layers.

3. Create two **new** layers with the following settings:

Layer	Color	Linetype
Construction	White	Continuous
Object	Blue	Continuous

4. Highlight the layer *Construction* in the list of layers.

5. Click on the **Current** button to set layer *Construction* as the *Current Layer*.

6. Click on the **Close** button to accept the settings and exit the *Layer Properties Manager* dialog box.

7. In the *Status Bar* area, reset the option buttons so that only *SNAP Mode* and *GRID Display* are switched **ON**.

Drawing *Construction* lines

❖ *Construction lines* are lines that extend to infinity. Construction lines are usually used as references for creating other objects. We will also place the construction lines on the *Construction* layer so that the layer can later be frozen or turned off.

1. Select the **Construction Line** icon in the *Draw* toolbar. In the command prompt area, the message "*_xline Specify a point or [Hor/Ver/Ang/Bisect/Offset]:*" is displayed.

   • To orient construction lines, we generally specify two points. Note that other orientation options are also available.

2. Select a location near the lower left corner of the graphics window. It is not necessary to align objects to the world coordinate origin. CAD systems provide us with many powerful tools to manipulate geometry. Our main goal is to use the CAD system as a flexible and powerful tool, and to be very efficient and effective with the systems.

3. Pick a location above the last point to create a **vertical construction line**.

4. Move the cursor toward the right of the first point and pick a location to create a **horizontal construction line**.

5. Inside the graphics window, **right-mouse-click** to end the Construction Line command.

6. In the *Status Bar* area, turn **OFF** the *SNAP* option.

Using the *OFFSET* command

1. Select the **Offset** icon in the *Modify* toolbar. In the command prompt area, the message "*Specify offset distance or [Through/Erase/Layer]:*" is displayed.

2. In the command prompt area, enter: **5.0 [ENTER]**.

3. In the command prompt area, the message "*Select object to offset or <exit>:*" is displayed. Pick the **vertical line** on the screen.

4. AutoCAD next asks us to identify the direction of the offset. Pick a location that is to the **right** of the vertical line.

5. Inside the graphics window, **right-mouse-click** and choose **Enter** to end the Offset command.

6. In the command prompt area, click on the small icon to access the list of recent commands.

7. Select **Offset** in the popup list, to repeat the Offset command.

8. In the command prompt area, enter: **2.5 [ENTER]**.

9. In the command prompt area, the message "*Select object to offset or <exit>:*" is displayed. Pick the **horizontal line** on the screen.

10. AutoCAD next asks us to identify the direction of the offset. Pick a location that is **above** the horizontal line.

11. Inside the graphics window, **right-mouse-click** to end the Offset command.

12. Repeat the **Offset** command and create the offset lines as shown.

Set layer *Object* as the current layer

1. On the *Layers* toolbar panel, choose the **Layer Control** box with the left-mouse-button.

2. Move the cursor over the name of the layer *Object*. The tool tip "*Object*" appears.

3. **Left-mouse-click once** and the layer *Object* is set as the *Current Layer*.

Using the *Running Object Snaps*

In **AutoCAD® 2013**, while using geometry construction commands, the cursor can be placed to points on objects such as endpoints, midpoints, centers, and intersections. In AutoCAD, this tool is called the ***Object Snap***.

Object snaps can be turned on in one of two ways:
- **Single Point (or override) Object Snaps**: Sets an object snap for one use.
- **Running Object Snaps**: Sets object snaps *active* until we turn them off.

The procedure we have used so far is the *Single Point Object Snaps* option, where we select the specific object snap from the *Object Snap* toolbar for one use only. The use of the *Running Object Snaps* option to assist the construction is illustrated next.

1. In the *Menu Bar*, select:

   [Tools] → [Drafting Settings]

2. In the *Drafting Settings* dialog box select the **Object Snap** tab.

The *Running Object Snap* options can be turned on or off by clicking the different options listed. Notice the different symbols associated with the different *Object Snap* options.

3. Turn **ON** the *Running Object Snap* by clicking the **Object Snap On** box, or hit the [**F3**] key once.

4. Confirm the ***Intersection***, ***Endpoint*** and ***Extension*** options are switched **ON** and click on the **OK** button to accept the settings and exit from the *Drafting Settings* dialog box.

❖ Notice in the *Status Bar* area the ***OSNAP*** button is switched ***ON***. We can toggle the *Running Object Snap* option on or off by clicking the *OSNAP* button.

5. Press the [**F3**] key once and notice the *OSNAP* button is switched ***OFF*** in the *Status Bar* area.

6. Press the [**F3**] key again and notice the *OSNAP* button is now switched ***ON*** in the *Status Bar* area.

➢ **AutoCAD® 2013** provides many input methods and shortcuts; you are encouraged to examine the different options and choose the option that best fits your own style.

Creating *Object* lines

> We will define the areas for the front view, top view and side view by adding object lines using the *Running Object Snap* option.

1. Select the **Line** command icon in the *Draw* toolbar. In the command prompt area, the message "*_line Specify first point:*" is displayed.

2. Move the cursor to the **intersection** of any two lines and notice the visual aid automatically displayed at the intersection.

3. Pick the four intersection points closest to the lower left corner to create the four sides of the area of the front view.

4. Inside the graphics window, right-mouse-click to activate the option menu and select **Enter** with the left-mouse-button to end the Line command.

5. Repeat the Line command to define the top view and side view as shown.

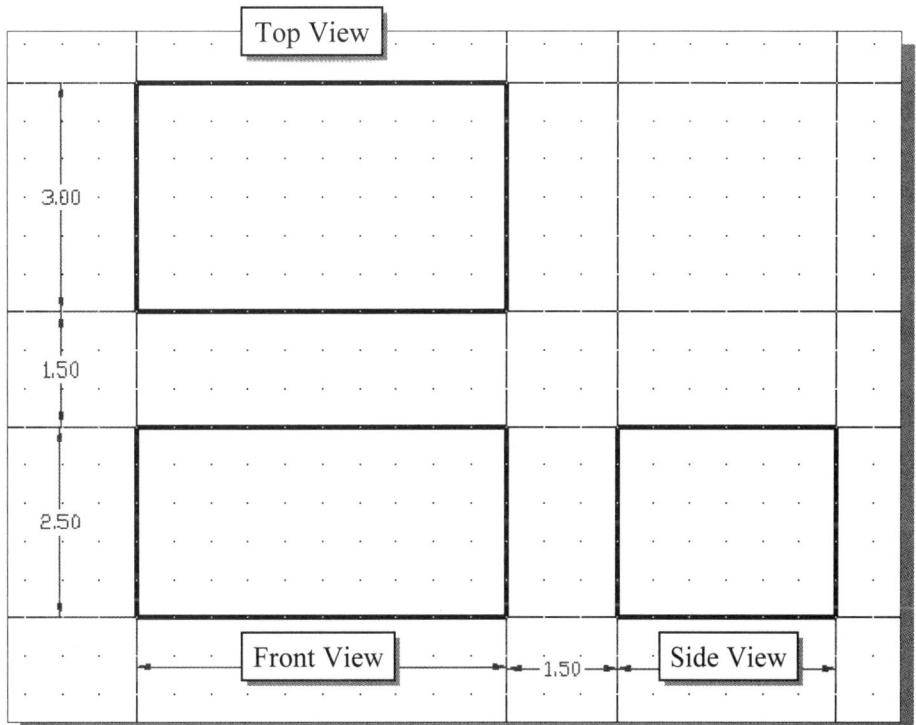

Turn *OFF* the Construction Lines layer

1. On the *Object Properties* toolbar, choose the *Layer Control* box with the left-mouse-button.

2. Move the cursor over the light-bulb icon for layer *Construction*. The tool tip "*Turn a layer On or Off*" appears.

3. **Left-mouse-click once** and notice the icon color is changed to gray, representing the layer (layer *Construction*) is turned *OFF*.

Adding more objects in the Front View

1. Use the **Offset** command and create the two parallel lines in the front view as shown.

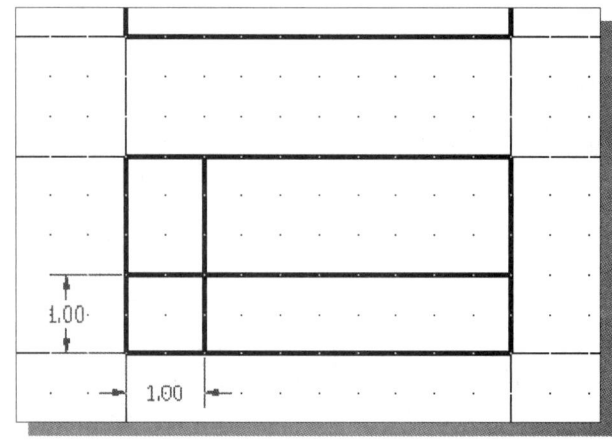

2. Use the **Trim** command and modify the front view as shown.

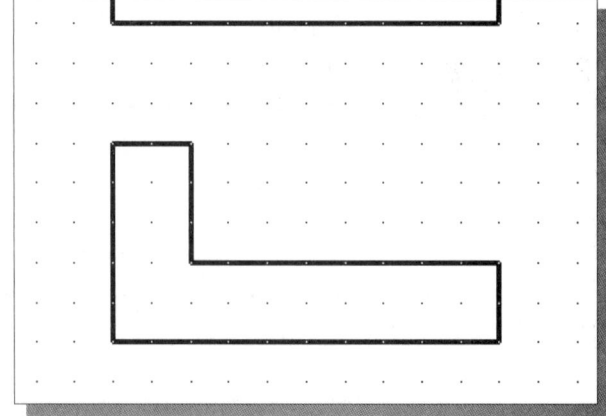

AutoCAD's *AutoSnap*™ and *AutoTrack*™ features

AutoCAD's *AutoSnap* and *AutoTrack* provide visual aids when the *Object Snap* options are switched *on*. The main advantages of *AutoSnap* and *AutoTrack* are as follows:

- **Symbols**: Automatically displays the *Object Snap* type at the object snap location.

- **Tooltips**: Automatically displays the *Object Snap* type below the cursor.

- **Magnet**: Locks the cursor onto a snap point when the cursor is near the point.

With ***Object Snap Tracking,*** the cursor can track along alignment paths based on other object snap points when specifying points in a command. To use *Object Snap Tracking*, one or more object snaps must be switched on. The basic rules of using the ***Object Snap Tracking*** option are as follows:

- To track from a *Running Object Snap* point, pause over the point while in a command.

- A tracking vector appears when we move the cursor.

- To stop tracking, pause over the point again.

- When multiple *Running Object Snaps* are on, press the **[TAB]** key to cycle through available snap points when the object snap aperture box is on an object.

1. In the *Status Bar* area, turn *ON* the *OTRACK* option.

2. Select the **Line** command icon in the *Draw* toolbar. In the command prompt area, the message "*_line Specify first point:*" is displayed.

3. Move the cursor near the top right corner of the vertical protrusion in the front view. Notice that *AutoSnap* automatically locks the cursor to the corner and displays the ***Endpoint*** symbol.

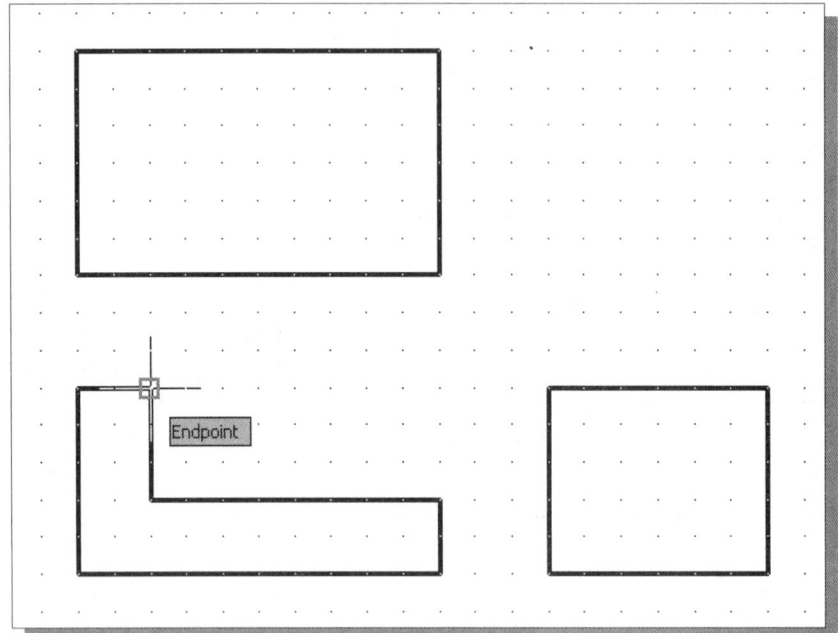

4. Move the cursor upward and notice that *Object Tracking* displays a dashed line, showing the alignment to the top right corner of the vertical protrusion in the front view. Move the cursor near the top horizontal line of the top view and **notice that** *AutoSnap* displays the intersection point.

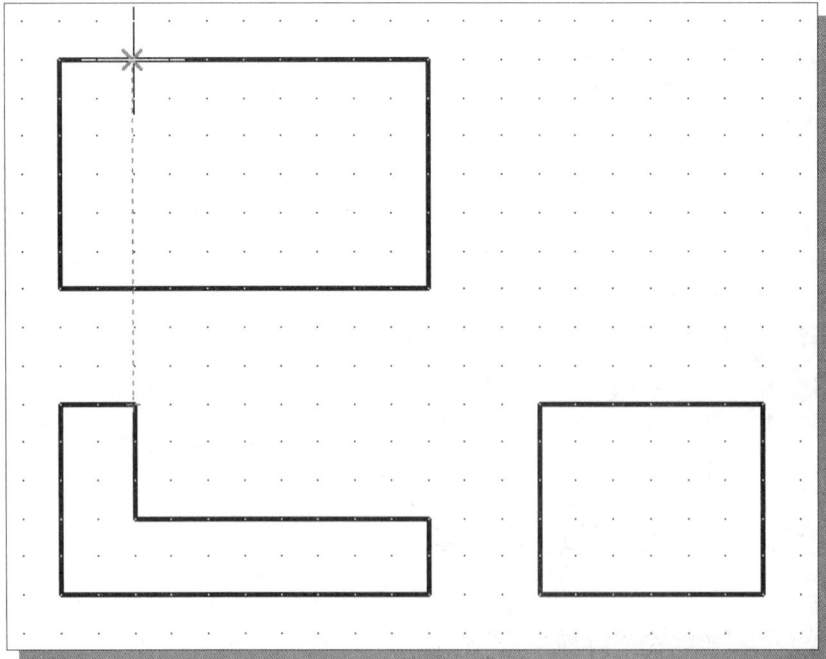

5. Left-mouse-click to place the starting point of a line at the intersection.

Orthographic Views in Multiview Drawings   16-13

6. Move the cursor to the top left corner of the front view to activate the tracking feature.

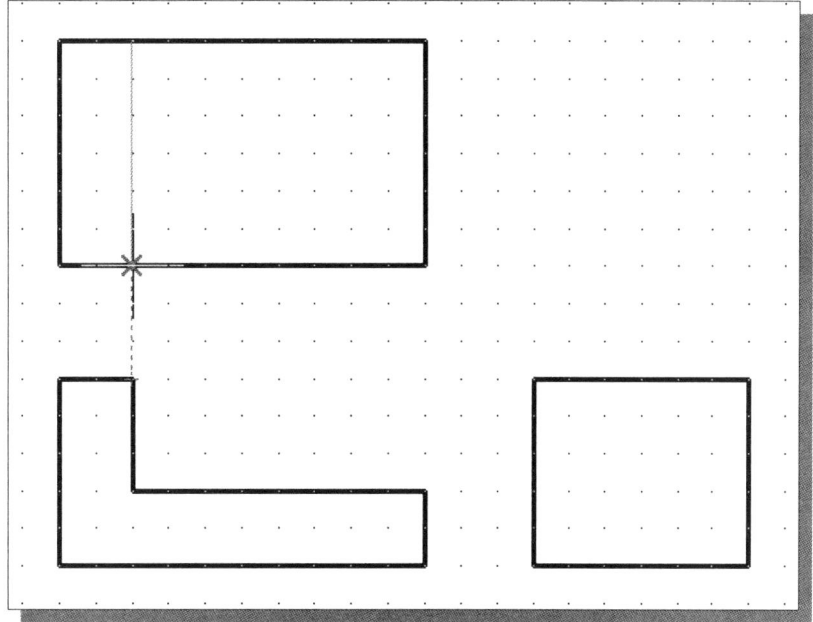

7. Create the line as shown in the above figure.

Adding more objects in the Top View

1. Use the **Offset** command and create the two parallel lines in the top view as shown.

2. On your own, select **[Tools]** → **[Toolbars]** → **[Object Snap]** to display the *Object Snap* toolbar on the screen.

3. Select the **Line** command icon in the *Draw* toolbar. In the command prompt area, the message "*_line Specify first point:*" is displayed.

4. In the *Object Snap* toolbar, pick **Snap From**. In the command prompt area, the message "*_from Base point*" is displayed. AutoCAD now expects us to select a geometric entity on the screen.

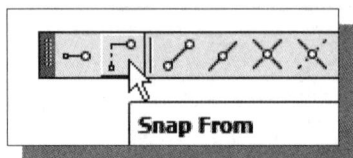

> The *Single Point Object Snap* overrides the *Running Object Snap* option.

5. We will measure relative to the lower right corner. Pick the corner as shown.

6. In the command prompt area, enter **@0,0.25** [ENTER].

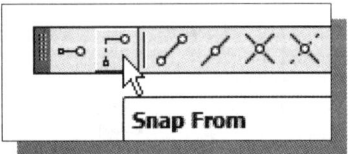

7. In the *Object Snap* toolbar, pick **Snap From**. Pick the lower right corner of the top view again.

8. In the command prompt area, enter **@-1.75,0** [ENTER].

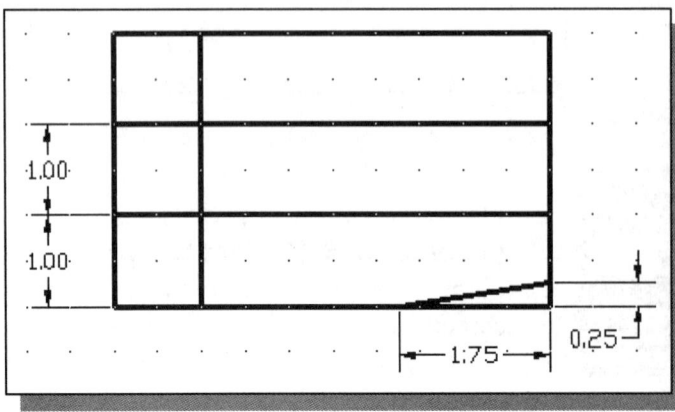

9. Inside the graphics window, right-mouse-click to activate the option menu and select **Enter** with the left-mouse-button to end the Line command.

10. Repeat the procedure and create the line on the top right corner as shown.

11. Using the *Snap From* option, create the circle (diameter **1.0**) as shown.

12. Select the **Trim** icon in the *Modify* toolbar. In the command prompt area, the message "*Select boundary edges... Select objects:*" is displayed.

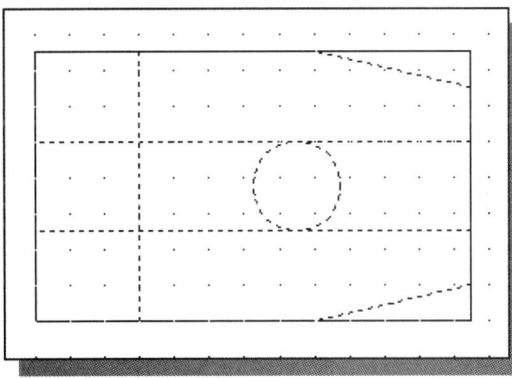

13. Pick the following objects as boundary edges: the circle, and the lines that are near the circle.

14. Inside the graphics window, **right-mouse-click** to accept the selected objects.

15. Select the unwanted portions and modify the objects as shown.

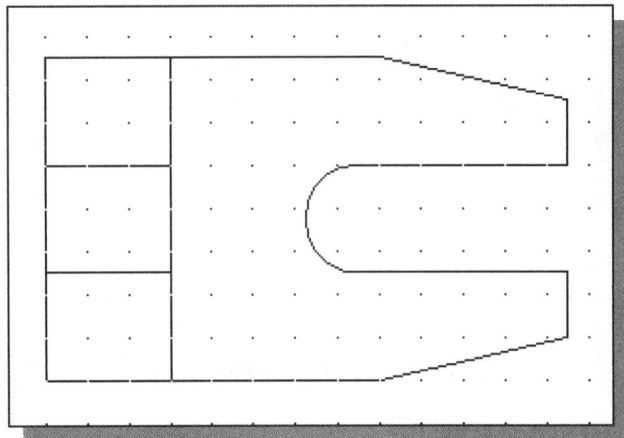

16. On your own, use the **Offset** and **Trim** commands and modify the top view as shown.

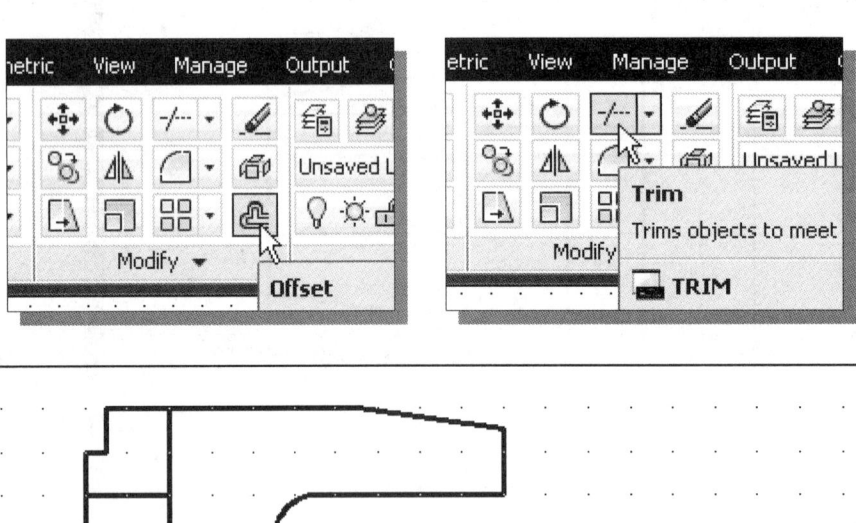

Drawing using the *Miter Line* method

❖ The *45° miter line* method is a simple and straightforward procedure to transfer measurements in between the top view and the side view.

1. On the *Layers* toolbar panel, choose the **Layer Control** box by clicking once with the left-mouse-button.

2. Move the cursor over the **light-bulb** icon for layer *Construction*. The tool tip "*Turn a layer On or Off*" appears.

3. **Left-mouse-click once** and notice the icon color is changed to a light color, representing the layer (layer *Construction*) is turned *ON*.

4. **Left-mouse-click once** over the name of the layer *Construction* to set it as the *Current Layer*.

5. Use the **Line** command and create the *miter line* by connecting the two intersections of the construction lines as shown.

6. Select the **Construction Line** command in the *Draw* toolbar as shown.

7. In the command prompt area, select the **Horizontal** option as shown.

8. On your own, create horizontal projection lines through all the corners in the top view as shown.

9. Use the **Trim** command and trim the projection lines as shown in the figure below.

10. On your own, create additional **Construction Lines** (vertical option) through all the intersection points that are on the *miter line*.

More Layers setup

1. Pick *Layer Properties Manager* in the *Layers* toolbar panel as shown in the figure below.

2. Click on the **New** icon to create new layers.

3. Create two **new layers** with the following settings:

Layer	*Color*	*Linetype*
Hidden	**Cyan**	**HIDDEN**
Center	**Red**	**CENTER**

- The default linetype is *Continuous*. To use other linetypes, click on the **Load** button in the *Select Linetype* dialog box and select the desired linetypes.

4. On your own, set the layer *Object* as the *Current Layer*.

Top View to Side View Projection

1. Using the *Running Object Snaps*, create the necessary **object-lines** in the side view.

2. Set layer *Hidden* as the *Current Layer* and create the two necessary hidden lines in the side view.

3. Set layer *Center* as the *Current Layer* and create the necessary centerlines in the side view.

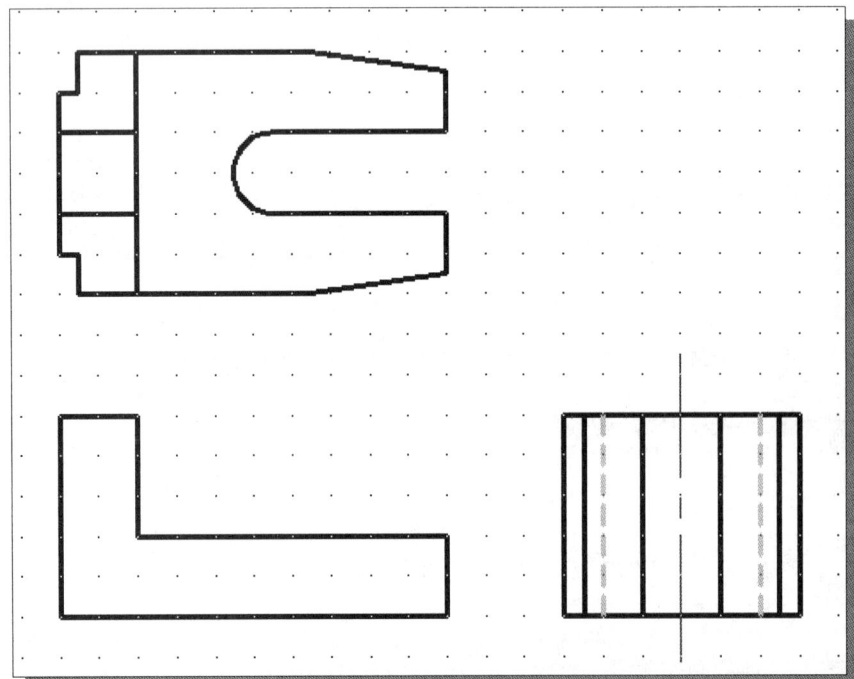

4. In the *Layer Control* box, turn **OFF** the **construction lines**.

5. Set layer **Object** as the *Current Layer*.

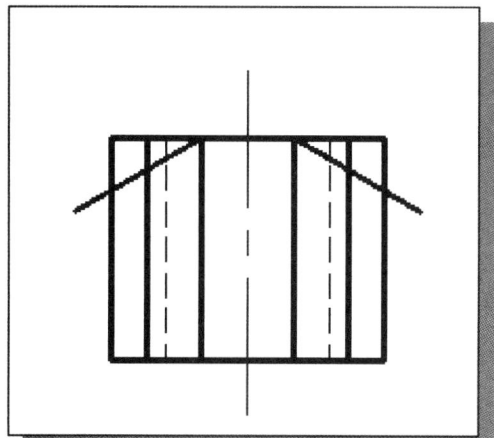

6. Use the **Line** command and create the two 30° inclined lines as shown.

   (Hint: Relative coordinate entries of **@2.0<-30** and **@2.0<210**.)

7. Use the Line command and create a horizontal line in the side view as shown.

8. On your own, use the **Trim** command and remove the unwanted portions in the side view. Refer to the image shown on the next page if necessary.

Completing the Front View

1. Select the **Line** command icon in the *Draw* toolbar. In the command prompt area, the message "*_line Specify first point:*" is displayed.

2. Move the cursor to the top left corner in the side view and the bottom left corner in the top view to activate the *Object Tracking* option to both corners.

3. Left-mouse-click once when the cursor is aligned to both corners as shown.

4. Create the **horizontal line** as shown.

5. Repeat the procedure and create the lines in the front view as shown.

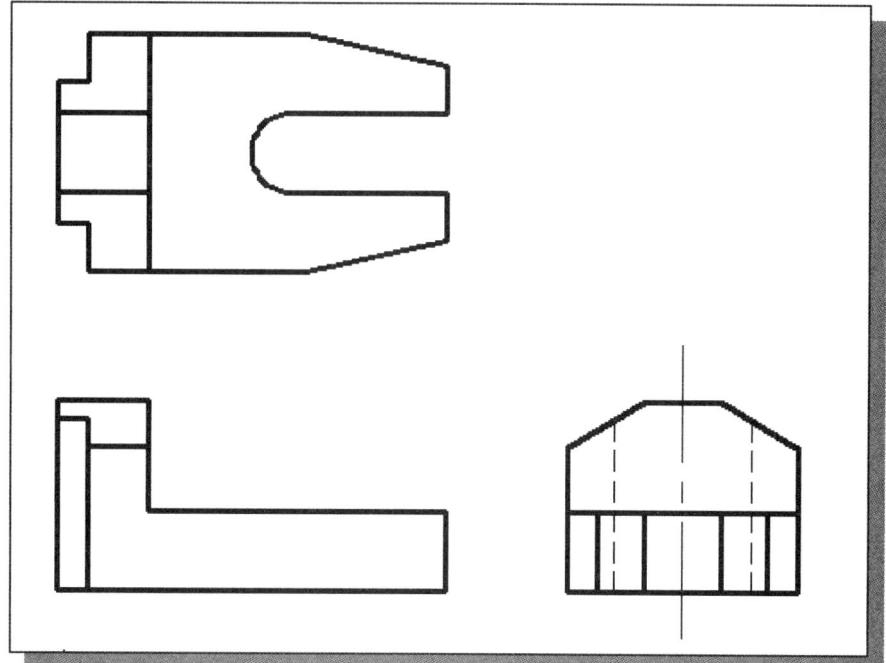

6. Add in any additional object lines that are necessary.

7. Set layer **Hidden** as the *Current Layer* and create the necessary hidden lines in the front view.

8. Set layer **Center** as the *Current Layer* and create the necessary centerlines in the top view and front view.

Object Information using the *LIST* command

- AutoCAD provides several tools that will allow us to get information about constructed geometric objects. The **List** command can be used to show detailed information about geometric objects.

1. Move the cursor to the side view and select the inclined line on the right, as shown in the figure.

2. In the *Properties* toolbar, click on the **List** icon to activate the command.

- Note the information regarding the selected object is displayed in the *AutoCAD Text Window* as shown.

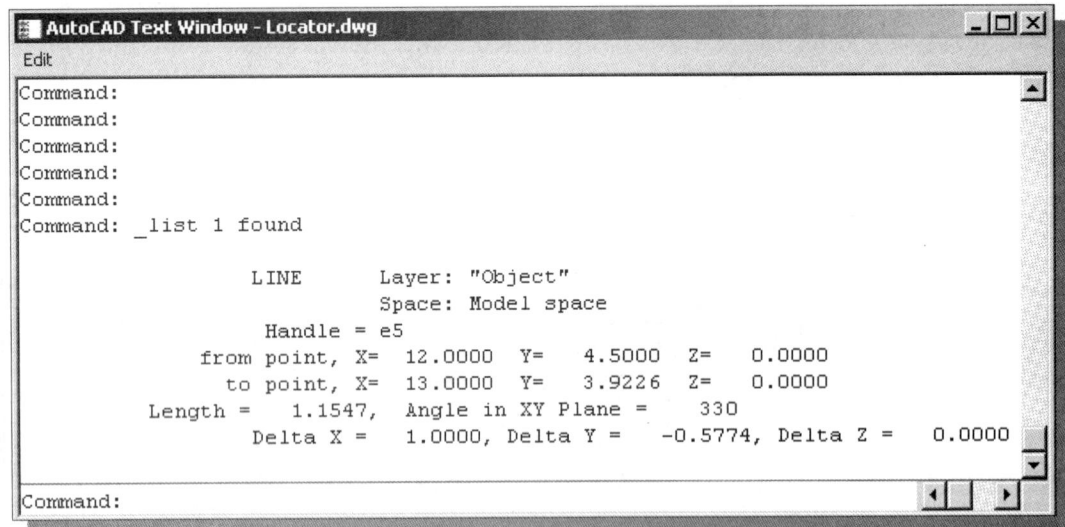

- Note the **List** command can be used to show detailed information about the selected line. The angle and length of the line, as well as the X, Y and Z components between the two endpoints are all listed in a separate window.

3. Press the [**F2**] key once to close the *AutoCAD Text Window*.

4. Press the [**Esc**] key once to deselect the selected line.

Object Information using the *PROPERTIES* command

- AutoCAD also provides tools that allow us to display and change properties of constructed geometric objects. The **Properties** command not only provides the detailed information about geometric objects, modifications can also be done very quickly.

1. In the *Ribbon* tabs area, left-mouse-click once on the **View** tab as shown.

2. In the *Palettes* toolbar, click on the **Properties** icon to activate the command.

3. Note the *Properties* panel appears on the screen. The "*No selection*" on top of the panel indicates no object has been selected.

4. Move the cursor to the side view and select the inclined line on the right, as shown in the figure.

5. The geometry information is listed at the bottom section. Note the line length is *1.1547* and at the angle of *330* degrees.

Geometry	
Start X	12.0000
Start Y	4.5000
Start Z	0.0000
End X	13.0000
End Y	3.9226
End Z	0.0000
Delta X	1.0000
Delta Y	-0.5774
Delta Z	0.0000
Length	1.1547
Angle	330

Review Questions: (Time: 20 minutes)

1. Explain what an orthographic view is and why it is important to engineering graphics.

2. What does the *Running Object Snaps* option allow us to do?

3. Explain how a *miter line* can assist us in creating orthographic views.

4. Describe the AutoCAD *AutoSnap* and *AutoTrack* options.

5. List and describe two AutoCAD commands that can be used to get geometric information about constructed objects.

6. List and describe two options you could use to quickly create a 2-inch line attached to a 2-inch circle, as shown in the below figure.

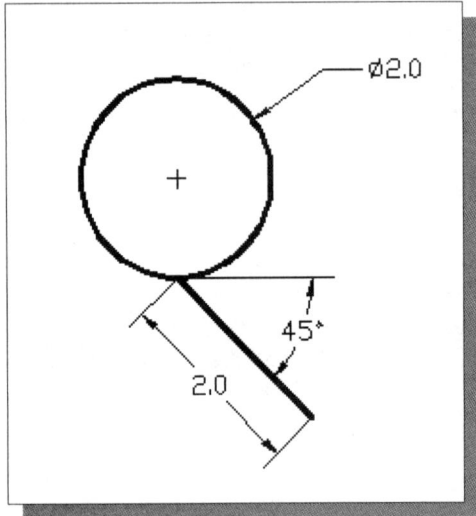

7. What are the length and angle of the inclined line, highlighted in the figure below, in the top view of the *Locator* design?

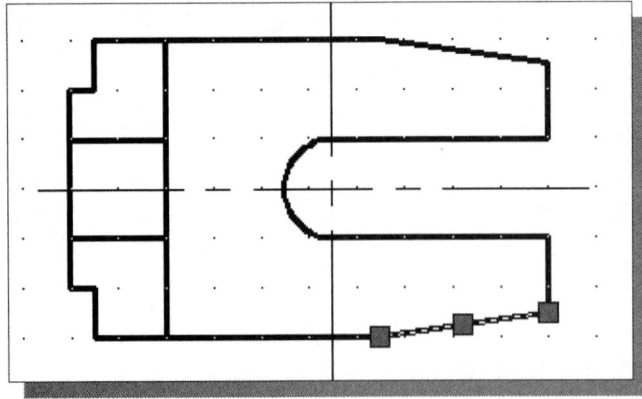

Exercises: (Time: 120 minutes)
(Unless otherwise specified, dimensions are in inches.)

1. Saddle Bracket

2. Anchor Base

3. Bearing Base

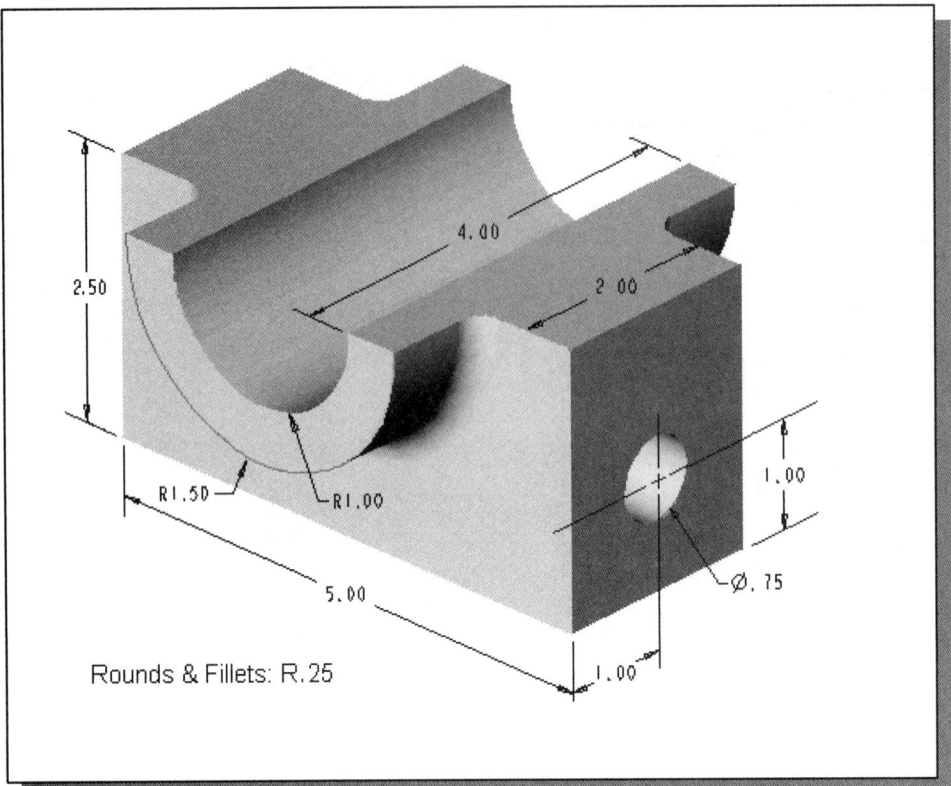

4. Shaft Support (Dimensions are in Millimeters.)

5. Connecting Rod

6. Tube Hanger

Notes:

Chapter 17
Basic Dimensioning and Notes

Learning Objectives

- Understand dimensioning nomenclature and basics
- Display and use the Dimension toolbar
- Use the AutoCAD Dimension Style Manager
- Create Center Marks
- Add Linear and Angular Dimensions
- Use the TEXT command
- Create SPECIAL CHARACTERS in Notes
- Using the AutoCAD Classic Workspace

Introduction

In order to manufacture a finalized design, the complete *shape* and *size* description must be shown on the drawings of the design. Thus far, the use of AutoCAD® 2013 to define the shape of designs has been illustrated. In this chapter, the procedures to convey the *size* definitions of designs using **AutoCAD® 2013** are discussed. The *tools of size description* are known as *dimensions* and *notes*.

Considerable experience and judgment is required for accurate size description. Detail drawings should contain only those dimensions that are necessary to make the design. Dimensions for the same feature of the design should be given only once in the same drawing. Nothing should be left to chance or guesswork on a drawing. Drawings should be dimensioned to avoid any possibility of questions. Dimensions should be carefully positioned; preferably near the profile of the feature being dimensioned. The designer and the CAD operator should be as familiar as possible with materials, methods of manufacturing, and shop processes.

Traditionally, detailing a drawing is the biggest bottleneck of the design process; and when doing board drafting, dimensioning is one of the most time consuming and tedious tasks. Today, most CAD systems provide what is known as an **auto-dimensioning feature**, where the CAD system automatically creates the extension lines, dimensional lines, arrowheads, and dimension values. Most CAD systems also provide an **associative dimensioning feature** so that the system automatically updates the dimensions when the drawing is modified.

The *Bracket* design

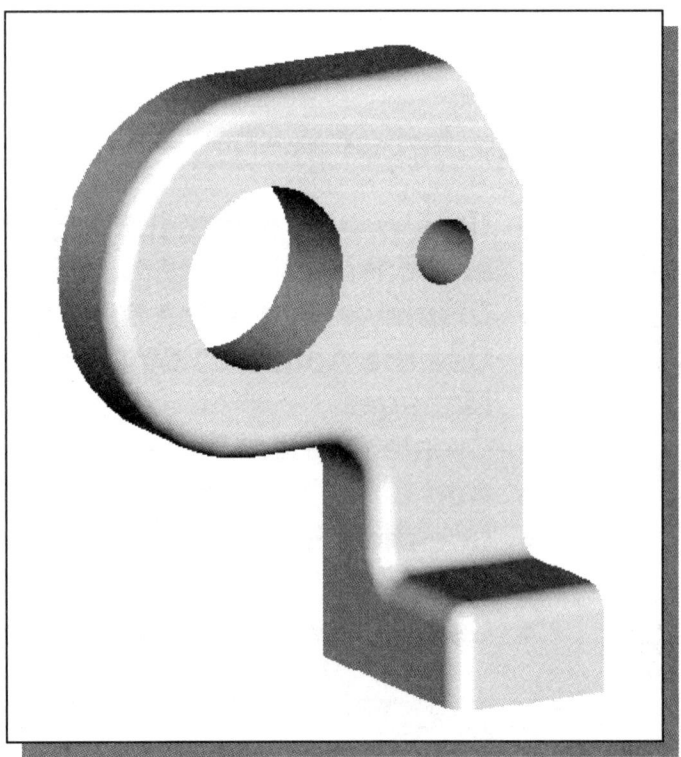

Starting Up AutoCAD 2013

1. Select the **AutoCAD 2013** option on the *Program* menu or select the **AutoCAD 2013** icon on the *Desktop*.

2. In the *Startup* window, select **Start from Scratch**, and select the **Imperial (feet and inches)** as the drawing units.

3. In the *Menu Bar*, select:

   [Tools] → **[Drafting Settings]**

4. In the *Drafting Settings* dialog box, select the **SNAP and GRID** tab if it is not the page on top.

5. Change *Grid Spacing* to **1.0** for both X and Y directions.

6. Also adjust the *Snap Spacing* to **0.5** for both X and Y directions.

7. Pick **OK** to exit the *Drafting Settings* dialog box.

8. In the *Status Bar* area, reset the option buttons so that only *SNAP Mode* and *GRID Display* are switched **ON**.

Layers setup

1. Pick *Layer Properties Manager* in the *Object Properties* toolbar.

2. In the *Layer Properties Manager* dialog box, click on the **New** button (or the key combination [**Alt+N**]) to create a new layer.

3. Create **layers** with the following settings:

Layer	Color	Linetype	Lineweight
Construction	Gray(9)	Continuous	Default
Object_Lines	Blue	Continuous	0.6mm
Hidden_Lines	Cyan	Hidden	0.3mm
Center_Lines	Red	Center	Default
Dimensions	Magenta	Continuous	Default
Section_Lines	White	Continuous	Default
CuttingPlane_Lines	Dark Gray	Phantom	0.6mm
Title_Block	Green	Continuous	1.2mm
Viewport	White	Continuous	Default

4. Highlight the layer *Construction* in the list of layers.

5. Click on the **Current** button to set layer *Construction* as the *Current Layer*.

6. Click on the **Close** button to accept the settings and exit the *Layer Properties Manager* dialog box.

The *Bracket* design

> Before going through the tutorial, make a rough sketch of a multiview drawing of the part. How many 2D views will be necessary to fully describe the part? Based on your knowledge of **AutoCAD® 2013** so far, how would you arrange and construct these 2D views? Take a few minutes to consider these questions and do preliminary planning by sketching on a piece of paper. You are also encouraged to construct the orthographic views on your own prior to going through the tutorial.

Drawing *Construction* lines

❖ We will place the construction lines on the *Construction* layer so that the layer can later be frozen or turned off.

1. Select the **Construction Line** icon in the *Draw* toolbar. In the command prompt area, the message "*_xline Specify a point or [Hor/Ver/Ang/Bisect/Offset]:*" is displayed.

    ➢ To orient construction lines, we generally specify two points, although other orientation options are also available.

2. Place the first point at world coordinate (**3,2**) on the screen.

3. Pick a location above the last point to create a **vertical line**.

4. Move the cursor toward the right of the first point and pick a location to create a **horizontal line**.

5. In the *Status Bar* area, turn **OFF** the *SNAP* option.

Using the *OFFSET* command

1. Select the **Offset** icon in the *Modify* toolbar. In the command prompt area, the message "*Specify offset distance or [Through]:*" is displayed.

2. In the command prompt area, enter: **2.875** [**ENTER**].

3. In the command prompt area, the message "*Select object to offset or <exit>:*" is displayed. Pick the **vertical line** on the screen.

4. AutoCAD next asks us to identify the direction of the offset. Pick a location that is to the **right** of the vertical line.

5. Inside the graphics window, right-mouse-click twice to **end** the Offset command.

6. In the command prompt area, click on the small icon to access the list of recent commands.

7. Select **Offset** in the popup list, to repeat the Offset command.

8. In the command prompt area, enter: **5.75 [ENTER]**.

9. In the command prompt area, the message "*Select object to offset or <exit>:*" is displayed. Pick the **horizontal line** on the screen.

10. AutoCAD next asks us to identify the direction of the offset. Pick a location that is **above** the horizontal line.

11. Inside the graphics window, right-mouse-click once to **end** the Offset command.

12. Repeat the **Offset** command and create the lines as shown.

Set layer *Object_Lines* as the *Current Layer*

1. On the *Object Properties* toolbar, choose the **Layer Control** box with the left-mouse-button.

2. Move the cursor over the name of layer **Object_Lines** and the tool tip "*Object_Lines*" appears.

3. **Left-mouse-click once** and layer *Object_Lines* is set as the *Current Layer*.

4. In the *Status Bar* area, turn *ON* the *Object SNAP, Object TRACKing*, and *Line Weight Display* options.

Creating *Object* lines

1. Select the **Line** command icon in the *Draw* toolbar. In the command prompt area, the message "*_line Specify first point:*" is displayed.

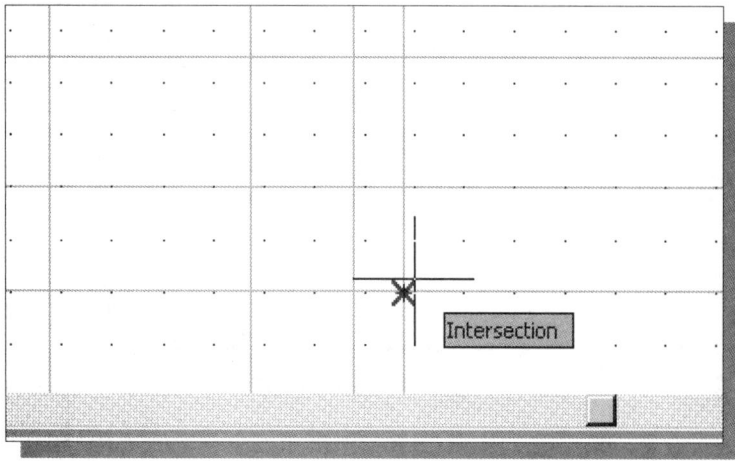

2. Move the cursor to the intersection of the construction lines at the lower right corner of the current sketch, and notice the visual aid automatically displayed at the intersection.

3. Create the object lines as shown below. (Hint: Use the *relative coordinate entry method* and the **Trim** command to construct the **30° line**.)

4. Use the Arc and Circle commands to complete the object lines as shown.

Creating *Hidden* lines

1. On the *Object Properties* toolbar, choose the *Layer Control* box with the left-mouse-button.

2. Move the cursor over the name of layer ***Hidden_Lines***, **left-mouse-click once**, and set layer *Hidden_lines* as the *Current Layer*.

3. On your own, create the five hidden lines in the side view as shown on the next page.

Creating *Center* lines

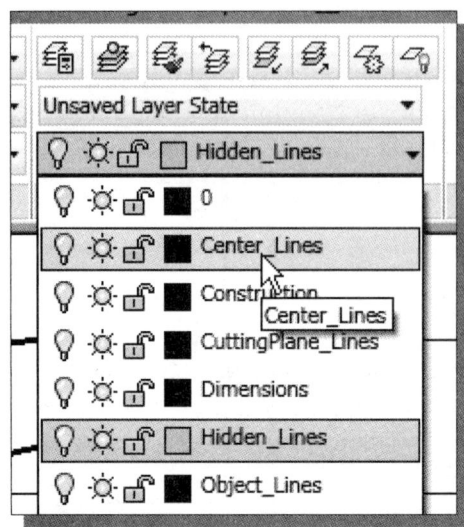

1. On the *Object Properties* toolbar, choose the *Layer Control* box to display the *Layer control list*.

2. Move the cursor over the name of layer **Center_Lines**, **left-mouse-click once** to set the layer as the *Current Layer*.

3. On your own, Create the center line in the side view as shown in the below figure. (The center lines in the front-view will be added using the *Center Mark* option.)

Turn *OFF* the Construction Lines

1. On the *Object Properties* toolbar, choose the *Layer Control* box with the left-mouse-button.

2. Move the cursor over the light-bulb icon for layer *Construction_Lines*, **left-mouse-click once**, and notice the icon color is changed to a gray tone color, representing the layer (layer *Construction_Lines*) is turned *OFF*.

3. Move the cursor over the name of layer **Object_Lines**, **left-mouse-click once**, and set layer *Object_Lines* as the *Current Layer*.

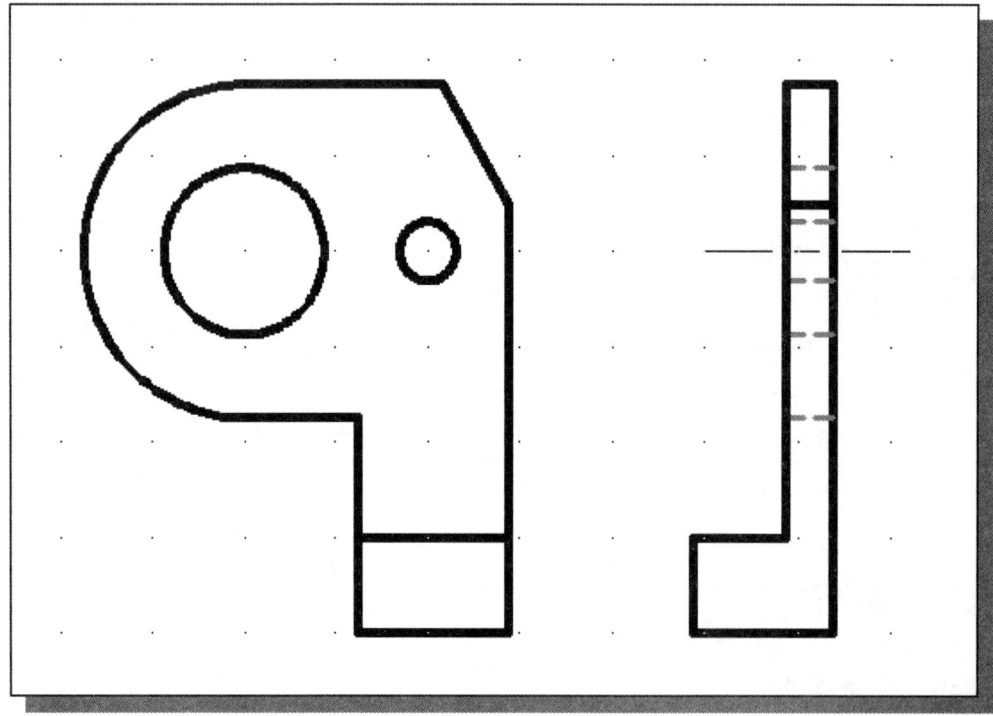

Basic Dimensioning and Notes   17-11

Using the *FILLET* command

1. Select the **Fillet** command icon in the *Modify* toolbar. In the command prompt area, the message "*Select first object or [Polyline/Radius/Trim]:*" is displayed.

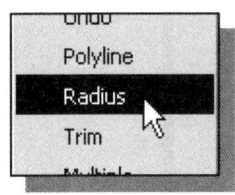

2. Inside the graphics window, right-mouse-click to activate the option menu and select the **Radius** option with the left-mouse-button to specify the radius of the fillet.

3. In the command prompt area, the message "*Specify fillet radius:*" is displayed.

   Specify fillet radius: **0.5** [**ENTER**].

4. Pick the **bottom horizontal line** of the front view as the first object to fillet.

5. Pick the **adjacent vertical line** connected to the arc to create a rounded corner as shown.

Radius *0.5*

6. Repeat the **Fillet** command and create the four rounded corners (radius **0.25**) as shown.

Radius *0.25*

Saving the Completed CAD Design

1. In the *Menu Bar*, select:
   [File] → [Save As]

2. In the *Save Drawing As* dialog box, select the folder in which you want to store the CAD file and enter **Bracket** in the *File name* box.

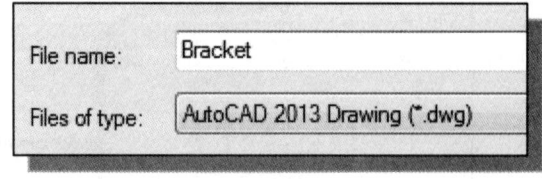

3. Click **Save** in the *Save Drawing As* dialog box to accept the selections and save the file.

Basic Dimensioning and Notes 17-13

Accessing the Dimensioning Commands

❖ The user interface in AutoCAD has gone through several renovations since it was first released back in 1982. The purpose of the renovations is to make commands more accessible. For example, the dimensioning commands can be accessed through several options:

➢ The **Menu Bar**: The majority of AutoCAD commands can be found in the *Menu Bar*. Specific task related commands are listed under the sub-items of the pull-down list. The commands listed under the *Menu Bar* are more complete, but it might take several clicks to reach the desired command.

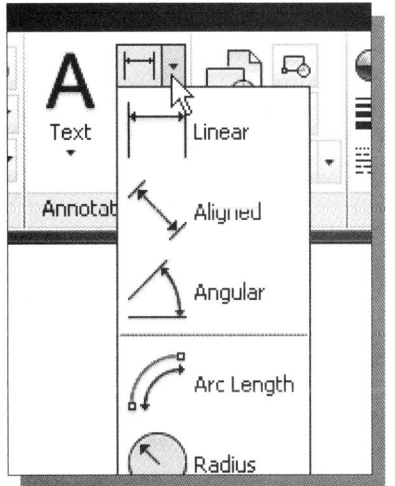

➢ The **Ribbon toolbar panels**: The more commonly used dimensioning commands are available in the *Annotation* toolbar as shown.

➢ The **Dimensions toolbar** under the **Annotate tab**: A more complete set of dimensioning commands.

➢ The **command prompt**: We can also type the command at the command prompt area. This option is always available, with or without displaying the toolbars.

The *Dimension* toolbar

> The *Dimension* toolbar offers the most flexible option to access the different dimensioning commands. The toolbar contains a more complete list than the *Ribbon* toolbars and this toolbar can be repositioned anywhere on the screen.

1. Move the cursor to the *Menu Bar* area and select:
   [Tools] → [Toolbars] → [AutoCAD] → [Dimension]

2. Move the cursor over the icons in the *Dimension* toolbar and read the brief description of each icon.

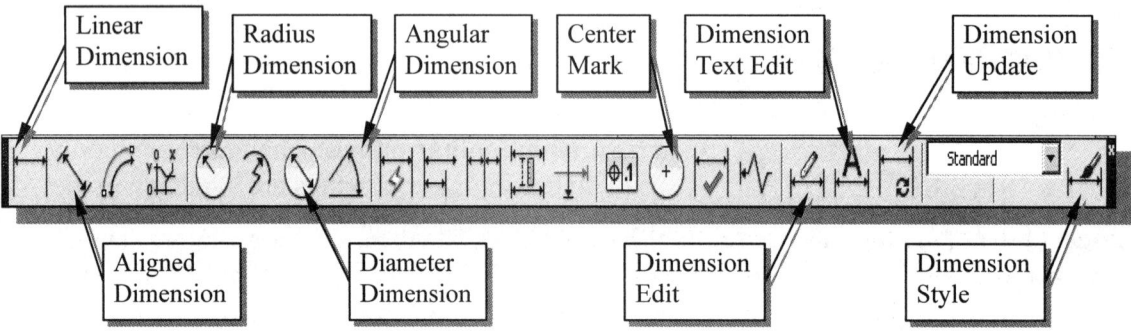

Using *Dimension Style Manager*

❖ The appearance of the dimensions are controlled by *dimension variables*, which we can set using the *Dimension Style Manager* dialog box.

1. In the *Dimension* toolbar, pick **Dimension Style**. The *Dimension Style Manager* dialog box appears on the screen.

Dimensions nomenclature and basics

As it was stated in *Chapter 1*, the rule for creating CAD designs and drawings is that they should be created **full size** using real-world units. The importance of this practice is evident when we begin applying dimensions to the geometry. The features that we specify for dimensioning are measured and displayed automatically.

Selecting and placing dimensions can be confusing at times. The two main things to consider are: (1) the function of the part and (2) the manufacturing operations. Detail drawings should contain only those dimensions that are necessary to make the design. Dimensions for the same feature of the design should be given only once in the same drawing. Nothing should be left to chance or guesswork on a drawing. Drawings should be dimensioned to avoid any possibility of questions. Dimensions should be carefully positioned; preferably near the profile of the feature being dimensioned.

Notice in the *Dimension Style Manager* dialog box, the AutoCAD default style name is *Standard*. We can create our own dimension style to fit the specific type of design we are working on, such as mechanical or architectual.

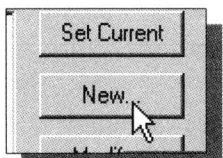

1. Click on the **New** button to create a new dimension style.

2. In the *Create New Dimension Style* dialog box, enter **Mechanical** as the dimension style name.

3. Click on the **Continue** button to proceed.

4. Click on the **Primary Units** tab.

5. Select *Fractional* as the *Unit format* under the **Primary Units** tab.

❖ On your own, examine the different options available; most of the settings are self-explanatory.

6. Select the **Fit** tab and notice the two options under *Scale for Dimension Features*.

❖ We can manually adjust the dimension scale factor or let AutoCAD automatically adjust the scale factor. For example, our current drawing will fit on A-size paper, and therefore we will use the scale factor of 1. If we decide to plot the same drawing on B-size paper, then we will need to set the dimension scale factor to 2.0. It is possible to let AutoCAD determine the scale factor based on the *layout* settings; we will discuss more about the *layout* in the next chapter.

7. Select the **Text** tab.

8. Set the *Text Height* to **0.125**.

9. Select the **Lines** tab and set *Extend beyond dim lines* to *0.125*.

10. Select the **Symbols and Arrows** tab and set *Arrow size* and *Center Marks* to *0.125*. Also set the *Center Marks* type to **Line**.

❖ Notice the different options available on this page, options that let us turn off one or both of extension lines, dimension lines, and arrowheads.

➢ The **Center Mark** option is used to control the appearance of center marks and centerlines for diameter and radial dimensions.

11. Click on the **OK** button to accept the settings and close the dialog box.

12. Pick the **Set Current** button to make the *Mechanical* dimension style the current dimension style.

13. Click on the **Close** button to accept the settings and close the *Dimension Style Manager* dialog box.

➢ The **Dimension Style Manager** allows us to easily control the appearance of the dimensions in the drawing.

Using the *CENTER MARK* command

1. On the *Object Properties* toolbar, choose the *Layer Control* box with the left-mouse-button.

2. Move the cursor over the name of layer *Center_Lines*, **left-mouse-click once**, and set layer *Center_lines* as the *Current Layer*.

3. In the *Dimension* toolbar, click on the **Center Mark** icon.

4. Pick the **radius 1.75 arc** in the front view and notice AutoCAD automatically places two centerlines through the center of the arc.

5. Repeat the **Center Mark** command and pick the **small circle** to place the centerlines as shown.

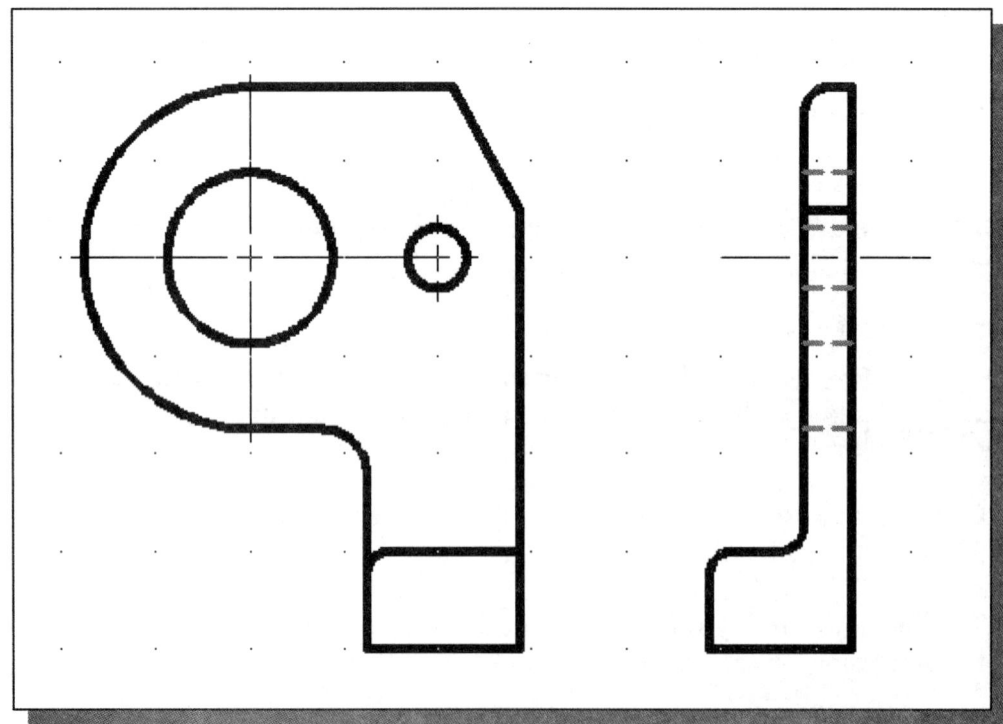

Basic Dimensioning and Notes   17-19

Adding *Linear* dimensions

1. On the *Object Properties* toolbar, choose the **Layer Control** box with the left-mouse-button.

2. Move the cursor over the name of layer *Dimensions*, **left-mouse-click once**, and set layer *Dimensions* as the *Current Layer*.

3. In the *Dimension* toolbar, click on the **Linear Dimension** icon.

 > The **Linear Dimension** command measures and annotates a feature with a horizontal or vertical dimension.

4. Pick the **lower left corner** of the front view of the part.

5. Pick the **lower right corner** of the front view of the part.

6. Pick a point that is about 0.5 inch below the bottom horizontal line of the front view to place the dimension text.

❖ Adding dimensions is this easy with AutoCAD's auto-dimensioning and associative-dimensioning features.

7. Repeat the **Linear Dimension** command and add the necessary linear dimensions as shown.

Adding an *Angular* dimension

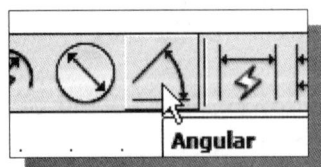

1. In the *Dimension* toolbar, click on the **Angular Dimension** icon.

   • The Angular Dimension command measures and annotates a feature with an angle dimension.

2. Pick the **inclined line** of the part in the front view.

3. Pick the **right vertical line** of the part in the front view.

4. Pick a point inside the desired quadrant and place the dimension text as shown.

Adding *Radius* and *Diameter* dimensions

1. In the *Dimension* toolbar, click on the **Radius Dimension** icon.

2. Pick the **large arc** in the front view.

3. Pick a point toward the left of the arc to place the dimension text.

4. Use the Radius Dimension and Diameter Dimension commands to add the necessary dimensions as shown.

Using the *MULTILINE TEXT* command

❖ AutoCAD provides two options to create notes. For simple entries, we can use the **Single Line Text** command. For longer entries with internal formatting, we can use the **Multiline Text** command. The procedures for both of these commands are self-explanatory. The **Single Line Text** command, also known as the **Text** command, can be used to enter several lines of text that can be rotated and resized. The text we are typing is displayed on the screen. Each line of text is treated as a separate object in AutoCAD. To end a line and begin another, press the [**ENTER**] key after entering characters. To end the Text command, press the [**ENTER**] key without entering any characters.

1. In the *Ribbon* toolbar panel, select:

    [**Multiline Text**]

2. In the command prompt area, the message "*Specify start point of text or [Justify/Style]:*" is displayed. Pick a location near the world coordinate (**1,1.5**).

3. Right-mouse-click once to bring up the option list and chose **Height**. In the command prompt area, the message "*Specify Height:*" is displayed. Enter **0.125** as the text height.

4. Click a position toward the right and create a rectangle representing roughly the area for the notes.

5. In the Edit Box, enter: **Rounds & Fillets R 1/4**

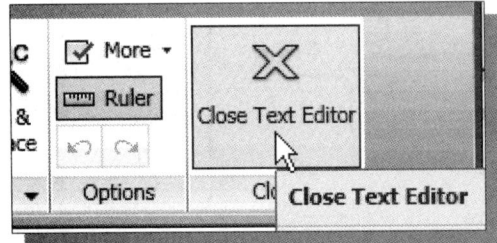

6. Note in the Ribbon toolbar area, the different command options are available to adjust the multiline text entered. Click [**Close Text Editor**] once to end the command.

Adding special characters

- We can add special text characters to the dimensioning text and notes. We can type in special characters during any text command and when entering the dimension text. The most common special characters have been given letters to make them easy to remember.

Code	Character	Symbol
%%C	Diameter symbol	⌀
%%D	Degree symbol	°
%%P	Plus/Minus sign	±

➢ On your own, create notes containing some of the special characters listed.

➢ On your own, switch on and off different layers to examine the information stored on each layer.

Saving the design

➢ In the *Standard Toolbar* area, select the **Save** icon.

A special note on Layers containing Dimensions

AutoCAD creates several hidden **BLOCKS** when we create associative dimensions and we will take a more in depth look at *blocks* in *Chapter 9*. AutoCAD treats **blocks** as a special type of object called a *named object*. Each kind of *named object* has a *symbol table* or a *dictionary*, and each table or dictionary can store multiple *named objects*. For example, if we create five dimension styles, our drawing's dimension style *symbol table* will have five dimension style records. In general, we do not work with *symbol tables* or *dictionaries* directly.

When we create dimensions in AutoCAD, most of the hidden blocks are placed in the same layer where the dimension was first defined. Some of the definitions are placed in the *DEFPOINTS* layer. When moving dimensions from one layer to another, AutoCAD does not move these definitions. When deleting layers, we cannot delete the current layer, *layer 0*, xref-dependent layers, or a layer that contains visible and/or invisible objects. Layers referenced by block definitions, along with the *DEFPOINTS* layer, cannot be deleted even if they do not contain visible objects.

To delete layers with hidden blocks, first use the **Purge** command **[Application → Drawing Utilities → Purge → Blocks]** to remove the invisible blocks. (We will have to remove all visible objects prior to using this command.) The empty layer can now be *deleted* or *purged*.

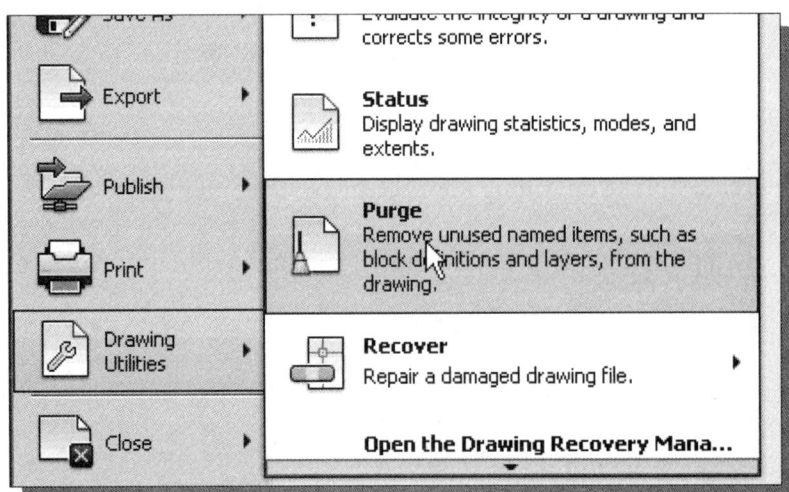

Review Questions: (Time: 25 minutes)

1. Why are dimensions and notes important to a technical drawing?

2. List and describe some of the general-dimensioning practices.

3. Describe the procedure in setting up a new *Dimension Style.*

4. What is the special way to create a diameter symbol when entering a dimension text?

5. What is the text code to create the **Diameter** symbol (Ø) in AutoCAD?

6. Which command can be used to delete layers with hidden blocks? Can we delete *Layer 0?*

7. Which quick-key is used to display and hide the *AutoCAD Text Window?*

8. What are the length and angle of the inclined line, highlighted in the figure below, in the front view of the *LBracket* design.

9. Construct the following drawing and measure the angle α

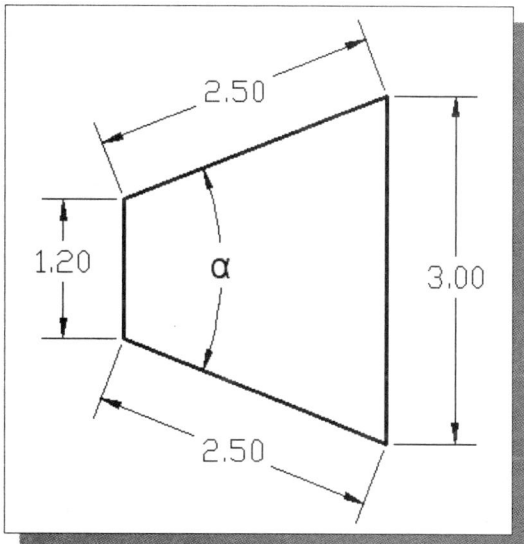

Exercises: (Time: 70 minutes)

1. **Shaft Guide** (Dimensions are in inches.)

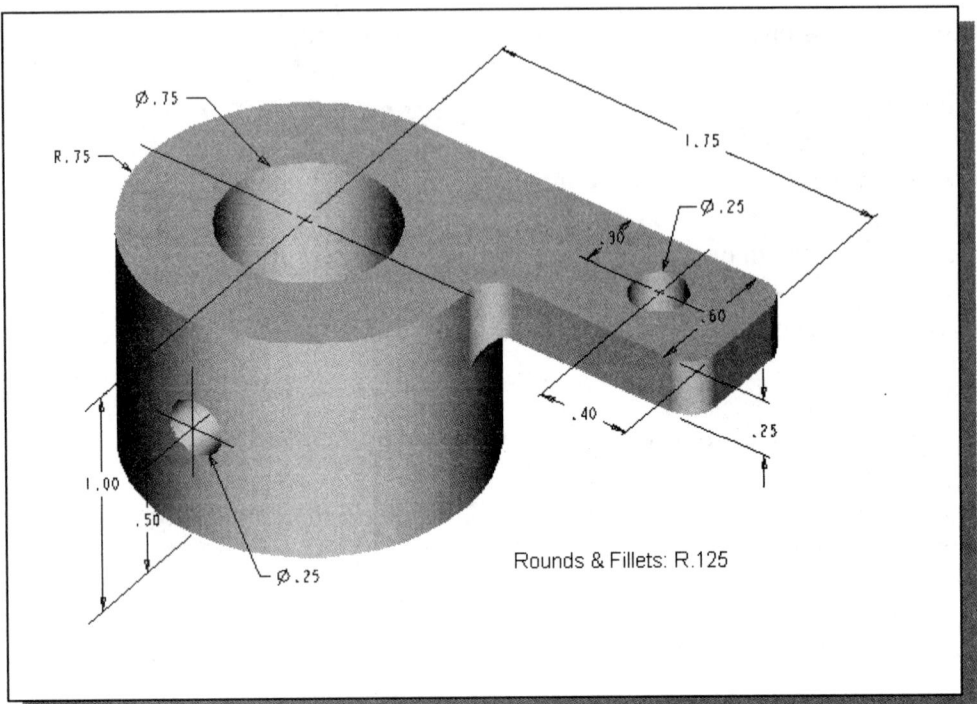

2. **Fixture Cap** (Dimensions are in millimeters.)

3. **Cylinder Support** (Dimensions are in inches.)

4. **Swivel Base** (Dimensions are in inches.)

Notes: